THE
DATA
VISUALIZATION
WORKSHOP

A self-paced, practical approach
to transforming your complex data
into compelling, captivating graphics

Mario Döbler and Tim Großmann

THE DATA VISUALIZATION WORKSHOP

Authors: Mario Döbler and Tim Großmann

Reviewers: Rohan Chikorde, Joshua Görner, Anshu Kumar, Piotr Malak, Ashish Pratik Patil, Narinder Kaur Saini, and Ankit Verma

Managing Editor: Aditya Shah

Acquisitions Editors: Manuraj Nair, Royluis Rodrigues, Kunal Sawant, Sneha Shinde, Anindya Sil, and Karan Wadekar

Production Editor: Roshan Kawale

Editorial Board: Megan Carlisle, Samuel Christa, Mahesh Dhyani, Heather Gopsill, Manasa Kumar, Alex Mazonowicz, Monesh Mirpuri, Bridget Neale, Dominic Pereira, Shiny Poojary, Abhishek Rane, Brendan Rodrigues, Erol Staveley, Ankita Thakur, Nitesh Thakur, and Jonathan Wray

First published: July 2020

Production reference: 2230221

ISBN: 978-1-80056-884-6

Published by Packt Publishing Ltd.

Livery Place, 35 Livery Street

Birmingham B3 2PB, UK

WHY LEARN WITH A PACKT WORKSHOP?

LEARN BY DOING

Packt Workshops are built around the idea that the best way to learn something new is by getting hands-on experience. We know that learning a language or technology isn't just an academic pursuit. It's a journey towards the effective use of a new tool—whether that's to kickstart your career, automate repetitive tasks, or just build some cool stuff.

That's why Workshops are designed to get you writing code from the very beginning. You'll start fairly small—learning how to implement some basic functionality—but once you've completed that, you'll have the confidence and understanding to move onto something slightly more advanced.

As you work through each chapter, you'll build your understanding in a coherent, logical way, adding new skills to your toolkit and working on increasingly complex and challenging problems.

CONTEXT IS KEY

All new concepts are introduced in the context of realistic use-cases, and then demonstrated practically with guided exercises. At the end of each chapter, you'll find an activity that challenges you to draw together what you've learned and apply your new skills to solve a problem or build something new.

We believe this is the most effective way of building your understanding and confidence. Experiencing real applications of the code will help you get used to the syntax and see how the tools and techniques are applied in real projects.

BUILD REAL-WORLD UNDERSTANDING

Of course, you do need some theory. But unlike many tutorials, which force you to wade through pages and pages of dry technical explanations and assume too much prior knowledge, Workshops only tell you what you actually need to know to be able to get started making things. Explanations are clear, simple, and to-the-point. So you don't need to worry about how everything works under the hood; you can just get on and use it.

Written by industry professionals, you'll see how concepts are relevant to real-world work, helping to get you beyond "Hello, world!" and build relevant, productive skills. Whether you're studying web development, data science, or a core programming language, you'll start to think like a problem solver and build your understanding and confidence through contextual, targeted practice.

ENJOY THE JOURNEY

Learning something new is a journey from where you are now to where you want to be, and this Workshop is just a vehicle to get you there. We hope that you find it to be a productive and enjoyable learning experience.

Packt has a wide range of different Workshops available, covering the following topic areas:

- Programming languages

- Web development

- Data science, machine learning, and artificial intelligence

- Containers

Once you've worked your way through this Workshop, why not continue your journey with another? You can find the full range online at http://packt.live/2MNkuyl.

If you could leave us a review while you're there, that would be great. We value all feedback. It helps us to continually improve and make better books for our readers, and also helps prospective customers make an informed decision about their purchase.

Thank you,
The Packt Workshop Team

Table of Contents

Chapter 3: A Deep Dive into Matplotlib   137

Chapter 4: Simplifying Visualizations Using Seaborn   203

Chapter 6: Making Things Interactive with Bokeh   305

PREFACE

ABOUT THE BOOK

Do you want to transform data into captivating images? Do you want to make it easy for your audience to process and understand the patterns, trends, and relationships hidden within your data?

The Data Visualization Workshop will guide you through the world of data visualization and help you to unlock simple secrets for transforming data into meaningful visuals with the help of exciting exercises and activities.

Starting with an introduction to data visualization, this book shows you how to first prepare raw data for visualization using NumPy and pandas operations. As you progress, you'll use plotting techniques, such as comparison and distribution, to identify relationships and similarities between datasets. You'll then work through practical exercises to simplify the process of creating visualizations using Python plotting libraries such as Matplotlib, and Seaborn. If you've ever wondered how popular companies like Uber and Airbnb use geoplotlib for geographical visualizations, this book has got you covered, helping you analyze and understand the process effectively. Finally, you'll use the Bokeh library to create dynamic visualizations that can be integrated into any web page.

By the end of this workshop, you'll have learned how to present engaging mission-critical insights by creating impactful visualizations with real-world data.

AUDIENCE

The Data Visualization Workshop is for beginners who want to learn data visualization, as well as developers and data scientists who are looking to enrich their practical data science skills. Prior knowledge of data analytics, data science, and visualization is not mandatory. Knowledge of Python basics and high-school-level math will help you grasp the concepts covered in this data visualization book more quickly and effectively.

ABOUT THE CHAPTERS

Chapter 1, The Importance of Data Visualization and Data Exploration, will introduce you to the basics of statistical analysis, along with basic operations for calculating the mean, median, and variance of different datasets with real-world datasets.

Chapter 2, All You Need to Know about Plots, will explain the design practices for certain plots. You will design attractive, tangible visualizations and learn to identify the best plot type for a given dataset and scenario.

Chapter 3, A Deep Dive into Matplotlib, will teach you the fundamentals of Matplotlib and how to create visualizations using the built-in plots that are provided by the library. You will also practice how to customize your visualization plots and write mathematical expressions using TeX.

Chapter 4, Simplifying Visualizations Using Seaborn, will extend your knowledge of Matplotlib by explaining the advantages of Seaborn in comparison to Matplotlib to show you how to design visually appealing and insightful plots efficiently.

Chapter 5, Plotting Geospatial Data, will teach you how to utilize Geoplotlib to create stunning geographical visualizations, identify the different types of geospatial charts, and create complex visualizations using tile providers and custom layers.

Chapter 6, Making Things Interactive with Bokeh, will introduce Bokeh, which is used to create insightful web-based visualizations that can be extended into beautiful, interactive visualizations that can easily be integrated into your web page.

Chapter 7, Combining What We Have Learned, will apply all the concepts that we will have learned in all the previous chapters, using three new datasets in combination with practical activities for Matplotlib, Seaborn, Geoplotlib, and Bokeh.

CONVENTIONS

Code words in text, database table names, folder names, filenames, file extensions, path names, dummy URLs, user input, and Twitter handles are shown as follows:

"Note that by simply passing the **axis** parameter in the **np.mean()** call, we can define the dimension our data will be aggregated on. **axis=0** is horizontal and **axis=1** is vertical."

Words that you see on the screen (for example, in menus or dialog boxes) appear in the same format.

A block of code is set as follows:

```
# slicing an intersection of 4 elements (2x2) of the first two rows and
first two columns
subsection_2x2 = dataset[1:3, 1:3]
np.mean(subsection_2x2)
```

New terms and important words are shown like this:

"In this book, you will learn how to use Python in combination with various libraries, such as **NumPy**, **pandas**, **Matplotlib**, **Seaborn**, and **geoplotlib**, to create impactful data visualizations using real-world data."

CODE PRESENTATION

Lines of code that span multiple lines are split using a backslash (\ ). When the code is executed, Python will ignore the backslash, and treat the code on the next line as a direct continuation of the current line.

For example:

```
history = model.fit(X, y, epochs=100, batch_size=5, verbose=1, \
                    validation_split=0.2, shuffle=False)
```

Comments are added into code to help explain specific bits of logic. Single-line comments are denoted using the **#** symbol, as follows:

```
# Print the sizes of the dataset
print("Number of Examples in the Dataset = ", X.shape[0])
print("Number of Features for each example = ", X.shape[1])
```

Multi-line comments are enclosed by triple quotes, as shown below:

```
"""
Define a seed for the random number generator to ensure the
result will be reproducible
"""
seed = 1
np.random.seed(seed)
random.set_seed(seed)
```

SETTING UP YOUR ENVIRONMENT

Before we explore the book in detail, we need to set up specific software and tools. In the following section, we shall see how to do that.

INSTALLING PYTHON

The following section will help you to install python in Windows, macOS and Linux systems.

INSTALLING PYTHON ON WINDOWS

Installing Python on Windows is done as follows:

1. Find your desired version of Python on the official installation page at https://www.anaconda.com/distribution/#windows.

2. Ensure you select Python 3.7 from the download page.

3. Ensure that you install a version relevant to the architecture of your system (either 32-bit or 64-bit). You can find out this information in the **System Properties** window of your OS.

4. After you download the installer, simply double-click on the file and follow the on-screen instructions.

INSTALLING PYTHON ON LINUX

To install Python on Linux, you have a couple of good options:

1. Open Command Prompt and verify that **p\Python 3** is not already installed by running **python3 --version**.

2. To install Python 3, run this:

```
sudo apt-get update
sudo apt-get install python3.7
```

3. Alternatively, you can install Python with the Anaconda Linux distribution by downloading the installer from https://www.anaconda.com/distribution/#linux and following the instructions.

INSTALLING PYTHON ON MACOS

Similar to Linux, you have a couple of methods for installing Python on a Mac. To install Python on macOS X, do the following:

1. Open the Terminal for Mac by pressing *CMD + Spacebar*, type **terminal** in the open search box, and hit *Enter*.

2. Install Xcode through the command line by running **xcode-select --install**.

3. The easiest way to install Python 3 is using Homebrew, which is installed through the command line by running **ruby -e "$(curl -fsSL https://raw. githubusercontent.com/Homebrew/install/master/install)"**.

4. Add Homebrew to your **$PATH** environment variable. Open your profile in the command line by running **sudo nano ~/.profile** and inserting **export PATH="/usr/local/opt/python/libexec/bin:$PATH"** at the bottom.

5. The final step is to install Python. In the command line, run **brew install python**.

6. You can also install Python using the Anaconda installer, available from https://www.anaconda.com/distribution/#macos.

INSTALLING LIBRARIES

pip comes pre-installed with Anaconda. Once Anaconda is installed on your machine, all the required libraries can be installed using **pip**, for example, **pip install numpy**. Alternatively, you can install all the required libraries using **pip install -r requirements.txt**. You can find the **requirements.txt** file at https://packt.live/3dgg8Hv.

The exercises and activities will be executed in Jupyter Notebooks. Jupyter is a Python library and can be installed in the same way as the other Python libraries – that is, with **pip install jupyter**, but fortunately, it comes pre-installed with Anaconda. To open a notebook, simply run the command **jupyter notebook** in the Anaconda Prompt.

WORKING WITH JUPYTERLAB AND JUPYTER NOTEBOOK

You'll be working on different exercises and activities in JupyterLab. These exercises and activities can be downloaded from the associated GitHub repository.

1. Download the repository from here: https://github.com/PacktWorkshops/The-Data-Visualization-Workshop.

2. You can either download it using GitHub Desktop or as a zipped folder by clicking on the green **Clone or download** button.

3. You can open a Jupyter Notebook using the Anaconda Navigator by clicking the **Launch** button under the Jupyter Notebook icon.

4. You can also open a Jupyter Notebook using the Anaconda Prompt. To do this, open the Anaconda Prompt and run the following command:

```
jupyter notebook
```

Jupyter Notebook will then be launched in your default browser.

5. Once you have launched Jupyter Notebook, a list of all files and folders will be presented. You can open the Jupyter Notebook file you wish to work with by simply double clicking it.

IMPORTING PYTHON LIBRARIES

Every exercise and activity in this book will make use of various libraries. Importing libraries into Python is very simple, as shown in the following steps:

1. To import libraries such as NumPy and pandas, run the following code. This will import the whole **numpy** library into your current file:

```
import numpy          # import numpy
```

2. In the first cells of the exercises and activities of this book, you will see the following code. Use **np** instead of **numpy** in our code to call methods from **numpy**:

```
import numpy as np       # import numpy and assign alias np
```

3. Partial imports can be done as shown in the following code:

```
from numpy import mean   # only import the mean method of numpy
```

This only loads the **mean** method from the library.

ACCESSING THE CODE FILES

You can find the complete code files of this book at https://packt.live/31USkof. You can also run many activities and exercises directly in your web browser by using the interactive lab environment at https://packt.live/37CIQ47.

We've tried to support interactive versions of all activities and exercises, but we recommend a local installation as well for instances where this support isn't available.

If you have any issues or questions about installation, please email us at workshops@packt.com.

1

THE IMPORTANCE OF DATA VISUALIZATION AND DATA EXPLORATION

OVERVIEW

This chapter introduces you to the basics of the statistical analysis of a dataset. We will look at basic operations for calculating the mean, median, and variance of different datasets and use NumPy and pandas to filter, sort, and shape the datasets to our requirements. The concepts we will cover will serve as a base of knowledge for the upcoming visualization chapters, in which we will work with real-world datasets. By the end of this chapter, you will be able to explain the importance of data visualization and calculate basic statistical values (such as median, mean, and variance), and use NumPy and pandas for data wrangling.

INTRODUCTION

Unlike machines, people are usually not equipped for interpreting a large amount of information from a random set of numbers and messages in each piece of data. Out of all our logical capabilities, we understand things best through the visual processing of information. When data is represented visually, the probability of understanding complex builds and numbers increases.

Python has recently emerged as a programming language that performs well for data analysis. It has applications across data science pipelines that convert data into a usable format (such as pandas), analyzes it (such as NumPy), and extract useful conclusions from the data to represent it in a visually appealing manner (such as Matplotlib or Bokeh). Python provides data visualization libraries that can help you assemble graphical representations efficiently.

In this book, you will learn how to use Python in combination with various libraries, such as **NumPy**, **pandas**, **Matplotlib**, **seaborn**, and **geoplotlib**, to create impactful data visualizations using real-world data. Besides that, you will also learn about the features of different types of charts and compare their advantages and disadvantages. This will help you choose the chart type that's suited to visualizing your data.

Once we understand the basics, we can cover more advanced concepts, such as interactive visualizations and how **Bokeh** can be used to create animated visualizations that tell a story. Upon completing this book, you will be able to perform **data wrangling**, extract relevant information, and visualize your findings descriptively.

INTRODUCTION TO DATA VISUALIZATION

Computers and smartphones store data such as names and numbers in a digital format. **Data representation** refers to the form in which you can store, process, and transmit data.

Representations can narrate a story and convey fundamental discoveries to your audience. Without appropriately modeling your information to use it to make meaningful findings, its value is reduced. Creating representations helps us achieve a more precise, more concise, and more direct perspective of information, making it easier for anyone to understand the data.

Information isn't equivalent to data. Representations are a useful apparatus to derive insights from the data. Thus, representations transform data into useful information.

THE IMPORTANCE OF DATA VISUALIZATION

Instead of just looking at data in the columns of an Excel spreadsheet, we get a better idea of what our data contains by using visualization. For instance, it's easy to see a pattern emerge from the numerical data that's given in the following scatter plot. It shows the correlation between body mass and the maximum longevity of various animals grouped by class. There is a positive correlation between body mass and maximum longevity:

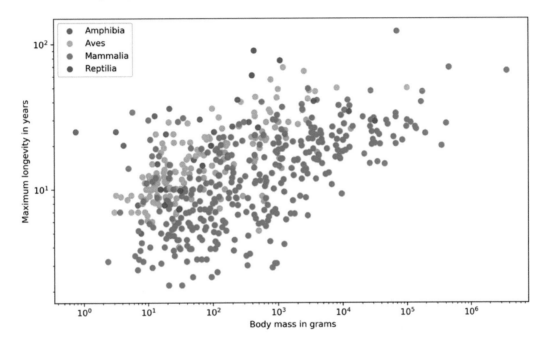

Figure 1.1: A simple example of data visualization

Visualizing data has many advantages, such as the following:

- Complex data can be easily understood.

- A simple visual representation of outliers, target audiences, and futures markets can be created.

- Storytelling can be done using dashboards and animations.

- Data can be explored through interactive visualizations.

DATA WRANGLING

Data wrangling is the process of transforming raw data into a suitable representation for various tasks. It is the discipline of augmenting, cleaning, filtering, standardizing, and enriching data in a way that allows it to be used in a downstream task, which in our case is data visualization.

Look at the following data wrangling process flow diagram to understand how accurate and actionable data can be obtained for business analysts to work on:

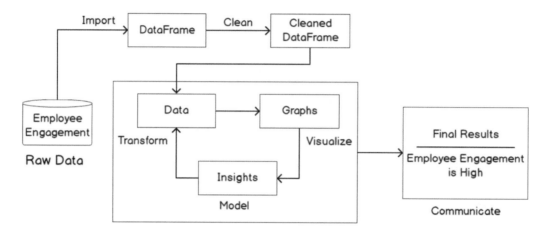

Figure 1.2: Data wrangling process to measure employee engagement

In relation to the preceding figure, the following steps explain the flow of the data wrangling process:

1. First, the Employee Engagement data is in its raw form.

2. Then, the data gets imported as a DataFrame and is later cleaned.

3. The cleaned data is then transformed into graphs, from which findings can be derived.

4. Finally, we analyze this data to communicate the final results.

For example, employee engagement can be measured based on raw data gathered from feedback surveys, employee tenure, exit interviews, one-on-one meetings, and so on. This data is cleaned and made into graphs based on parameters such as referrals, faith in leadership, and scope of promotions. The percentages, that is, information derived from the graphs, help us reach our result, which is to determine the measure of employee engagement.

TOOLS AND LIBRARIES FOR VISUALIZATION

There are several approaches to creating data visualizations. Depending on your requirements, you might want to use a non-coding tool such as **Tableau**, which allows you to get a good feel for your data. Besides Python, which will be used in this book, **MATLAB** and **R** are widely used in data analytics.

However, Python is the most popular language in the industry. Its ease of use and the speed at which you can manipulate and visualize data, combined with the availability of a number of libraries, make Python the best choice for data visualization.

> **NOTE**
>
> MATLAB (https://www.mathworks.com/products/matlab.html), R (https://www.r-project.org), and Tableau (https://www.tableau.com) are not part of this book; we will only cover the relevant tools and libraries for Python.

OVERVIEW OF STATISTICS

Statistics is a combination of the analysis, collection, interpretation, and representation of numerical data. **Probability** is a measure of the likelihood that an event will occur and is quantified as a number between 0 and 1.

A **probability distribution** is a function that provides the probability for every possible event. A probability distribution is frequently used for statistical analysis. The higher the probability, the more likely the event. There are two types of probability distributions, namely discrete and continuous.

A **discrete probability distribution** shows all the values that a random variable can take, together with their probability. The following diagram illustrates an example of a discrete probability distribution. If we have a six-sided die, we can roll each number between 1 and 6. We have six events that can occur based on the number that's rolled. There is an equal probability of rolling any of the numbers, and the individual probability of any of the six events occurring is 1/6:

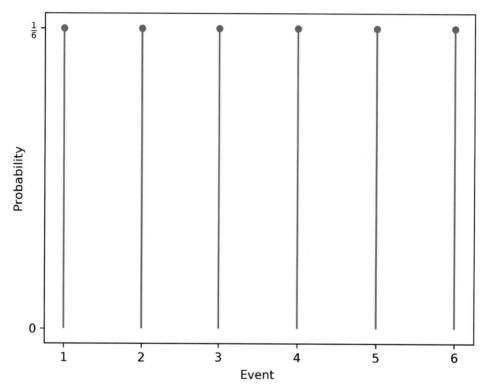

Figure 1.3: Discrete probability distribution for die rolls

A **continuous probability distribution** defines the probabilities of each possible value of a continuous random variable. The following diagram provides an example of a continuous probability distribution. This example illustrates the distribution of the time needed to drive home. In most cases, around 60 minutes is needed, but sometimes, less time is needed because there is no traffic, and sometimes, much more time is needed if there are traffic jams:

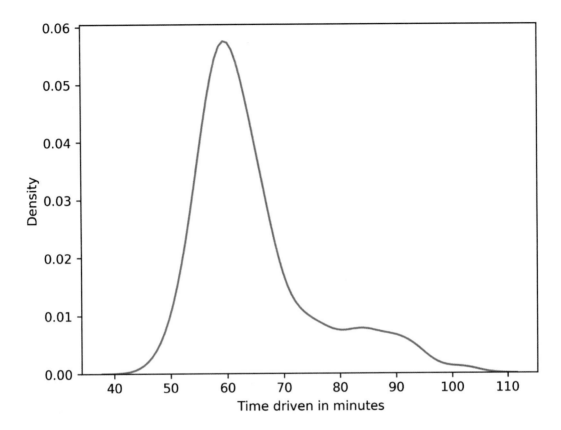

Figure 1.4: Continuous probability distribution for the time taken to reach home

MEASURES OF CENTRAL TENDENCY

Measures of central tendency are often called **averages** and describe central or typical values for a probability distribution. We are going to discuss three kinds of averages in this chapter:

- **Mean**: The arithmetic average is computed by summing up all measurements and dividing the sum by the number of observations. The mean is calculated as follows:

$$\mu = \frac{1}{N} \sum_{i=1}^{N} x_i$$

Figure 1.5: Formula for mean

- **Median**: This is the middle value of the ordered dataset. If there is an even number of observations, the median will be the average of the two middle values. The median is less prone to outliers compared to the mean, where outliers are distinct values in data.

- **Mode**: Our last measure of central tendency, the mode is defined as the most frequent value. There may be more than one mode in cases where multiple values are equally frequent.

For example, a die was rolled 10 times, and we got the following numbers: 4, 5, 4, 3, 4, 2, 1, 1, 2, and 1.

The mean is calculated by summing all the events and dividing them by the number of observations: *(4+5+4+3+4+2+1+1+2+1)/10=2.7.*

To calculate the median, the die rolls have to be ordered according to their values. The ordered values are as follows: 1, 1, 1, 2, 2, 3, 4, 4, 4, 5. Since we have an even number of die rolls, we need to take the average of the two middle values. The average of the two middle values is *(2+3)/2=2.5.*

The modes are 1 and 4 since they are the two most frequent events.

MEASURES OF DISPERSION

Dispersion, also called **variability**, is the extent to which a probability distribution is stretched or squeezed.

The different measures of dispersion are as follows:

- **Variance**: The variance is the expected value of the squared deviation from the mean. It describes how far a set of numbers is spread out from their mean. Variance is calculated as follows:

$$Var(X) = \frac{1}{N} \sum_{i=1}^{N} (x_i - \mu)^2$$

Figure 1.6: Formula for mean

- **Standard deviation**: This is the square root of the variance.
- **Range**: This is the difference between the largest and smallest values in a dataset.
- **Interquartile range**: Also called the **midspread** or **middle 50%**, this is the difference between the 75th and 25th percentiles, or between the upper and lower quartiles.

CORRELATION

The measures we have discussed so far only considered single variables. In contrast, **correlation** describes the statistical relationship between two variables:

- In a positive correlation, both variables move in the same direction.
- In a negative correlation, the variables move in opposite directions.
- In zero correlation, the variables are not related.

> **NOTE**
>
> One thing you should be aware of is that correlation does not imply causation. Correlation describes the relationship between two or more variables, while causation describes how one event is caused by another. For example, consider a scenario in which ice cream sales are correlated with the number of drowning deaths. But that doesn't mean that ice cream consumption causes drowning. There could be a third variable, say temperature, that may be responsible for this correlation. Higher temperatures may cause an increase in both ice cream sales and more people engaging in swimming, which may be the real reason for the increase in deaths due to drowning.

Example

Consider you want to find a decent apartment to rent that is not too expensive compared to other apartments you've found. The other apartments (all belonging to the same locality) you found on a website are priced as follows: $700, $850, $1,500, and $750 per month. Let's calculate some values statistical measures to help us make a decision:

- The mean is *($700 + $850 + $1,500 + $750) / 4 = $950*.

- The median is *($750 + $850) / 2 = $800*.

- The standard deviation is $\sqrt{\frac{(\$700-\$950)^2+(\$850-\$950)^2+(\$1500-\$950)^2+(\$750-\$950)^2}{4}} = \$322.10$.

- The range is *$1,500 - $700 = $800*.

As an exercise, you can try and calculate the variance as well. However, note that compared with all the above values, the median value ($800) is a better statistical measure in this case since it is less prone to outliers (the rent amount of $1,500). Given that all apartments belong to the same locality, you can clearly see that the apartment costing $1500 is definitely priced much higher as compared with other apartments. A simple statistical analysis helped us to narrow down our choices.

TYPES OF DATA

It is important to understand what kind of data you are dealing with so that you can select both the right statistical measure and the right visualization. We categorize data as categorical/qualitative and numerical/quantitative. Categorical data describes characteristics, for example, the color of an object or a person's gender. We can further divide categorical data into nominal and ordinal data. In contrast to nominal data, ordinal data has an order.

Numerical data can be divided into discrete and continuous data. We speak of discrete data if the data can only have certain values, whereas continuous data can take any value (sometimes limited to a range).

Another aspect to consider is whether the data has a temporal domain – in other words, is it bound to time or does it change over time? If the data is bound to a location, it might be interesting to show the spatial relationship, so you should keep that in mind as well. The following flowchart classifies the various data types:

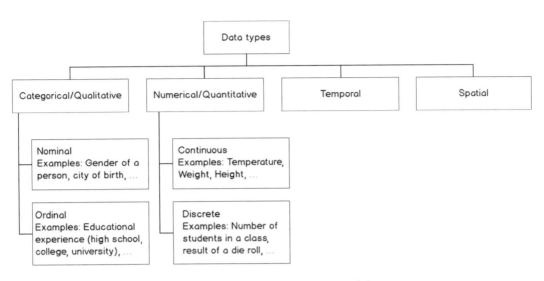

Figure 1.7: Classification of types of data

SUMMARY STATISTICS

In real-world applications, we often encounter enormous datasets. Therefore, **summary statistics** are used to summarize important aspects of data. They are necessary to communicate large amounts of information in a compact and simple way.

We have already covered measures of central tendency and dispersion, which are both summary statistics. It is important to know that measures of central tendency show a center point in a set of data values, whereas measures of dispersion show how much the data varies.

The following table gives an overview of which measure of central tendency is best suited to a particular type of data:

Data type	Best measure of central tendency
Nominal	Mode
Ordinal	Median
Numerical	Mean/Median

Figure 1.8: Best suited measures of central tendency for different types of data

In the next section, we will learn about the NumPy library and implement a few exercises using it.

NUMPY

When handling data, we often need a way to work with multidimensional arrays. As we discussed previously, we also have to apply some basic mathematical and statistical operations on that data. This is exactly where **NumPy** positions itself. It provides support for large n-dimensional arrays and has built-in support for many high-level mathematical and statistical operations.

> **NOTE**
>
> Before NumPy, there was a library called **Numeric**. However, it's no longer used, because NumPy's signature **ndarray** allows the performant handling of large and high-dimensional matrices.

Ndarrays are the essence of NumPy. They are what makes it faster than using Python's built-in lists. Other than the built-in list data type, ndarrays provide a stridden view of memory (for example, `int[]` in Java). Since they are homogeneously typed, meaning all the elements must be of the same type, the stride is consistent, which results in less memory wastage and better access times.

The **stride** is the number of locations between the beginnings of two adjacent elements in an array. They are normally measured in bytes or in units of the size of the array elements. A stride can be larger or equal to the size of the element, but not smaller; otherwise, it would intersect the memory location of the next element.

> **NOTE**
>
> Remember that NumPy arrays have a defined data type. This means you are not able to insert strings into an integer type array. NumPy is mostly used with double-precision data types.

The following are some of the built-in methods that we will use in the exercises and activities of this chapter.

mean

NumPy provides implementations of all the mathematical operations we covered in the *Overview of Statistics* section of this chapter. The mean, or average, is the one we will look at in more detail in the upcoming exercise:

> **NOTE**
>
> The # symbol in the code snippet below denotes a code comment. Comments are added into code to help explain specific bits of logic.

```
# mean value for the whole dataset
np.mean(dataset)

# mean value of the first row
np.mean(dataset[0])

# mean value of the whole first column
np.mean(dataset[:, 0]

# mean value of the first 10 elements of the second row
np.mean(dataset[1, 0:10])
```

median

Several of the mathematical operations have the same interface. This makes them easy to interchange if necessary. The **median**, **var**, and **std** methods will be used in the upcoming exercises and activities:

```
# median value for the whole dataset
np.median(dataset)

# median value of the last row using reverse indexing
np.median(dataset[-1])

# median value of values of rows >5 in the first column
np.median(dataset[5:, 0])
```

Note that we can index every element from the end of our dataset as we can from the front by using **reverse indexing**. It's a simple way to get the last or several of the last elements of a list. Instead of **[0]** for the first/last element, it starts with **dataset[-1]** and then decreases until **dataset[-len(dataset)]**, which is the first element in the dataset.

var

As we mentioned in the *Overview of Statistics* section, the variance describes how far a set of numbers is spread out from their mean. We can calculate the variance using the **var** method of NumPy:

```
# variance value for the whole dataset
np.var(dataset)

# axis used to get variance per column
np.var(dataset, axis=0)

# axis used to get variance per row
np.var(dataset, axis=1)
```

std

One of the advantages of the standard deviation is that it remains in the scalar system of the data. This means that the unit of the deviation will have the same unit as the data itself. The **std** method works just like the others:

```
# standard deviation for the whole dataset
np.std(dataset)

# std value of values from the 2 first rows and columns
np.std(dataset[:2, :2])

# axis used to get standard deviation per row
np.std(dataset, axis=1)
```

Now we will do an exercise to load a dataset and calculate the mean using these methods.

> **NOTE**
>
> All the exercises and activities in this chapter will be developed in Jupyter Notebooks. Please download the GitHub repository with all the prepared templates from https://packt.live/31USkof. Make sure you have installed all the libraries as mentioned in the preface.

EXERCISE 1.01: LOADING A SAMPLE DATASET AND CALCULATING THE MEAN USING NUMPY

In this exercise, we will be loading the **normal_distribution.csv** dataset and calculating the mean of each row and each column in it:

1. Using the Anaconda Navigator launch either Jupyter Labs or Jupyter Notebook. In the directory of your choice, create a **Chapter01/Exercise1.01** folder.

2. Create a new Jupyter Notebook and save it as **Exercise1.01.ipynb** in the **Chapter01/Exercise1.01** folder.

3. Now, begin writing the code for this exercise as shown in the steps below. We begin with the import statements. Import **numpy** with an alias:

```
import numpy as np
```

4. Use the **genfromtxt** method of NumPy to load the dataset:

> **NOTE**
>
> The code snippet shown here uses a backslash (\ ) to split the logic across multiple lines. When the code is executed, Python will ignore the backslash, and treat the code on the next line as a direct continuation of the current line.

```
dataset = \
np.genfromtxt('../../Datasets/normal_distribution.csv', \
              delimiter=',')
```

> **NOTE**
>
> In the preceding snippet, and for the rest of the book, we will be using a relative path to load the datasets. However, for the preceding code to work as intended, you need to follow the folder arrangement as present in this link: https://packt.live/3ftUu3P. Alternatively, you can also use the absolute path; for example, **dataset = np.genfromtxt('C:/Datasets/ normal_distribution.csv', delimiter=',')**. If your Jupyter Notebook is saved in the same folder as the dataset, then you can simply use the filename: **dataset = np.genfromtxt('normal_ distribution.csv', delimiter=',')**

The **genfromtxt** method helps load the data from a given text or **.csv** file. If everything works as expected, the generation should run through without any error or output.

> **NOTE**
>
> The **numpy.genfromtext** method is less efficient than the **pandas. read_csv** method. We shall refrain from going into the details of why this is the case as this explanation is beyond the scope of this text.

5. Check the data you just imported by simply writing the name of the ndarray in the next cell. Simply executing a cell that returns a value, such as an ndarray, will use Jupyter formatting, which looks nice and, in most cases, displays more information than using **print**:

```
# looking at the dataset
dataset
```

A section of the output resulting from the preceding code is as follows:

```
array([[ 99.14931546, 104.03852715, 107.43534677,  97.85230675,
         98.74986914,  98.80833412,  96.81964892,  98.56783189],
       [ 92.02628776,  97.10439252,  99.32066924,  97.24584816,
         92.9267508 ,  92.65657752, 105.7197853 , 101.23162942],
       [ 95.66253664,  95.17750125,  90.93318132, 110.18889465,
         98.80084371, 105.95297652,  98.37481387, 106.54654286],
       [ 91.37294597, 100.96781394, 100.40118279, 113.42090475,
        105.48508838,  91.6604946 , 106.1472841 ,  95.08715803],
       [101.20862522, 103.5730309 , 100.28690912, 105.85269352,
         93.37126331, 108.57980357, 100.79478953,  94.20019732],
       [102.80387079,  98.29687616,  93.24376389,  97.24130034,
         89.03452725,  96.2832753 , 104.60344836, 101.13442416],
       [106.71751618, 102.97585605,  98.45723272, 100.72418901,
        106.39798503,  95.46493436,  94.35373179, 106.83273763],
       [ 96.02548256, 102.82360856, 106.47551845, 101.34745901,
        102.45651798,  98.74767493,  97.57544275,  92.5748759 ],
       [105.30350449,  92.87730812, 103.19258339, 104.40518318,
        101.29326772, 100.85447132, 101.2226037 , 106.03868807],
       [110.44484313,  93.87155456, 101.5363647 ,  97.65393524,
         92.75048583, 101.72074646,  96.96851209, 103.29147111],
       [101.3514185 , 100.37372248, 106.6471081 , 100.61742813,
        105.0320535 ,  99.35999981,  98.87007532,  95.85284217],
       [ 97.21315663. 107.02874163. 102.17642112,  96.74630281,
```

Figure 1.9: The first few rows of the normal_distribution.csv file

6. Print the shape using the **dataset.shape** command to get a quick overview of our dataset. This will give us output in the form (rows, columns):

```
dataset.shape
```

We can also call the rows as instances and the columns as features. This means that our dataset has 24 instances and 8 features. The output of the preceding code is as follows:

```
(24,8)
```

7. Calculate the mean after loading and checking our dataset. The first row in a NumPy array can be accessed by simply indexing it with zero; for example, **dataset[0]**. As we mentioned previously, NumPy has some built-in functions for calculations such as the mean. Call **np.mean()** and pass in the dataset's first row to get the result:

```
# calculating the mean for the first row
np.mean(dataset[0])
```

The output of the preceding code is as follows:

```
100.177647525
```

8. Now, calculate the mean of the first column by using **np.mean()** in combination with the column indexing **dataset[:, 0]**:

```
np.mean(dataset[:, 0])
```

The output of the preceding code is as follows:

```
99.76743510416668
```

Whenever we want to define a range to select from a dataset, we can use a colon, **:**, to provide start and end values for the to be selected range. If we don't provide start and end values, the default of *0* to *n* is used, where n is the length of the current axis.

9. Calculate the mean for every single row, aggregated in a list, using the **axis** tools of NumPy. Note that by simply passing the **axis** parameter in the **np.mean()** call, we can define the dimension our data will be aggregated on. **axis=0** is horizontal and **axis=1** is vertical. Get the result for each row by using **axis=1**:

```
np.mean(dataset, axis=1)
```

The output of the preceding code is as follows:

```
array([[100.17764752,  97.27899259, 100.20466135, 100.56785907,
        100.98341406,  97.83018578, 101.49052285,  99.75332252,
        101.89845125,  99.77973914, 101.013081  , 100.54961696,
         98.48256886,  98.49816126, 101.85956927,  97.05201872,
        102.62147483, 101.21177037,  99.58777968,  98.96533534,
        103.85792812, 101.89050288,  99.07192574,  99.34233101]])
```

Figure 1.10: Mean of the elements of each row

Get the mean of each column by using **axis=0**:

```
np.mean(dataset, axis=0)
```

The output of the preceding code is as follows:

```
array([ 99.7674351 ,  99.61229127, 101.14584656, 101.8449316 ,
        99.04871791,  99.67838931,  99.7848489 , 100.44049274])
```

Figure 1.11: Mean of elements for each column

10. Calculate the mean of the whole matrix by summing all the values we retrieved in the previous steps:

```
np.mean(dataset)
```

The output of the preceding code is as follows:

```
100.16536917390624
```

> **NOTE**
>
> To access the source code for this specific section, please refer to https://packt.live/30IkAMp.
>
> You can also run this example online at https://packt.live/2Y4yHK1.

You are already one step closer to using NumPy in combination with plotting libraries and creating impactful visualizations. Since we've now covered the very basics and calculated the mean, it's now up to you to solve the upcoming activity.

ACTIVITY 1.01: USING NUMPY TO COMPUTE THE MEAN, MEDIAN, VARIANCE, AND STANDARD DEVIATION OF A DATASET

In this activity, we will use the skills we've learned to import datasets and perform some basic calculations (mean, median, variance, and standard deviation) to compute our tasks.

Perform the following steps to implement this activity:

1. Open the **Activity1.01.ipynb** Jupyter Notebook from the **Chapter01** folder to do this activity. Import NumPy and give it the alias **np**.

2. Load the **normal_distribution.csv** dataset by using the **genfromtxt** method from NumPy.

3. Print a subset of the first two rows of the dataset.

4. Load the dataset and calculate the mean of the third row. Access the third row by using index 2, **dataset[2]**.

5. Index the last element of an ndarray in the same way a regular Python list can be accessed. **dataset[:, -1]** will give us the last column of every row.

6. Get a submatrix of the first three elements of every row of the first three columns by using the double-indexing mechanism of NumPy.

7. Calculate the median for the last row of the dataset.

8. Use reverse indexing to define a range to get the last three columns. We can use **dataset[:, -3:]** here.

9. Aggregate the values along an **axis** to calculate the rows. We can use **axis=1** here.

10. Calculate the variance for each column using **axis 0**.

11. Calculate the variance of the intersection of the last two rows and the first two columns.

12. Calculate the standard deviation for the dataset.

> **NOTE**
>
> The solution for this activity can be found on page 388.

You have now completed your first activity using NumPy. In the following activities, this knowledge will be consolidated further.

BASIC NUMPY OPERATIONS

In this section, we will learn about basic NumPy operations such as indexing, slicing, splitting, and iterating and implement them in an exercise.

INDEXING

Indexing elements in a NumPy array, at a high level, works the same as with built-in Python lists. Therefore, we can index elements in multi-dimensional matrices:

```
# index single element in outermost dimension
dataset[0]

# index in reversed order in outermost dimension
dataset[-1]

# index single element in two-dimensional data
dataset[1, 1]

# index in reversed order in two-dimensional data
dataset[-1, -1]
```

SLICING

Slicing has also been adapted from Python's lists. Being able to easily slice parts of lists into new ndarrays is very helpful when handling large amounts of data:

```
# rows 1 and 2
dataset[1:3]

# 2x2 subset of the data
dataset[:2, :2]

# last row with elements reversed
dataset[-1, ::-1]

# last 4 rows, every other element up to index 6
dataset[-5:-1, :6:2]
```

SPLITTING

Splitting data can be helpful in many situations, from plotting only half of your time-series data to separating test and training data for machine learning algorithms.

There are two ways of splitting your data, horizontally and vertically. Horizontal splitting can be done with the **hsplit** method. Vertical splitting can be done with the **vsplit** method:

```
# split horizontally in 3 equal lists
np.hsplit(dataset, (3))


# split vertically in 2 equal lists
np.vsplit(dataset, (2))
```

ITERATING

Iterating the NumPy data structures, ndarrays, is also possible. It steps over the whole list of data one after another, visiting every single element in the ndarray once. Considering that they can have several dimensions, indexing gets very complex.

The **nditer** is a multi-dimensional iterator object that iterates over a given number of arrays:

```
# iterating over whole dataset (each value in each row)
for x in np.nditer(dataset):
    print(x)
```

The **ndenumerate** will give us exactly this index, thus returning (**0**, **1**) for the second value in the first row:

> **NOTE**
>
> The triple-quotes (**"""**) shown in the code snippet below are used to denote the start and end points of a multi-line code comment. Comments are added into code to help explain specific bits of logic.

```
"""
iterating over the whole dataset with indices matching the
position in the dataset
"""
for index, value in np.ndenumerate(dataset):
    print(index, value)
```

Now, we will perform an exercise using these basic NumPy operations.

EXERCISE 1.02: INDEXING, SLICING, SPLITTING, AND ITERATING

In this exercise, we will use the features of NumPy to index, slice, split, and iterate ndarrays to consolidate what we've learned. A client has provided us with a dataset, **normal_distribution_splittable.csv**, wants us to confirm that the values in the dataset are closely distributed around the mean value of 100.

> **NOTE**
>
> You can obviously plot a distribution and show the spread of data, but here we want to practice implementing the aforementioned operations using the NumPy library.

Let's use the features of NumPy to index, slice, split, and iterate ndarrays.

Indexing

1. Create a new Jupyter Notebook and save it as **Exercise1.02.ipynb** in the **Chapter01/Exercise1.02** folder.

2. Import the necessary libraries:

```
import numpy as np
```

3. Load the **normal_distribution.csv** dataset using NumPy. Have a look at the ndarray to verify that everything works:

```
dataset = np.genfromtxt('../../Datasets/'\
                        'normal_distribution_splittable.csv', \
                        delimiter=',')
```

> **NOTE**
>
> As mentioned in the previous exercise, here too we have used a relative path to load the dataset. You can change the path depending on where you have saved the Jupyter Notebook and the dataset.

Remember that we need to show that our dataset is closely distributed around a mean of 100; that is, whatever value we wish to show/calculate should be around 100. For this purpose, first we will calculate the mean of the values of the second and the last row.

4. Use simple indexing for the second row, as we did in our first exercise. For a clearer understanding, all the elements of the second row are saved to a variable and then we calculate the mean of these elements:

```
second_row = dataset[1]
np.mean(second_row)
```

The output of the preceding code is as follows:

```
96.90038836444445
```

5. Now, reverse index the last row and calculate the mean of that row. Always remember that providing a negative number as the index value will index the list from the end:

```
last_row = dataset[-1]
np.mean(last_row)
```

The output of the preceding code is as follows:

```
100.18096645222221
```

From the outputs obtained in *step 4* and *5*, we can say that these values indeed are close to 100. To further convince our client, we will access the first value of the first row and the last value of the second last row.

6. Index the first value of the first row using the Python standard syntax of [0][0]:

```
first_val_first_row = dataset[0][0]
np.mean(first_val_first_row)
```

The output of the preceding code is as follows:

```
99.14931546
```

7. Use reverse indexing to access the last value of the second last row (we want to use the combined access syntax here). Remember that **−1** means the last element:

```
last_val_second_last_row = dataset[-2, -1]
np.mean(last_val_second_last_row)
```

The output of the preceding code is as follows:

```
101.2226037
```

> **NOTE**
>
> For *steps 6* and *7*, even if you had not used **np.mean()**, you would have got the same values as presently shown. This is because the mean of a single value will be the value itself. You can try the above steps with the following code:
>
> ```
> first_val_first_row = dataset[0][0]
> first_val_first_row
> last_val_second_last_row = dataset[-2, -1]
> last_val_second_last_row
> ```

From all the preceding outputs, we can confidently say that the values we obtained hover around a mean of 100. Next, we'll use slicing, splitting, and iterating to achieve our goal.

Slicing

1. Create a 2x2 matrix that starts at the second row and second column using **[1:3, 1:3]**:

```
"""
slicing an intersection of 4 elements (2x2) of the
first two rows and first two columns
"""
subsection_2x2 = dataset[1:3, 1:3]
np.mean(subsection_2x2)
```

The output of the preceding code is as follows:

```
95.63393608250001
```

2. In this task, we want to have every other element of the fifth row. Provide indexing of **::2** as our second element to get every second element of the given row:

```
every_other_elem = dataset[4, ::2]
np.mean(every_other_elem)
```

The output of the preceding code is as follows:

```
98.35235805800001
```

Introducing the second column into the indexing allows us to add another layer of complexity. The third value allows us to only select certain values (such as every other element) by providing a value of 2. This means it skips the values between and only takes each second element from the used list.

3. Reverse the elements in a slice using negative numbers:

```
reversed_last_row = dataset[-1, ::-1]
np.mean(reversed_last_row)
```

The output of the preceding code is as follows:

```
100.18096645222222
```

Splitting

1. Use the **hsplit** method to split our dataset into three equal parts:

```
hor_splits = np.hsplit(dataset,(3))
```

Note that if the dataset can't be split with the given number of slices, it will throw an error.

2. Split the first third into two equal parts vertically. Use the **vsplit** method to vertically split the dataset in half. It works like **hsplit**:

```
ver_splits = np.vsplit(hor_splits[0],(2))
```

3. Compare the shapes. We can see that the subset has the required half of the rows and the third half of the columns:

```
print("Dataset", dataset.shape)
print("Subset", ver_splits[0].shape)
```

The output of the preceding code is as follows:

```
Dataset (24, 9)
Subset (12, 3)
```

Iterating

1. Iterate over the whole dataset (each value in each row):

```
curr_index = 0
for x in np.nditer(dataset):
    print(x, curr_index)
    curr_index += 1
```

The output of the preceding code is as follows:

```
99.14931546 0
104.03852715 1
107.43534677 2
97.85230675 3
98.74986914 4
98.80833412 5
96.81964892 6
98.56783189 7
101.34745901 8
92.02628776 9
97.10439252 10
```

Figure 1.12: Iterating the entire dataset

Looking at the given piece of code, we can see that the index is simply incremented with each element. This only works with one-dimensional data. If we want to index multi-dimensional data, this won't work.

2. Use the **ndenumerate** method to iterate over the whole dataset. It provides two positional values, **index** and **value**:

```
for index, value in np.ndenumerate(dataset):
    print(index, value)
```

The output of the preceding code is as follows:

```
(0, 0) 99.14931546
(0, 1) 104.03852715
(0, 2) 107.43534677
(0, 3) 97.85230675
(0, 4) 98.74986914
(0, 5) 98.80833412
(0, 6) 96.81964892
(0, 7) 98.56783189
(0, 8) 101.34745901
(1, 0) 92.02628776
(1, 1) 97.10439252
(1, 2) 99.32066924
(1, 3) 97.24584816
(1, 4) 92.9267508
(1, 5) 92.65657752
```

Figure 1.13: Enumerating the dataset with multi-dimensional data

Notice that all the output values we obtained are close to our mean value of 100. Thus, we have successfully managed to convince our client using several NumPy methods that our data is closely distributed around the mean value of 100.

> **NOTE**
>
> To access the source code for this specific section, please refer to https://packt.live/2Neteuh.
>
> You can also run this example online at https://packt.live/3e7K0qq.

We've already covered most of the basic data wrangling methods for NumPy. In the next section, we'll take a look at more advanced features that will give you the tools you need to get better at analyzing your data.

ADVANCED NUMPY OPERATIONS

In this section, we will learn about advanced NumPy operations such as filtering, sorting, combining, and reshaping and then implement them in an exercise.

FILTERING

Filtering is a very powerful tool that can be used to clean up your data if you want to avoid outlier values.

In addition to the **dataset[dataset > 10]** shorthand notation, we can use the built-in NumPy **extract** method, which does the same thing using a different notation, but gives us greater control with more complex examples.

If we only want to extract the indices of the values that match our given condition, we can use the built-in **where** method. For example, **np.where(dataset > 5)** will return a list of indices of the values from the initial dataset that is bigger than 5:

```
# values bigger than 10
dataset[dataset > 10]

# alternative - values smaller than 3
np.extract((dataset < 3), dataset)

# values bigger 5 and smaller 10
dataset[(dataset > 5) & (dataset < 10)]

# indices of values bigger than 5 (rows and cols)
np.where(dataset > 5)
```

SORTING

Sorting each row of a dataset can be really useful. Using NumPy, we are also able to sort on other dimensions, such as columns.

In addition, **argsort** gives us the possibility to get a list of indices, which would result in a sorted list:

```
# values sorted on last axis
np.sort(dataset)


# values sorted on axis 0
np.sort(dataset, axis=0)


# indices of values in sorted list
np.argsort(dataset)
```

COMBINING

Stacking rows and columns onto an existing dataset can be helpful when you have two datasets of the same dimension saved to different files.

Given two datasets, we use **vstack** to stack **dataset_1** on top of **dataset_2**, which will give us a combined dataset with all the rows from **dataset_1**, followed by all the rows from **dataset_2**.

If we use **hstack**, we stack our datasets "next to each other," meaning that the elements from the first row of **dataset_1** will be followed by the elements of the first row of **dataset_2**. This will be applied to each row:

```
# combine datasets vertically
np.vstack([dataset_1, dataset_2])


# combine datasets horizontally
np.hstack([dataset_1, dataset_2])


# combine datasets on axis 0
np.stack([dataset_1, dataset_2], axis=0)
```

RESHAPING

Reshaping can be crucial for some algorithms. Depending on the nature of your data, it might help you to reduce dimensionality to make visualization easier:

```
# reshape dataset to two columns x rows
dataset.reshape(-1, 2)


# reshape dataset to one row x columns
np.reshape(dataset, (1, -1))
```

Here, **-1** is an unknown dimension that NumPy identifies automatically. NumPy will figure out the length of any given array and the remaining dimensions and will thus make sure that it satisfies the required standard.

Next, we will perform an exercise using advanced NumPy operations.

EXERCISE 1.03: FILTERING, SORTING, COMBINING, AND RESHAPING

This final exercise for NumPy provides some more complex tasks to consolidate our learning. It will also combine most of the previously learned methods as a recap. We'll use the filtering features of NumPy for sorting, stacking, combining, and reshaping our data:

1. Create a new Jupyter Notebook and save it as **Exercise1.03.ipynb** in the **Chapter01/Exercise1.03** folder.

2. Import the necessary libraries:

```
import numpy as np
```

3. Load the **normal_distribution_splittable.csv** dataset using NumPy. Make sure that everything works by having a look at the ndarray:

```
dataset = np.genfromtxt('../../Datasets/'\
                        'normal_distribution_splittable.csv', \
                        delimiter=',')
dataset
```

4. You will obtain the following output:

```
array([[ 99.14931546, 104.03852715, 107.43534677,  97.85230675,
         98.74986914,  98.80833412,  96.81964892,  98.56783189,
        101.34745901],
       [ 92.02628776,  97.10439252,  99.32066924,  97.24584816,
         92.9267508 ,  92.65657752, 105.7197853 , 101.23162942,
         93.87155456],
       [ 95.66253664,  95.17750125,  90.93318132, 110.18889465,
         98.80084371, 105.95297652,  98.37481387, 106.54654286,
        107.22482426],
       [ 91.37294597, 100.96781394, 100.40118279, 113.42090475,
        105.48508838,  91.6604946 , 106.1472841 ,  95.08715803,
        103.40412146],
       [101.20862522, 103.5730309 , 100.28690912, 105.85269352,
         93.37126331, 108.57980357, 100.79478953,  94.20019732,
         96.10020311],
       [102.80387079,  98.29687616,  93.24376389,  97.24130034,
         89.03452725,  96.2832753 , 104.60344836, 101.13442416,
         97.62787811],
       [106.71751618, 102.97585605,  98.45723272, 100.72418901,
        106.39798503,  95.46493436,  94.35373179, 106.83273763,
        100.07721494],
       [ 96.02548256, 102.82360856, 106.47551845, 101.34745901,
        102.45651798,  98.74767493,  97.57544275,  92.5748759 ,
         91.37294597],
       [105.30350449,  92.87730812, 103.19258339, 104.40518318,
        101.29326772, 100.85447132, 101.2226037 , 106.03868807,
         97.85230675],
```

Figure 1.14: Rows and columns of the dataset

NOTE

For ease of presentation, we have shown only a part of the output.

Filtering

1. Get values greater than 105 by supplying the condition **> 105** in the brackets:

```
vals_greater_five = dataset[dataset > 105]
vals_greater_five
```

You will obtain the following output:

```
array([107.43534677, 105.7197853 , 110.18889465, 105.95297652,
       106.54654286, 107.22482426, 113.42090475, 105.48508838,
       106.1472841 , 105.85269352, 108.57980357, 106.71751618,
       106.39798503, 106.83273763, 106.47551845, 105.30350449,
       106.03868807, 110.44484313, 106.6471081 , 105.0320535 ,
       107.02874163, 105.07475277, 106.57364584, 107.22482426,
       107.19119932, 108.09423367, 109.40523174, 106.11454989,
       106.57052697, 105.13668343, 105.37011896, 110.44484313,
       105.86078488, 106.89005002, 106.57364584, 107.40064604,
       106.38276709, 106.46476468, 110.43976681, 105.02389857,
       106.05042487, 106.89005002])
```

Figure 1.15: Filtered dataset displaying values greater than 105

You can see in the preceding figure that all the values in the output are greater than 105.

2. Extract the values of our dataset that are between the values 90 and 95. To use more complex conditions, we might want to use the **extract** method of NumPy:

```
vals_between_90_95 = np.extract((dataset > 90) \
                     & (dataset < 95), dataset)
vals_between_90_95
```

You will obtain the following output:

```
array([92.02628776, 92.9267508 , 92.65657752, 93.87155456, 90.93318132,
       91.37294597, 91.6604946 , 93.37126331, 94.20019732, 93.24376389,
       94.35373179, 92.5748759 , 91.37294597, 92.87730812, 93.87155456,
       92.75048583, 93.97853495, 91.32093303, 92.0108226 , 93.18884302,
       93.83969256, 94.5081787 , 94.59300658, 93.04610867, 91.6779221 ,
       91.37294597, 94.76253572, 94.57421727, 94.11176915, 93.97853495])
```

Figure 1.16: Filtered dataset displaying values between 90 and 95

The preceding output clearly shows that only values lying between 90 and 95 are printed.

3. Use the **where** method to get the indices of values that have a delta of less than 1; that is, *[individual value] – 100* should be less than 1. Use those indices (**row, col)** in a list comprehension and print them out:

```
rows, cols = np.where(abs(dataset - 100) < 1)
one_away_indices = [[rows[index], \
                    cols[index]] for (index, _) \
                    in np.ndenumerate(rows)]
one_away_indices
```

The **where** method from NumPy allows us to get **indices (rows, cols)** for each of the matching values.

Observe the following truncated output:

```
[[0, 0],
 [1, 2],
 [3, 1],
 [3, 2],
 [4, 2],
 [4, 6],
 [6, 3],
 [6, 8],
 [8, 5],
 [9, 8],
 [10, 1],
 [10, 3],
 [10, 5],
 [12, 8],
 [13, 0],
 [13, 4],
```

Figure 1.17: Indices of the values that have a delta of less than 1

Let us confirm if we indeed obtained the right indices. The first set of indices **0 , 0** refer to the very first value in the output shown in *Figure 1.14*. Indeed, this is the correct value as **abs (99.14931546 – 100) < 1**. We can quickly check this for a couple of more values and conclude that indeed the code has worked as intended.

> **NOTE**
>
> **List comprehensions** are Python's way of mapping over data. They're a handy notation for creating a new list with some operation applied to every element of the old list.
>
> For example, if we want to double the value of every element in this list, **list = [1, 2, 3, 4, 5]**, we would use list comprehensions like this: **doubled_list=[x*x for x in list]**. This gives us the following list: **[1, 4, 9, 16, 25]**. To get a better understanding of list comprehensions, please visit https://docs.python.org/3/tutorial/datastructures.html#list-comprehensions.

Sorting

1. Sort each row in our dataset by using the **sort** method:

```
row_sorted = np.sort(dataset)
row_sorted
```

As described before, by default, the **last axis** will be used. In a two-dimensional dataset, this is axis 1 which represents the rows. So, we can omit the **axis=1** argument in the **np.sort** method call. You will obtain the following output:

```
array([[ 96.81964892,  97.85230675,  98.56783189,  98.74986914,
         98.80833412,  99.14931546, 101.34745901, 104.03852715,
        107.43534677],
       [ 92.02628776,  92.65657752,  92.9267508 ,  93.87155456,
         97.10439252,  97.24584816,  99.32066924, 101.23162942,
        105.7197853 ],
       [ 90.93318132,  95.17750125,  95.66253664,  98.37481387,
         98.80084371, 105.95297652, 106.54654286, 107.22482426,
        110.18889465],
       [ 91.37294597,  91.6604946 ,  95.08715803, 100.40118279,
        100.96781394, 103.40412146, 105.48508838, 106.1472841 ,
        113.42090475],
       [ 93.37126331,  94.20019732,  96.10020311, 100.28690912,
        100.79478953, 101.20862522, 103.5730309 , 105.85269352,
        108.57980357],
       [ 89.03452725,  93.24376389,  96.2832753 ,  97.24130034,
         97.62787811,  98.29687616, 101.13442416, 102.80387079,
        104.60344836],
       [ 94.35373179,  95.46493436,  98.45723272, 100.07721494,
        100.72418901, 102.97585605, 106.39798503, 106.71751618,
        106.83273763],
       [ 91.37294597,  92.5748759 ,  96.02548256,  97.57544275,
         98.74767493, 101.34745901, 102.45651798, 102.82360856,
        106.47551845],
```

Figure 1.18: Dataset with sorted rows

Compare the preceding output with that in *Figure 1.14*. What do you observe? The values along the rows have been sorted in an ascending order as expected.

2. With multi-dimensional data, we can use the **axis** parameter to define which dataset should be sorted. Use the **0** axes to sort the values by column:

```
col_sorted = np.sort(dataset, axis=0)
col_sorted
```

A truncated version of the output is as follows:

```
array([[ 91.37294597,  88.80221141,  90.93318132,  93.18884302,
         85.98839623,  91.6604946 ,  91.32093303,  92.5748759 ,
         91.37294597],
       [ 92.02628776,  91.6779221 ,  93.24376389,  94.59300658,
         89.03452725,  92.65657752,  93.04610867,  94.20019732,
         91.37294597],
       [ 94.11176915,  92.0108226 ,  93.83969256,  96.74630281,
         92.75048583,  95.19184343,  94.35373179,  94.76253572,
         93.87155456],
       [ 95.65982034,  92.87730812,  94.5081787 ,  97.24130034,
         92.9267508 ,  95.46493436,  96.50342927,  95.08715803,
         93.97853495],
       [ 95.66253664,  93.87155456,  97.75887636,  97.24584816,
         93.37126331,  95.62359311,  96.81964892,  95.85284217,
         95.19184343],
       [ 96.02548256,  94.57421727,  98.45723272,  97.62787811,
         93.97853495,  96.2832753 ,  96.89244283,  97.59572169,
         96.10020311],
```

Figure 1.19: Dataset with sorted columns

As expected, the values along the columns (91.37294597, 91.02628776, 94.11176915, and so on) are now sorted in an ascending order.

3. Create a sorted index list and use fancy indexing to get access to sorted elements easily. To keep the order of our dataset and obtain only the values of a sorted dataset, we will use **argsort**:

```
index_sorted = np.argsort(dataset[0])
dataset[0][index_sorted]
```

The output is as follows:

```
array([ 96.81964892,  97.85230675,  98.56783189,  98.74986914,
        98.80833412,  99.14931546, 101.34745901, 104.03852715,
       107.43534677])
```

Figure 1.20: First row with sorted values from argsort

As can be seen from the preceding output, we have obtained the first row with sorted values.

Combining

4. Use the combining features to add the second half of the first column back together, add the second column to our combined dataset, and add the third column to our combined dataset.

```
thirds = np.hsplit(dataset, (3))
halfed_first = np.vsplit(thirds[0], (2))


halfed_first[0]
```

The output of the preceding code is as follows:

```
array([[ 99.14931546, 104.03852715, 107.43534677],
       [ 92.02628776,  97.10439252,  99.32066924],
       [ 95.66253664,  95.17750125,  90.93318132],
       [ 91.37294597, 100.96781394, 100.40118279],
       [101.20862522, 103.5730309 , 100.28690912],
       [102.80387079,  98.29687616,  93.24376389],
       [106.71751618, 102.97585605,  98.45723272],
       [ 96.02548256, 102.82360856, 106.47551845],
       [105.30350449,  92.87730812, 103.19258339],
       [110.44484313,  93.87155456, 101.5363647 ],
       [101.3514185 , 100.37372248, 106.6471081 ],
       [ 97.21315663, 107.02874163, 102.17642112]])
```

Figure 1.21: Splitting the dataset

5. Use **vstack** to vertically combine the **halfed_first** datasets:

```
first_col = np.vstack([halfed_first[0], halfed_first[1]])
first_col
```

The output of the preceding code is as follows:

```
array([[ 99.14931546, 104.03852715, 107.43534677],
       [ 92.02628776,  97.10439252,  99.32066924],
       [ 95.66253664,  95.17750125,  90.93318132],
       [ 91.37294597, 100.96781394, 100.40118279],
       [101.20862522, 103.5730309 , 100.28690912],
       [102.80387079,  98.29687616,  93.24376389],
       [106.71751618, 102.97585605,  98.45723272],
       [ 96.02548256, 102.82360856, 106.47551845],
       [105.30350449,  92.87730812, 103.19258339],
       [110.44484313,  93.87155456, 101.5363647 ],
       [101.3514185 , 100.37372248, 106.6471081 ],
       [ 97.21315663, 107.02874163, 102.17642112],
       [ 95.65982034, 107.22482426, 107.19119932],
       [100.39303522,  92.0108226 ,  97.75887636],
       [103.1521596 , 109.40523174,  93.83969256],
       [106.11454989,  88.80221141,  94.5081787 ],
       [ 96.78266211,  99.84251605, 104.03478031],
       [101.86186193, 103.61720152,  99.57859892],
       [ 97.49594839,  96.59385486, 104.63817694],
       [ 96.76814836,  91.6779221 , 101.79132774],
       [106.89005002, 106.57364584, 102.26648279],
       [ 99.80873105, 101.63973121, 106.46476468],
       [ 96.10020311,  94.57421727, 100.80409326],
       [ 94.11176915,  99.62387832, 104.51786419]])
```

Figure 1.22: Vertically combining the dataset

After stacking the second half of our split dataset, we have one-third of our initial dataset stacked together again. Now, we want to add the other two remaining datasets to our **first_col** dataset.

6. Use the **hstack** method to combine our already combined **first_col** with the second of the three split datasets:

```
first_second_col = np.hstack([first_col, thirds[1]])
first_second_col
```

A truncated version of the output resulting from the preceding code is as follows:

```
array([[ 99.14931546, 104.03852715, 107.43534677,  97.85230675,
         98.74986914,  98.80833412],
       [ 92.02628776,  97.10439252,  99.32066924,  97.24584816,
         92.9267508 ,  92.65657752],
       [ 95.66253664,  95.17750125,  90.93318132, 110.18889465,
         98.80084371, 105.95297652],
       [ 91.37294597, 100.96781394, 100.40118279, 113.42090475,
        105.48508838,  91.6604946 ],
       [101.20862522, 103.5730309 , 100.28690912, 105.85269352,
         93.37126331, 108.57980357],
       [102.80387079,  98.29687616,  93.24376389,  97.24130034,
         89.03452725,  96.2832753 ],
       [106.71751618, 102.97585605,  98.45723272, 100.72418901,
        106.39798503,  95.46493436],
       [ 96.02548256, 102.82360856, 106.47551845, 101.34745901,
        102.45651798,  98.74767493],
       [105.30350449,  92.87730812, 103.19258339, 104.40518318,
        101.29326772, 100.85447132],
       [110.44484313,  93.87155456, 101.5363647 ,  97.65393524,
         92.75048583, 101.72074646],
       [101.3514185 , 100.37372248, 106.6471081 , 100.61742813,
        105.0320535 ,  99.35999981],
```

Figure 1.23: Horizontally combining the dataset

7. Use **hstack** to combine the last one-third column with our dataset. This is the same thing we did with our second-third column in the previous step:

```
full_data = np.hstack([first_second_col, thirds[2]])
full_data
```

A truncated version of the output resulting from the preceding code is as follows:

```
array([[ 99.14931546, 104.03852715, 107.43534677,  97.85230675,
         98.74986914,  98.80833412,  96.81964892,  98.56783189,
        101.34745901],
       [ 92.02628776,  97.10439252,  99.32066924,  97.24584816,
         92.9267508 ,  92.65657752, 105.7197853 , 101.23162942,
         93.87155456],
       [ 95.66253664,  95.17750125,  90.93318132, 110.18889465,
         98.80084371, 105.95297652,  98.37481387, 106.54654286,
        107.22482426],
       [ 91.37294597, 100.96781394, 100.40118279, 113.42090475,
        105.48508838,  91.6604946 , 106.1472841 ,  95.08715803,
        103.40412146],
       [101.20862522, 103.5730309 , 100.28690912, 105.85269352,
         93.37126331, 108.57980357, 100.79478953,  94.20019732,
         96.10020311],
       [102.80387079,  98.29687616,  93.24376389,  97.24130034,
         89.03452725,  96.2832753 , 104.60344836, 101.13442416,
         97.62787811],
       [106.71751618, 102.97585605,  98.45723272, 100.72418901,
        106.39798503,  95.46493436,  94.35373179, 106.83273763,
        100.07721494],
       [ 96.02548256, 102.82360856, 106.47551845, 101.34745901,
        102.45651798,  98.74767493,  97.57544275,  92.5748759 ,
         91.37294597],
       [105.30350449,  92.87730812, 103.19258339, 104.40518318,
        101.29326772, 100.85447132, 101.2226037 , 106.03868807,
         97.85230675],
```

Figure 1.24: The complete dataset

Reshaping

1. Reshape our dataset into a single list using the **reshape** method:

```
single_list = np.reshape(dataset, (1, -1))
single_list
```

A truncated version of the output resulting from the preceding code is as follows:

```
array([[ 99.14931546, 104.03852715, 107.43534677,  97.85230675,
         98.74986914,  98.80833412,  96.81964892,  98.56783189,
        101.34745901,  92.02628776,  97.10439252,  99.32066924,
         97.24584816,  92.9267508 ,  92.65657752, 105.7197853 ,
        101.23162942,  93.87155456,  95.66253664,  95.17750125,
         90.93318132, 110.18889465,  98.80084371, 105.95297652,
         98.37481387, 106.54654286, 107.22482426,  91.37294597,
        100.96781394, 100.40118279, 113.42090475, 105.48508838,
         91.6604946 , 106.1472841 ,  95.08715803, 103.40412146,
        101.20862522, 103.5730309 , 100.28690912, 105.85269352,
         93.37126331, 108.57980357, 100.79478953,  94.20019732,
         96.10020311, 102.80387079,  98.29687616,  93.24376389,
         97.24130034,  89.03452725,  96.2832753 , 104.60344836,
        101.13442416,  97.62787811, 106.71751618, 102.97585605,
         98.45723272, 100.72418901, 106.39798503,  95.46493436,
         94.35373179, 106.83273763, 100.07721494,  96.02548256,
        102.82360856, 106.47551845, 101.34745901, 102.45651798,
         98.74767493,  97.57544275,  92.5748759 ,  91.37294597,
```

Figure 1.25: Reshaped dataset

2. Provide a **−1** for the dimension. This tells NumPy to figure the dimension out itself:

```
# reshaping to a matrix with two columns
two_col_dataset = dataset.reshape(-1, 2)
two_col_dataset
```

A truncated version of the output resulting from the preceding code is as follows:

```
array([[ 99.14931546, 104.03852715],
       [107.43534677,  97.85230675],
       [ 98.74986914,  98.80833412],
       [ 96.81964892,  98.56783189],
       [101.34745901,  92.02628776],
       [ 97.10439252,  99.32066924],
       [ 97.24584816,  92.9267508 ],
       [ 92.65657752, 105.7197853 ],
       [101.23162942,  93.87155456],
       [ 95.66253664,  95.17750125],
       [ 90.93318132, 110.18889465],
       [ 98.80084371, 105.95297652],
       [ 98.37481387, 106.54654286],
       [107.22482426,  91.37294597],
       [100.96781394, 100.40118279],
       [113.42090475, 105.48508838],
       [ 91.6604946 , 106.1472841 ],
       [ 95.08715803, 103.40412146],
       [101.20862522, 103.5730309 ],
       [100.28690912, 105.85269352],
       [ 93.37126331, 108.57980357],
       [100.79478953,  94.20019732],
       [ 96.10020311, 102.80387079],
       [ 98.29687616,  93.24376389],
       [ 97.24130034,  89.03452725],
       [ 96.2832753 , 104.60344836],
       [101.13442416,  97.62787811],
       [106.71751618, 102.97585605],
```

Figure 1.26: The dataset in a two-column format

> **NOTE**
>
> To access the source code for this specific section, please refer to https://packt.live/2YD4AZn.
>
> You can also run this example online at https://packt.live/3e6F7Ol.

You have now used many of the basic operations that are needed so that you can analyze a dataset. Next, we will be learning about pandas, which will provide several advantages when working with data that is more complex than simple multi-dimensional numerical data. pandas also support different data types in datasets, meaning that we can have columns that hold strings and others that have numbers.

NumPy, as you've seen, has some powerful tools. Some of them are even more powerful when combined with pandas DataFrames.

PANDAS

The **pandas** Python library provides data structures and methods for manipulating different types of data, such as numerical and temporal data. These operations are easy to use and highly optimized for performance.

Data formats, such as **CSV** and **JSON**, and databases can be used to create **DataFrames**. DataFrames are the internal representations of data and are very similar to tables but are more powerful since they allow you to efficiently apply operations such as multiplications, aggregations, and even joins. Importing and reading both files and in-memory data is abstracted into a user-friendly interface. When it comes to handling missing data, pandas provide built-in solutions to clean up and augment your data, meaning it fills in missing values with reasonable values.

Integrated indexing and label-based slicing in combination with fancy indexing (what we already saw with NumPy) make handling data simple. More complex techniques, such as **reshaping**, **pivoting,** and **melting** data, together with the possibility of easily **joining** and **merging** data, provide powerful tooling so that you can handle your data correctly.

If you're working with **time-series data**, operations such as **date range generation**, **frequency conversion**, and **moving window statistics** can provide an advanced interface for data wrangling.

> **NOTE**
>
> The installation instructions for pandas can be found here: https://pandas.pydata.org/. The latest version is v0.25.3 (used in this book); however, every v0.25.x should be suitable.

ADVANTAGES OF PANDAS OVER NUMPY

The following are some of the advantages of pandas:

- **High level of abstraction**: pandas have a higher abstraction level than NumPy, which gives it a simpler interface for users to interact with. It abstracts away some of the more complex concepts, such as high-performance matrix multiplications and joining tables, and makes it easier to use and understand.

- **Less intuition**: Many methods, such as joining, selecting, and loading files, are used without much intuition and without taking away much of the powerful nature of pandas.

- **Faster processing**: The internal representation of DataFrames allows faster processing for some operations. Of course, this always depends on the data and its structure.

- **Easy DataFrame design**: DataFrames are designed for operations with and on large datasets.

DISADVANTAGES OF PANDAS

The following are some of the disadvantages of pandas:

- **Less applicable**: Due to its higher abstraction, it's generally less applicable than NumPy. Especially when used outside of its scope, operations can get complex.

- **More disk space**: Due to the internal representation of DataFrames and the way pandas trades disk space for a more performant execution, the memory usage of complex operations can spike.

- **Performance problems**: Especially when doing heavy joins, which is not recommended, memory usage can get critical and might lead to performance problems.

- **Hidden complexity**: Less experienced users often tend to overuse methods and execute them several times instead of reusing what they've already calculated. This hidden complexity makes users think that the operations themselves are simple, which is not the case.

> **NOTE**
>
> Always try to think about how to design your workflows instead of excessively using operations.

Now, we will do an exercise to load a dataset and calculate the mean using pandas.

EXERCISE 1.04 LOADING A SAMPLE DATASET AND CALCULATING THE MEAN USING PANDAS

In this exercise, we will be loading the **world_population.csv** dataset and calculating the mean of some rows and columns. Our dataset holds the yearly population density for every country. Let's use pandas to perform this exercise:

1. Create a new Jupyter Notebook and save it as **Exercise1.04.ipynb** in the **Chapter01/Exercise1.04** folder.

2. Import the **pandas** libraries:

```
import pandas as pd
```

3. Use the **read_csv** method to load the aforementioned dataset. We want to use the first column, containing the country names, as our index. We will use the **index_col** parameter for that:

```
dataset = \
pd.read_csv('../../Datasets/world_population.csv', \
            index_col=0)
```

4. Now, check the data you just imported by simply writing the name of the dataset in the next cell. pandas uses a data structure called DataFrames. Print some of the rows. To avoid filling the screen, use the pandas **head()** method:

```
dataset.head()
```

The output of the preceding code is as follows:

Country Name	Country Code	Indicator Name	Indicator Code	1960	1961	1962	1963	1964	1965
Aruba	ABW	Population density (people per sq. km of land ...	EN.POP.DNST	NaN	307.972222	312.366667	314.983333	316.827778	318.666667
Andorra	AND	Population density (people per sq. km of land ...	EN.POP.DNST	NaN	30.587234	32.714894	34.914894	37.170213	39.470213
Afghanistan	AFG	Population density (people per sq. km of land ...	EN.POP.DNST	NaN	14.038148	14.312061	14.599692	14.901579	15.218206
Angola	AGO	Population density (people per sq. km of land ...	EN.POP.DNST	NaN	4.305195	4.384299	4.464433	4.544558	4.624228
Albania	ALB	Population density (people per sq. km of land ...	EN.POP.DNST	NaN	60.576642	62.456898	64.329234	66.209307	68.058066

Figure 1.27: The first five rows of our dataset

Both **head()** and **tail()** let you provide a number, **n**, as a parameter, which describes how many rows should be returned.

> **NOTE**
>
> Simply executing a cell that returns a value such as a DataFrame will use Jupyter formatting, which looks nicer and, in most cases, displays more information than using **print**.

5. Print out the shape of the dataset to get a quick overview using the **dataset. shape** command. This works the same as it does with NumPy ndarrays. It will give us the output in the form **(rows, columns)**:

```
dataset.shape
```

The output of the preceding code is as follows:

```
(264, 60)
```

6. Index the column with the year 1961. pandas DataFrames have built-in functions for calculations, such as the **mean**. This means we can simply call **dataset. mean()** to get the result.

The printed output should look as follows:

```
dataset["1961"].mean()
```

The output of the preceding code is as follows:

```
176.91514132840555
```

7. Check the difference in population density over the years by repeating the previous step with the column for the year 2015 (the population more than doubled in the given time range):

```
# calculating the mean for 2015 column
dataset["2015"].mean()
```

The output of the preceding code is as follows:

```
368.70660104001837
```

8. To get the mean for every single country (row), we can make use of pandas **axis** tools. Use the **mean()** method on the dataset on **axis=1**, meaning all the rows, and return the first 10 rows using the **head()** method:

```
dataset.mean(axis=1).head(10)
```

The output of the preceding code is as follows:

```
Country Name
Aruba                     413.944949
Andorra                   106.838839
Afghanistan                25.373379
Angola                      9.649583
Albania                    99.159197
Arab World                 16.118586
United Arab Emirates       31.321721
Argentina                  11.634028
Armenia                   103.415539
American Samoa            211.855636
dtype: float64
```

Figure 1.28: Mean of elements in the first 10 countries (rows)

9. Get the mean for each column and return the last 10 entries:

```
dataset.mean(axis=0).tail(10)
```

The output of the preceding code is as follows:

```
2007      331.995474
2008      338.688417
2009      343.649206
2010      347.967029
2011      351.942027
2012      357.787305
2013      360.985726
2014      364.849194
2015      368.706601
2016             NaN
dtype:  float64
```

Figure 1.29: Mean of elements for the last 10 years (columns)

10. Calculate the mean of the whole DataFrame:

```
# calculating the mean for the whole matrix
dataset.mean()
```

The output of the preceding code is as follows:

```
1960         NaN
1961    176.915141
1962    180.703231
1963    184.572413
1964    188.461797
1965    192.412363
1966    196.145042
1967    200.118063
1968    203.879464
1969    207.336102
1970    210.607871
1971    213.489694
1972    215.998475
1973    218.438708
1974    220.621210
1975    223.046375
1976    224.960258
1977    227.006734
1978    229.187306
1979    232.510772
1980    236.185357
1981    240.789508
1982    246.175178
1983    251.342389
1984    256.647822
```

Figure 1.30: Mean of elements for each column

Since pandas DataFrames can have different data types in each column, aggregating this value on the whole dataset out of the box makes no sense. By default, **axis=0** will be used, which means that this will give us the same result as the cell prior to this.

> **NOTE**
>
> To access the source code for this specific section, please refer to https://packt.live/37z3Us1.
>
> You can also run this example online at https://packt.live/2Bb0ks8.

We've now seen that the interface of pandas has some similar methods to NumPy, which makes it really easy to understand. We have now covered the very basics, which will help you solve the first exercise using pandas. In the following exercise, you will consolidate your basic knowledge of pandas and use the methods you just learned to solve several computational tasks.

EXERCISE 1.05: USING PANDAS TO COMPUTE THE MEAN, MEDIAN, AND VARIANCE OF A DATASET

In this exercise, we will take the previously learned skills of importing datasets and basic calculations and apply them to solve the tasks of our first exercise using pandas.

Let's use pandas features such as **mean**, **median**, and **variance** to make some calculations on our data:

1. Create a new Jupyter Notebook and save it as **Exercise1.05.ipynb** in the **Chapter01/Exercise1.05** folder.

2. Import the necessary libraries:

```
import pandas as pd
```

3. Use the **read_csv** method to load the aforementioned dataset and use the **index_col** parameter to define the first column as our index:

```
dataset = \
pd.read_csv('../../Datasets/world_population.csv', \
            index_col=0)
```

4. Print the first two rows of our dataset:

```
dataset[0:2]
```

The output of the preceding code is as follows:

Country Name	Country Code	Indicator Name	Indicator Code	1960	1961	1962	1963	1964
Aruba	ABW	Population density (people per sq. km of land ...	EN.POP.DNST	NaN	307.972222	312.366667	314.983333	316.827778
Andorra	AND	Population density (people per sq. km of land ...	EN.POP.DNST	NaN	30.587234	32.714894	34.914894	37.170213

2 rows × 60 columns

Figure 1.31: The first two rows, printed

5. Now, index the third row by using **dataset.iloc[[2]]**. Use the **axis** parameter to get the mean of the country rather than the yearly column:

```
dataset.iloc[[2]].mean(axis=1)
```

The output of the preceding code is as follows:

```
Country Name
Afghanistan     25.373379
dtype: float64
```

Figure 1.32: Calculating the mean of the third row

6. Index the last element of the DataFrame using **-1** as the index for the **iloc()** method:

```
dataset.iloc[[-1]].mean(axis=1)
```

The output of the preceding code is as follows:

```
Country Name
Zimbabwe     24.520532
dtype: float64
```

Figure 1.33: Calculating the mean of the last row

7. Calculate the mean value of the values labeled as Germany using **loc**, which works based on the index column:

```
dataset.loc[["Germany"]].mean(axis=1)
```

The output of the preceding code is as follows:

```
Country Name
Germany    227.773688
dtype: float64
```

Figure 1.34: Indexing a country and calculating the mean of Germany

8. Calculate the median value of the last row by using reverse indexing and **axis=1** to aggregate the values in the row:

```
dataset.iloc[[-1]].median(axis=1)
```

The output of the preceding code is as follows:

```
Country Name
Zimbabwe    25.505431
dtype: float64
```

Figure 1.35: Usage of the median method on the last row

9. Use reverse indexing to get the last three columns with **dataset[-3:]** and calculate the median for each of them:

```
dataset[-3:].median(axis=1)
```

The output of the preceding code is as follows:

```
Country Name
Congo, Dem. Rep.    14.419050
Zambia              10.352668
Zimbabwe            25.505431
dtype: float64
```

Figure 1.36: Median of the last three columns

10. Calculate the median population density values for the first 10 countries of the list using the **head** and **median** methods:

```
dataset.head(10).median(axis=1)
```

The output of the preceding code is as follows:

```
Country Name
Aruba                  348.022222
Andorra                107.300000
Afghanistan             19.998926
Angola                   8.458253
Albania                106.001058
Arab World              15.307283
United Arab Emirates    19.305072
Argentina               11.618238
Armenia                105.898033
American Samoa         220.245000
dtype: float64
```

Figure 1.37: Usage of the axis to calculate the median of the first 10 rows

When handling larger datasets, the order in which methods are executed matters. Think about what **head(10)** does for a moment. It simply takes your dataset and returns the first 10 rows in it, cutting down your input to the **mean()** method drastically.

The last method we'll cover here is the variance. pandas provide a consistent API, which makes it easy to use.

11. Calculate the variance of the dataset and return only the last five columns:

```
dataset.var().tail()
```

The output of the preceding code is as follows:

```
2012    3.063475e+06
2013    3.094597e+06
2014    3.157111e+06
2015    3.220634e+06
2016             NaN
dtype: float64
```

Figure 1.38: Variance of the last five columns

12. Calculate the mean for the year 2015 using both NumPy and pandas separately:

```
# NumPy pandas interoperability
import numpy as np
print("pandas", dataset["2015"].mean())
print("numpy", np.mean(dataset["2015"]))
```

The output of the preceding code is as follows:

Pandas 368.7066010400187
NumPy 368.7066010400187

Figure 1.39: Using NumPy's mean method with a pandas DataFrame

NOTE

To access the source code for this specific section, please refer to https://packt.live/2N7E2Kh.

You can also run this example online at https://packt.live/2Y3B2Fa.

This exercise of how to use NumPy's **mean** method with a pandas DataFrame shows that, in some cases, NumPy has better functionality. However, the DataFrame format of pandas is more applicable, so we combine both libraries to get the best out of both.

You've completed your first exercise with pandas, which showed you some of the similarities, and also differences when working with NumPy and pandas. In the following exercise, this knowledge will be consolidated. You'll also be introduced to more complex features and methods of pandas.

BASIC OPERATIONS OF PANDAS

In this section, we will learn about the basic pandas operations, such as indexing, slicing, and iterating, and implement them with an exercise.

INDEXING

Indexing with pandas is a bit more complex than with NumPy. We can only access columns with a single bracket. To use the indices of the rows to access them, we need the **iloc** method. If we want to access them with **index_col** (which was set in the **read_csv** call), we need to use the **loc** method:

```
# index the 2000 col
dataset["2000"]

# index the last row
dataset.iloc[-1]

# index the row with index Germany
dataset.loc["Germany"]

# index row Germany and column 2015
dataset[["2015"]].loc[["Germany"]]
```

SLICING

Slicing with pandas is even more powerful. We can use the default slicing syntax we've already seen with NumPy or use multi-selection. If we want to slice different rows or columns by name, we can simply pass a list into the brackets:

```
# slice of the first 10 rows
dataset.iloc[0:10]

# slice of rows Germany and India
dataset.loc[["Germany", "India"]]

# subset of Germany and India with years 1970/90
dataset.loc[["Germany", "India"]][["1970", "1990"]]
```

ITERATING

Iterating DataFrames is also possible. Considering that they can have several **dimensions** and **dtypes**, the indexing is very high level and iterating over each row has to be done separately:

```
# iterating the whole dataset
for index, row in dataset.iterrows():
    print(index, row)
```

SERIES

A pandas Series is a one-dimensional labeled array that is capable of holding any type of data. We can create a Series by loading datasets from a **.csv** file, Excel spreadsheet, or SQL database. There are many different ways to create them, such as the following:

- NumPy arrays:

```
# import pandas
import pandas as pd
# import numpy
import numpy as np
# creating a numpy array
numarr = np.array(['p','y','t','h','o','n'])
ser = pd.Series(numarr)
print(ser)
```

- pandas lists:

```
# import pandas
import pandas as pd
# creating a pandas list
plist = ['p','y','t','h','o','n']
ser = pd.Series(plist)
print(ser)
```

Now, we will use basic pandas operations in an exercise.

EXERCISE 1.06: INDEXING, SLICING, AND ITERATING USING PANDAS

In this exercise, we will use the previously discussed pandas features to index, slice, and iterate DataFrames using pandas Series. To derive some insights from our dataset, we need to be able to explicitly index, slice, and iterate our data. For example, we can compare several countries in terms of population density growth.

Let's use the indexing, slicing, and iterating operations to display the population density of Germany, Singapore, United States, and India for years 1970, 1990, and 2010.

Indexing

1. Create a new Jupyter Notebook and save it as **Exercise1.06.ipynb** in the **Chapter01/Exercise1.06** folder.

2. Import the necessary libraries:

```
import pandas as pd
```

3. Use the **read_csv** method to load the **world_population.csv** dataset and use the first column, (containing the country names) as our index using the **index_col** parameter:

```
dataset = \
pd.read_csv('../../Datasets/world_population.csv', \
            index_col=0)
```

4. Index the row with the **index_col "United States"** using the **loc** method:

```
dataset.loc[["United States"]].head()
```

The output of the preceding code is as follows:

	Country Code	Indicator Name	Indicator Code	1960	1961	1962	1963	1964	1965	1966	...
Country Name											
United States	USA	Population density (people per sq. km of land ...	EN.POP.DNST	NaN	20.05588	20.366723	20.661953	20.950959	21.214527	21.460952	...

1 rows × 60 columns

Figure 1.40: A few columns from the output showing indexing United States with the loc method

5. Use reverse indexing in pandas to index the second to last row using the **iloc** method:

```
dataset.iloc[[-2]]
```

The output of the preceding code is as follows:

	Country Code	Indicator Name	Indicator Code	1960	1961	1962	1963	1964	1965	1966	...	2007
Country Name												
Zambia	ZMB	Population density (people per sq. km of land ...	EN.POP.DNST	NaN	4.227724	4.359305	4.496824	4.639914	4.788452	4.942343	...	17.13592

1 rows × 60 columns

Figure 1.41: Indexing the second to last row

6. Columns are indexed using their header. This is the first line of the CSV file. Index the column with the header of **2000** as a Series:

```
dataset["2000"].head()
```

The output of the preceding code is as follows:

```
Country Name
Aruba          504.766667
Andorra        139.146809
Afghanistan     30.177894
Angola          12.078798
Albania        112.738212
Name: 2000, dtype: float64
```

Figure 1.42: Indexing all 2000 columns

Remember, the **head()** method simply returns the first five rows.

7. First, get the data for the year 2000 as a DataFrame and then select India using the **loc()** method using chaining:

```
dataset[["2000"]].loc[["India"]]
```

The output of the preceding code is as follows:

2000

Country Name

India   354.326858

Figure 1.43: Getting the population density of India in 2000

Since the double brackets notation returns a DataFrame once again, we can chain method calls to get distinct elements.

8. Use the single brackets notation to get the distinct value for the population density of India in 2000:

```
dataset["2000"].loc["India"]
```

If we want to only retrieve a Series object, we must replace the double brackets with single ones. The output of the preceding code is as follows:

```
354.326858357522
```

Slicing

1. Create a slice with the rows 2 to 5 using the `iloc()` method again:

```
# slicing countries of rows 2 to 5
dataset.iloc[1:5]
```

The output of the preceding code is as follows:

Country Name	Country Code	Indicator Name	Indicator Code	1960	1961	1962	1963
Andorra	AND	Population density (people per sq. km of land ...	EN.POP.DNST	NaN	30.587234	32.714894	34.914894
Afghanistan	AFG	Population density (people per sq. km of land ...	EN.POP.DNST	NaN	14.038148	14.312061	14.599692
Angola	AGO	Population density (people per sq. km of land ...	EN.POP.DNST	NaN	4.305195	4.384299	4.464433
Albania	ALB	Population density (people per sq. km of land ...	EN.POP.DNST	NaN	60.576642	62.456898	64.329234

4 rows × 60 columns

Figure 1.44: The countries in rows 2 to 5

2. Use the `loc()` method to access several rows in the DataFrame and use the nested brackets to provide a list of elements. Slice the dataset to get the rows for Germany, Singapore, United States, and India:

```
dataset.loc[["Germany", "Singapore", "United States", "India"]]
```

The output of the preceding code is as follows:

Country Name	Country Code	Indicator Name	Indicator Code	1960	1961	1962	1963
Germany	DEU	Population density (people per sq. km of land ...	EN.POP.DNST	NaN	210.172807	212.029284	214.001527
Singapore	SGP	Population density (people per sq. km of land ...	EN.POP.DNST	NaN	2540.895522	2612.238806	2679.104478
United States	USA	Population density (people per sq. km of land ...	EN.POP.DNST	NaN	20.055880	20.366723	20.661953
India	IND	Population density (people per sq. km of land ...	EN.POP.DNST	NaN	154.275864	157.424902	160.679256

4 rows × 60 columns

Figure 1.45: Slicing Germany, Singapore, United States, and India

3. Use chaining to get the rows for Germany, Singapore, United States, and India and return only the values for the years 1970, 1990, and 2010. Since the double bracket queries return new DataFrames, we can chain methods and therefore access distinct subframes of our data:

```
country_list = ["Germany", "Singapore", "United States", "India"]


dataset.loc[country_list][["1970", "1990", "2010"]]
```

The output of the preceding code is as follows:

Country Name	1970	1990	2010
Germany	223.897371	227.517054	234.606908
Singapore	3096.268657	4547.958209	7231.811966
United States	22.388131	27.254514	33.817936
India	186.312757	292.817404	414.028200

Figure 1.46: Slices some of the countries and their population density
for 1970, 1990, and 2010

Iterating

1. Iterate our dataset and print out the countries up until **Angola** using the **iterrows()** method. The index will be the name of our row, and the row will hold all the columns:

```
for index, row in dataset.iterrows():
    # only printing the rows until Angola
    if index == 'Angola':
        break
    print(index, '\n', \
        row[["Country Code", "1970", "1990", "2010"]], '\n')
```

The output of the preceding code is as follows:

```
Aruba
  Country Code        ABW
1970              328.139
1990              345.267
2010              564.428
Name: Aruba, dtype: object

Andorra
  Country Code        AND
1970              51.6574
1990              115.981
2010              179.615
Name: Andorra, dtype: object

Afghanistan
  Country Code        AFG
1970              17.0344
1990              18.4842
2010              42.8303
Name: Afghanistan, dtype: object
```

Figure 1.47: Iterating all countries until Angola

> **NOTE**
>
> To access the source code for this specific section, please refer to
> https://packt.live/2YKqHNM.
>
> You can also run this example online at https://packt.live/2YD56Xo.

We've already covered most of the underlying data wrangling methods using pandas. In the next exercise, we'll take a look at more advanced features such as filtering, sorting, and reshaping to prepare you for the next chapter.

ADVANCED PANDAS OPERATIONS

In this section, we will learn about some advanced pandas operations such as filtering, sorting, and reshaping and implement them in an exercise.

FILTERING

Filtering in pandas has a higher-level interface than NumPy. You can still use the simple brackets-based **conditional filtering**. However, you're also able to use more complex queries, for example, filter rows based on labels using likeness, which allows us to search for a substring using the **like** argument and even full regular expressions using **regex**:

```
# only column 1994
dataset.filter(items=["1990"])


# countries population density < 10 in 1999
dataset[(dataset["1990"] < 10)]


# years containing an 8
dataset.filter(like="8", axis=1)


# countries ending with a
dataset.filter(regex="a$", axis=0)
```

SORTING

Sorting each row or column based on a given row or column will help you analyze your data better and find the ranking of a given dataset. With pandas, we are able to do this pretty easily. Sorting in ascending and descending order can be done using the parameter known as **ascending**. The default sorting order is **ascending**. Of course, you can do more complex sorting by providing more than one value in the **by = [ ]** list. Those will then be used to sort values for which the first value is the same:

```
# values sorted by 1999
dataset.sort_values(by=["1999"])
# values sorted by 1999 descending
dataset.sort_values(by=["1994"], ascending=False)
```

RESHAPING

Reshaping can be crucial for easier visualization and algorithms. However, depending on your data, this can get really complex:

```
dataset.pivot(index=["1999"] * len(dataset), \
              columns="Country Code", values="1999")
```

Now, we will use advanced pandas operations to perform an exercise.

EXERCISE 1.07: FILTERING, SORTING, AND RESHAPING

This exercise provides some more complex tasks and also combines most of the methods we learned about previously as a recap. After this exercise, you should be able to read the most basic pandas code and understand its logic.

Let's use pandas to filter, sort, and reshape our data.

Filtering

1. Create a new Jupyter Notebook and save it as **Exercise1.07.ipynb** in the **Chapter01/Exercise1.07** folder.

2. Import the necessary libraries:

```
# importing the necessary dependencies
import pandas as pd
```

3. Use the **read_csv** method to load the dataset, again defining our first column as an index column:

```
# loading the dataset
dataset = \
pd.read_csv('../../Datasets/world_population.csv', \
            index_col=0)
```

4. Use **filter** instead of using the bracket syntax to filter for specific items. Filter the dataset for columns 1961, 2000, and 2015 using the items parameter:

```
# filtering columns 1961, 2000, and 2015
dataset.filter(items=["1961", "2000", "2015"]).head()
```

The output of the preceding code is as follows:

Country Name	1961	2000	2015
Aruba	307.972222	504.766667	577.161111
Andorra	30.587234	139.146809	149.942553
Afghanistan	14.038148	30.177894	49.821649
Angola	4.305195	12.078798	20.070565
Albania	60.576642	112.738212	105.444051

Figure 1.48: Filtering data for 1961, 2000, and 2015

5. Use conditions to get all the countries that had a higher population density than **500** in **2000**. Simply pass this condition in brackets:

```
"""
filtering countries that had a greater population density
than 500 in 2000
"""
dataset[(dataset["2000"] > 500)][["2000"]]
```

The output of the preceding code is as follows:

Country Name	2000
Aruba	504.766667
Bangladesh	1008.532988
Bahrain	939.232394
Bermuda	1236.660000
Barbados	627.530233
Channel Islands	766.623711
Gibraltar	2735.100000
Hong Kong SAR, China	6347.619048
Macao SAR, China	21595.350000
St. Martin (French part)	521.764706
Monaco	16040.500000

Figure 1.49: Filtering out values that are greater than 500 in the 2000 column

6. Search for arbitrary columns or rows (depending on the index given) that match a certain **regex**. Get all the columns that start with 2 by passing **^2** (meaning that it starts at **2**):

```
dataset.filter(regex="^2", axis=1).head()
```

The output of the preceding code is as follows:

Country Name	2000	2001	2002	2003	2004
Aruba	504.766667	516.077778	527.750000	538.972222	548.566667
Andorra	139.146809	144.191489	151.161702	159.112766	166.674468
Afghanistan	30.177894	31.448029	32.912231	34.475030	35.995236
Angola	12.078798	12.483188	12.921871	13.388462	13.873025
Albania	112.738212	111.685146	111.350730	110.934891	110.472226

Figure 1.50: Retrieving all columns starting with 2

7. Filter the rows instead of the columns by passing **axis=0**. This will be helpful for situations when we want to filter all the rows that start with **A**:

```
dataset.filter(regex="^A", axis=0).head()
```

The output of the preceding code is as follows:

Country Name	Country Code	Indicator Name	Indicator Code	1960	1961	1962	1963
Aruba	ABW	Population density (people per sq. km of land ...	EN.POP.DNST	NaN	307.972222	312.366667	314.983333
Andorra	AND	Population density (people per sq. km of land ...	EN.POP.DNST	NaN	30.587234	32.714894	34.914894
Afghanistan	AFG	Population density (people per sq. km of land ...	EN.POP.DNST	NaN	14.038148	14.312061	14.599692
Angola	AGO	Population density (people per sq. km of land ...	EN.POP.DNST	NaN	4.305195	4.384299	4.464433
Albania	ALB	Population density (people per sq. km of land ...	EN.POP.DNST	NaN	60.576642	62.456898	64.329234

5 rows × 60 columns

Figure 1.51: Retrieving the rows that start with A

8. Use the **like** query to find only the countries that contain the word **land**, such as Switzerland:

```
dataset.filter(like="land", axis=0).head()
```

The output of the preceding code is as follows:

Country Name	Country Code	Indicator Name	Indicator Code	1960	1961	1962	1963
Switzerland	CHE	Population density (people per sq. km of land ...	EN.POP.DNST	NaN	137.479609	141.009285	144.056036
Channel Islands	CHI	Population density (people per sq. km of land ...	EN.POP.DNST	NaN	569.067010	574.551546	580.386598
Cayman Islands	CYM	Population density (people per sq. km of land ...	EN.POP.DNST	NaN	33.441667	33.925000	34.283333
Finland	FIN	Population density (people per sq. km of land ...	EN.POP.DNST	NaN	14.645934	14.745865	14.850484
Faroe Islands	FRO	Population density (people per sq. km of land ...	EN.POP.DNST	NaN	24.878223	25.181232	25.465616

5 rows × 60 columns

Figure 1.52: Retrieving all countries containing the word "land"

Sorting

1. Use the **sort_values** or **sort_index** method to get the countries with the lowest population density for the year 1961:

```
dataset.sort_values(by=["1961"])[["1961"]].head(10)
```

The output of the preceding code is as follows:

Country Name	1961
Greenland	0.098625
Mongolia	0.632212
Namibia	0.749775
Libya	0.843320
Mauritania	0.856916
Botswana	0.946793
United Arab Emirates	1.207955
Australia	1.364565
Iceland	1.785825
Oman	1.825186

Figure 1.53: Sorting by the values for the year 1961

2. Just for comparison, carry out sorting for **2015**:

```
dataset.sort_values(by=["2015"])[["2015"]].head(10)
```

The output of the preceding code is as follows:

Country Name	2015
Greenland	0.136713
Mongolia	1.904744
Namibia	2.986590
Australia	3.095579
Iceland	3.299980
Suriname	3.480609
Libya	3.568227
Guyana	3.896800
Canada	3.942567
Mauritania	3.946409

Figure 1.54: Sorting based on the values of 2015

We can see that the order of the countries with the lowest population density has changed a bit, but that the first three entries remain unchanged.

3. Sort column 2015 in **descending** order to show the biggest values first:

```
dataset.sort_values(by=["2015"], \
                    ascending=False)[["2015"]].head(10)
```

The output of the preceding code is as follows:

Country Name	2015
Macao SAR, China	19392.937294
Monaco	18865.500000
Singapore	7828.857143
Hong Kong SAR, China	6957.809524
Gibraltar	3221.700000
Bahrain	1788.619481
Maldives	1363.876667
Malta	1347.915625
Bermuda	1304.700000
Bangladesh	1236.810648

Figure 1.55: Sorting in descending order

Reshaping

1. Get a DataFrame where the columns are **country codes** and the only row is the year **2015**. Since we only have one **2015** label, we need to duplicate it as many times as our dataset's length:

```
# reshaping to 2015 as row and country codes as columns
dataset_2015 = dataset[["Country Code", "2015"]]
dataset_2015.pivot(index=["2015"] * len(dataset_2015), \
                columns="Country Code", values="2015")
```

The output of the preceding code is as follows:

Country Code	ABW	AFG	AGO	ALB	AND	ARB	ARE	ARG	ARM
2015	577.161111	49.821649	20.070565	105.444051	149.942553	28.779858	109.53305	15.864696	105.996207

1 rows × 264 columns

Figure 1.56: Reshaping the dataset into a single row for the values of 2015

> **NOTE**
>
> To access the source code for this specific section, please refer to https://packt.live/2N0xHQZ.
>
> You can also run this example online at https://packt.live/30Jeziw.

You now know the basic functionality of pandas and have already applied it to a real-world dataset. In the final activity for this chapter, we will try to analyze a forest fire dataset to get a feeling for mean forest fire sizes and whether the temperature of each month is proportional to the number of fires.

ACTIVITY 1.02: FOREST FIRE SIZE AND TEMPERATURE ANALYSIS

In this activity, we will use pandas features to derive some insights from a forest fire dataset. We will get the mean size of forest fires, what the largest recorded fire in our dataset is, and whether the amount of forest fires grows proportionally to the temperature in each month.

Our forest fires dataset has the following structure:

- **X**: X-axis spatial coordinate within the Montesinho park map: 1 to 9

- **Y**: Y-axis spatial coordinate within the Montesinho park map: 2 to 9

- **month**: Month of the year: 'jan' to 'dec'

- **day**: Day of the week: 'mon' to 'sun'

- **FFMC**: FFMC index from the FWI system: 18.7 to 96.20

- **DMC**: DMC index from the FWI system: 1.1 to 291.3

- **DC**: DC index from the FWI system: 7.9 to 860.6

- **ISI**: ISI index from the FWI system: 0.0 to 56.10

- **temp**: Temperature in degrees Celsius: 2.2 to 33.30

- **RH**: Relative humidity in %: 15.0 to 100

- **wind**: Wind speed in km/h: 0.40 to 9.40

- **rain**: Outside rain in mm/m²: 0.0 to 6.4

- **area**: The burned area of the forest (in ha): 0.00 to 1090.84

> **NOTE**
>
> We will only be using the **month**, **temp**, and **area** columns in this activity.

The following are the steps for this activity:

1. Open the **Activity1.02.ipynb** Jupyter Notebook from the **Chapter01** folder to complete this activity. Import **pandas** using the **pd** alias.

2. Load the **forestfires.csv** dataset using pandas.

3. Print the first two rows of the dataset to get a feeling for its structure.

Derive insights from the sizes of forest fires

1. Filter the dataset so that it only contains entries that have an area larger than 0.

2. Get the mean, min, max, and std of the area column and see what information this gives you.

3. Sort the filtered dataset using the area column and print the last 20 entries using the **tail** method to see how many huge values it holds.

4. Then, get the median of the area column and visually compare it to the mean value.

Finding the month with the most forest fires

1. Get a list of unique values from the month column of the dataset.

2. Get the number of entries for the month of March using the **shape** member of our DataFrame.

3. Now, iterate over all the months, filter our dataset for the rows containing the given month, and calculate the mean temperature. Print a statement with the number of fires, the mean temperature, and the month.

> **NOTE**
>
> The solution for this activity can be found on page 391.

You have now completed this topic all about pandas, which concludes this chapter. We have learned about the essential tools that help you wrangle and work with data. pandas is an incredibly powerful and widely used tool for wrangling and understanding data.

SUMMARY

NumPy and pandas are essential tools for data wrangling. Their user-friendly interfaces and performant implementation make data handling easy. Even though they only provide a little insight into our datasets, they are valuable for wrangling, augmenting, and cleaning our datasets. Mastering these skills will improve the quality of your visualizations.

In this chapter, we learned about the basics of NumPy, pandas, and statistics. Even though the statistical concepts we covered are basic, they are necessary to enrich our visualizations with information that, in most cases, is not directly provided in our datasets. This hands-on experience will help you implement the exercises and activities in the following chapters.

In the next chapter, we will focus on the different types of visualizations and how to decide which visualization would be best for our use case. This will give you theoretical knowledge so that you know when to use a specific chart type and why. It will also lay down the fundamentals of the remaining chapters in this book, which will focus on teaching you how to use Matplotlib and seaborn to create the plots we have discussed here. After we have covered basic visualization techniques with Matplotlib and seaborn, we will dive more in-depth and explore the possibilities of interactive and animated charts, which will introduce an element of storytelling into our visualizations.

2

ALL YOU NEED TO KNOW ABOUT PLOTS

OVERVIEW

This chapter will teach you the fundamentals of the various types of plots such as line charts, bar charts, bubble plots, radar charts, and so on. For each plot type that we discuss, we will also describe best practices and use cases. The activities presented in this chapter will enable you to apply the knowledge gained. By the end of this chapter, you will be equipped with the important skill of identifying the best plot type for a given dataset and scenario.

INTRODUCTION

In the previous chapter, we learned how to work with new datasets and get familiar with their data and structure. We also got hands-on experience of how to analyze and transform them using different data wrangling techniques such as filtering, sorting, and reshaping. All of these techniques will come in handy when working with further real-world datasets in the coming activities.

In this chapter, we will focus on various visualizations and identify which visualization is best for showing certain information for a given dataset. We will describe every visualization in detail and give practical examples, such as comparing different stocks over time or comparing the ratings for different movies. Starting with comparison plots, which are great for comparing multiple variables over time, we will look at their types (such as line charts, bar charts, and radar charts).

We will then move onto relation plots, which are handy for showing relationships among variables. We will cover scatter plots for showing the relationship between two variables, bubble plots for three variables, correlograms for variable pairs, and finally, heatmaps for visualizing multivariate data.

The chapter will further explain composition plots (used to visualize variables that are part of a whole), as well as pie charts, stacked bar charts, stacked area charts, and Venn diagrams. To give you a deeper insight into the distribution of variables, we will discuss distribution plots, describing histograms, density plots, box plots, and violin plots.

Finally, we will talk about dot maps, connection maps, and choropleth maps, which can be categorized into geoplots. Geoplots are useful for visualizing geospatial data. Let's start with the family of comparison plots, including line charts, bar charts, and radar charts.

> **NOTE**
>
> The data used in this chapter has been provided to demonstrate the different types of plots available to you. In each case, the data itself will be revisited and explained more fully in a later chapter.

COMPARISON PLOTS

Comparison plots include charts that are ideal for comparing multiple variables or variables over time. Line charts are great for visualizing variables over time. For comparison among items, bar charts (also called column charts) are the best way to go. For a certain time period (say, fewer than 10-time points), vertical bar charts can be used as well. Radar charts or spider plots are great for visualizing multiple variables for multiple groups.

LINE CHART

Line charts are used to display quantitative values over a continuous time period and show information as a series. A line chart is ideal for a time series that is connected by straight-line segments.

The value being measured is placed on the y-axis, while the x-axis is the timescale.

USES

- Line charts are great for comparing multiple variables and visualizing trends for both single as well as multiple variables, especially if your dataset has many time periods (more than 10).

- For smaller time periods, vertical bar charts might be the better choice.

The following diagram shows a trend of real estate prices (per million US dollars) across two decades. Line charts are ideal for showing data trends:

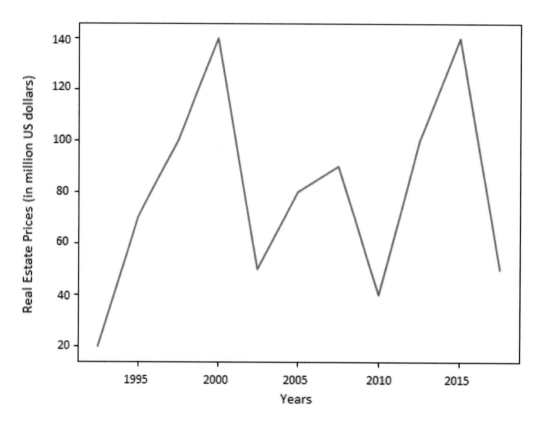

Figure 2.1: Line chart for a single variable

EXAMPLE

The following figure is a multiple-variable line chart that compares the stock-closing prices for Google, Facebook, Apple, Amazon, and Microsoft. A line chart is great for comparing values and visualizing the trend of the stock. As we can see, Amazon shows the highest growth:

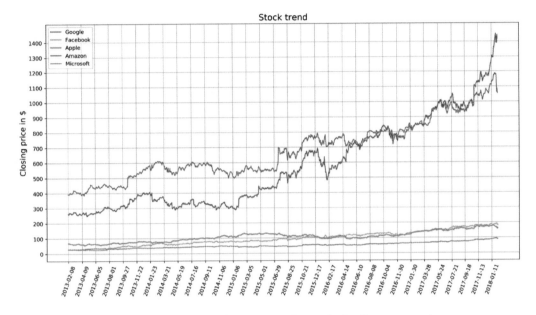

Figure 2.2: Line chart showing stock trends for five companies

DESIGN PRACTICES

- Avoid too many lines per chart.

- Adjust your scale so that the trend is clearly visible.

> **NOTE**
>
> For plots with multiple variables, a legend should be given to describe each variable.

BAR CHART

In a bar chart, the bar length encodes the value. There are two variants of bar charts: vertical bar charts and horizontal bar charts.

USE

While they are both used to compare numerical values across categories, vertical bar charts are sometimes used to show a single variable over time.

DON'TS OF BAR CHARTS

- Don't confuse vertical bar charts with histograms. Bar charts compare different variables or categories, while histograms show the distribution for a single variable. Histograms will be discussed later in this chapter.

- Another common mistake is to use bar charts to show central tendencies among groups or categories. Use box plots or violin plots to show statistical measures or distributions in these cases.

EXAMPLES

The following diagram shows a vertical bar chart. Each bar shows the marks out of 100 that 5 students obtained in a test:

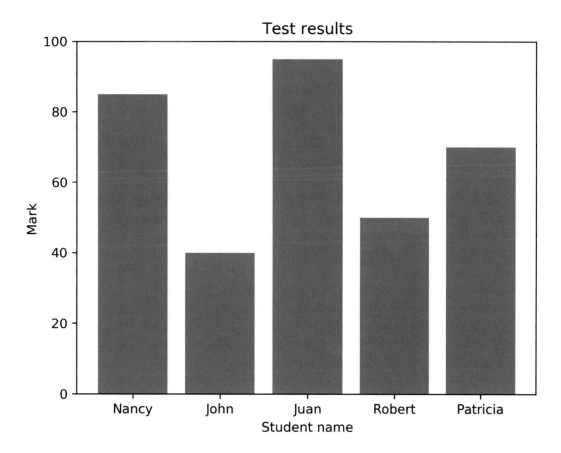

Figure 2.3: Vertical bar chart using student test data

The following diagram shows a horizontal bar chart. Each bar shows the marks out of 100 that 5 students obtained in a test:

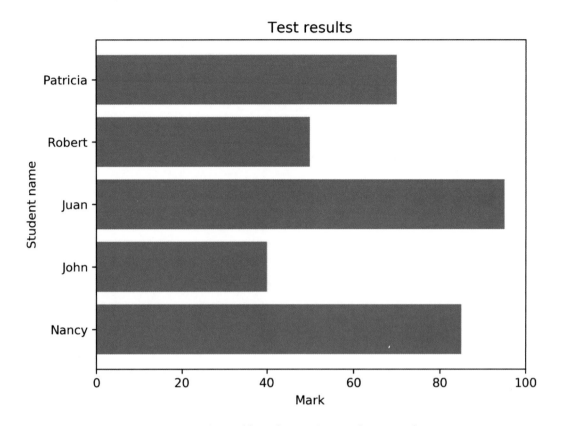

Figure 2.4: Horizontal bar chart using student test data

The following diagram compares movie ratings, giving two different scores. The Tomatometer is the percentage of approved critics who have given a positive review for the movie. The Audience Score is the percentage of users who have given a score of 3.5 or higher out of 5. As we can see, **The Martian** is the only movie with both a high Tomatometer and Audience Score. **The Hobbit: An Unexpected Journey** has a relatively high Audience Score compared to the Tomatometer score, which might be due to a huge fan base:

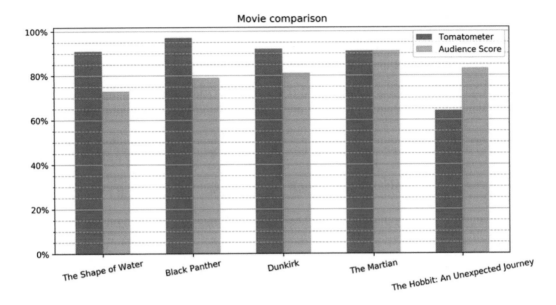

Figure 2.5: Comparative bar chart

DESIGN PRACTICES

- The axis corresponding to the numerical variable should start at zero. Starting with another value might be misleading, as it makes a small value difference look like a big one.

- Use horizontal labels—that is, as long as the number of bars is small, and the chart doesn't look too cluttered.

- The labels can be rotated to different angles if there isn't enough space to present them horizontally. You can see this on the labels of the x-axis of the preceding diagram.

RADAR CHART

Radar charts (also known as **spider** or **web charts**) visualize multiple variables with each variable plotted on its own axis, resulting in a polygon. All axes are arranged radially, starting at the center with equal distances between one another, and have the same scale.

USES

- Radar charts are great for comparing multiple quantitative variables for a single group or multiple groups.

- They are also useful for showing which variables score high or low within a dataset, making them ideal for visualizing performance.

EXAMPLES

The following diagram shows a radar chart for a single variable. This chart displays data about a student scoring marks in different subjects:

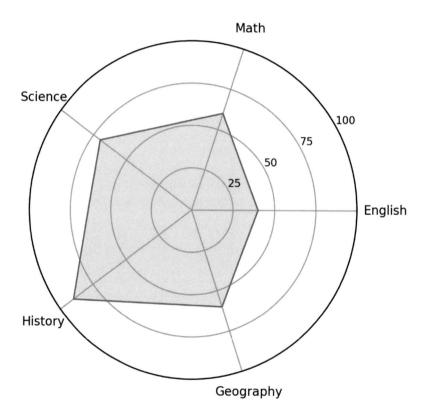

Figure 2.6: Radar chart for one variable (student)

The following diagram shows a radar chart for two variables/groups. Here, the chart explains the marks that were scored by two students in different subjects:

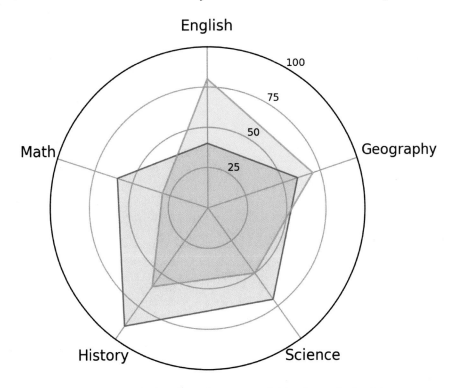

Figure 2.7: Radar chart for two variables (two students)

The following diagram shows a radar chart for multiple variables/groups. Each chart displays data about a student's performance in different subjects:

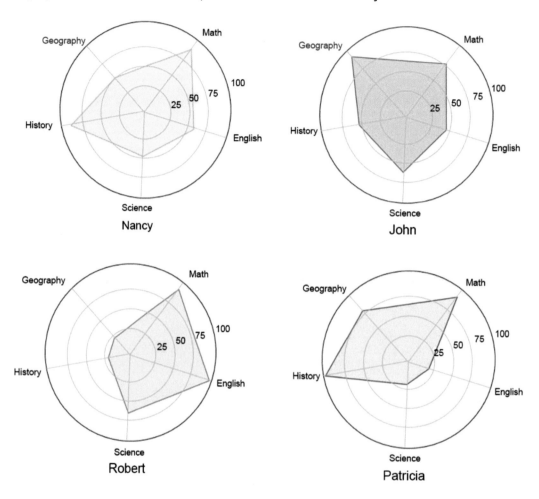

Figure 2.8: Radar chart with faceting for multiple variables (multiple students)

DESIGN PRACTICES

- Try to display 10 factors or fewer on a single radar chart to make it easier to read.

- Use **faceting** (displaying each variable in a separate plot) for multiple variables/ groups, as shown in the preceding diagram, in order to maintain clarity.

In the first section, we learned which plots are suitable for comparing items. Line charts are great for comparing something over time, whereas bar charts are for comparing different items. Last but not least, radar charts are best suited for visualizing multiple variables for multiple groups. In the following activity, you can check whether you understood which plot is best for which scenario.

ACTIVITY 2.01: EMPLOYEE SKILL COMPARISON

You are given scores of four employees (Alex, Alice, Chris, and Jennifer) for five attributes: efficiency, quality, commitment, responsible conduct, and cooperation. Your task is to compare the employees and their skills. This activity will foster your skills in choosing the best visualization when it comes to comparing items.

1. Which charts are suitable for this task?

2. You are given the following bar and radar charts. List the advantages and disadvantages of both charts. Which is the better chart for this task in your opinion, and why?

   The following diagram shows a bar chart for the employee skills:

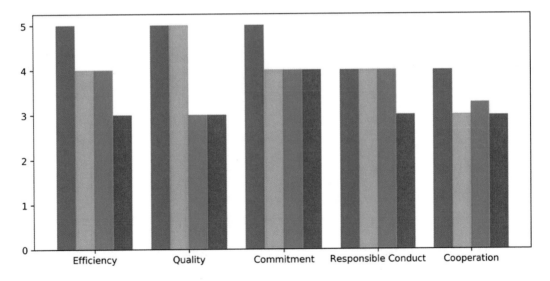

Figure 2.9: Employee skills comparison with a bar chart

The following diagram shows a radar chart for the employee skills:

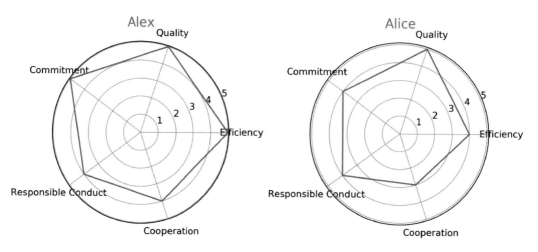

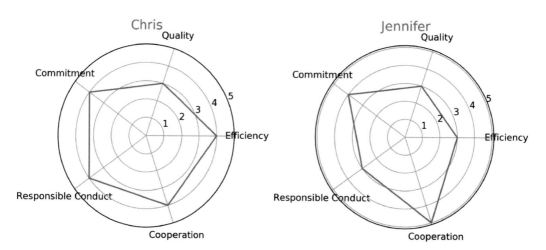

Figure 2.10: Employee skills comparison with a radar chart

3. What could be improved in the respective visualizations?

NOTE

The solution to this activity can be found on page 397.

Concluding the activity, you hopefully have a good understanding of deciding which comparison plots are best for the situation. In the next section, we will discuss different relation plots.

RELATION PLOTS

Relation plots are perfectly suited to showing relationships among variables. A scatter plot visualizes the correlation between two variables for one or multiple groups. Bubble plots can be used to show relationships between three variables. The additional third variable is represented by the dot size. Heatmaps are great for revealing patterns or correlations between two qualitative variables. A correlogram is a perfect visualization for showing the correlation among multiple variables.

SCATTER PLOT

Scatter plots show data points for two numerical variables, displaying a variable on both axes.

USES

- You can detect whether a correlation (relationship) exists between two variables.

- They allow you to plot the relationship between multiple groups or categories using different colors.

- A bubble plot, which is a variation of the scatter plot, is an excellent tool for visualizing the correlation of a third variable.

EXAMPLES

The following diagram shows a scatter plot of **height** and **weight** of persons belonging to a single group:

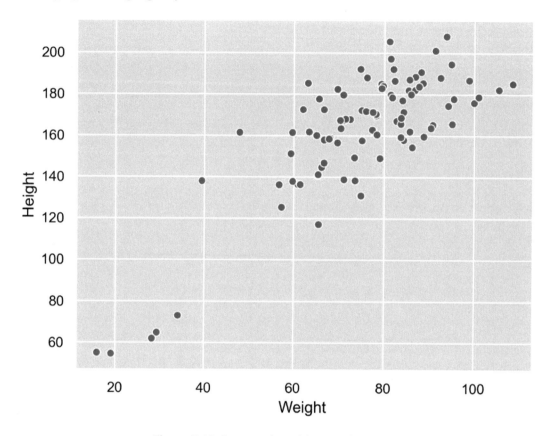

Figure 2.11: Scatter plot with a single group

The following diagram shows the same data as in the previous plot but differentiates between groups. In this case, we have different groups: **A**, **B**, and **C**:

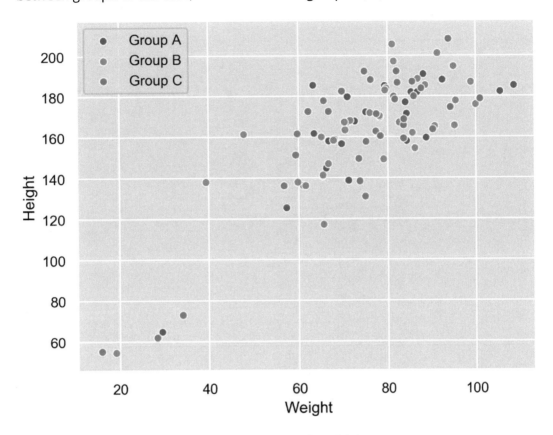

Figure 2.12: Scatter plot with multiple groups

The following diagram shows the correlation between body mass and the maximum longevity for various animals grouped by their classes. There is a positive correlation between body mass and maximum longevity:

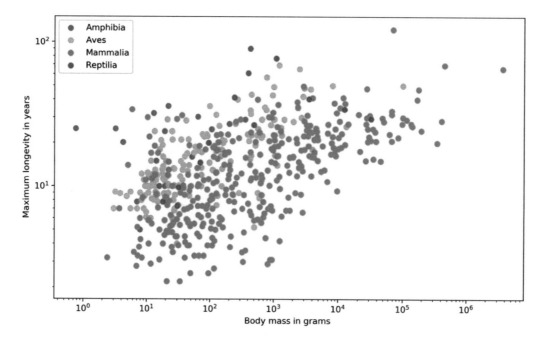

Figure 2.13: Correlation between body mass and maximum longevity for animals

DESIGN PRACTICES

- Start both axes at zero to represent data accurately.

- Use contrasting colors for data points and avoid using symbols for scatter plots with multiple groups or categories.

VARIANTS: SCATTER PLOTS WITH MARGINAL HISTOGRAMS

In addition to the scatter plot, which visualizes the correlation between two numerical variables, you can plot the marginal distribution for each variable in the form of histograms to give better insight into how each variable is distributed.

EXAMPLES

The following diagram shows the correlation between body mass and the maximum longevity for animals in the **Aves** class. The marginal histograms are also shown, which helps to get a better insight into both variables:

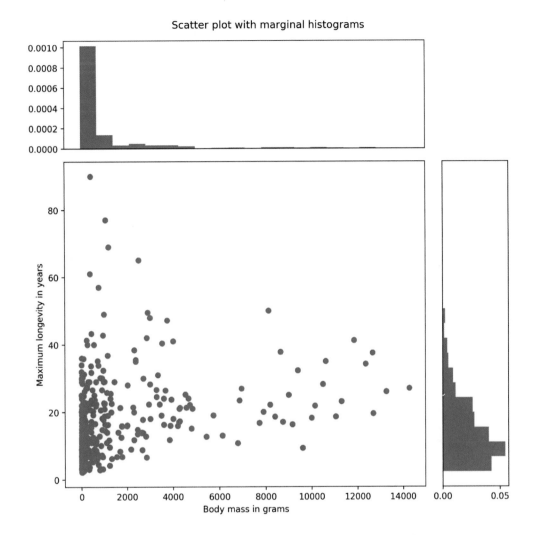

Figure 2.14: Correlation between body mass and maximum longevity
of the Aves class with marginal histograms

BUBBLE PLOT

A **bubble plot** extends a scatter plot by introducing a third numerical variable. The value of the variable is represented by the size of the dots. The area of the dots is proportional to the value. A legend is used to link the size of the dot to an actual numerical value.

USE

Bubble plots help to show a correlation between three variables.

EXAMPLE

The following diagram shows a bubble plot that highlights the relationship between heights and age of humans to get the weight of each person, which is represented by the size of the bubble:

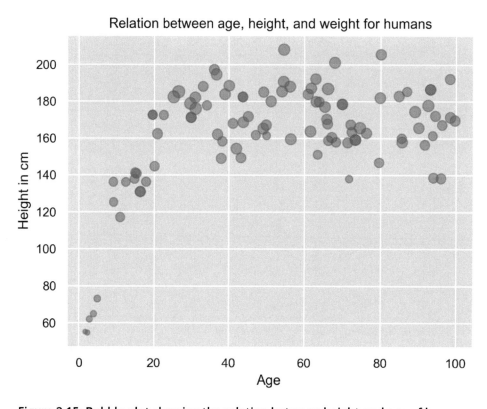

Figure 2.15: Bubble plot showing the relation between height and age of humans

DESIGN PRACTICES

- The design practices for the scatter plot are also applicable to the bubble plot.
- Don't use bubble plots for very large amounts of data, since too many bubbles make the chart difficult to read.

CORRELOGRAM

A **correlogram** is a combination of scatter plots and histograms. Histograms will be discussed in detail later in this chapter. A correlogram or correlation matrix visualizes the relationship between each pair of numerical variables using a scatter plot.

The diagonals of the correlation matrix represent the distribution of each variable in the form of a histogram. You can also plot the relationship between multiple groups or categories using different colors. A correlogram is a great chart for exploratory data analysis to get a feel for your data, especially the correlation between variable pairs.

EXAMPLES

The following diagram shows a correlogram for the height, weight, and age of humans. The diagonal plots show a histogram for each variable. The off-diagonal elements show scatter plots between variable pairs:

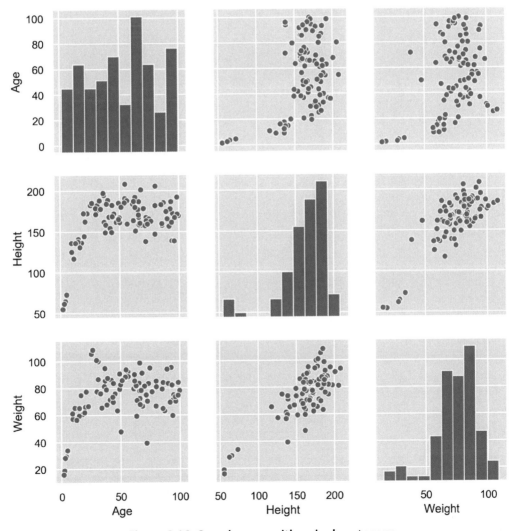

Figure 2.16: Correlogram with a single category

The following diagram shows the correlogram with data samples separated by color into different groups:

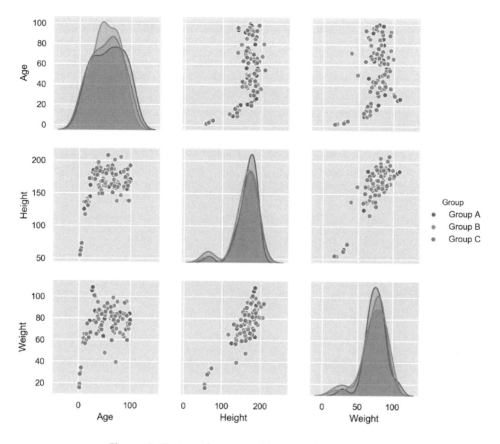

Figure 2.17: Correlogram with multiple categories

DESIGN PRACTICES

- Start both axes at zero to represent data accurately.

- Use contrasting colors for data points and avoid using symbols for scatter plots with multiple groups or categories.

HEATMAP

A **heatmap** is a visualization where values contained in a matrix are represented as colors or color saturation. Heatmaps are great for visualizing multivariate data (data in which analysis is based on more than two variables per observation), where categorical variables are placed in the rows and columns and a numerical or categorical variable is represented as colors or color saturation.

USE

The visualization of multivariate data can be done using heatmaps as they are great for finding patterns in your data.

EXAMPLES

The following diagram shows a heatmap for the most popular products on the electronics category page across various e-commerce websites, where the color shows the number of units sold. In the following diagram, we can analyze that the darker colors represent more units sold, as shown in the key:

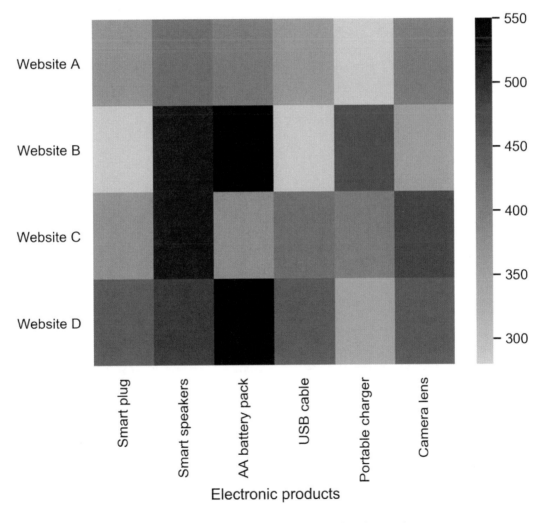

Figure 2.18: Heatmap for popular products in the electronics category

Variants: Annotated Heatmaps

Let's see the same example we saw previously in an annotated heatmap, where the color shows the number of units sold:

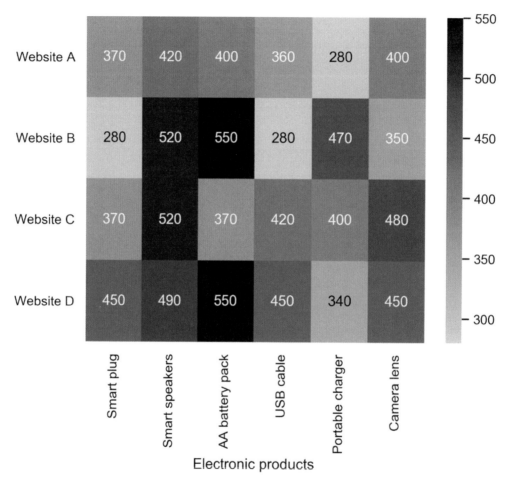

Figure 2.19: Annotated heatmap for popular products in the electronics category

DESIGN PRACTICE

- Select colors and contrasts that will be easily visible to individuals with vision problems so that your plots are more inclusive.

In this section, we introduced various plots for relating a variable to other variables and looked at their uses, and multiple examples for the different relation plots were given. The following activity will give you some practice in working with heatmaps.

ACTIVITY 2.02: ROAD ACCIDENTS OCCURRING OVER TWO DECADES

You are given a diagram that provides information about the road accidents that have occurred over the past two decades during the months of January, April, July, and October. The aim of this activity is to understand how you can use heatmaps to visualize multivariate data.

1. Identify the two years during which the number of road accidents occurring was the least.

2. For the past two decades, identify the month for which accidents showed a marked decrease:

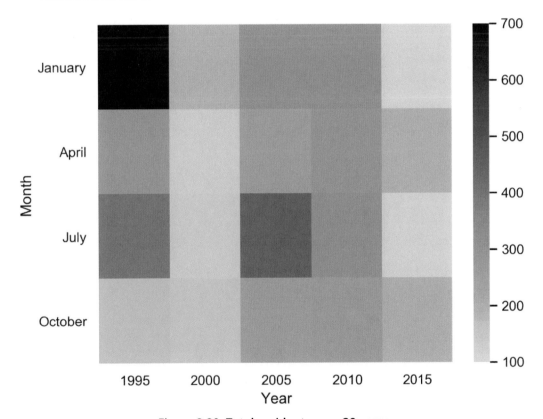

Figure 2.20: Total accidents over 20 years

> **NOTE**
>
> The solution to this activity can be found on page 397.

COMPOSITION PLOTS

Composition plots are ideal if you think about something as a part of a whole. For static data, you can use pie charts, stacked bar charts, or Venn diagrams. **Pie charts** or **donut charts** help show proportions and percentages for groups. If you need an additional dimension, stacked bar charts are great. Venn diagrams are the best way to visualize overlapping groups, where each group is represented by a circle. For data that changes over time, you can use either stacked bar charts or stacked area charts.

PIE CHART

Pie charts illustrate numerical proportions by dividing a circle into slices. Each arc length represents a proportion of a category. The full circle equates to 100%. For humans, it is easier to compare bars than arc lengths; therefore, it is recommended to use bar charts or stacked bar charts the majority of the time.

USE

To compare items that are part of a whole.

EXAMPLES

The following diagram shows household water usage around the world:

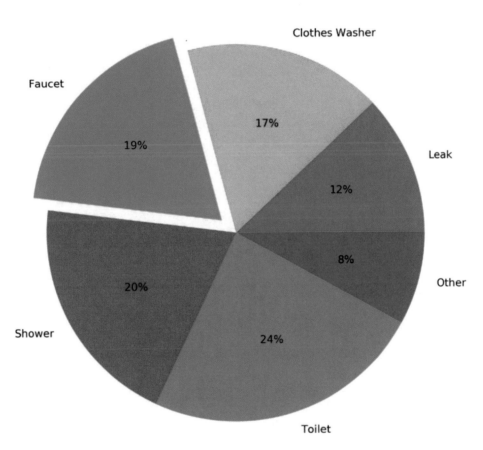

Figure 2.21: Pie chart for global household water usage

DESIGN PRACTICES

- Arrange the slices according to their size in increasing/decreasing order, either in a clockwise or counterclockwise manner.

- Make sure that every slice has a different color.

VARIANTS: DONUT CHART

An alternative to a pie chart is a **donut chart**. In contrast to pie charts, it is easier to compare the size of slices, since the reader focuses more on reading the length of the arcs instead of the area. Donut charts are also more space-efficient because the center is cut out, so it can be used to display information or further divide groups into subgroups.

The following diagram shows a basic donut chart:

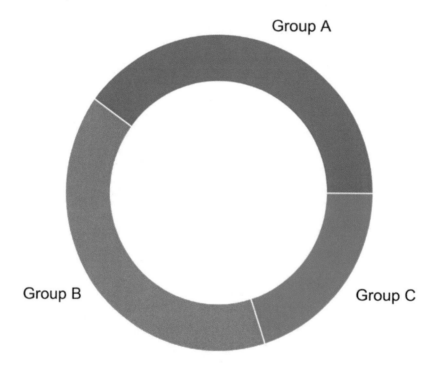

Figure 2.22: Donut chart

The following diagram shows a donut chart with subgroups:

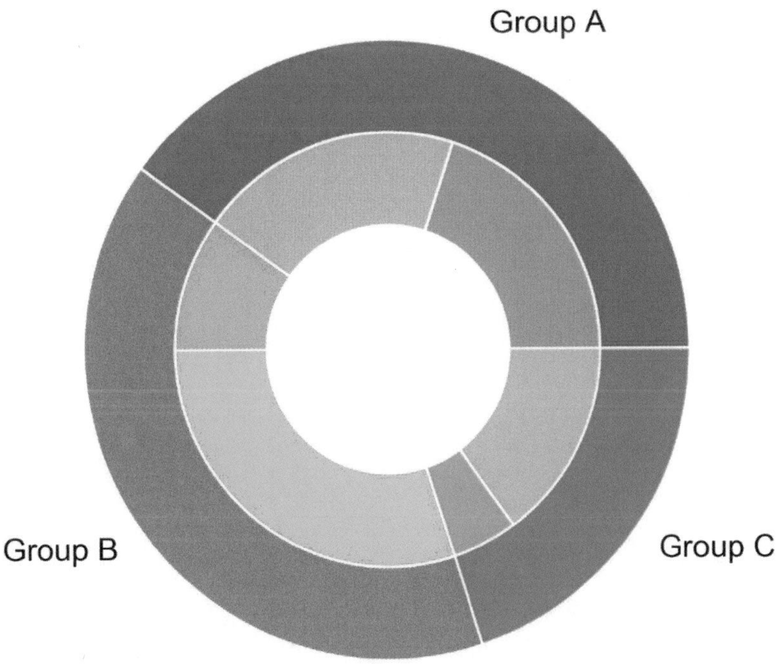

Figure 2.23: Donut chart with subgroups

DESIGN PRACTICE

- Use the same color that's used for the category for the subcategories. Use varying brightness levels for the different subcategories.

STACKED BAR CHART

Stacked bar charts are used to show how a category is divided into subcategories and the proportion of the subcategory in comparison to the overall category. You can either compare total amounts across each bar or show a percentage of each group. The latter is also referred to as a **100% stacked bar chart** and makes it easier to see relative differences between quantities in each group.

USE

- To compare variables that can be divided into sub-variables

EXAMPLES

The following diagram shows a generic stacked bar chart with five groups:

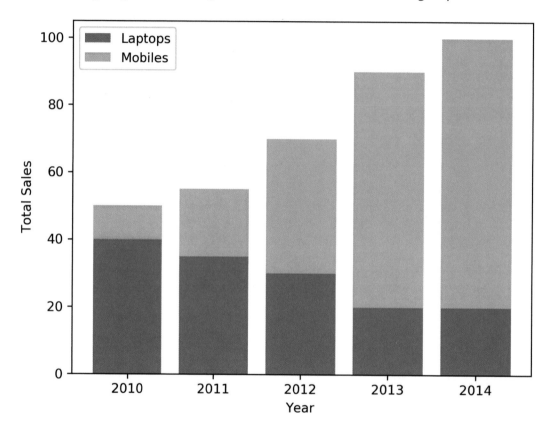

Figure 2.24: Stacked bar chart to show sales of laptops and mobiles

The following diagram shows a 100% stacked bar chart with the same data that was used in the preceding diagram:

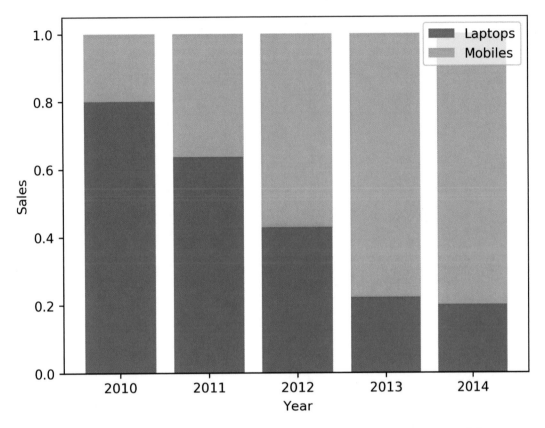

Figure 2.25: 100% stacked bar chart to show sales of laptops, PCs, and mobiles

The following diagram illustrates the daily total sales of a restaurant over several days. The daily total sales of non-smokers are stacked on top of the daily total sales of smokers:

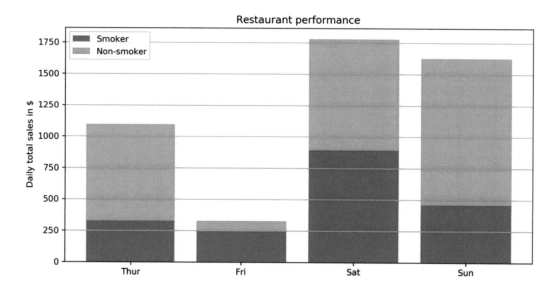

Figure 2.26: Daily total restaurant sales categorized by smokers and non-smokers

DESIGN PRACTICES

- Use contrasting colors for stacked bars.

- Ensure that the bars are adequately spaced to eliminate visual clutter. The ideal space guideline between each bar is half the width of a bar.

- Categorize data alphabetically, sequentially, or by value, to uniformly order it and make things easier for your audience.

STACKED AREA CHART

Stacked area charts show trends for part-of-a-whole relations. The values of several groups are illustrated by stacking individual area charts on top of one another. It helps to analyze both individual and overall trend information.

USE

To show trends for time series that are part of a whole.

EXAMPLES

The following diagram shows a stacked area chart with the net profits of Google, Facebook, Twitter, and Snapchat over a decade:

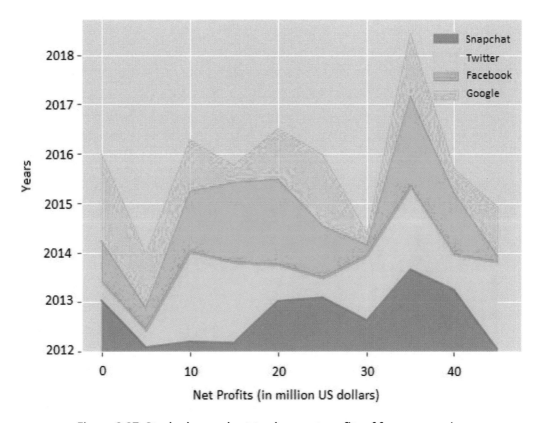

Figure 2.27: Stacked area chart to show net profits of four companies

DESIGN PRACTICE

- Use transparent colors to improve information visibility. This will help you to analyze the overlapping data and you will also be able to see the grid lines.

In this section, we covered various composition plots and we will conclude this section with the following activity.

ACTIVITY 2.03: SMARTPHONE SALES UNITS

You want to compare smartphone sales units for the five biggest smartphone manufacturers over time and see whether there is any trend. In this activity, we also want to look at the advantages and disadvantages of stacked area charts compared to line charts:

1. Looking at the following line chart, analyze the sales of each manufacturer and identify the one whose fourth-quarter performance is exceptional when compared to the third quarter.

2. Analyze the performance of all manufacturers and make a prediction about two companies whose sales units will show a downward and an upward trend:

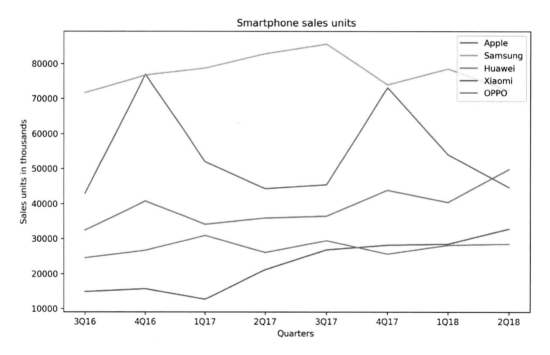

Figure 2.28: Line chart of smartphone sales units

3. What would be the advantages and disadvantages of using a stacked area chart instead of a line chart?

> **NOTE**
>
> The solution to this activity can be found on page 398.

VENN DIAGRAM

Venn diagrams, also known as **set diagrams**, show all possible logical relations between a finite collection of different sets. Each set is represented by a circle. The circle size illustrates the importance of a group. The size of overlap represents the intersection between multiple groups.

USE

To show overlaps for different sets.

EXAMPLE

Visualizing the intersection of the following diagram shows a Venn diagram for students in two groups taking the same class in a semester:

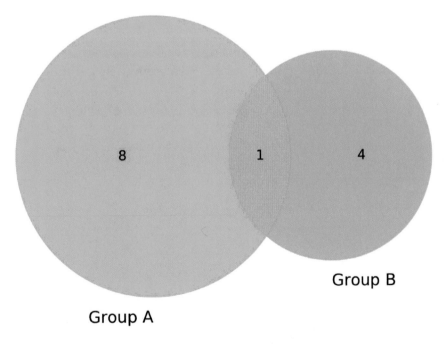

Figure 2.29: Venn diagram showing students taking the same class

From the preceding diagram, we can note that there are eight students in just group A, four students in just group B, and one student in both groups.

DESIGN PRACTICE

- It is not recommended to use Venn diagrams if you have more than three groups. It would become difficult to understand.

Moving on from composition plots, we will cover distribution plots in the following section.

DISTRIBUTION PLOTS

Distribution plots give a deep insight into how your data is distributed. For a single variable, a histogram is effective. For multiple variables, you can either use a box plot or a violin plot. The violin plot visualizes the densities of your variables, whereas the box plot just visualizes the median, the interquartile range, and the range for each variable.

HISTOGRAM

A **histogram** visualizes the distribution of a single numerical variable. Each bar represents the frequency for a certain interval. Histograms help get an estimate of statistical measures. You see where values are concentrated, and you can easily detect outliers. You can either plot a histogram with absolute frequency values or, alternatively, normalize your histogram. If you want to compare distributions of multiple variables, you can use different colors for the bars.

USE

Get insights into the underlying distribution for a dataset.

EXAMPLE

The following diagram shows the distribution of the **Intelligence Quotient (IQ)** for a test group. The dashed lines represent the standard deviation each side of the mean (the solid line):

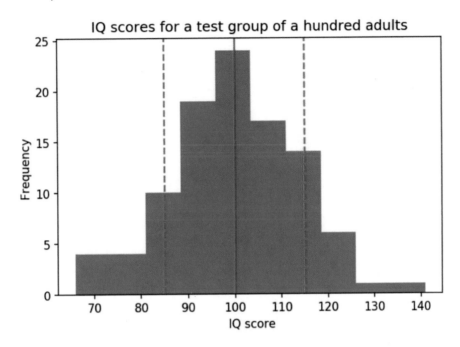

Figure 2.30: Distribution of IQ for a test group of a hundred adults

DESIGN PRACTICE

- Try different numbers of bins (data intervals), since the shape of the histogram can vary significantly.

DENSITY PLOT

A **density plot** shows the distribution of a numerical variable. It is a variation of a histogram that uses **kernel smoothing**, allowing for smoother distributions. One advantage these have over histograms is that density plots are better at determining the distribution shape since the distribution shape for histograms heavily depends on the number of bins (data intervals).

USE

To compare the distribution of several variables by plotting the density on the same axis and using different colors.

EXAMPLE

The following diagram shows a basic density plot:

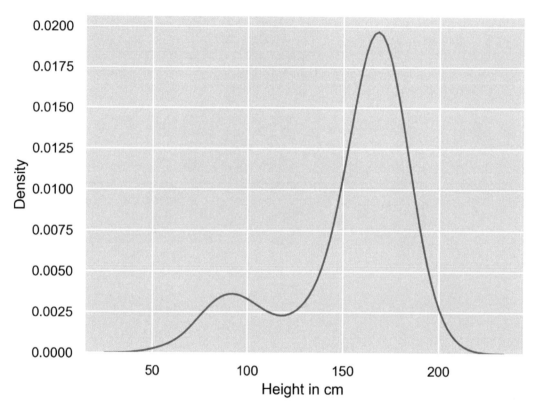

Figure 2.31: Density plot

The following diagram shows a basic multi-density plot:

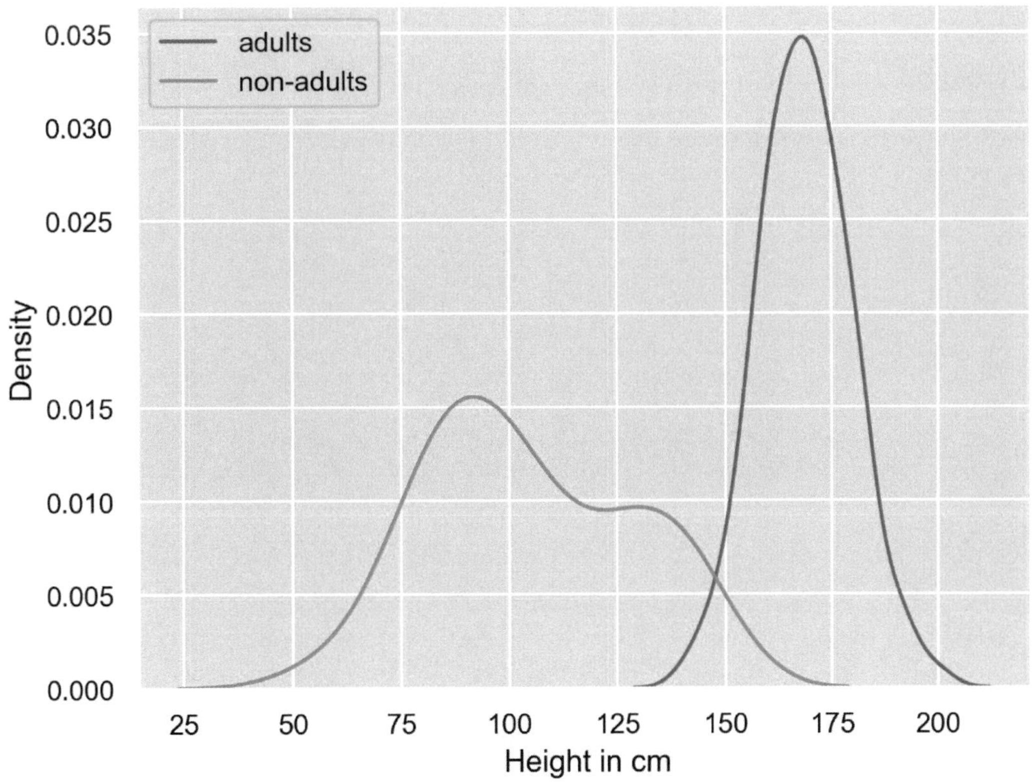

Figure 2.32: Multi-density plot

DESIGN PRACTICE

- Use contrasting colors to plot the density of multiple variables.

BOX PLOT

The **box plot** shows multiple statistical measurements. The box extends from the lower to the upper quartile values of the data, thus allowing us to visualize the interquartile range (IQR). The horizontal line within the box denotes the median. The parallel extending lines from the boxes are called **whiskers**; they indicate the variability outside the lower and upper quartiles. There is also an option to show data **outliers**, usually as circles or diamonds, past the end of the whiskers.

USE

Compare statistical measures for multiple variables or groups.

EXAMPLES

The following diagram shows a basic box plot that shows the height of a group of people:

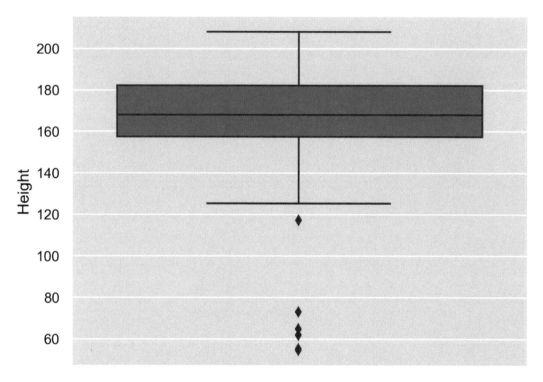

Figure 2.33: Box plot showing a single variable

The following diagram shows a basic box plot for multiple variables. In this case, it shows heights for two different groups – adults and non-adults:

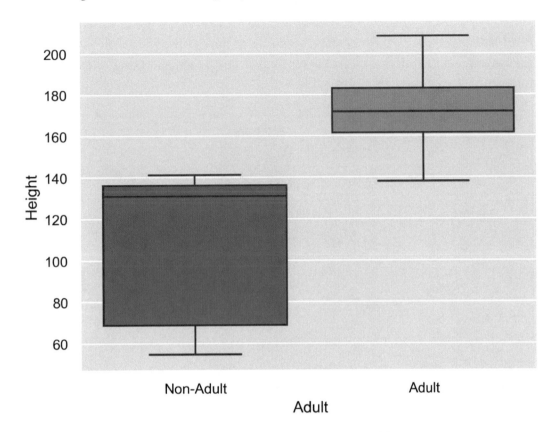

Figure 2.34: Box plot for multiple variables

In the next section, we will learn what the features, uses, and best practices are of the violin plot.

VIOLIN PLOT

Violin plots are a combination of box plots and density plots. Both the statistical measures and the distribution are visualized. The thick black bar in the center represents the interquartile range, while the thin black line corresponds to the whiskers in a box plot. The white dot indicates the median. On both sides of the centerline, the density is visualized.

USE

Compare statistical measures and density for multiple variables or groups.

EXAMPLES

The following diagram shows a violin plot for a single variable and shows how students have performed in **Math**:

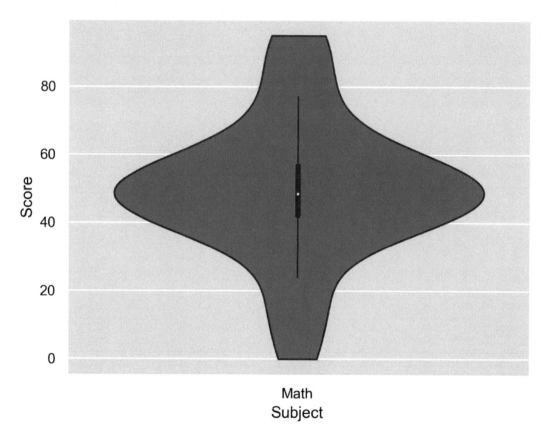

Figure 2.35: Violin plot for a single variable (Math)

From the preceding diagram, we can analyze that most of the students have scored around 40-60 in the **Math** test.

The following diagram shows a violin plot for two variables and shows the performance of students in **English** and **Math**:

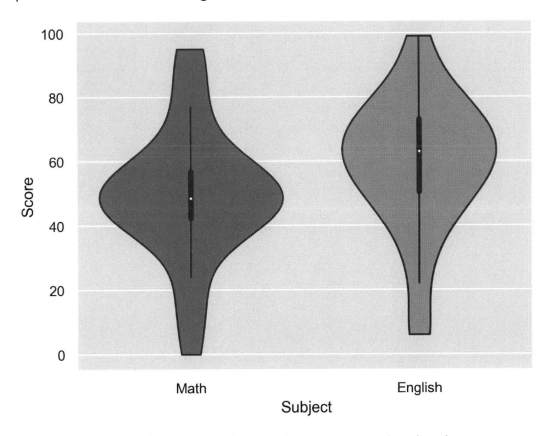

Figure 2.36: Violin plot for multiple variables (English and Math)

From the preceding diagram, we can say that on average, the students have scored more in **English** than in **Math**, but the highest score was secured in **Math**.

The following diagram shows a violin plot for a single variable divided into three groups, and shows the performance of three divisions of students in **English** based on their score:

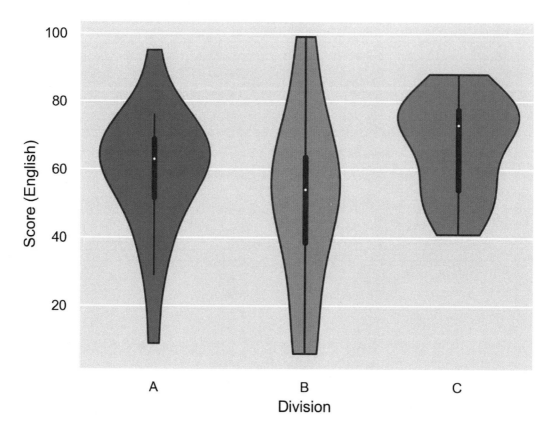

Figure 2.37: Violin plot with multiple categories (three groups of students)

From the preceding diagram, we can note that on average, division C has scored the highest, division B has scored the lowest, and division A is, on average, in between divisions B and C.

DESIGN PRACTICE

• Scale the axes accordingly so that the distribution is clearly visible and not flat.

In this section, distribution plots were introduced. In the following activity, we will have a closer look at histograms.

ACTIVITY 2.04: FREQUENCY OF TRAINS DURING DIFFERENT TIME INTERVALS

You are provided with a histogram that states the number of trains arriving at different time intervals in the afternoon to determine the maximum number of trains arriving in 2-hour time intervals. The goal of this activity is to gain a deeper insight into histograms:

1. Looking at the following histogram, can you identify the interval during which a maximum number of trains arrive?

2. How would the histogram change if in the morning, the same total number of trains arrive as in the afternoon, and if you have the same frequencies for all time intervals?

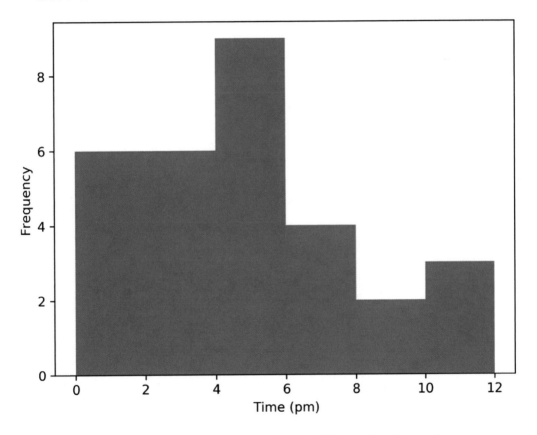

Figure 2.38: Frequency of trains during different time intervals

NOTE

The solution to this activity can be found on page 398.

With that activity, we conclude the section about distribution plots and we will introduce geoplots in the next section.

GEOPLOTS

Geological plots are a great way to visualize geospatial data. Choropleth maps can be used to compare quantitative values for different countries, states, and so on. If you want to show connections between different locations, connection maps are the way to go.

DOT MAP

In a **dot map**, each dot represents a certain number of observations. Each dot has the same size and value (the number of observations each dot represents). The dots are not meant to be counted; they are only intended to give an impression of magnitude. The size and value are important factors for the effectiveness and impression of the visualization. You can use different colors or symbols for the dots to show multiple categories or groups.

USE

To visualize geospatial data.

EXAMPLE

The following diagram shows a dot map where each dot represents a certain amount of bus stops throughout the world:

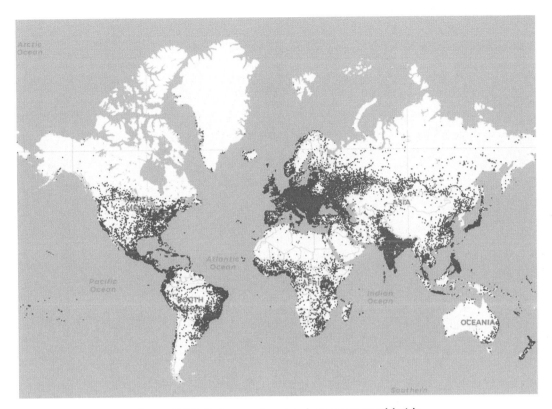

Figure 2.39: Dot map showing bus stops worldwide

DESIGN PRACTICES

- Do not show too many locations. You should still be able to see the map to get a feel for the actual location.

- Choose a dot size and value so that in dense areas, the dots start to blend. The dot map should give a good impression of the underlying spatial distribution.

CHOROPLETH MAP

In a **choropleth map**, each tile is colored to encode a variable. For example, a tile represents a geographic region for counties and countries. Choropleth maps provide a good way to show how a variable varies across a geographic area. One thing to keep in mind for choropleth maps is that the human eye naturally gives more attention to larger areas, so you might want to normalize your data by dividing the map area-wise.

USE

To visualize geospatial data grouped into geological regions—for example, states or countries.

EXAMPLE

The following diagram shows a choropleth map of a weather forecast in the USA:

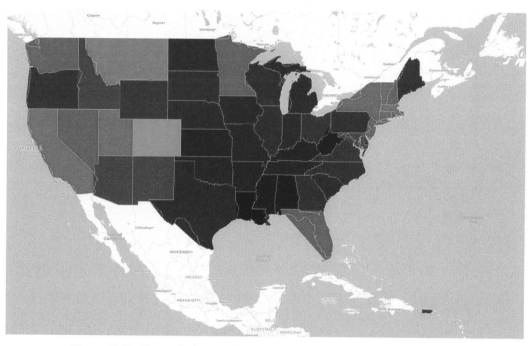

Figure 2.40: Choropleth map showing a weather forecast for the USA

DESIGN PRACTICES

- Use darker colors for higher values, as they are perceived as being higher in magnitude.

- Limit the color gradation, since the human eye is limited in how many colors it can easily distinguish between. Seven color gradations should be enough.

CONNECTION MAP

In a **connection map**, each line represents a certain number of connections between two locations. The link between the locations can be drawn with a straight or rounded line, representing the shortest distance between them.

Each line has the same thickness and value (the number of connections each line represents). The lines are not meant to be counted; they are only intended to give an impression of magnitude. The size and value of a connection line are important factors for the effectiveness and impression of the visualization.

You can use different colors for the lines to show multiple categories or groups, or you can use a colormap to encode the length of the connection.

USE

To visualize connections.

EXAMPLES

The following diagram shows a connection map of flight connections around the world:

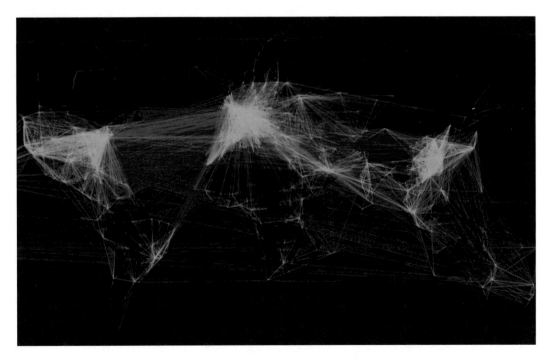

Figure 2.41: Connection map showing flight connections around the world

DESIGN PRACTICES

- Do not show too many connections as it will be difficult for you to analyze the data. You should still see the map to get a feel for the actual locations of the start and end points.

- Choose a line thickness and value so that the lines start to blend in dense areas. The connection map should give a good impression of the underlying spatial distribution.

Geoplots are special plots that are great for visualizing geospatial data. In the following section, we want to briefly talk about what's generally important when it comes to creating good visualizations.

WHAT MAKES A GOOD VISUALIZATION?

There are multiple aspects to what makes a good visualization:

- Most importantly, the visualization should be self-explanatory and visually appealing. To make it self-explanatory, use a legend, descriptive labels for your x-axis and y-axis, and titles.

- A visualization should tell a story and be designed for your audience. Before creating your visualization, think about your target audience; create simple visualizations for a non-specialist audience and more technical detailed visualizations for a specialist audience. Think about a story to tell with your visualization so that your visualization leaves an impression on the audience.

COMMON DESIGN PRACTICES

- Use colors to differentiate variables/subjects rather than symbols, as colors are more perceptible.

- To show additional variables on a 2D plot, use color, shape, and size.

- Keep it simple and don't overload the visualization with too much information.

ACTIVITY 2.05: ANALYZING VISUALIZATIONS

The following visualizations are not ideal as they do not represent data well. Answer the following questions for each visualization. The aim of this activity is to sharpen your skills with regard to choosing the best suitable plot for a scenario.

1. What are the bad aspects of these visualizations?

2. How could we improve the visualizations? Sketch the right visualization for both scenarios.

The first visualization is supposed to illustrate the top 30 YouTube music channels according to their number of subscribers:

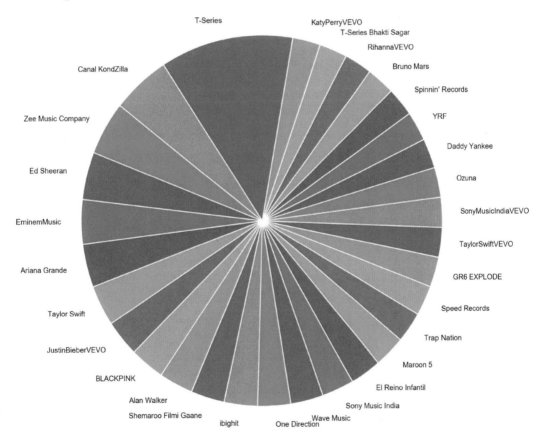

Figure 2.42: Pie chart showing the top 30 YouTube music channels

The second visualization is supposed to illustrate the number of people playing a certain game in a casino over 2 days:

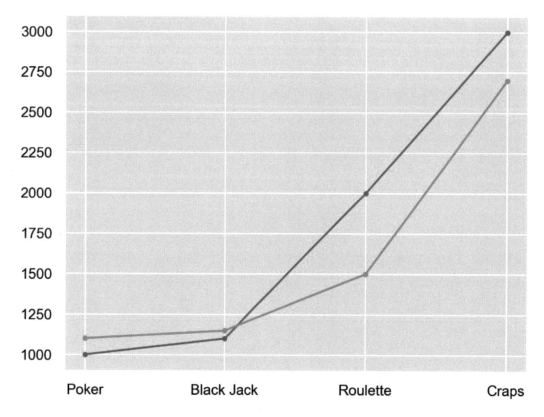

Figure 2.43: Line chart displaying casino data for 2 days

NOTE

The solution to this activity can be found on page 399.

ACTIVITY 2.06: CHOOSING A SUITABLE VISUALIZATION

In this activity, we are using a dataset to visualize the median, the interquartile ranges, and the underlying density of populations from different income groups. Following is the link to the dataset that we have used: https://population.un.org/wpp/ Download/Files/1_Indicators%20(Standard)/EXCEL_FILES/1_Population/WPP2019_POP_ F07_1_POPULATION_BY_AGE_BOTH_SEXES.xlsx. Select the best suitable plot from the following plots.

The following diagram shows the population by different income groups using a density plot:

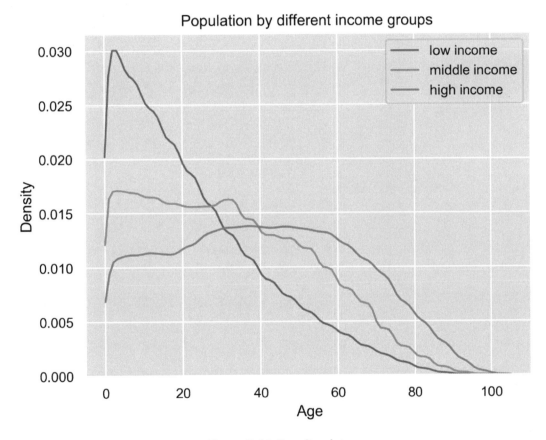

Figure 2.44: Density plot

The following diagram shows the population by different income groups using a box plot:

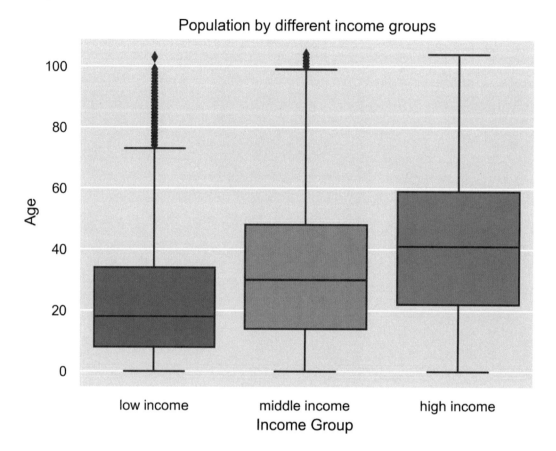

Figure 2.45: Box plot

The following diagram shows the population by different income groups using a violin plot:

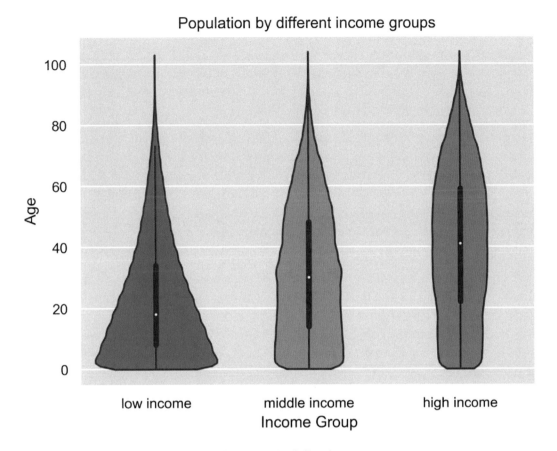

Figure 2.46: Violin plot

NOTE

The solution to this activity can be found on page 401.

SUMMARY

This chapter covered the most important visualizations, categorized into comparison, relation, composition, distribution, and geological plots. For each plot, a description, practical examples, and design practices were given. Comparison plots, such as line charts, bar charts, and radar charts, are well suited to comparing multiple variables or variables over time. Relation plots are perfectly suited to show relationships between variables. Scatter plots, bubble plots, which are an extension of scatter plots, correlograms, and heatmaps were considered.

Composition plots are ideal if you need to think about something as part of a whole. We first covered pie charts and continued with stacked bar charts, stacked area charts, and Venn diagrams. For distribution plots that give a deep insight into how your data is distributed, histograms, density plots, box plots, and violin plots were considered. Regarding geospatial data, we discussed dot maps, connection maps, and choropleth maps. Finally, some remarks were provided on what makes a good visualization.

In the next chapter, we will dive into Matplotlib and create our own visualizations. We will start by introducing the basics, followed by talking about how you can add text and annotations to make your visualizations more comprehensible. We will continue creating simple plots and using layouts to include multiple plots within a visualization. At the end of the next chapter, we will explain how you can use Matplotlib to visualize images.

3

A DEEP DIVE INTO MATPLOTLIB

OVERVIEW

This chapter describes the fundamentals of Matplotlib and teaches you how to create visualizations using the built-in plots that are provided by the library. Specifically, you will create various visualizations such as bar plots, pie charts, radar plots, histograms, and scatter plots through various exercises and activities. You will also learn basic skills such as loading, saving, plotting, and manipulating the color scale of images. You will also be able to customize your visualization plots and write mathematical expressions using TeX.

INTRODUCTION

In the previous chapter, we focused on various visualizations and identified which visualization is best suited to show certain information for a given dataset. We learned about the features, uses, and best practices for following various plots such as comparison plots, relation plots, composition plots, distribution plots, and geoplots.

Matplotlib is probably the most popular plotting library for Python. It is used for data science and machine learning visualizations all around the world. John Hunter was an American neurobiologist who began developing Matplotlib in 2003. It aimed to emulate the commands of the **MATLAB** software, which was the scientific standard back then. Several features, such as the global style of MATLAB, were introduced into Matplotlib to make the transition to Matplotlib easier for MATLAB users. This chapter teaches you how to best utilize the various functions and methods of Matplotlib to create insightful visualizations.

Before we start working with Matplotlib to create our first visualizations, we will need to understand the hierarchical structure of plots in Matplotlib. We will then cover the basic functionality, such as creating, displaying, and saving Figures. Before covering the most common visualizations, text and legend functions will be introduced. After that, layouts will be covered, which enable multiple plots to be combined into one. We will end the chapter by explaining how to plot images and how to use mathematical expressions.

OVERVIEW OF PLOTS IN MATPLOTLIB

Plots in Matplotlib have a hierarchical structure that nests Python objects to create a tree-like structure. Each plot is encapsulated in a **Figure** object. This **Figure** is the top-level container of the visualization. It can have multiple axes, which are basically individual plots inside this top-level container.

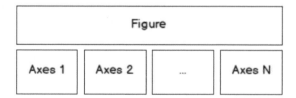

Figure 3.1: A Figure contains at least one axes object

Furthermore, we again find Python objects that control axes, tick marks, legends, titles, text boxes, the grid, and many other objects. All of these objects can be customized.

The two main components of a plot are as follows:

- **Figure**

  The Figure is an outermost container that allows you to draw multiple plots within it. It not only holds the **Axes** object but also has the ability to configure the **Title**.

- **Axes**

  The axes are an actual plot, or subplot, depending on whether you want to plot single or multiple visualizations. Its sub-objects include the x-axis, y-axis, spines, and legends.

Observing this design, we can see that this hierarchical structure allows us to create a complex and customizable visualization.

When looking at the "anatomy" of a Figure (shown in the following diagram), we get an idea about the complexity of a visualization. Matplotlib gives us the ability not only to display data, but also design the whole **Figure** around it by adjusting the **Grid**, **X** and **Y ticks**, **tick labels**, and the **Legend**.

This implies that we can modify every single bit of a plot, starting from the **Title** and **Legend**, right down to the major and minor ticks on the spines:

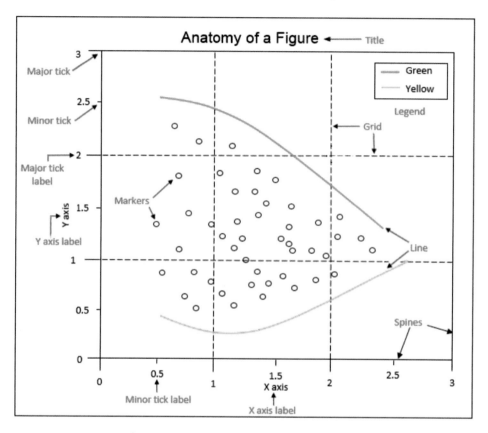

Figure 3.2: Anatomy of a Matplotlib Figure

Taking a deeper look into the anatomy of a **Figure** object, we can observe the following components:

- **Spines**: Lines connecting the axis tick marks
- **Title**: Text label of the whole Figure object
- **Legend**: Describes the content of the plot
- **Grid**: Vertical and horizontal lines used as an extension of the tick marks
- **X/Y axis label**: Text labels for the X and Y axes below the spines
- **Minor tick**: Small value indicators between the major tick marks
- **Minor tick label**: Text label that will be displayed at the minor ticks

- **Major tick**: Major value indicators on the spines
- **Major tick label**: Text label that will be displayed at the major ticks
- **Line**: Plotting type that connects data points with a line
- **Markers**: Plotting type that plots every data point with a defined marker

In this book, we will focus on Matplotlib's submodule, **pyplot**, which provides MATLAB-like plotting.

PYPLOT BASICS

pyplot contains a simpler interface for creating visualizations that allow the users to plot the data without explicitly configuring the **Figure** and **Axes** themselves. They are automatically configured to achieve the desired output. It is handy to use the alias **plt** to reference the imported submodule, as follows:

```
import matplotlib.pyplot as plt
```

The following sections describe some of the common operations that are performed when using pyplot.

CREATING FIGURES

You can use **plt.figure()** to create a new **Figure**. This function returns a Figure instance, but it is also passed to the backend. Every Figure-related command that follows is applied to the current Figure and does not need to know the Figure instance.

By default, the Figure has a width of 6.4 inches and a height of 4.8 inches with a **dpi** (dots per inch) of 100. To change the default values of the Figure, we can use the parameters **figsize** and **dpi**.

The following code snippet shows how we can manipulate a Figure:

```
#To change the width and the height
plt.figure(figsize=(10, 5))

#To change the dpi
plt.figure(dpi=300)
```

Even though it is not necessary to explicitly create a Figure, this is a good practice if you want to create multiple Figures at the same time.

CLOSING FIGURES

Figures that are no longer used should be closed by explicitly calling **plt.close()**, which also cleans up memory efficiently.

If nothing is specified, the **plt.close()** command will close the current Figure. To close a specific Figure, you can either provide a reference to a Figure instance or provide the Figure number. To find the **number** of a Figure object, we can make use of the **number** attribute, as follows:

```
plt.gcf().number
```

The **plt.close('all')** command is used to close all active Figures. The following example shows how a Figure can be created and closed:

```
#Create Figure with Figure number 10
plt.figure(num=10)

#Close Figure with Figure number 10
plt.close(10)
```

For a small Python script that only creates a visualization, explicitly closing a Figure isn't required, since the memory will be cleaned in any case once the program terminates. But if you create lots of Figures, it might make sense to close Figures in between so as to save memory.

FORMAT STRINGS

Before we actually plot something, let's quickly discuss **format strings**. They are a neat way to specify **colors**, **marker types**, and **line styles**. A format string is specified as **[color][marker][line]**, where each item is optional. If the **color** argument is the only argument of the format string, you can use **matplotlib.colors**. Matplotlib recognizes the following formats, among others:

- RGB or RGBA float tuples (for example, (0.2, 0.4, 0.3) or (0.2, 0.4, 0.3, 0.5))

- RGB or RGBA hex strings (for example, '#0F0F0F' or '#0F0F0F0F')

The following table is an example of how a color can be represented in one particular format:

Colors	Color
'b'	blue
'r'	red
'g'	green
'm'	magenta
'c'	cyan
'k'	black
'w'	white
'y'	yellow

Figure 3.3: Color specified in string format

All the available marker options are illustrated in the following figure:

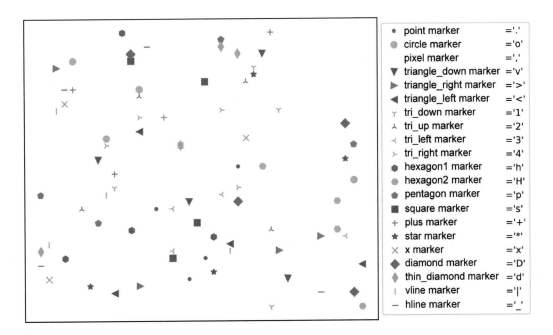

Figure 3.4: Markers in format strings

All the available line styles are illustrated in the following diagram. In general, solid lines should be used. We recommend restricting the use of dashed and dotted lines to either visualize some bounds/targets/goals or to depict uncertainty, for example, in a forecast:

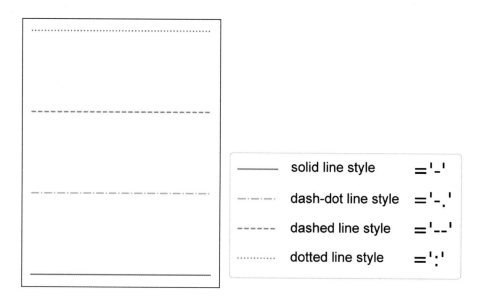

Figure 3.5: Line styles

To conclude, format strings are a handy way to quickly customize colors, marker types, and line styles. It is also possible to use arguments, such as **color**, **marker**, and **linestyle**.

PLOTTING

With **plt.plot([x], y, [fmt])**, you can plot data points as lines and/or markers. The function returns a list of **Line2D** objects representing the plotted data. By default, if you do not provide a format string (**fmt**), the data points will be connected with straight, solid lines. **plt.plot([0, 1, 2, 3], [2, 4, 6, 8])** produces a plot, as shown in the following diagram. Since **x** is optional and the default values are **[0, ..., N-1]**, **plt.plot([2, 4, 6, 8])** results in the same plot:

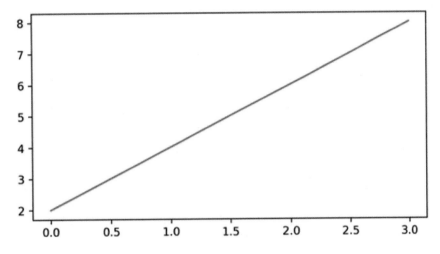

Figure 3.6: Plotting data points as a line

If you want to plot markers instead of lines, you can just specify a format string with any marker type. For example, `plt.plot([0, 1, 2, 3], [2, 4, 6, 8], 'o')` displays data points as circles, as shown in the following diagram:

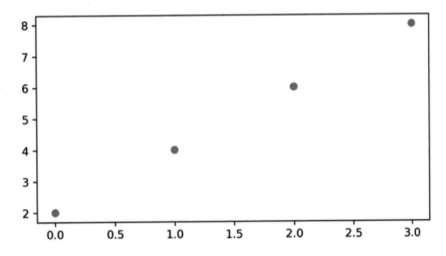

Figure 3.7: Plotting data points with markers (circles)

To plot multiple data pairs, the syntax **plt.plot([x], y, [fmt], [x], y2, [fmt2], …)** can be used. **plt.plot([2, 4, 6, 8], 'o', [1, 5, 9, 13], 's')** results in the following diagram. Similarly, you can use **plt.plot** multiple times, since we are working on the same Figure and Axes:

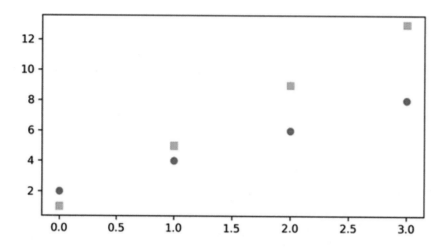

Figure 3.8: Plotting data points with multiple markers

Any **Line2D** properties can be used instead of format strings to further customize the plot. For example, the following code snippet shows how we can additionally specify the **linewidth** and **markersize** arguments:

```
plt.plot([2, 4, 6, 8], color='blue', marker='o', \
         linestyle='dashed', linewidth=2, markersize=12)
```

Besides providing data using lists or NumPy arrays, it might be handy to use pandas DataFrames, as explained in the next section.

PLOTTING USING PANDAS DATAFRAMES

It is pretty straightforward to use **pandas.DataFrame** as a data source. Instead of providing **x** and **y** values, you can provide the **pandas.DataFrame** in the data parameter and give keys for **x** and **y**, as follows:

```
plt.plot('x_key', 'y_key', data=df)
```

If your data is already a pandas DataFrame, this is the preferred way.

TICKS

Tick locations and labels can be set manually if Matplotlib's default isn't sufficient. Considering the previous plot, it might be preferable to only have ticks at multiples of ones at the x-axis. One way to accomplish this is to use **plt.xticks()** and **plt.yticks()** to either get or set the ticks manually.

plt.xticks(ticks, [labels], [kwargs])** sets the current tick locations and labels of the x-axis.

Parameters:

- **ticks**: List of tick locations; if an empty list is passed, ticks will be disabled.

- **labels** (optional): You can optionally pass a list of labels for the specified locations.

- ****kwargs** (optional): **matplotlib.text.Text()** properties can be used to customize the appearance of the tick labels. A quite useful property is **rotation**; this allows you to rotate the tick labels to use space more efficiently.

Example:

Consider the following code to plot a graph with custom ticks:

```
import numpy as np
plt.figure(figsize=(6, 3))
plt.plot([2, 4, 6, 8], 'o', [1, 5, 9, 13], 's')
plt.xticks(ticks=np.arange(4))
```

This will result in the following plot:

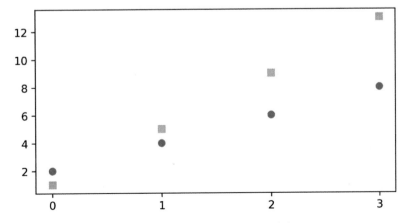

Figure 3.9: Plot with custom ticks

It's also possible to specify tick labels, as follows:

```
plt.figure(figsize=(6, 3))
plt.plot([2, 4, 6, 8], 'o', [1, 5, 9, 13], 's')
plt.xticks(ticks=np.arange(4), \
        labels=['January', 'February', 'March', 'April'], \
        rotation=20)
```

This will result in the following plot:

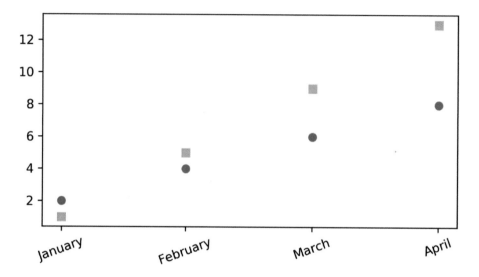

Figure 3.10: Plot with custom tick labels

If you want to do even more sophisticated things with ticks, you should look into tick locators and formatters. For example, **ax.xaxis.set_major_locator(plt.NullLocator())** would remove the major ticks of the x-axis, and **ax.xaxis.set_major_formatter(plt.NullFormatter())** would remove the major tick labels, but not the tick locations of the x-axis.

DISPLAYING FIGURES

plt.show() is used to display a Figure or multiple Figures. To display Figures within a Jupyter Notebook, simply set the **%matplotlib inline** command at the beginning of the code.

If you forget to use **plt.show()**, the plot won't show up. We will learn how to save the Figure in the next section.

SAVING FIGURES

The **plt.savefig(fname)** saves the current Figure. There are some useful optional parameters you can specify, such as **dpi**, **format**, or **transparent**. The following code snippet gives an example of how you can save a Figure:

```
plt.figure()
plt.plot([1, 2, 4, 5], [1, 3, 4, 3], '-o')
#bbox_inches='tight' removes the outer white margins
plt.savefig('lineplot.png', dpi=300, bbox_inches='tight')
```

The following is the output of the code:

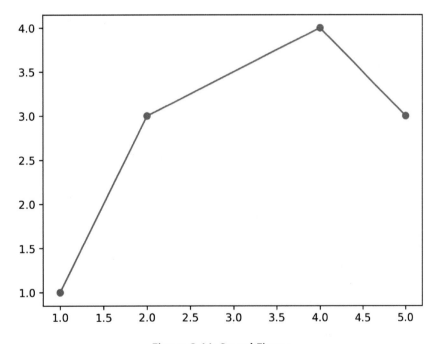

Figure 3.11: Saved Figure

Let's create a simple visualization in our next exercise.

EXERCISE 3.01: CREATING A SIMPLE VISUALIZATION

In this exercise, we will create our first simple plot using Matplotlib. The purpose of this exercise is for you to create your first simple line plot using Matplotlib, including the customization of the plot with format strings.

1. Create a new **Exercise3.01.ipynb** Jupyter Notebook in the **Chapter03/ Exercise3.01** folder to implement this exercise.

2. Import the necessary modules and enable plotting within the Jupyter Notebook:

```
import numpy as np
import matplotlib.pyplot as plt

%matplotlib inline
```

3. Explicitly create a Figure and set the **dpi** to 200:

```
plt.figure(dpi=200)
```

4. Plot the following data pairs **(x, y)** as circles, which are connected via line segments: **(1, 1)**, **(2, 3)**, **(4, 4)**, and **(5, 3)**. Then, visualize the plot:

```
plt.plot([1, 2, 4, 5], [1, 3, 4, 3], '-o')
plt.show()
```

Your output should look similar to this:

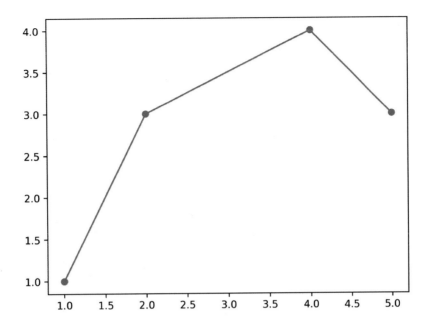

Figure 3.12: A simple visualization created with the help of given data pairs and connected via line segments

5. Save the plot using the **plt.savefig()** method. Here, we can either provide a filename within the method or specify the full path:

```
plt.savefig('Exercise3.01.png', bbox_inches='tight')
```

> **NOTE**
>
> To access the source code for this specific section, please refer to https://packt.live/2URkzlE.
>
> You can also run this example online at https://packt.live/2YI3A6t.

This exercise showed you how to create a line plot in Matplotlib and how to use format strings to quickly customize the appearance of the specified data points. Don't forget to use **bbox_inches='tight'** to remove the outer white margins. In the following section, we will cover how to further customize plots by adding text and a legend.

BASIC TEXT AND LEGEND FUNCTIONS

All of the functions we discuss in this topic, except for the legend, create and return a **matplotlib.text.Text()** instance. We are mentioning it here so that you know that all of the properties discussed can be used for the other functions as well. All text functions are illustrated in *Figure 3.13*.

LABELS

Matplotlib provides a few **label** functions that we can use for setting labels to the x- and y-axes. The **plt.xlabel()** and **plt.ylabel()** functions are used to set the label for the current axes. The **set_xlabel()** and **set_ylabel()** functions are used to set the label for specified axes.

Example:

```
ax.set_xlabel('X Label')
ax.set_ylabel('Y Label')
```

You should (always) add labels to make a visualization more self-explanatory. The same is valid for titles, which will be discussed now.

TITLES

A **title** describes a particular chart/graph. The titles are placed above the axes in the center, left edge, or right edge. There are two options for titles – you can either set the **Figure title** or the title of an **Axes**. The **suptitle()** function sets the title for the current and specified Figure. The **title()** function helps in setting the title for the current and specified axes.

Example:

```
fig = plt.figure()
fig.suptitle('Suptitle', fontsize=10, fontweight='bold')
```

This creates a bold Figure title with a text subtitle and a font size of 10:

```
plt.title('Title', fontsize=16)
```

The **plt.title** function will add a title to the Figure with text as **Title** and font size of **16** in this case.

TEXT

There are two options for **text** – you can either add text to a Figure or text to an Axes. The **figtext(x, y, text)** and **text(x, y, text)** functions add text at locations **x** or **y** for a Figure.

Example:

```
ax.text(4, 6, 'Text in Data Coords', \
        bbox={'facecolor': 'yellow', 'alpha':0.5, 'pad':10})
```

This creates a yellow text box with the text **Text in Data Coords**.

Text can be used to provide additional textual information to a visualization. To annotate something, Matplotlib offers annotations.

ANNOTATIONS

Compared to text that is placed at an arbitrary position on the Axes, **annotations** are used to annotate some features of the plot. In annotations, there are two locations to consider: the annotated location, **xy**, and the location of the annotation, text **xytext**. It is useful to specify the parameter **arrowprops**, which results in an arrow pointing to the annotated location.

Example:

```
ax.annotate('Example of Annotate', xy=(4,2), \
            xytext=(8,4), \
            arrowprops=dict(facecolor='green', shrink=0.05))
```

This creates a green arrow pointing to the data coordinates (4, 2) with the text **Example of Annotate** at data coordinates (8, 4):

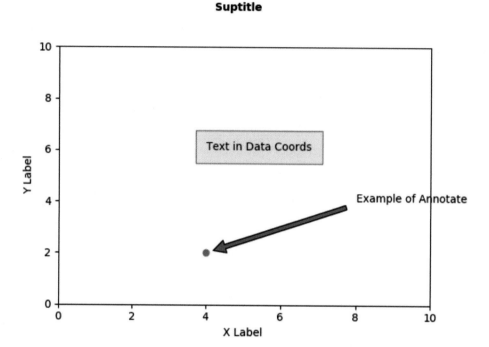

Figure 3.13: Implementation of text commands

LEGENDS

Legend describes the content of the plot. To add a **legend** to your Axes, we have to specify the **label** parameter at the time of plot creation. Calling **plt.legend()** for the current Axes or **Axes.legend()** for a specific Axes will add the legend. The **loc** parameter specifies the location of the legend.

Example:

```
plt.plot([1, 2, 3], label='Label 1')
plt.plot([2, 4, 3], label='Label 2')
plt.legend()
```

This example is illustrated in the following diagram:

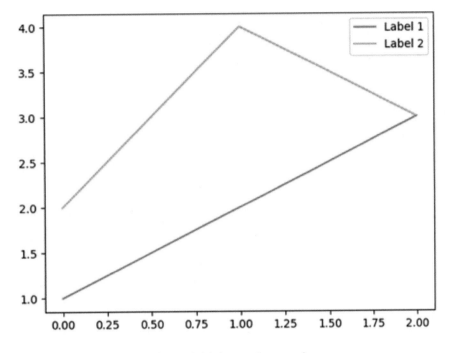

Figure 3.14: Legend example

Labels, titles, text, annotations, and a legend are great ways to add textual information to visualization and therefore make it more understandable and self-explanatory. But don't overdo it. Too much text can be overwhelming. The following activity gives you the opportunity to consolidate the theoretical foundations learned in this section.

ACTIVITY 3.01: VISUALIZING STOCK TRENDS BY USING A LINE PLOT

In this activity, we will create a line plot to show stock trends. The aim of this activity is to not just visualize the data but to use labels, a title, and a legend to make the visualization self-explanatory and "complete."

Let's look at the following scenario: you are interested in investing in stocks. You downloaded the stock prices for the "big five": Amazon, Google, Apple, Facebook, and Microsoft. You want to visualize the closing prices in dollars to identify trends. This dataset is available in the **Datasets** folder that you had downloaded initially. The following are the steps to perform:

1. Import the necessary modules and enable plotting within a Jupyter Notebook.

2. Use pandas to read the datasets (**GOOGL_data.csv**, **FB_data.csv**, **AAPL_data.csv**, **AMZN_data.csv**, and **MSFT_data.csv**) located in the **Datasets** folder. The **read_csv()** function reads a **.csv** file into a DataFrame.

3. Use Matplotlib to create a line chart visualizing the closing prices for the past 5 years (whole data sequence) for all five companies. Add labels, titles, and a legend to make the visualization self-explanatory. Use **plt.grid()** to add a grid to your plot. If necessary, adjust the ticks in order to make them readable.

   After executing the preceding steps, the expected output should be as follows:

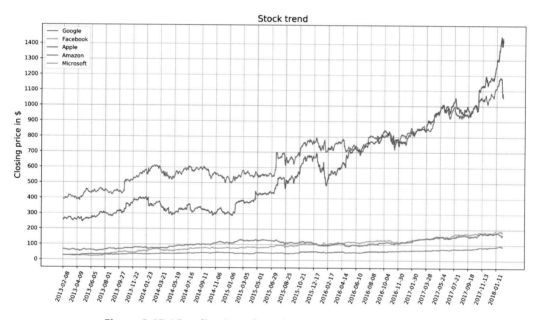

Figure 3.15: Visualization of stock trends of five companies

> **NOTE**
>
> The solution to this activity can be found on page 402.

This covers the most important things about pyplot. In the following section, we will talk about how to create various plots in Matplotlib.

BASIC PLOTS

In this section, we are going to go through the different types of simple plots. This includes bar charts, pie charts, stacked bar, and area charts, histograms, box plots, scatter plots and bubble plots. Please refer to the previous chapter to get more details about these plots. More sophisticated plots, such as violin plots, will be covered in the next chapter, using Seaborn instead of Matplotlib.

BAR CHART

The `plt.bar(x, height, [width])` creates a vertical bar plot. For horizontal bars, use the `plt.barh()` function.

Important parameters:

- **x**: Specifies the x coordinates of the bars

- **height**: Specifies the height of the bars

- **width** (optional): Specifies the width of all bars; the default is 0.8

Example:

```
plt.bar(['A', 'B', 'C', 'D'], [20, 25, 40, 10])
```

The preceding code creates a bar plot, as shown in the following diagram:

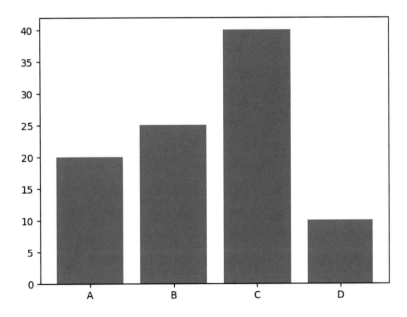

Figure 3.16: A simple bar chart

If you want to have subcategories, you have to use the **plt.bar()** function multiple times with shifted x-coordinates. This is done in the following example and illustrated in the figure that follows. The **arange()** function is a method in the **NumPy** package that returns evenly spaced values within a given interval. The **gca()** function helps in getting the instance of current axes on any current Figure. The **set_xticklabels()** function is used to set the x-tick labels with the list of given string labels.

Example:

```
labels = ['A', 'B', 'C', 'D']
x = np.arange(len(labels))
width = 0.4
plt.bar(x - width / 2, [20, 25, 40, 10], width=width)
plt.bar(x + width / 2, [30, 15, 30, 20], width=width)
# Ticks and tick labels must be set manually
plt.xticks(x)
ax = plt.gca()
ax.set_xticklabels(labels)
```

This creates a bar chart as shown in the following diagram:

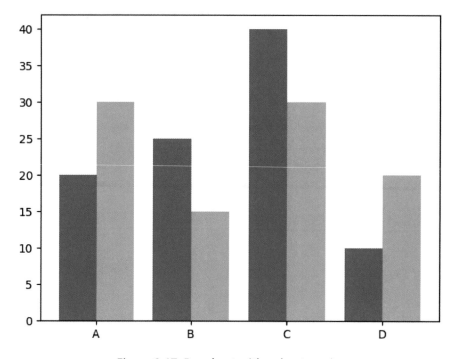

Figure 3.17: Bar chart with subcategories

After providing the theoretical foundation for creating bar charts in Matplotlib, you can apply your acquired knowledge in practice with the following activity.

ACTIVITY 3.02: CREATING A BAR PLOT FOR MOVIE COMPARISON

In this activity, we will create visually appealing bar plots. We will use a bar plot to compare movie scores. You are given five movies with scores from Rotten Tomatoes. The Tomatometer is the percentage of approved Tomatometer critics who have given a positive review for the movie. The Audience Score is the percentage of users who have given a score of 3.5 or higher out of 5. Compare these two scores among the five movies.

The following are the steps to perform:

1. Import the necessary modules and enable plotting within a Jupyter Notebook.

2. Use pandas to read the data located in the **Datasets** subfolder.

3. Use Matplotlib to create a visually appealing bar plot comparing the two scores for all five movies.

4. Use the movie titles as labels for the x-axis. Use percentages at intervals of 20 for the y-axis and minor ticks at intervals of 5. Add a legend and a suitable title to the plot.

5. Use functions that are required to explicitly specify the axes. To get the reference to the current axes, use **ax = plt.gca()**. To add minor y-ticks, use **Axes. set_yticks([ticks], minor=True)**. To add a horizontal grid for major ticks, use **Axes.yaxis.grid(which='major')**, and to add a dashed horizontal grid for minor ticks, use **Axes.yaxis.grid(which='minor', linestyle='--')**.

The expected output is as follows:

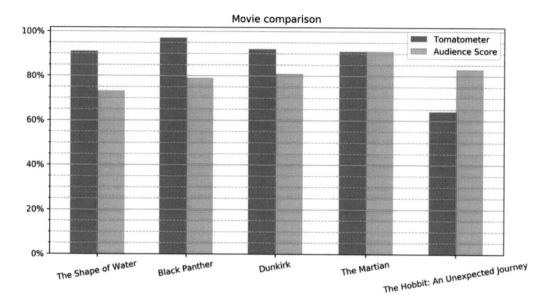

Figure 3.18: Bar plot comparing scores of five movies

> **NOTE**
>
> The solution to this activity can be found on page 404.

After practicing the creation of bar plots, we will discuss how to create pie charts in Matplotlib in the following section.

PIE CHART

The `plt.pie(x, [explode], [labels], [autopct])` function creates a pie chart.

Important parameters:

- **x**: Specifies the slice sizes.

- **explode** (optional): Specifies the fraction of the radius offset for each slice. The **explode-array** must have the same length as the **x-array**.

- **`labels`** (optional): Specifies the labels for each slice.

- **`autopct`** (optional): Shows percentages inside the slices according to the specified format string. Example: **`'%1.1f%%'`**.

Example:

```
plt.pie([0.4, 0.3, 0.2, 0.1], explode=(0.1, 0, 0, 0), \
        labels=['A', 'B', 'C', 'D'])
```

The result of the preceding code is visualized in the following diagram:

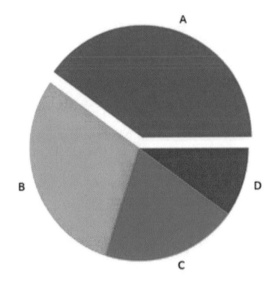

Figure 3.19: Basic pie chart

After this short introduction to pie charts, we will create a more sophisticated pie chart that visualizes the water usage in a common household in the following exercise.

EXERCISE 3.02: CREATING A PIE CHART FOR WATER USAGE

In this exercise, we will use a pie chart to visualize water usage. There has been a shortage of water in your locality in the past few weeks. To understand the reason behind it, generate a visual representation of water usage using pie charts.

The following are the steps to perform:

1. Create an **Exercise3.02.ipynb** Jupyter Notebook in the **Chapter03/ Exercise3.02** folder to implement this exercise.

2. Import the necessary modules and enable plotting within the Jupyter Notebook:

```
# Import statements
import pandas as pd
import matplotlib.pyplot as plt


%matplotlib inline
```

3. Use pandas to read the data located in the **Datasets** subfolder:

```
# Load dataset
data = pd.read_csv('../../Datasets/water_usage.csv')
```

4. Use a pie chart to visualize water usage. Highlight one usage of your choice using the **explode** parameter. Show the percentages for each slice and add a title:

```
# Create figure
plt.figure(figsize=(8, 8), dpi=300)
# Create pie plot
plt.pie('Percentage', explode=(0, 0, 0.1, 0, 0, 0), \
        labels='Usage', data=data, autopct='%.0f%%')
# Add title
plt.title('Water usage')
# Show plot
plt.show()
```

The output is as follows:

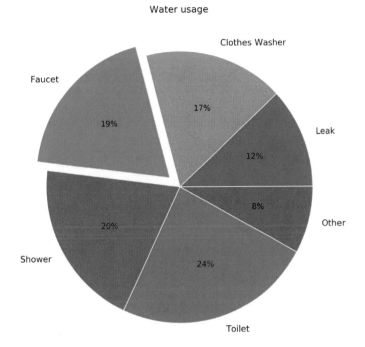

Figure 3.20: Pie chart for water usage

Pie charts are a common way to show part-of-a-whole relationships, as you've seen in the previous exercise. Another visualization that falls into this category are stacked bar charts.

> **NOTE**
>
> To access the source code for this specific section, please refer to https://packt.live/3frXRrZ.
>
> You can also run this example online at https://packt.live/2Y4D1cd.

In the next section, we will learn how to generate a stacked bar chart and implement an activity on it.

STACKED BAR CHART

A **stacked bar chart** uses the same **plt.bar** function as bar charts. For each stacked bar, the **plt.bar** function must be called, and the **bottom** parameter must be specified, starting with the second stacked bar. This will become clear with the following example:

```
plt.bar(x, bars1)
plt.bar(x, bars2, bottom=bars1)
plt.bar(x, bars3, bottom=np.add(bars1, bars2))
```

The result of the preceding code is visualized in the following diagram:

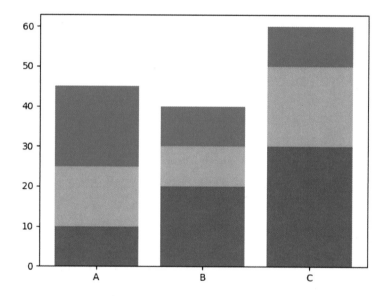

Figure 3.21: A stacked bar chart

Let's get some more practice with stacked bar charts in the following activity.

ACTIVITY 3.03: CREATING A STACKED BAR PLOT TO VISUALIZE RESTAURANT PERFORMANCE

In this activity, we will use a stacked bar plot to visualize the performance of a restaurant. Let's look at the following scenario: you are the owner of a restaurant and, due to a new law, you have to introduce a *No Smoking Day*. To make as few losses as possible, you want to visualize how many sales are made every day, categorized by smokers and non-smokers.

Use the dataset tips from Seaborn, which contains multiple entries of restaurant bills, and create a matrix where the elements contain the sum of the total bills for each day and smokers/non-smokers:

> **NOTE**
>
> For this exercise, we will import the Seaborn library as `import seaborn as sns`. The dataset can be loaded using this code: `bills = sns.load_dataset('tips')`.
>
> We will learn in detail about this in *Chapter 4, Simplifying Visualizations Using Seaborn*.

1. Import all the necessary dependencies and load the **tips** dataset. Note that we have to import the Seaborn library to load the dataset.

2. Use the given dataset and create a matrix where the elements contain the sum of the total bills for each day and split according to smokers/non-smokers.

3. Create a stacked bar plot, stacking the summed total bills separated according to smoker and non-smoker for each day.

4. Add a legend, labels, and a title.

   After executing the preceding steps, the expected output should be as follows:

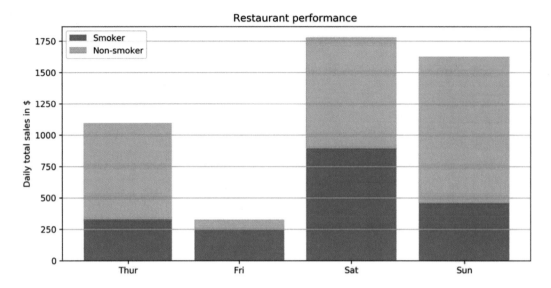

Figure 3.22: Stacked bar chart showing the performance
of a restaurant on different days

> **NOTE**
>
> The solution to this activity can be found on page 406.

In the following section, stacked area charts will be covered, which, in comparison to stacked bar charts, are suited to visualizing part-of-a-whole relationships for time series data.

STACKED AREA CHART

`plt.stackplot(x, y)` creates a stacked area plot.

Important parameters:

- **x**: Specifies the x-values of the data series.

- **y**: Specifies the y-values of the data series. For multiple series, either as a 2D array or any number of 1D arrays, call the following function: `plt.stackplot(x, y1, y2, y3, …)`.

- **labels** (optional): Specifies the labels as a list or tuple for each data series.

Example:

```
plt.stackplot([1, 2, 3, 4], [2, 4, 5, 8], [1, 5, 4, 2])
```

The result of the preceding code is shown in the following diagram:

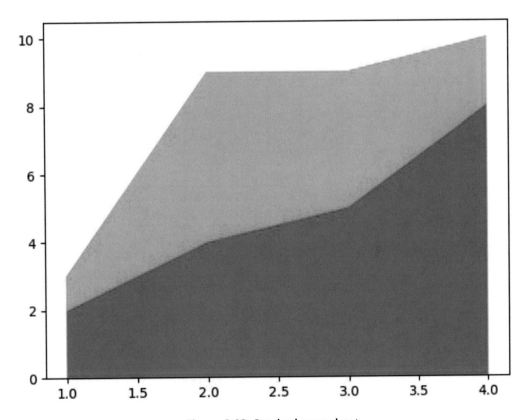

Figure 3.23: Stacked area chart

Let's get some more practice regarding stacked area charts in the following activity.

ACTIVITY 3.04: COMPARING SMARTPHONE SALES UNITS USING A STACKED AREA CHART

In this activity, we will compare smartphone sales units using a stacked area chart. Let's look at the following scenario: you want to invest in one of the five biggest smartphone manufacturers. Looking at the quarterly sales units as part of a whole may be a good indicator of which company to invest in:

1. Import the necessary modules and enable plotting within a Jupyter Notebook.

2. Use pandas to read the **smartphone_sales.csv** dataset located in the **Datasets** subfolder.

3. Create a visually appealing stacked area chart. Add a legend, labels, and a title.

   After executing the preceding steps, the expected output should be as follows:

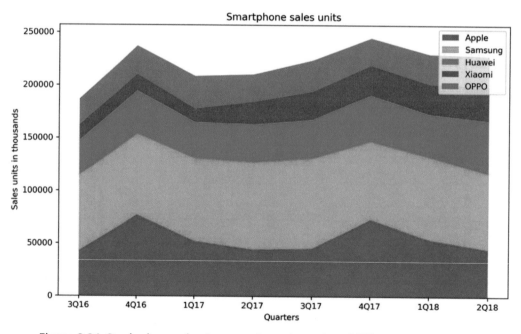

Figure 3.24: Stacked area chart comparing sales units of different smartphone manufacturers

> **NOTE**
>
> The solution to this activity can be found on page 409.

In the following section, the histogram will be covered, which helps to visualize the distribution of a single numerical variable.

HISTOGRAM

A histogram visualizes the distribution of a single numerical variable. Each bar represents the frequency for a certain interval. The **plt.hist(x)** function creates a histogram.

Important parameters:

- **x**: Specifies the input values.

- **bins**: (optional): Specifies the number of bins as an integer or specifies the bin edges as a list.

- **range**: (optional): Specifies the lower and upper range of the bins as a tuple.

- **density**: (optional): If true, the histogram represents a probability density.

Example:

```
plt.hist(x, bins=30, density=True)
```

The result of the preceding code is shown in the following diagram:

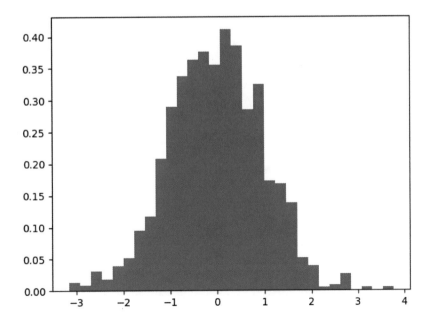

Figure 3.25: Histogram

plt.hist2d(x, y) creates a 2D histogram. 2D histograms can be used to visualize the frequency of two-dimensional data. The data is plotted on the xy-plane and the frequency is indicated by the color. An example of a 2D histogram is shown in the following diagram:

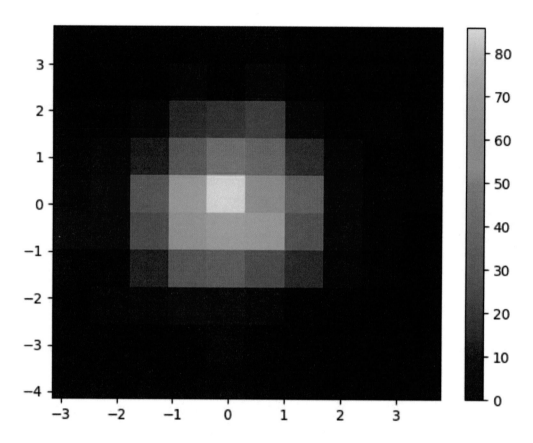

Figure 3.26: 2D histogram with color bar

Histograms are a good way to visualize an estimated density of your data. If you're only interested in summary statistics, such as central tendency or dispersion, the following covered box plots are more interesting.

BOX PLOT

The box plot shows multiple statistical measurements. The box extends from the lower to the upper quartile values of the data, thereby allowing us to visualize the interquartile range. For more details regarding the plot, refer to the previous chapter. The **plt.boxplot(x)** function creates a box plot.

Important parameters:

- **x**: Specifies the input data. It specifies either a 1D array for a single box, or a sequence of arrays for multiple boxes.

- **notch**: (optional) If true, notches will be added to the plot to indicate the confidence interval around the median.

- **labels**: (optional) Specifies the labels as a sequence.

- **showfliers**: (optional) By default, it is true, and outliers are plotted beyond the caps.

- **showmeans**: (optional) If true, arithmetic means are shown.

Example:

```
plt.boxplot([x1, x2], labels=['A', 'B'])
```

The result of the preceding code is shown in the following diagram:

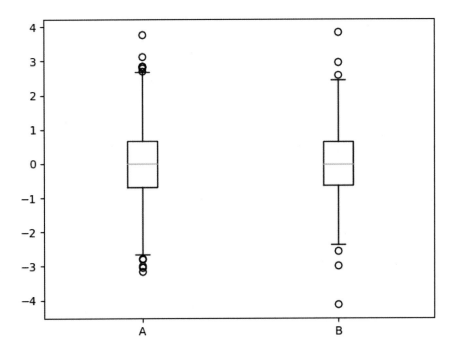

Figure 3.27: Box plot

Now that we've introduced histograms and box plots in Matplotlib, our theoretical knowledge can be practiced in the following activity, where both charts are used to visualize data regarding the intelligence quotient.

ACTIVITY 3.05: USING A HISTOGRAM AND A BOX PLOT TO VISUALIZE INTELLIGENCE QUOTIENT

In this activity, we will visualize the **intelligence quotient** (**IQ**) of 100 applicants using histogram and box plots. 100 people have come for an interview in a company. To place an individual applicant in the overall group, a histogram and a box plot shall be used.

> **NOTE**
>
> The `plt.axvline(x, [color=…], [linestyle=…])` function draws a vertical line at position `x`.

1. Import the necessary modules and enable plotting within a Jupyter Notebook.

2. Use the following IQ scores to create the plots:

```
# IQ samples
iq_scores = [126,  89,  90, 101, 102,  74,  93, 101,  66, \
             120, 108,  97,  98, 105, 119,  92, 113,  81, \
             104, 108,  83, 102, 105, 111, 102, 107, 103,  \
              89,  89, 110,  71, 110, 120,  85, 111,  83, 122, \
             120, 102, 84, 118, 100, 100, 114,  81, 109,  69,  \
              97,  95, 106, 116, 109, 114,  98,  90,  92,  98,  \
              91,  81,  85,  86, 102,  93, 112,  76, 89, 110,  \
              75, 100,  90,  96,  94, 107, 108,  95,  96,  96, \
             114,  93,  95, 117, 141, 115,  95,  86, 100, 121, \
             103,  66,  99,  96, 111, 110, 105, 110, 91, 112, \
             102, 112,  75]
```

3. Plot a histogram with 10 bins for the given IQ scores. IQ scores are normally distributed with a mean of 100 and a standard deviation of 15. Visualize the mean as a vertical solid red line, and the standard deviation using dashed vertical lines. Add labels and a title. The expected output is as follows:

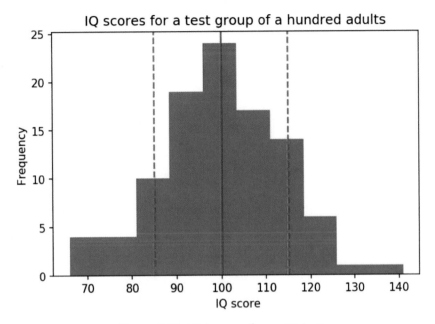

Figure 3.28: Histogram for an IQ test

4. Create a box plot to visualize the same IQ scores. Add labels and a title. The expected output is as follows:

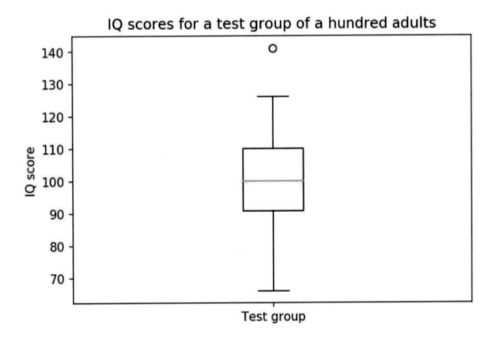

Figure 3.29: Box plot for IQ scores

5. Create a box plot for each of the IQ scores of the different test groups. Add labels and a title. The following are IQ scores for different test groups that we can use as data:

```
group_a = [118, 103, 125, 107, 111,  96, 104,  97,  96, \
           114,  96,  75, 114, 107,  87, 117, 117, 114, \
           117, 112, 107, 133,  94,  91, 118, 110, 117,  \
            86, 143,  83, 106,  86,  98, 126, 109,  91, 112, \
           120, 108, 111, 107,  98,  89, 113, 117,  81, 113, \
           112,  84, 115,  96,  93, 128, 115, 138, 121,  87, \
           112, 110,  79, 100,  84, 115,  93, 108, 130, 107, \
           106, 106, 101, 117,  93,  94, 103, 112,  98, 103,  \
            70, 139,  94, 110, 105, 122,  94,  94, 105, 129, \
           110, 112,  97, 109, 121, 106, 118, 131,  88, 122, \
           125,  93,  78]

group_b = [126,  89,  90, 101, 102,  74,  93, 101,  66, \
           120, 108,  97,  98, 105, 119,  92, 113,  81, \
           104, 108,  83, 102, 105, 111, 102, 107, 103,  \
            89,  89, 110,  71, 110, 120,  85, 111,  83, \
           122, 120, 102,  84, 118, 100, 100, 114,  81, \
           109,  69,  97,  95, 106, 116, 109, 114,  98,  \
            90,  92,  98,  91,  81,  85,  86, 102,  93, 112,  \
            76,  89, 110,  75, 100,  90,  96,  94, 107, 108,  \
            95,  96,  96, 114,  93,  95, 117, 141, 115,  95,  \
            86, 100, 121, 103,  66,  99,  96, 111, 110, 105, \
           110,  91, 112, 102, 112,  75]

group_c = [108,  89, 114, 116, 126, 104, 113,  96,  69, 121, \
           109, 102, 107, 122, 104, 107, 108, 137, 107, 116,  \
            98, 132, 108, 114,  82,  93,  89,  90,  86,  91,  \
            99,  98,  83,  93, 114,  96,  95, 113, 103, 81, \
           107,  85, 116,  85, 107, 125, 126, 123, 122, 124, \
           115, 114,  93,  93, 114, 107, 107,  84, 131,  91, \
           108, 127, 112, 106, 115,  82,  90, 117, 108, 115, \
           113, 108, 104, 103,  90, 110, 114,  92, 101,  72, \
           109,  94, 122,  90, 102,  86, 119, 103, 110,  96,  \
```

```
            90, 110,  96,  69,  85, 102,  69,  96, 101,  90]

group_d = [93,  99,  91, 110,  80, 113, 111, 115,  98,  74, \
            96,  80,  83, 102,  60,  91,  82,  90,  97, 101, \
            89,  89, 117,  91, 104, 104, 102, 128, 106, 111, \
            79,  92,  97, 101, 106, 110,  93,  93, 106, 108, \
            85,  83, 108,  94,  79,  87, 113, 112, 111, 111, \
            79, 116, 104,  84, 116, 111, 103, 103, 112,  68, \
            54,  80,  86, 119,  81,  84,  91,  96, 116, 125, \
            99,  58, 102,  77,  98, 100,  90, 106, 109, 114, \
           102, 102, 112, 103,  98,  96,  85,  97, 110, 131, \
            92,  79, 115, 122,  95, 105,  74,  85,  85,  95]
```

The expected output is as follows:

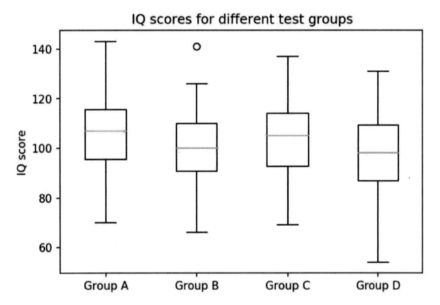

Figure 3.30: Box plot for IQ scores of different test groups

> **NOTE**
>
> The solution to this activity can be found on page 411.

In the next section, we will learn how to generate a scatter plot.

SCATTER PLOT

Scatter plots show data points for two numerical variables, displaying a variable on both axes. **plt.scatter(x, y)** creates a scatter plot of **y** versus **x**, with optionally varying marker size and/or color.

Important parameters:

- **x, y**: Specifies the data positions.

- **s**: (optional) Specifies the marker size in points squared.

- **c**: (optional) Specifies the marker color. If a sequence of numbers is specified, the numbers will be mapped to the colors of the color map.

Example:

```
plt.scatter(x, y)
```

The result of the preceding code is shown in the following diagram:

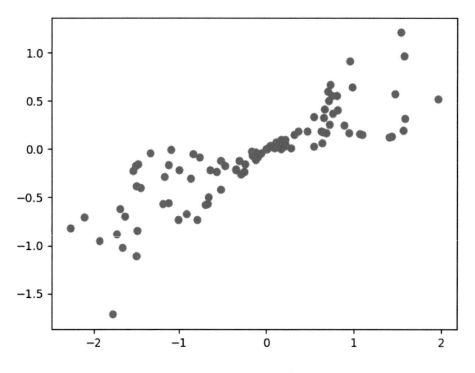

Figure 3.31: Scatter plot

Let's implement a scatter plot in the following exercise.

EXERCISE 3.03: USING A SCATTER PLOT TO VISUALIZE CORRELATION BETWEEN VARIOUS ANIMALS

In this exercise, we will use a scatter plot to show correlation within a dataset. Let's look at the following scenario: You are given a dataset containing information about various animals. Visualize the correlation between the various animal attributes such as *Maximum longevity in years* and *Body mass in grams*.

> **NOTE**
>
> The **Axes.set_xscale('log')** and the **Axes.set_yscale('log')** change the scale of the x-axis and y-axis to a logarithmic scale, respectively.

Let's visualize the correlation between various animals with the help of a scatter plot:

1. Create an **Exercise3.03.ipynb** Jupyter Notebook in the **Chapter03/Exercise3.03** folder to implement this exercise.

2. Import the necessary modules and enable plotting within the Jupyter Notebook:

```
# Import statements
import pandas as pd
import numpy as np
import matplotlib.pyplot as plt
%matplotlib inline
```

3. Use pandas to read the data located in the **Datasets** folder:

```
# Load dataset
data = pd.read_csv('../../Datasets/anage_data.csv')
```

4. The given dataset is not complete. Filter the data so that you end up with samples containing a body mass and a maximum longevity. Sort the data according to the animal class; here, the **isfinite()** function (to check whether the number is finite or not) checks for the finiteness of the given element:

```
# Preprocessing
longevity = 'Maximum longevity (yrs)'
mass = 'Body mass (g)'
data = data[np.isfinite(data[longevity]) \
        & np.isfinite(data[mass])]
```

```
# Sort according to class
amphibia = data[data['Class'] == 'Amphibia']
aves = data[data['Class'] == 'Aves']
mammalia = data[data['Class'] == 'Mammalia']
reptilia = data[data['Class'] == 'Reptilia']
```

5. Create a scatter plot visualizing the correlation between the body mass and the maximum longevity. Use different colors to group data samples according to their class. Add a legend, labels, and a title. Use a log scale for both the x-axis and y-axis:

```
# Create figure
plt.figure(figsize=(10, 6), dpi=300)
# Create scatter plot
plt.scatter(amphibia[mass], amphibia[longevity], \
            label='Amphibia')
plt.scatter(aves[mass], aves[longevity], \
            label='Aves')
plt.scatter(mammalia[mass], mammalia[longevity], \
            label='Mammalia')
plt.scatter(reptilia[mass], reptilia[longevity], \
            label='Reptilia')
# Add legend
plt.legend()
# Log scale
ax = plt.gca()
ax.set_xscale('log')
ax.set_yscale('log')
# Add labels
plt.xlabel('Body mass in grams')
plt.ylabel('Maximum longevity in years')
# Show plot
plt.show()
```

The following is the output of the code:

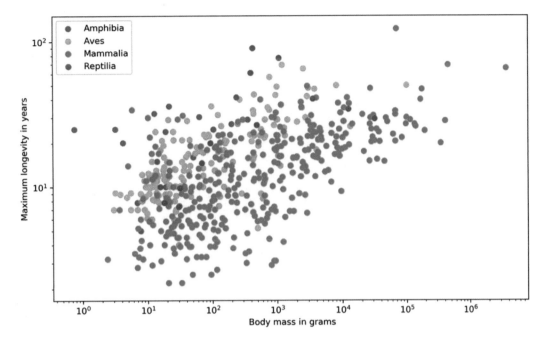

Figure 3.32: Scatter plot on animal statistics

From the preceding output, we can visualize the correlation between various animals based on the maximum longevity in years and body mass in grams.

> **NOTE**
>
> To access the source code for this specific section, please refer to https://packt.live/3fsozRf.
>
> You can also run this example online at https://packt.live/37yk0C7.

Next, we will learn how to generate a bubble plot.

BUBBLE PLOT

The **plt.scatter** function is used to create a bubble plot. To visualize a third or fourth variable, the parameters **s** (scale) and **c** (color) can be used.

Example:

```
plt.scatter(x, y, s=z*500, c=c, alpha=0.5)
plt.colorbar()
```

The **colorbar** function adds a colorbar to the plot, which indicates the value of the color. The result is shown in the following diagram:

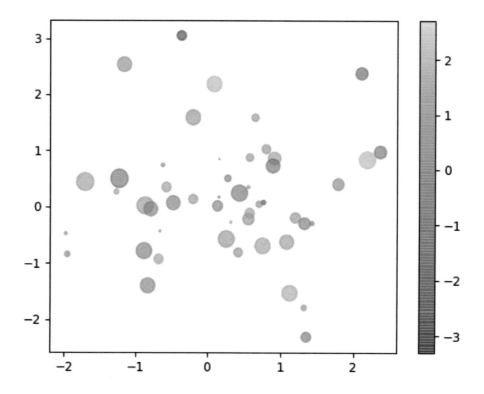

Figure 3.33: Bubble plot with color bar

LAYOUTS

There are multiple ways to define a visualization layout in Matplotlib. By layout, we mean the arrangement of multiple Axes within a Figure. We will start with **subplots** and how to use the **tight layout** to create visually appealing plots and then cover **GridSpec**, which offers a more flexible way to create multi-plots.

SUBPLOTS

It is often useful to display several plots next to one another. Matplotlib offers the concept of subplots, which are multiple Axes within a Figure. These plots can be grids of plots, nested plots, and so on.

Explore the following options to create subplots:

- The **plt.subplots(, ncols)** function creates a Figure and a set of subplots. **nrows, ncols** define the number of rows and columns of the subplots, respectively.

- The **plt.subplot(nrows, ncols, index)** function or, equivalently, **plt.subplot(pos)** adds a subplot to the current Figure. The index starts at 1. The **plt.subplot(2, 2, 1)** function is equivalent to **plt.subplot(221)**.

- The **Figure.subplots(nrows, ncols)** function adds a set of subplots to the specified Figure.

- The **Figure.add_subplot(nrows, ncols, index)** function or, equivalently, **Figure.add_subplot(pos)**, adds a subplot to the specified Figure.

To share the x-axis or y-axis, the parameters **sharex** and **sharey** must be set, respectively. The axis will have the same limits, ticks, and scale.

plt.subplot and **Figure.add_subplot** have the option to set a projection. For a polar projection, either set the **projection='polar'** parameter or the **parameter polar=True** parameter.

Example 1:

```
fig, axes = plt.subplots(2, 2)
axes = axes.ravel()
for i, ax in enumerate(axes):
    ax.plot(series[i])
# [...]
for i in range(4):
    plt.subplot(2, 2, i+1)
    plt.plot(series[i])
```

Both examples yield the same result, as shown in the following diagram:

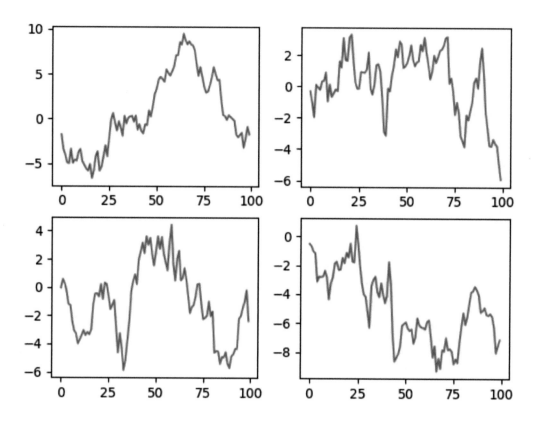

Figure 3.34: Subplots

Example 2:

```
fig, axes = plt.subplots(2, 2, sharex=True, sharey=True)
axes = axes.ravel()
for i, ax in enumerate(axes):
    ax.plot(series[i])
```

Setting **sharex** and **sharey** to **True** results in the following diagram. This allows for a better comparison:

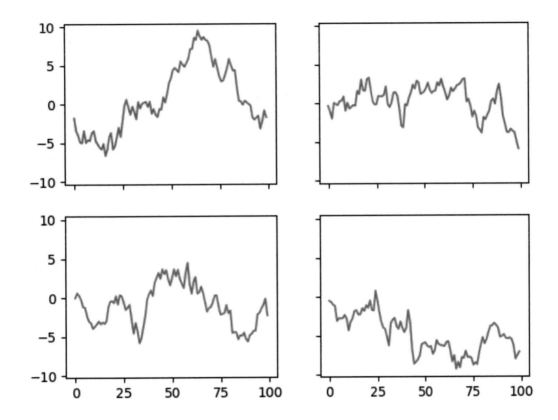

Figure 3.35: Subplots with a shared x- and y-axis

Subplots are an easy way to create a Figure with multiple plots of the same size placed in a grid. They are not really suited for more sophisticated layouts.

TIGHT LAYOUT

The **plt.tight_layout()** adjusts subplot parameters (primarily padding between the Figure edge and the edges of subplots, and padding between the edges of adjacent subplots) so that the subplots fit well in the Figure.

Examples:

If you do not use **plt.tight_layout()**, subplots might overlap:

```
fig, axes = plt.subplots(2, 2)
axes = axes.ravel()
for i, ax in enumerate(axes):
    ax.plot(series[i])
    ax.set_title('Subplot ' + str(i))
```

The result of the preceding code is shown in the following diagram:

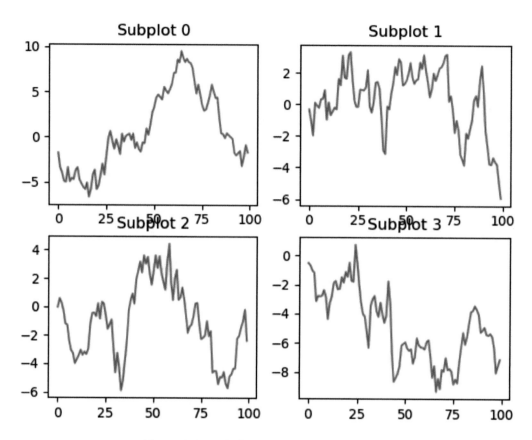

Figure 3.36: Subplots with no layout option

Using **plt.tight_layout()** results in no overlapping of the subplots:

```
fig, axes = plt.subplots(2, 2)
axes = axes.ravel()
for i, ax in enumerate(axes):
    ax.plot(series[i])
    ax.set_title('Subplot ' + str(i))
plt.tight_layout()
```

The result of the preceding code is shown in the following diagram:

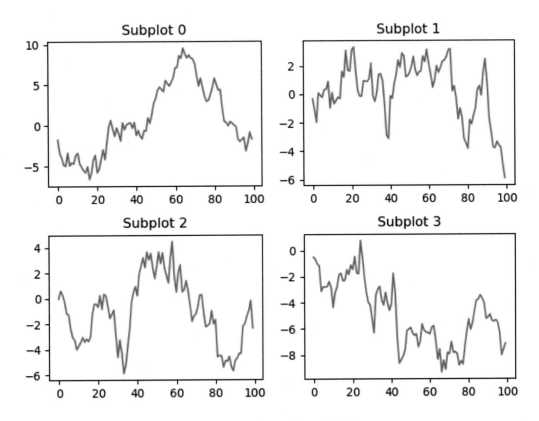

Figure 3.37: Subplots with a tight layout

RADAR CHARTS

Radar charts, also known as **spider** or **web charts**, visualize multiple variables, with each variable plotted on its own axis, resulting in a polygon. All axes are arranged radially, starting at the center with equal distance between each other, and have the same scale.

EXERCISE 3.04: WORKING ON RADAR CHARTS

As a manager of a team, you have to award a "Star Performer" trophy to an employee for the month of December. You come to the conclusion that the best way to understad the performance of your team members would be to visualize the performance of your team members in a radar chart. Thus, in this exercise, we will show you how to create a radar chart. The following are the steps to perform this exercise:

1. Create an **Exercise3.04.ipynb** Jupyter Notebook in the **Chapter03/ Exercise3.04** folder to implement this exercise.

2. Import the necessary modules and enable plotting within a Jupyter Notebook:

```
# Import settings
import numpy as np
import pandas as pd
import matplotlib.pyplot as plt
%matplotlib inline
```

3. The following dataset contains ratings of five different attributes for four employees:

```
"""
Sample data
Attributes: Efficiency, Quality, Commitment, Responsible Conduct,
Cooperation
"""
data = \
pd.DataFrame({'Employee': ['Alex', 'Alice', \
                           'Chris', 'Jennifer'], \
              'Efficiency': [5, 4, 4, 3,],
              'Quality': [5, 5, 3, 3],
              'Commitment': [5, 4, 4, 4],
              'Responsible Conduct': [4, 4, 4, 3],
              'Cooperation': [4, 3, 4, 5]})
```

4. Create angle values and close the plot:

```
attributes = list(data.columns[1:])
values = list(data.values[:, 1:])
employees = list(data.values[:, 0])
angles = [n / float(len(attributes)) * 2 \
          * np.pi for n in range(len(attributes))]
# Close the plot
angles += angles[:1]
values = np.asarray(values)
values = np.concatenate([values, values[:, 0:1]], axis=1)
```

5. Create subplots with the polar projection. Set a tight layout so that nothing overlaps:

```
# Create figure
plt.figure(figsize=(8, 8), dpi=150)
# Create subplots
for i in range(4):
    ax = plt.subplot(2, 2, i + 1, polar=True)
    ax.plot(angles, values[i])
    ax.set_yticks([1, 2, 3, 4, 5])
    ax.set_xticks(angles)
    ax.set_xticklabels(attributes)
    ax.set_title(employees[i], fontsize=14, color='r')
# Set tight layout
plt.tight_layout()
# Show plot
plt.show()
```

The following diagram shows the output of the preceding code:

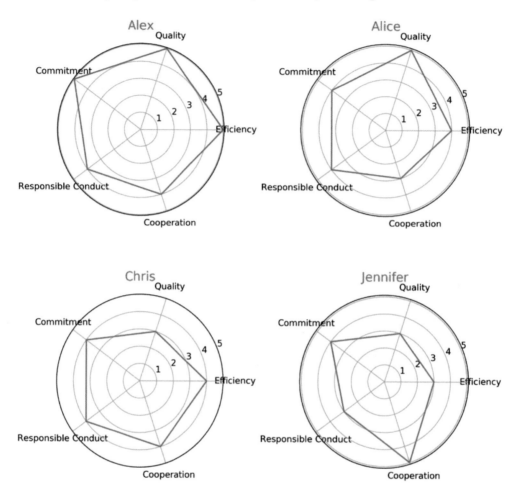

Figure 3.38: Radar charts

From the preceding output, we can clearly see how the various team members have performed in terms of metrics such as Quality, Efficiency, Cooperation, Responsible Conduct, and Commitment. You can easily draw the conclusion that Alex outperforms his collegues when all metrics are considered. In the next section, we will learn how to use the **GridSpec** function.

GRIDSPEC

The **matplotlib.gridspec.GridSpec(nrows, ncols)** function specifies the geometry of the grid in which a subplot will be placed. For example, you can specify a grid with three rows and four columns. As a next step, you have to define which elements of the gridspec are used by a subplot; elements of a gridspec are accessed in the same way as NumPy arrays. You could, for example, only use a single element of a gridspec for a subplot and therefore end up with 12 subplots in total. Another possibility, as shown in the following example, is to create a bigger subplot using 3x3 elements of the gridspec and another three subplots with a single element each.

Example:

```
gs = matplotlib.gridspec.GridSpec(3, 4)
ax1 = plt.subplot(gs[:3, :3])
ax2 = plt.subplot(gs[0, 3])
ax3 = plt.subplot(gs[1, 3])
ax4 = plt.subplot(gs[2, 3])
ax1.plot(series[0])
ax2.plot(series[1])
ax3.plot(series[2])
ax4.plot(series[3])
plt.tight_layout()
```

The result of the preceding code is shown in the following diagram:

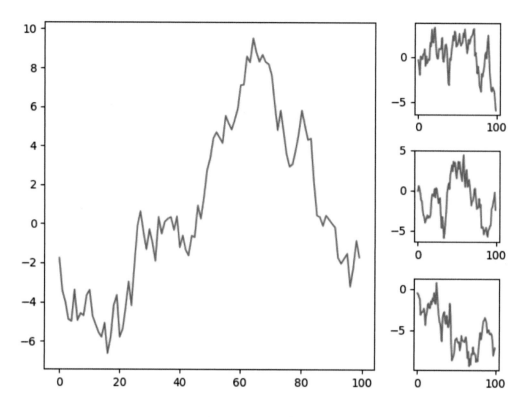

Figure 3.39: GridSpec

Next, we will implement an activity to implement `GridSpec`.

ACTIVITY 3.06: CREATING A SCATTER PLOT WITH MARGINAL HISTOGRAMS

In this activity, we will make use of **GridSpec** to visualize a **scatter plot** with **marginal histograms**. Let's look at the following scenario: you are given a dataset containing information about various animals. Visualize the correlation between the various animal attributes using scatter plots and marginal histograms.

The following are the steps to perform:

1. Import the necessary modules and enable plotting within a Jupyter Notebook.

2. Filter the data so that you end up with samples containing a body mass and maximum longevity as the given dataset, **AnAge**, which was used in the previous exercise, is not complete. Select all of the samples of the **Aves** class with a body mass of less than 20,000.

3. Create a Figure with a constrained layout. Create a gridspec of size 4x4. Create a scatter plot of size 3x3 and marginal histograms of size 1x3 and 3x1. Add labels and a Figure title.

    After executing the preceding steps, the expected output should be as follows:

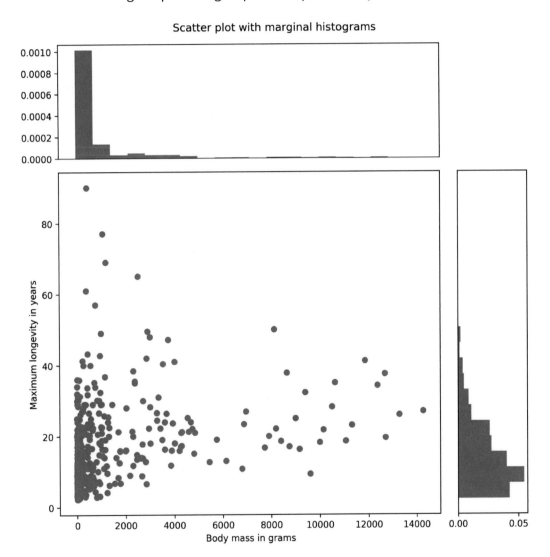

Figure 3.40: Scatter plots with marginal histograms

NOTE

The solution to this activity can be found on page 415.

Next, we will learn how to work with image data in our visualizations.

IMAGES

If you want to include images in your visualizations or work with image data, Matplotlib offers several functions for you. In this section, we will show you how to **load**, **save**, and **plot** images with Matplotlib.

> **NOTE**
>
> The images that are used in this section are sourced from https://unsplash.com/.

BASIC IMAGE OPERATIONS

The following are the basic operations for designing an image.

Loading Images

If you encounter image formats that are not supported by Matplotlib, we recommend using the **Pillow** library to load the image. In Matplotlib, loading images is part of the **image** submodule. We use the alias **mpimg** for the submodule, as follows:

```
import matplotlib.image as mpimg
```

The **mpimg.imread(fname)** reads an image and returns it as a **numpy.array** object. For grayscale images, the returned array has a shape (height, width), for RGB images (height, width, 3), and for RGBA images (height, width, 4). The array values range from 0 to 255.

We can also load the image in the following manner:

```
img_filenames = os.listdir('../../Datasets/images')
imgs = \
[mpimg.imread(os.path.join('../../Datasets/images', \
                           img_filename)) \
                   for img_filename in img_filenames]
```

The **os.listdir()** method in Python is used to get the list of all files and directories in the specified directory and then the **os.path.join()** function is used to join one or more path components intelligently.

Saving Images

The **mpimg.imsave(fname, array)** saves a **numpy.array** object as an image file. If the **format** parameter is not given, the format is deduced from the filename extension. With the optional parameters **vmin** and **vmax**, the color limits can be set manually. For a grayscale image, the default for the optional parameter, **cmap**, is **'viridis'**; you might want to change it to **'gray'**.

Plotting a Single Image

The **plt.imshow(img)** displays an image and returns an **AxesImage** object. For grayscale images with shape (height, width), the image array is visualized using a colormap. The default colormap is **'viridis'**, as illustrated in *Figure 3.41*. To actually visualize a grayscale image, the colormap has to be set to **'gray'** (that is, **plt.imshow(img, cmap='gray')**, which is illustrated in *Figure 3.42*. Values for grayscale, RGB, and RGBA images can be either **float** or **uint8**, and range from **[0...1]** or **[0...255]**, respectively. To manually define the value range, the parameters **vmin** and **vmax** must be specified. A visualization of an RGB image is shown in the following figures:

Figure 3.41: Grayscale image with a default viridis colormap

The following figure shows a grayscale image with a gray colormap:

Figure 3.42: Grayscale image with a gray colormap

The following figure shows an RGB image:

Figure 3.43: RGB image

Sometimes, it might be helpful to get an insight into the color values. We can simply add a color bar to the image plot. It is recommended to use a colormap with high contrast—for example, **jet**:

```
plt.imshow(img, cmap='jet')
plt.colorbar()
```

The preceding example is illustrated in the following figure:

Figure 3.44: Image with a jet colormap and color bar

Another way to get insight into the image values is to plot a histogram, as shown in the following diagram. To plot the histogram for an image array, the array has to be flattened using **numpy.ravel**:

```
plt.hist(img.ravel(), bins=256, range=(0, 1))
```

The following diagram shows the output of the preceding code:

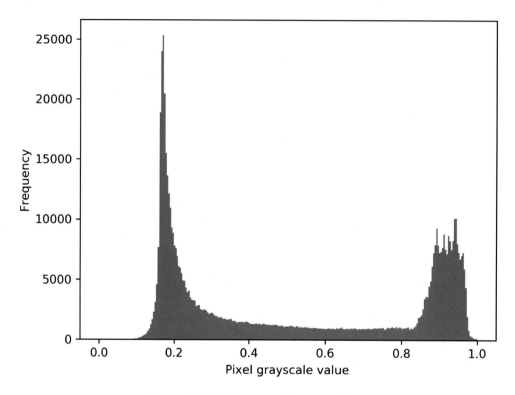

Figure 3.45: Histogram of image values

Plotting Multiple Images in a Grid

To plot multiple images in a grid, we can simply use **plt.subplots** and plot an image per **Axes**:

```
fig, axes = plt.subplots(1, 2)
for i in range(2):
    axes[i].imshow(imgs[i])
```

The result of the preceding code is shown in the following diagram:

Figure 3.46: Multiple images within a grid

In some situations, it would be neat to remove the ticks and add labels. **axes.set_xticks([])** and **axes.set_yticks([])** remove x-ticks and y-ticks, respectively. **axes.set_xlabel('label')** adds a label:

```
fig, axes = plt.subplots(1, 2)
labels = ['coast', 'beach']
for i in range(2):
    axes[i].imshow(imgs[i])
    axes[i].set_xticks([])
    axes[i].set_yticks([])
    axes[i].set_xlabel(labels[i])
```

The result of the preceding code is shown in the following diagram:

Figure 3.47: Multiple images with labels

Let's go through an activity for grid images.

ACTIVITY 3.07: PLOTTING MULTIPLE IMAGES IN A GRID

In this activity, we will plot images in a grid. You are a developer in a social media company. Management has decided to add a feature that helps the customer to upload images in a 2x2 grid format. Develop some standard code to generate grid-formatted images and add this new feature to your company's website.

The following are the steps to perform:

1. Import the necessary modules and enable plotting within a Jupyter Notebook.

2. Load all four images from the **Datasets** subfolder.

3. Visualize the images in a 2x2 grid. Remove the axes and give each image a label.

   After executing the preceding steps, the expected output should be as follows:

Figure 3.48: Visualizing images in a 2x2 grid

NOTE

The solution to this activity can be found on page 418.

In this activity, we have plotted images in a 2x2 grid. In the next section, we will learn the basics of how to write and plot a mathematical expression.

WRITING MATHEMATICAL EXPRESSIONS

In case you need to write mathematical expressions within the code, Matplotlib supports **TeX**, one of the most popular typesetting systems, especially for typesetting mathematical formulas. You can use it in any text by placing your mathematical expression in a pair of dollar signs. There is no need to have TeX installed since Matplotlib comes with its own parser.

An example of this is given in the following code:

```
plt.xlabel(,$x$')
plt.ylabel(,$\cos(x)$')
```

The following diagram shows the output of the preceding code:

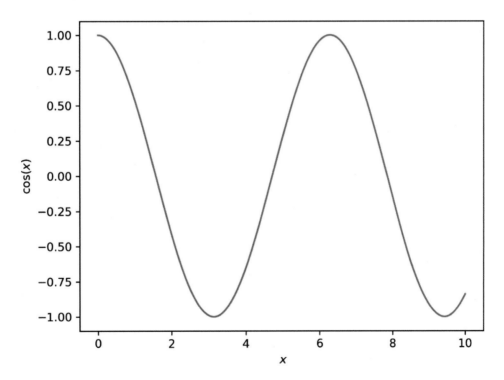

Figure 3.49: Diagram demonstrating mathematical expressions

TeX examples:

- `'$\alpha_i>\beta_i$'` produces $\alpha_i > \beta_i$.

- `'$\sum_{i=0}^\infty x_i$'` produces $\sum_{i=0}^{\infty} x_i$.

- `'$\sqrt[3]{8}$'` produces $\sqrt[3]{8}$.

- `'$\frac{3 - \frac{x}{2}}{5}$'` produces $\frac{3 - \frac{x}{2}}{5}$.

In this section, we learned how to write a basic mathematical expression and generate a plot using it.

SUMMARY

In this chapter, we provided a detailed introduction to Matplotlib, one of the most popular visualization libraries for Python. We started off with the basics of pyplot and its operations, and then followed up with a deep insight into the numerous possibilities that help to enrich visualizations with text. Using practical examples, this chapter covered the most popular plotting functions that Matplotlib offers, including comparison charts, and composition and distribution plots. It concluded with how to visualize images and write mathematical expressions.

In the next chapter, we will learn about the Seaborn library. Seaborn is built on top of Matplotlib and provides a higher-level abstraction to create visualizations in an easier way. One neat feature of Seaborn is the easy integration of DataFrames from the pandas library. Furthermore, Seaborn offers a few more plots out of the box, including more advanced visualizations, such as violin plots.

SIMPLIFYING VISUALIZATIONS USING SEABORN

OVERVIEW

In this chapter, we will see how Seaborn differs from Matplotlib and construct effective plots leveraging the advantages of Seaborn. Specifically, you will use Seaborn to plot bivariate distributions, heatmaps, pairwise relationships, and so on. This chapter also teaches you how to use **FacetGrid** for visualizing plots for multiple variables separately. By the end of this chapter, you will be able to explain the advantages Seaborn has compared to Matplotlib and design visually appealing and insightful plots efficiently.

INTRODUCTION

In the previous chapter, we took an in-depth look at Matplotlib, one of the most popular plotting libraries for Python. Various plot types were covered, and we looked into customizing plots to create aesthetic plots.

Unlike **Matplotlib**, **Seaborn** is not a standalone Python library. It is built on top of Matplotlib and provides a higher-level abstraction to make visually appealing statistical visualizations. A neat feature of Seaborn is the ability to integrate with DataFrames from the pandas library.

With Seaborn, we attempt to make visualization a central part of data exploration and understanding. Internally, Seaborn operates on DataFrames and arrays that contain the complete dataset. This enables it to perform semantic mappings and statistical aggregations that are essential for displaying informative visualizations. Seaborn can also be used to simply change the style and appearance of Matplotlib visualizations.

The most prominent features of Seaborn are as follows:

- Beautiful out-of-the-box plots with different themes

- Built-in color palettes that can be used to reveal patterns in the dataset

- A dataset-oriented interface

- A high-level abstraction that still allows for complex visualizations

ADVANTAGES OF SEABORN

Working with DataFrames using Matplotlib adds some inconvenient overhead. For example, simply exploring your dataset can take up a lot of time, since you require some additional data wrangling to be able to plot the data from the DataFrames using Matplotlib.

Seaborn, however, is built to operate on DataFrames and full dataset arrays, which makes this process simpler. It internally performs the necessary semantic mappings and statistical aggregation to produce informative plots.

> **NOTE**
>
> The American Community Survey (ACS) Public-Use Microdata Samples (PUMS) dataset (one-year estimate from 2017) from https://www.census.gov/programs-surveys/acs/technical-documentation/pums/documentation.2017.html is used in this chapter. This dataset is later used in *Chapter 07, Combining What We Have Learned*. This dataset can also be downloaded from GitHub. Here is the link: https://packt.live/3bzApYN.

The following is an example of plotting using the Seaborn library:

```
import seaborn as sns
import pandas as pd
sns.set(style="ticks")
data = pd.read_csv("../../Datasets/salary.csv")[:1000]
sns.relplot(x="Salary", y="Age", hue="Education", \
            style="Education", col="Gender", data=data)
```

This creates the following plot:

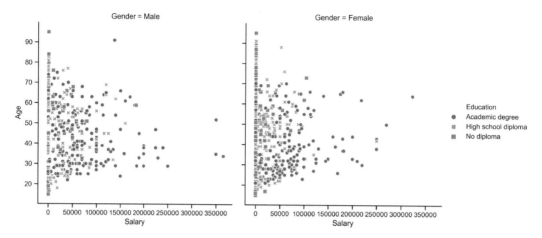

Figure 4.1: Seaborn relation plot

Seaborn uses Matplotlib to draw plots. Even though many tasks can be accomplished with just Seaborn, further customization might require the usage of Matplotlib. We only provided the names of the variables in the dataset and the roles they play in the plot. Unlike in Matplotlib, it is not necessary to translate the variables into parameters of the visualization.

Other potential obstacles are the default Matplotlib parameters and configurations. The default parameters in Seaborn provide better visualizations without additional customization. We will look at these default parameters in detail in the upcoming topics.

For users who are already familiar with Matplotlib, the extension with Seaborn is self-evident, since the core concepts are mostly similar.

CONTROLLING FIGURE AESTHETICS

As we mentioned previously, Matplotlib is highly customizable. But it also has the effect that it is very inconvenient, as it can take a long time to adjust all necessary parameters to get your desired visualization. In Seaborn, we can use customized themes and a high-level interface for controlling the appearance of Matplotlib figures.

The following code snippet creates a simple line plot in Matplotlib:

```
%matplotlib inline
import matplotlib.pyplot as plt
plt.figure()
x1 = [10, 20, 5, 40, 8]
x2 = [30, 43, 9, 7, 20]
plt.plot(x1, label='Group A')
plt.plot(x2, label='Group B')
plt.legend()
plt.show()
```

This is what the plot looks with Matplotlib's default parameters:

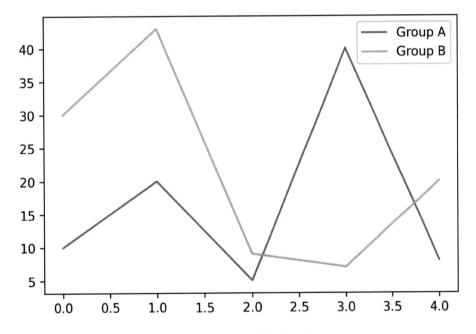

Figure 4.2: Matplotlib line plot

To switch to the Seaborn defaults, simply call the **set()** function:

```
%matplotlib inline
import matplotlib.pyplot as plt
import seaborn as sns
sns.set()
plt.figure()
x1 = [10, 20, 5, 40, 8]
x2 = [30, 43, 9, 7, 20]
plt.plot(x1, label='Group A')
plt.plot(x2, label='Group B')
plt.legend()
plt.show()
```

Following is the output of the code:

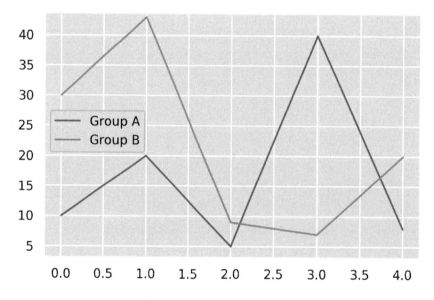

Figure 4.3: Seaborn line plot

Seaborn categorizes Matplotlib's parameters into two groups. The first group contains parameters for the aesthetics of the plot, while the second group scales various elements of the plot so that it can be easily used in different contexts, such as visualizations that are used for presentations and posters.

SEABORN FIGURE STYLES

To control the plot style, Seaborn provides two methods: **set_style(style, [rc])** and **axes_style(style, [rc])**.

seaborn.set_style(style, [rc]) sets the aesthetic style of the plots.

Parameters:

- **style**: A dictionary of parameters or the name of one of the following preconfigured sets: **darkgrid**, **whitegrid**, **dark**, **white**, or **ticks**

- **rc** (optional): Parameter mappings to override the values in the preset Seaborn-style dictionaries

Here is an example:

```
%matplotlib inline
import matplotlib.pyplot as plt
import seaborn as sns
sns.set_style("whitegrid")
plt.figure()
x1 = [10, 20, 5, 40, 8]
x2 = [30, 43, 9, 7, 20]
plt.plot(x1, label='Group A')
plt.plot(x2, label='Group B')
plt.legend()
plt.show()
```

This results in the following plot:

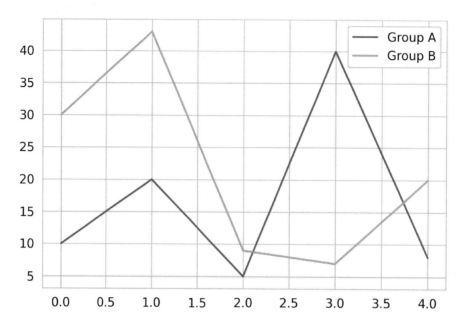

Figure 4.4: Seaborn line plot with whitegrid style

seaborn.axes_style(style, [rc]) returns a parameter dictionary for the aesthetic style of the plots. The function can be used in a **with** statement to temporarily change the style parameters.

Here are the parameters:

- **style**: A dictionary of parameters or the name of one of the following pre-configured sets: **darkgrid**, **whitegrid**, **dark**, **white**, or **ticks**

- **rc** (optional): Parameter mappings to override the values in the preset Seaborn-style dictionaries

Here is an example:

```
%matplotlib inline
import matplotlib.pyplot as plt
import seaborn as sns
sns.set()
plt.figure()
x1 = [10, 20, 5, 40, 8]
```

```
x2 = [30, 43, 9, 7, 20]
with sns.axes_style('dark'):
    plt.plot(x1, label='Group A')
    plt.plot(x2, label='Group B')
plt.legend()
plt.show()
```

The aesthetics are only changed temporarily. The result is shown in the following diagram:

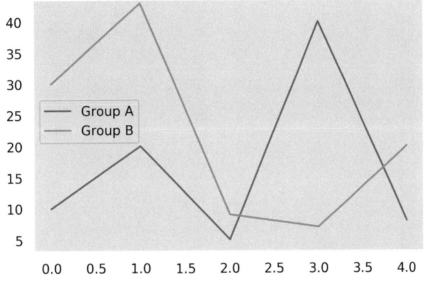

Figure 4.5: Seaborn line plot with dark axes style

For further customization, you can pass a dictionary of parameters to the **rc** argument. You can only override parameters that are part of the style definition.

REMOVING AXES SPINES

Sometimes, it might be desirable to remove the top and right axes spines. The **despine()** function is used to remove the top and right axes spines from the plot:

```
seaborn.despine(fig=None, ax=None, top=True, right=True, \
                left=False, bottom=False, \
                offset=None, trim=False)
```

The following code helps to remove the axes spines:

```
%matplotlib inline
import matplotlib.pyplot as plt
import seaborn as sns
sns.set_style("white")
plt.figure()
x1 = [10, 20, 5, 40, 8]
x2 = [30, 43, 9, 7, 20]
plt.plot(x1, label='Group A')
plt.plot(x2, label='Group B')
sns.despine()
plt.legend()
plt.show()
```

This results in the following plot:

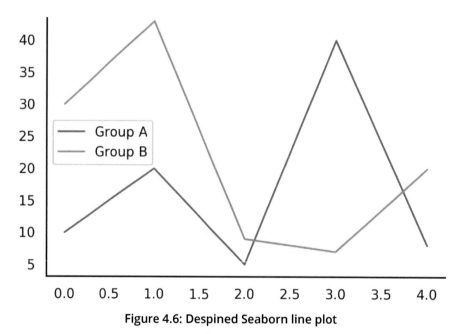

Figure 4.6: Despined Seaborn line plot

In the next section, we will learn to control the scale of plot elements.

CONTROLLING THE SCALE OF PLOT ELEMENTS

A separate set of parameters controls the scale of plot elements. This is a handy way to use the same code to create plots that are suited for use in contexts where larger or smaller plots are necessary. To control the context, two functions can be used.

seaborn.set_context(context, [font_scale], [rc]) sets the plotting context parameters. This does not change the overall style of the plot but affects things such as the size of the labels and lines. The base context is a **notebook**, and the other contexts are **paper**, **talk**, and **poster**—versions of the **notebook** parameters scaled by 0.8, 1.3, and 1.6, respectively.

Here are the parameters:

- **context**: A dictionary of parameters or the name of one of the following preconfigured sets: **paper**, **notebook**, **talk**, or **poster**

- **font_scale** (optional): A scaling factor to independently scale the size of font elements

- **rc** (optional): Parameter mappings to override the values in the preset Seaborn context dictionaries

The following code helps set the context:

```
%matplotlib inline
import matplotlib.pyplot as plt
import seaborn as sns
sns.set_context("poster")
plt.figure()
x1 = [10, 20, 5, 40, 8]
x2 = [30, 43, 9, 7, 20]
plt.plot(x1, label='Group A')
plt.plot(x2, label='Group B')
plt.legend()
plt.show()
```

The preceding code generates the following output:

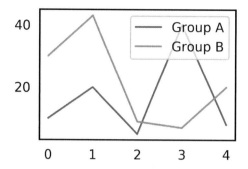

Figure 4.7: Seaborn line plot with poster context

`seaborn.plotting_context(context, [font_scale], [rc])` returns a parameter dictionary to scale elements of the Figure. This function can be used with a statement to temporarily change the context parameters.

Here are the parameters:

- **context**: A dictionary of parameters or the name of one of the following pre-configured sets: **paper, notebook, talk,** or **poster**

- **font_scale** (optional): A scaling factor to independently scale the size of font elements

- **rc** (optional): Parameter mappings to override the values in the preset Seaborn context dictionaries

Contexts are an easy way to use preconfigured scales of plot elements for different use cases. We will apply them in the following exercise, which uses a box plot to compare the IQ scores of different test groups.

> **NOTE**
>
> All the exercises and activities in this chapter are developed using Jupyter Notebook. The files can be downloaded from the following link: https://packt. live/2ONDmLI. All the datasets used in this chapter can be found at https://packt.live/3bzApYN.

EXERCISE 4.01: COMPARING IQ SCORES FOR DIFFERENT TEST GROUPS BY USING A BOX PLOT

In this exercise, we will generate a box plot using Seaborn. We will compare IQ scores among different test groups using a box plot of the Seaborn library to demonstrate how easy and efficient it is to create plots with Seaborn provided that we have a proper DataFrame. This exercise also shows how to quickly change the style and context of a Figure using the pre-configurations supplied by Seaborn.

Let's compare IQ scores among different test groups using the Seaborn library:

1. Create an **Exercise4.01.ipynb** Jupyter Notebook in the **Chapter04/ Exercise4.01** folder to implement this exercise.

2. Import the necessary modules and enable plotting within the **Exercise4.01. ipynb** file:

```
%matplotlib inline
import numpy as np
import pandas as pd
import matplotlib.pyplot as plt
import seaborn as sns
```

3. Use the pandas **read_csv()** function to read the data located in the **Datasets** folder:

```
mydata = pd.read_csv("../../Datasets/iq_scores.csv")
```

4. Access the data of each test group in the column. Convert this into a list using the **tolist()** method. Once the data of each test group has been converted into a list, assign this list to variables of each respective test group:

```
group_a = mydata[mydata.columns[0]].tolist()
group_b = mydata[mydata.columns[1]].tolist()
group_c = mydata[mydata.columns[2]].tolist()
group_d = mydata[mydata.columns[3]].tolist()
```

5. Print the values of each group to check whether the data inside it is converted into a list. This can be done with the help of the **print()** function:

```
print(group_a)
```

The data values of Group A are shown in the following screenshot:

```
[118, 103, 125, 107, 111, 96, 104, 97, 96, 114, 96, 75, 114, 107, 87, 117, 117, 114, 117, 112, 107, 133, 9
4, 91, 118, 110, 117, 86, 143, 83, 106, 86, 98, 126, 109, 91, 112, 120, 108, 111, 107, 98, 89, 113, 117, 8
1, 113, 112, 84, 115, 96, 93, 128, 115, 138, 121, 87, 112, 110, 79, 100, 84, 115, 93, 108, 130, 107, 106,
106, 101, 117, 93, 94, 103, 112, 98, 103, 70, 139, 94, 110, 105, 122, 94, 94, 105, 129, 110, 112, 97, 109,
121, 106, 118, 131, 88, 122, 125, 93, 78]
```

Figure 4.8: Values of Group A

The following is the code for printing Group B:

```
print(group_b)
```

The data values of Group B are shown in the following screenshot:

```
[126, 89, 90, 101, 102, 74, 93, 101, 66, 120, 108, 97, 98, 105, 119, 92, 113, 81, 104, 108, 83, 102, 105,
111, 102, 107, 103, 89, 89, 110, 71, 110, 120, 85, 111, 83, 122, 120, 102, 84, 118, 100, 100, 114, 81, 10
9, 69, 97, 95, 106, 116, 109, 114, 98, 90, 92, 98, 91, 81, 85, 86, 102, 93, 112, 76, 89, 110, 75, 110, 90,
96, 94, 107, 108, 95, 96, 96, 114, 93, 95, 117, 141, 115, 95, 86, 100, 121, 103, 66, 99, 96, 111, 110, 10
5, 110, 91, 112, 102, 112, 75]
```

Figure 4.9: Values of Group B

The following is the code for printing Group C:

```
print(group_c)
```

The data values of Group C are shown in the following screenshot:

```
[108, 89, 114, 116, 126, 104, 113, 96, 69, 121, 109, 102, 107, 122, 104, 107, 108, 137, 107, 116, 98, 132,
108, 114, 82, 93, 89, 90, 86, 91, 99, 98, 83, 93, 114, 96, 95, 113, 103, 81, 107, 85, 116, 85, 107, 125, 1
26, 123, 122, 124, 115, 114, 93, 93, 114, 107, 107, 84, 131, 91, 108, 127, 112, 106, 115, 82, 90, 117, 10
8, 115, 113, 108, 104, 103, 90, 110, 114, 92, 101, 72, 109, 94, 122, 90, 102, 86, 119, 103, 110, 96, 90, 1
10, 96, 69, 85, 102, 69, 96, 101, 90]
```

Figure 4.10: Values of Group C

The following is the code for printing Group D:

```
print(group_d)
```

The data values of Group D are shown in the following screenshot:

```
[93, 99, 91, 110, 80, 113, 111, 115, 98, 74, 96, 80, 83, 102, 60, 91, 82, 90, 97, 101, 89, 89, 117, 91, 10
4, 104, 102, 128, 106, 111, 79, 92, 97, 101, 106, 110, 93, 93, 106, 108, 85, 83, 108, 94, 79, 87, 113, 11
2, 111, 111, 79, 116, 104, 84, 116, 111, 103, 103, 112, 68, 54, 80, 86, 119, 81, 84, 91, 96, 116, 125, 99,
58, 102, 77, 98, 100, 90, 106, 109, 114, 102, 102, 112, 103, 98, 96, 85, 97, 110, 131, 92, 79, 115, 122, 9
5, 105, 74, 85, 85, 95]
```

Figure 4.11: Values of Group D

6. Once we have the data for each test group, we need to construct a DataFrame from this data. This can be done with the help of the **pd.DataFrame()** function, which is provided by pandas:

```
data = pd.DataFrame({'Groups': ['Group A'] \
                    * len(group_a) + ['Group B'] \
                    * len(group_b) + ['Group C'] \
                    * len(group_c) + ['Group D'] \
                    * len(group_d),\
                    'IQ score': group_a + group_b \
                    + group_c + group_d})
```

7. If you don't create your own DataFrame, it is often helpful to print the column names, which is done by calling **print(data.columns)**. The output is as follows:

$$Index(['Groups', 'IQ score'], dtype='object')$$

Figure 4.12: Column labels

You can see that our DataFrame has two variables with the labels **Groups** and **IQ score**. This is especially interesting since we can use them to specify which variable to plot on the x-axis and which one on the y-axis.

8. Now, since we have the DataFrame, we need to create a box plot using the **boxplot()** function provided by Seaborn. Within this function, specify the variables for both the axes along with the DataFrame. Make **Groups** the variable to plot on the x-axis, and **IQ score** the variable for the y-axis. Pass **data** as a parameter. Here, **data** is the DataFrame that we obtained from the previous step. Moreover, use the **whitegrid** style, set the context to **talk**, and remove all axes spines, except the one on the bottom:

```
plt.figure(dpi=150)
# Set style
sns.set_style('whitegrid')
# Create boxplot
sns.boxplot('Groups', 'IQ score', data=data)
# Despine
sns.despine(left=True, right=True, top=True)
# Add title
plt.title('IQ scores for different test groups')
# Show plot
plt.show()
```

The **despine()** function helps in removing the top and right spines from the plot by default (without passing any arguments to the function). Here, we have also removed the left spine. Using the **title()** function, we have set the title for our plot. The **show()** function visualizes the plot.

After executing the preceding steps, the final output should be as follows:

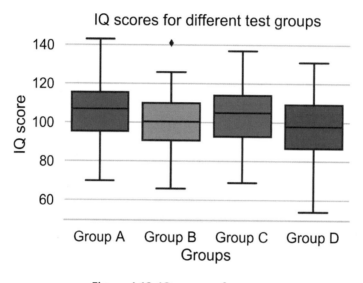

Figure 4.13: IQ scores of groups

From the preceding diagram, we can conclude that Seaborn offers visually appealing plots out of the box and allows easy customization, such as changing the style, context, and spines. Once a suitable DataFrame exists, the plotting is achieved with a single function. Column names are automatically used for labeling the axis. Even categorical variables are supported out of the box.

> **NOTE**
>
> To access the source code for this specific section, please refer to https://packt.live/3hwvR8m.
>
> You can also run this example online at https://packt.live/2Y6TTPy.

Another great advantage of Seaborn is color palettes, which are introduced in the following section.

COLOR PALETTES

Color is a very important factor for your visualization. Color can reveal patterns in data if used effectively or hide patterns if used poorly. Seaborn makes it easy to select and use **color palettes** that are suited to your task. The `color_palette()` function provides an interface for many of the possible ways to generate color palettes.

The `seaborn.color_palette([palette], [n_colors], [desat])` command returns a list of colors, thus defining a color palette.

The parameters are as follows:

- `palette` (optional): Name of palette or **None** to return the current palette.

- `n_colors` (optional): Number of colors in the palette. If the specified number of colors is larger than the number of colors in the palette, the colors will be cycled.

- `desat` (optional): The proportion to desaturate each color by.

You can set the palette for all plots with `set_palette()`. This function accepts the same arguments as `color_palette()`. In the following sections, we will explain how color palettes are divided into different groups.

Choosing the best color palette is not straightforward and, to some extent, subjective. To make a good decision, you have to know the characteristics of your data. There are three general groups of color palettes, namely, categorical, sequential, and diverging, which we will break down in the following sections.

CATEGORICAL COLOR PALETTES

Categorical palettes (or qualitative color palettes) are best suited for distinguishing categorical data that does not have an inherent ordering. The color palette should have colors as distinct from one another as possible, resulting in palettes where mainly the hue changes. When it comes to human perception, there is a limit to how many different colors are perceived. A rule of thumb is that if you have double-digit categories, it is advisable to divide the categories into groups. Different shades of color could be used for a group. Another way to keep groups apart could be to use hues that are close together in the color wheel within a group and hues that are far apart for different groups.

Some examples where it is suitable to use categorical color palettes are line charts showing stock trends for different companies, and a bar chart with subcategories; basically, any time you want to group your data.

There are six default themes in Seaborn: **deep, muted, bright, pastel, dark,** and **colorblind**. The code and output for each theme are provided in the following diagram. Out of these color palettes, it doesn't really matter which one you use. Choose the one you prefer and the one that best fits the overall theme of the visualization. It's never a bad idea to use the colorblind palette to account for colorblind people. The following is the code to create a deep color palette:

```
import seaborn as sns
palette1 = sns.color_palette("deep")
sns.palplot(palette1)
```

The following diagram shows the output of the code:

Figure 4.14: Deep color palette

The following code creates a muted color palette:

```
palette2 = sns.color_palette("muted")
sns.palplot(palette2)
```

The following is the output of the code:

Figure 4.15: Muted color palette

The following code creates a bright color palette:

```
palette3 = sns.color_palette("bright")
sns.palplot(palette3)
```

The following is the output of the code:

Figure 4.16: Bright color palette

The following code creates a pastel color palette:

```
palette4 = sns.color_palette("pastel")
sns.palplot(palette4)
```

Here is the output showing a pastel color palette:

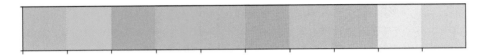

Figure 4.17: Pastel color palette

The following code creates a dark color palette:

```
palette5 = sns.color_palette("dark")
sns.palplot(palette5)
```

The following diagram shows a dark color palette:

Figure 4.18: Dark color palette

The following code creates a colorblind palette:

```
palette6 = sns.color_palette("colorblind")
sns.palplot(palette6)
```

Here is the output of the code:

Figure 4.19: Colorblind color palette

SEQUENTIAL COLOR PALETTES

Sequential color palettes are appropriate for sequential data ranges from low to high values, or vice versa. It is recommended to use bright colors for low values and dark ones for high values. Some examples of sequential data are absolute temperature, weight, height, or the number of students in a class.

One of the sequential color palettes that Seaborn offers is cubehelix palettes. They have a linear increase or decrease in brightness and some variation in hue, meaning that even when converted to black and white, the information is preserved.

The default palette returned by **cubehelix_palette()** is illustrated in the following diagram. To customize the cubehelix palette, the hue at the start of the helix can be set with **start** (a value between 0 and 3), or the number of rotations around the hue wheel can be set with **rot**:

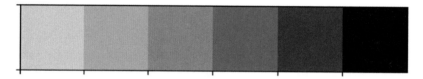

Figure 4.20: Cubehelix palette

Creating custom sequential palettes that only produce colors that start at either light or dark desaturated colors and end with a specified color can be accomplished with **light_palette()** or **dark_palette()**. Two examples are given in the following:

```
custom_palette2 = sns.light_palette("magenta")
sns.palplot(custom_palette2)
```

The following diagram shows the output of the code:

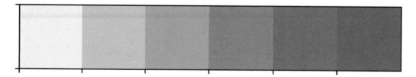

Figure 4.21: Custom magenta color palette

The preceding palette can also be reversed by setting the **reverse** parameter to **True** in the following code:

```
custom_palette3 = sns.light_palette("magenta", reverse=True)
sns.palplot(custom_palette3)
```

The following diagram shows the output of the code:

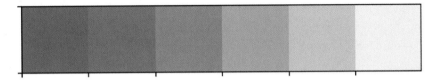

Figure 4.22: Custom reversed magenta color palette

By default, creating a color palette only returns a list of colors. If you want to use it as a colormap object, for example, in combination with a heatmap, set the **as_cmap=True** argument, as demonstrated in the following example:

```
x = np.arange(25).reshape(5, 5)
ax = sns.heatmap(x, cmap=sns.cubehelix_palette(as_cmap=True))
```

This creates the following heatmap:

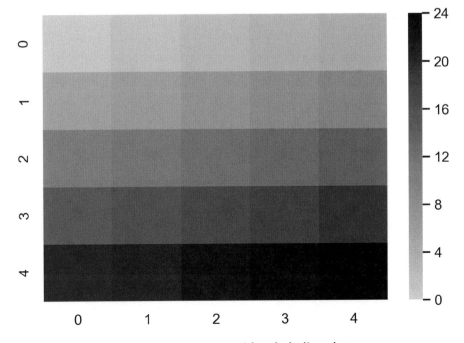

Figure 4.23: Heatmap with cubehelix palette

In the next section, we will learn about diverging color palettes.

DIVERGING COLOR PALETTES

Diverging color palettes are used for data that consists of a well-defined midpoint. An emphasis is placed on both high and low values. For example, if you are plotting any population changes for a particular region from some baseline population, it is best to use diverging colormaps to show the relative increase and decrease in the population. The following code snippet and output provides a better understanding of diverging plots, wherein we use the **coolwarm** template, which is built into Matplotlib:

```
custom_palette4 = sns.color_palette("coolwarm", 7)
sns.palplot(custom_palette4)
```

The following diagram shows the output of the code:

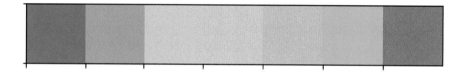

Figure 4.24: Coolwarm color palette

You can use the **diverging_palette()** function to create custom-diverging palettes. We can pass two **hues** in degrees as parameters, along with the total number of palettes. The following code snippet and output provides a better insight:

```
custom_palette5 = sns.diverging_palette(120, 300, n=7)
sns.palplot(custom_palette5)
```

The following diagram shows the output of the code:

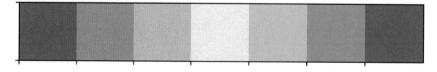

Figure 4.25: Custom diverging color palette

As we already mentioned, colors, when used effectively, can reveal patterns in data. Spend some time thinking about which color palette is best for certain data. Let's apply color palettes to visualize temperature changes in the following exercise.

EXERCISE 4.02: SURFACE TEMPERATURE ANALYSIS

In this exercise, we will generate a heatmap using Seaborn. The goal of this exercise is to choose an appropriate color palette for the given data. You are asked to visualize the surface temperature change for the Northern Hemisphere for past years. Data from the GISS Surface Temperature Analysis is used, which contains estimates of global surface temperature change (in degree Celsius) for every month. The dataset contains temperature anomalies for every month from 1880 to the present. Temperature anomalies indicate how much warmer or colder it is than normal. For the GISS analysis, normal means the average over the 30-year period 1951-1980.

> **NOTE**
>
> The dataset used for this exercise is used from https://data.giss.nasa.gov/gistemp/ (accessed January 7, 2020). For more details about the dataset, visit the website, looking at the FAQs in particular. This dataset is also available in your **Datasets** folder.

Following are the steps to perform:

1. Create an **Exercise4.02.ipynb** Jupyter Notebook in the **Chapter04/Exercise4.02** folder to implement this exercise.

2. Import the necessary modules and enable plotting:

```
%matplotlib inline
import numpy as np
import pandas as pd
import matplotlib.pyplot as plt
import seaborn as sns
sns.set()
```

3. Use the pandas **read_csv()** function to read the **northern_surface_temperature.csv** dataset located in the **Datasets** folder. After successful loading, transpose the dataset so that it is in a suitable structure:

```
data = pd.read_csv("../../Datasets/"\
                   "northern_surface_temperature.csv", \
                   index_col=['Year'])
data = data.transpose()
```

4. Create a custom-diverging palette that diverges to blue (240 degrees on the hue wheel) for low values and to red (15 degrees on the hue wheel) for high values. Set the saturation as **s=99**. Make sure that the **diverging_palette()** function returns a colormap by setting **as_cmap=True**:

```
heat_colormap = sns.diverging_palette(240, 15, s=99, \
                                      as_cmap=True)
```

5. Plot the heatmap for every 5 years. To ensure that the neutral color corresponds to no temperature change (the value is zero), set **center=0**:

```
plt.figure(dpi=200)
sns.heatmap(data.iloc[:, ::5], cmap=heat_colormap, center=0)
plt.title("Temperature Changes from 1880 to 2015 " \
          "(base period 1951-1980)")
plt.savefig('temperature_change.png', dpi=300, \
            bbox_inches='tight')
```

The following is the output of the preceding code:

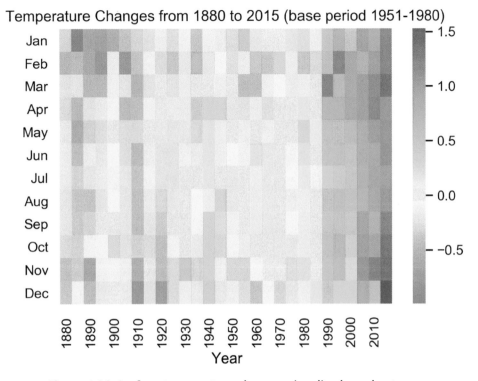

Figure 4.26: Surface temperature changes visualized as a heatmap

The preceding diagram helps us to visualize the surface temperature change for the Northern Hemisphere for past years.

> **NOTE**
>
> To access the source code for this specific section, please refer to https://packt.live/3fracg8.
>
> You can also run this example online at https://packt.live/3d4u5bd.

Let's now perform an activity to create a heatmap using a real-life dataset with various color palettes.

ACTIVITY 4.01: USING HEATMAPS TO FIND PATTERNS IN FLIGHT PASSENGERS' DATA

In this activity, we will use a heatmap to find patterns in the flight passengers' data. The goal of this activity is to apply your knowledge about color palettes to choose a suitable color palette for this data.

The following are the steps to perform:

1. Use pandas to read the **flight_details.csv** dataset located in the **Datasets** folder. The given dataset contains the monthly figures for flight passengers for the years 1949 to 1960. This dataset originates from the Seaborn library.

2. Use a heatmap to visualize the given data.

3. Use your own appropriate colormap. Make sure that the lowest value is the brightest, and the highest the darkest, color. After executing the preceding steps, the expected output should be as follows:

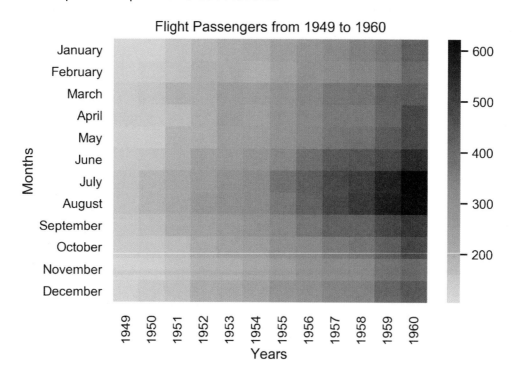

Figure 4.27: Heatmap of flight passengers' data

NOTE

The solution to this activity can be found on page 420.

After the in-depth discussion about various color palettes, we will introduce some more advanced plots that Seaborn offers in the following section.

ADVANCED PLOTS IN SEABORN

In the previous chapter, we discussed various plots in Matplotlib, but there are still a few visualizations left that we want to discuss. First, we will revise bar plots since Seaborn offers some neat additional features for them. Moreover, we will cover kernel density estimation, correlograms, and violin plots.

BAR PLOTS

In the last chapter, we already explained how to create bar plots with Matplotlib. Creating bar plots with subgroups was quite tedious, but Seaborn offers a very convenient way to create various bar plots. They can also be used in Seaborn to represent estimates of central tendency with the height of each bar, while uncertainty is indicated by error bars at the top of the bar.

The following example gives you a good idea of how this works:

```
import pandas as pd
import seaborn as sns
data = pd.read_csv("../Datasets/salary.csv")
sns.set(style="whitegrid")
sns.barplot(x="Education", y="Salary", hue="District", data=data)
```

The result is shown in the following diagram:

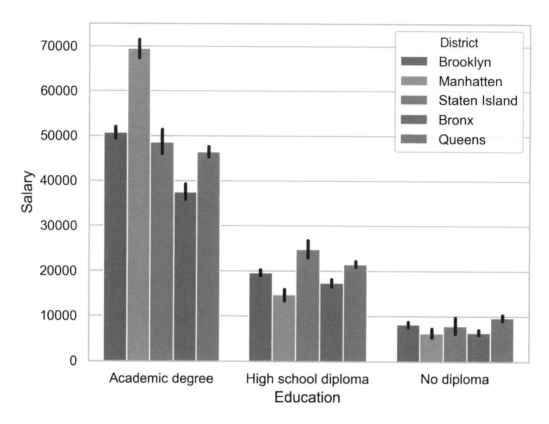

Figure 4.28: Seaborn bar plot

Let's get some practice with Seaborn bar plots in the following activity.

ACTIVITY 4.02: MOVIE COMPARISON REVISITED

In this activity, we will generate a bar plot to compare movie scores. You will be given five movies with scores from Rotten Tomatoes. The Tomatometer is the percentage of approved Tomatometer critics who have given a positive review for a movie. The Audience Score is the percentage of users who have given a score of 3.5 or higher, out of 5. Compare these two scores among the five movies:

1. Use pandas to read the **movie_scores.csv** dataset located in the **Datasets** folder.

2. Transform the data into a useable format for Seaborn's **barplot** function.

3. Use Seaborn to create a visually appealing bar plot that compares the two scores for all five movies.

After executing the preceding steps, the expected output should appear as follows:

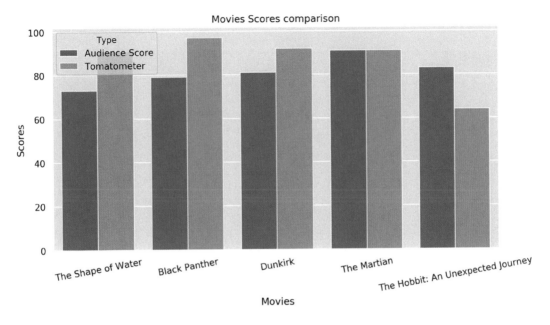

Figure 4.29: Movie Scores comparison

NOTE

The solution to this activity can be found on page 422.

KERNEL DENSITY ESTIMATION

It is often useful to visualize how variables of a dataset are distributed. Seaborn offers handy functions to examine univariate and bivariate distributions. One possible way to look at a univariate distribution in Seaborn is by using the **distplot()** function. This will draw a histogram and fit a **kernel density estimate** (**KDE**), as illustrated in the following example:

```
%matplotlib inline
import numpy as np
import pandas as pd
import matplotlib.pyplot as plt
data = pd.read_csv('../../Datasets/age_salary_hours.csv')
```

```
sns.distplot(data.loc[:, 'Age'])
plt.xlabel('Age')
plt.ylabel('Density')
```

The result is shown in the following diagram:

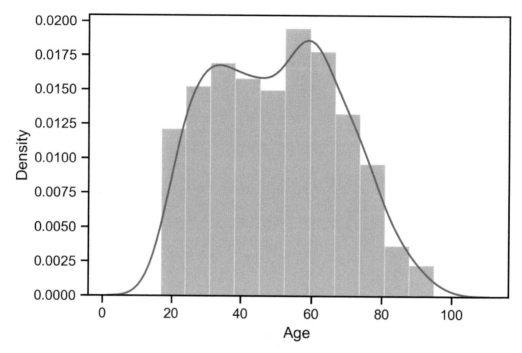

Figure 4.30: KDE with a histogram for a univariate distribution

To just visualize the KDE, Seaborn provides the **kdeplot()** function:

```
sns.kdeplot(data.loc[:, 'Age'], shade=True)
plt.xlabel('Age')
plt.ylabel('Density')
```

The KDE plot is shown in the following diagram, along with a shaded area under the curve:

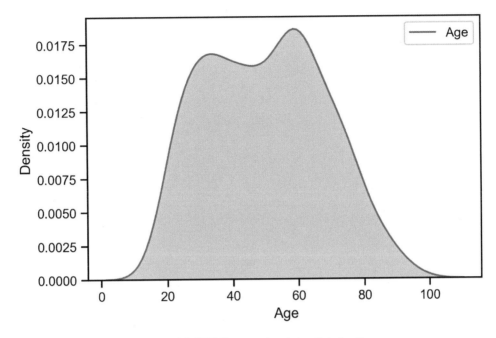

Figure 4.31: KDE for a univariate distribution

In the next section, we will learn how to plot bivariate distributions.

PLOTTING BIVARIATE DISTRIBUTIONS

For visualizing **bivariate distributions**, we will introduce three different plots. The first two plots use the `jointplot()` function, which creates a multi-panel figure that shows both the joint relationship between both variables and the corresponding marginal distributions.

A scatter plot shows each observation as points on the **x** and **y** axes. Additionally, a histogram for each variable is shown:

```
import pandas as pd
import seaborn as sns
data = pd.read_csv('../../Datasets/age_salary_hours.csv')
sns.set(style="white")
sns.jointplot(x="Annual Salary", y="Age", data=data))
```

The scatter plot with marginal histograms is shown in the following diagram:

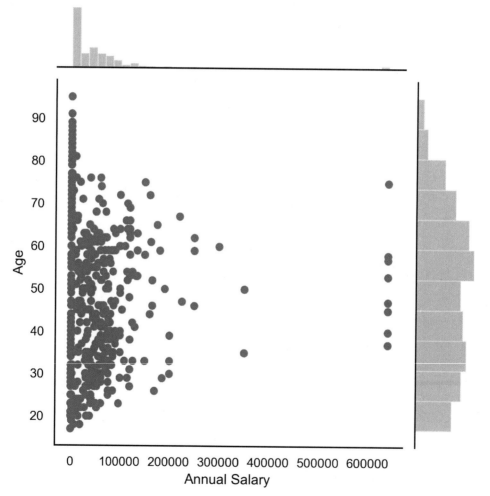

Figure 4.32: Scatter plot with marginal histograms

It is also possible to use the KDE procedure to visualize bivariate distributions. The joint distribution is shown as a contour plot, as demonstrated in the following code:

```
sns.jointplot('Annual Salary', 'Age', data=subdata, \
              kind='kde', xlim=(0, 500000), ylim=(0, 100))
```

The result is shown in the following diagram:

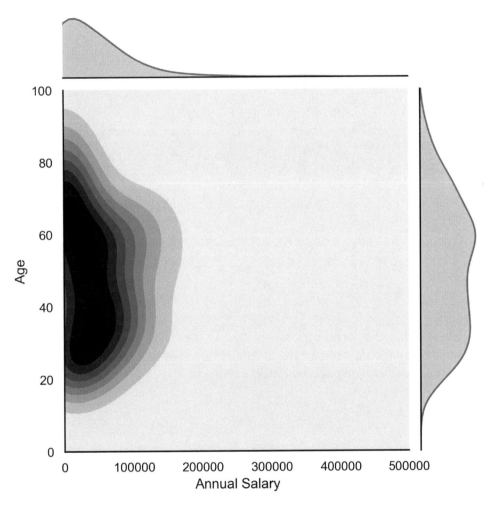

Figure 4.33: Contour plot

The joint distribution is shown as a contour plot in the center of the diagram. The darker the color, the higher the density. The marginal distributions are visualized on the top and on the right.

VISUALIZING PAIRWISE RELATIONSHIPS

For visualizing multiple pairwise relationships in a dataset, Seaborn offers the **pairplot()** function. This function creates a matrix where off-diagonal elements visualize the relationship between each pair of variables and the diagonal elements show the marginal distributions.

The following example gives us a better understanding of this:

```
%matplotlib inline
import numpy as np
import pandas as pd
import matplotlib.pyplot as plt
import seaborn as sns
data = pd.read_csv('../../Datasets/age_salary_hours.csv')
sns.set(style="ticks", color_codes=True)
g = sns.pairplot(data, hue='Education')
```

> **NOTE**
>
> The **age_salary_hours** dataset is derived from https://www.census.gov/programs-surveys/acs/technical-documentation/pums/documentation.2017.html.

A pair plot, also called a **correlogram**, is shown in the following diagram. Scatter plots are shown for all variable pairs on the off-diagonal, while KDEs are shown on the diagonal. Groups are highlighted by different colors:

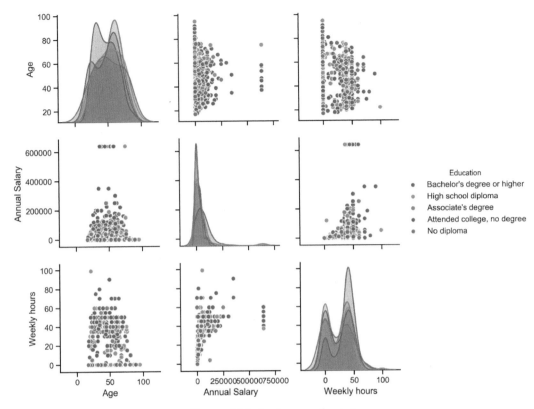

Figure 4.34: Seaborn pair plot

VIOLIN PLOTS

A different approach to visualizing statistical measures is by using **violin plots**. They combine box plots with the kernel density estimation procedure that we described previously. It provides a richer description of the variable's distribution. Additionally, the quartile and whisker values from the box plot are shown inside the violin.

The following example demonstrates the usage of violin plots:

```
import pandas as pd
import seaborn as sns
data = pd.read_csv("../../Datasets/salary.csv")
sns.set(style="whitegrid")
sns.violinplot('Education', 'Salary', hue='Gender', \
               data=data, split=True, cut=0)
```

The result appears as follows:

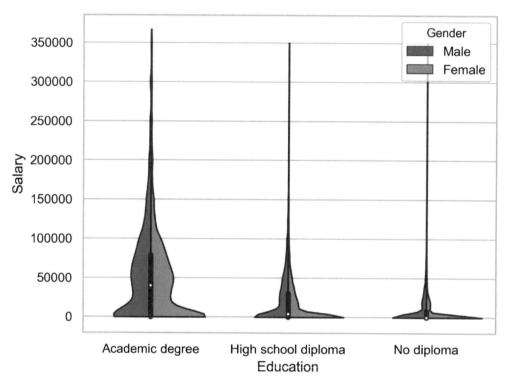

Figure 4.35: Seaborn violin plot

The violin plot shows both statistical measures and the probability distribution. The data is divided into education groups, which are shown on the x-axis, and gender groups, which are highlighted by different colors.

With the next activity, we will conclude the section about advanced plots. In this section, multi-plots in Seaborn are introduced.

ACTIVITY 4.03: COMPARING IQ SCORES FOR DIFFERENT TEST GROUPS BY USING A VIOLIN PLOT

In this activity, we will compare the IQ scores among four different test groups by using the violin plot that's provided by the Seaborn library. The following steps will help you to complete this activity:

1. Use pandas to read the **iq_scores.csv** dataset located in the **Datasets** folder.

2. Access the data of each group in the column, convert it into a list, and assign appropriate variables.

3. Create a pandas DataFrame from the data for each respective group.

4. Create a box plot for the IQ scores of the different test groups using Seaborn's **violinplot** function.

5. Use the **whitegrid** style, set the context to **talk**, and remove all axes spines, except the one on the bottom. Add a title to the plot.

   After executing the preceding steps, the final output should appear as follows:

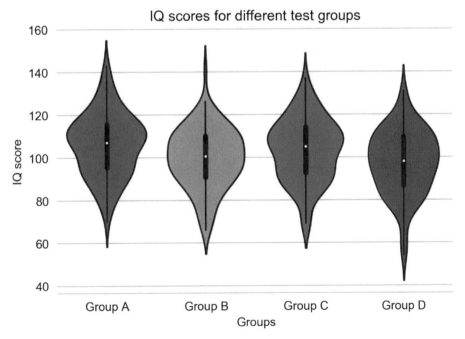

Figure 4.36: Violin plot showing IQ scores of different groups

> **NOTE**
>
> The solution to this activity can be found on page 424.

In the next section, we will learn about multi-plots in Seaborn.

MULTI-PLOTS IN SEABORN

In the previous topic, we introduced a multi-plot, namely, the pair plot. In this topic, we want to talk about a different way to create flexible multi-plots.

FACETGRID

The **FacetGrid** is useful for visualizing a certain plot for multiple variables separately. A FacetGrid can be drawn with up to three dimensions: **row**, **col**, and **hue**. The first two have the obvious relationship with the rows and columns of an array. The **hue** is the third dimension and is shown in different colors. The **FacetGrid** class has to be initialized with a DataFrame, and the names of the variables that will form the row, column, or hue dimensions of the grid. These variables should be **categorical** or **discrete**.

The `seaborn.FacetGrid(data, row, col, hue, …)` command initializes a multi-plot grid for plotting conditional relationships.

Here are some interesting parameters:

- **data**: A tidy ("long-form") DataFrame where each column corresponds to a variable, and each row corresponds to an observation

- **row, col, hue**: Variables that define subsets of the given data, which will be drawn on separate facets in the grid

- **sharex, sharey** (optional): Share **x**/**y** axes across rows/columns

- **height** (optional): Height (in inches) of each facet

Initializing the grid does not draw anything on it yet. To visualize data on this grid, the `FacetGrid.map()` method has to be used. You can provide any plotting function and the name(s) of the variable(s) in the DataFrame to the plot:

FacetGrid.map(func, *args, **kwargs) applies a plotting function to each facet of the grid.

Here are the parameters:

- **func**: A plotting function that takes data and keyword arguments.

- ***args**: The column names in data that identify variables to plot. The data for each variable is passed to **func** in the order in which the variables are specified.

- ****kwargs**: Keyword arguments that are passed to the plotting function.

The following example visualizes **FacetGrid** with scatter plots:

```
import pandas as pd
import matplotlib.pyplot as plt
import seaborn as sns
data = pd.read_csv("../../Datasets/salary.csv")[:1000]
g = sns.FacetGrid(data, col='District')
g.map(plt.scatter, 'Salary', 'Age')
```

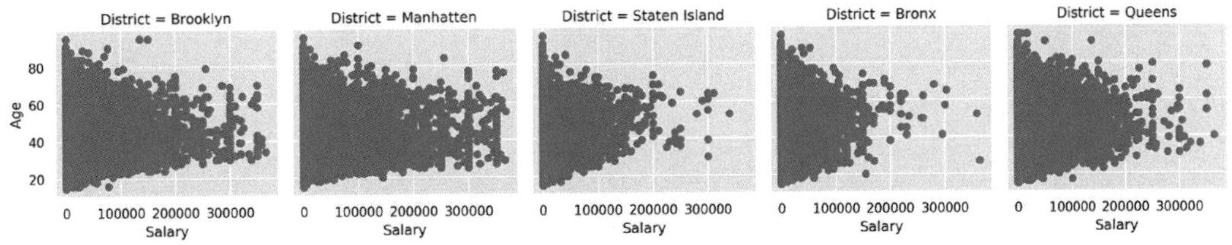

Figure 4.37: FacetGrid with scatter plots

We will conclude FacetGrids with the following activity.

ACTIVITY 4.04: VISUALIZING THE TOP 30 MUSIC YOUTUBE CHANNELS USING SEABORN'S FACETGRID

In this activity, we will generate a FacetGrid plot using the Seaborn library. We will visualize the total number of subscribers and the total number of views for the top 30 YouTube channels (as of January 2020) in the music category by using the **FacetGrid()** function that's provided by the Seaborn library.

Visualize the given data using a FacetGrid with two columns. The first column should show the number of subscribers for each YouTube channel, whereas the second column should show the number of views. The goal of this activity is to get some practice working with FacetGrids. The following are the steps to implement this activity:

1. Use pandas to read the **YouTube.csv** dataset located in the **Datasets** folder.

2. Access the data of each group in the column, convert this into a list, and assign this list to variables of each respective group.

3. Create a pandas DataFrame with the preceding data, using the data of each respective group.

4. Create a FacetGrid with two columns to visualize the data.

    After executing the preceding steps, the final output should appear as follows:

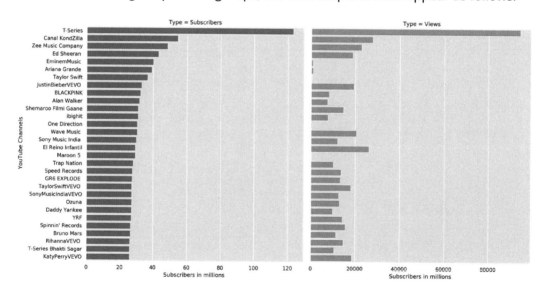

Figure 4.38: Subscribers and views of the top 30 YouTube channels

> **NOTE**
>
> The solution to this activity can be found on page 427.

In the next section, we will learn how to plot a regression plot using Seaborn.

REGRESSION PLOTS

Regression is a technique in which we estimate the relationship between a dependent variable (mostly plotted along the Y – axis) and an independent variable (mostly plotted along the X – axis). Given a dataset, we can assign independent and dependent variables and then use various regression methods to find out the relation between these variables. Here, we will only cover linear regression; however, Seaborn provides a wider range of regression functionality if needed.

The **regplot()** function offered by Seaborn helps to visualize linear relationships, determined through linear regression. The following code snippet gives a simple example:

```
import numpy as np
import seaborn as sns
x = np.arange(100)
# normal distribution with mean 0 and a standard deviation of 5
y = x + np.random.normal(0, 5, size=100)
sns.regplot(x, y)
```

The **regplot()** function draws a scatter plot, a regression line, and a 95% confidence interval for that regression, as shown in the following diagram:

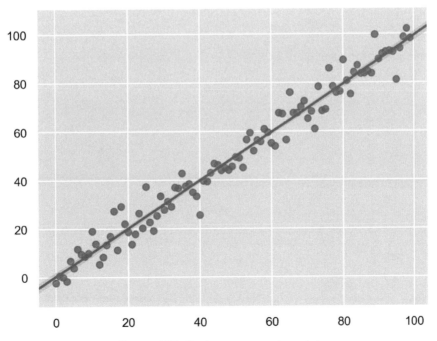

Figure 4.39: Seaborn regression plot

Let's have a look at a more practical example in the following activity.

ACTIVITY 4.05: LINEAR REGRESSION FOR ANIMAL ATTRIBUTE RELATIONS

In this activity, we will generate a regression plot to visualize a real-life dataset using the Seaborn library. You have a dataset pertaining to various animals, including their body mass and maximum longevity. To discover whether there is any linear relationship between these two variables, a regression plot will be used.

> **NOTE**
>
> The dataset used is from http://genomics.senescence.info/download.html#anage. The dataset can also be downloaded from GitHub. Here is the link to it: https://packt.live/3bzApYN.

The following are the steps to perform:

1. Use pandas to read the **anage_data.csv** dataset located in the **Datasets** folder.

2. Filter the data so that you end up with samples containing a body mass and maximum longevity. Only consider samples for the **Mammalia** class and a body mass of less than 200,000.

3. Create a regression plot to visualize the linear relationship between the variables.

After executing the preceding steps, the output should appear as follows:

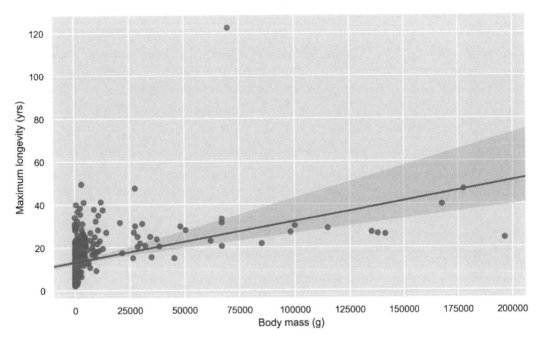

Figure 4.40: Linear regression for animal attribute relations

> **NOTE**
>
> The solution to this activity can be found on page 430.

In the next section, we will learn how to plot Squarify using Seaborn.

SQUARIFY

At this point, we will briefly talk about **tree maps**. Tree maps display hierarchical data as a set of nested rectangles. Each group is represented by a rectangle, of which its area is proportional to its value. Using color schemes, it is possible to represent hierarchies (groups, subgroups, and so on). Compared to pie charts, tree maps use space efficiently. Matplotlib and Seaborn do not offer tree maps, and so the **Squarify** library that is built on top of Matplotlib is used. Seaborn is a great addition for creating color palettes.

> **NOTE**
>
> To install Squarify, first launch the command prompt from the Anaconda Navigator. Then, execute the following command:
> `pip install squarify`.

The following code snippet is a basic tree map example. It requires the **squarify** library:

```
%matplotlib inline
import matplotlib.pyplot as plt
import seaborn as sns
import squarify
colors = sns.light_palette("brown", 4)
squarify.plot(sizes=[50, 25, 10, 15], \
              label=["Group A", "Group B", "Group C", "Group D"], \
              color=colors)
plt.axis("off")
plt.show()
```

The result is shown in the following diagram:

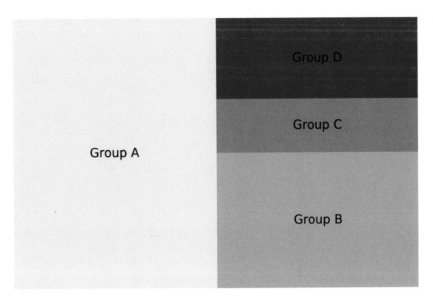

Figure 4.41: Tree map

Now, let's have a look at a real-world example that uses tree maps in the following exercise.

EXERCISE 4.03: WATER USAGE REVISITED

In this exercise, we will create a tree map using the Squarify and Seaborn libraries. Consider the scenario where you want to save water. Therefore, you visualize your household's water usage by using a tree map, which can be created with the help of the Squarify library.

> **NOTE**
>
> Before beginning the exercise, make sure you have installed Squarify by executing `pip install squarify` on your command prompt. The `water_usage.csv` dataset used is this exercise is sourced from this link: https://www.epa.gov/watersense/how-we-use-water. Their data originates from https://www.waterrf.org/research/projects/residential-end-uses-water-version-2. This dataset is also available in your **Datasets** folder.

Following are the steps to perform:

1. Create an **Exercise4.03.ipynb** Jupyter Notebook in the **Chapter04/ Exercise4.03** folder to implement this exercise.

2. Import the necessary modules and enable plotting within the **Exercise4.03. ipynb** file:

```
%matplotlib inline
import numpy as np
import pandas as pd
import matplotlib.pyplot as plt
import seaborn as sns
import squarify
```

3. Use the **read_csv()** function of pandas to read the **water_usage.csv** dataset located in the **Datasets** folder:

```
mydata = pd.read_csv("../../Datasets/water_usage.csv", \
                     index_col=0)
```

4. Create a list of labels by accessing each column from the preceding dataset. Here, the **astype('str')** function is used to cast the fetched data into a type string:

```
labels = mydata['Usage'] \
         + ' (' + mydata['Percentage'].astype('str') + '%)'
```

5. To create a tree map visualization of the given data, use the **plot()** function of the **squarify** library. This function takes three parameters. The first parameter is a list of all the percentages, and the second parameter is a list of all the labels, which we got in the previous step. The third parameter is the colormap that can be created by using the **light_palette()** function of the Seaborn library:

```
# Create figure
plt.figure(dpi=200)
# Create tree map
squarify.plot(sizes=mydata['Percentage'], \
              label=labels, \
              color=sns.light_palette('green', mydata.shape[0]))
```

```
plt.axis('off')
# Add title
plt.title('Water usage')
# Show plot
plt.show()
```

Following is the output of the code:

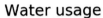

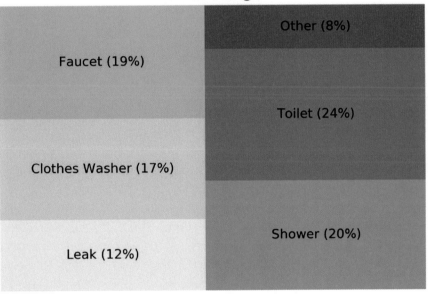

Figure 4.42: Tree map visualizing the water usage in a household

To conclude this exercise, you can see that tree maps are great for visualizing part-of-a-whole relationships. We immediately see that using the toilet requires the most water, followed by showers.

ACTIVITY 4.06: VISUALIZING THE IMPACT OF EDUCATION ON ANNUAL SALARY AND WEEKLY WORKING HOURS

In this activity, we will generate multiple plots using a real-life dataset. You're asked to get insights on whether the education of people has an influence on their annual salary and weekly working hours. You ask 500 people in the state of New York about their age, annual salary, weekly working hours, and their education. You first want to know the percentage for each education type, so therefore you use a tree map. Two violin plots will be used to visualize the annual salary and weekly working hours. Compare in each case to what extent education has an impact.

It should also be taken into account that all visualizations in this activity are designed to be suitable for colorblind people. In principle, this is always a good idea to bear in mind.

> **NOTE**
>
> The American Community Survey (ACS) Public-Use Microdata Samples (PUMS) dataset (one-year estimate from 2017) from https://www.census.gov/programs-surveys/acs/technical-documentation/pums/documentation.2017.html is used in this activity. This dataset is later used in *Chapter 07, Combining What We Have Learned*. This dataset can also be downloaded from GitHub. Here is the link: https://packt.live/3bzApYN.

The following are the steps to perform:

1. Use pandas to read the **age_salary_hours.csv** dataset located in the **Datasets** folder.

2. Use a tree map to visualize the percentages for each education type. After executing the preceding steps, the outputs should appear as follows:

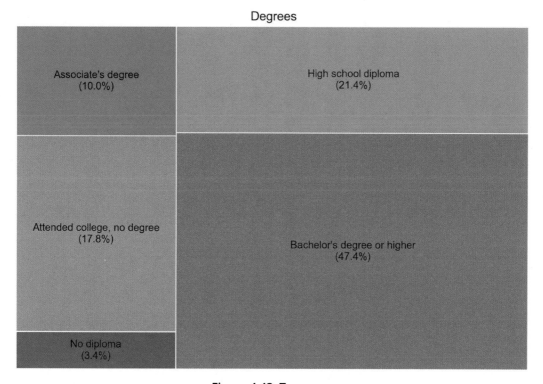

Figure 4.43: Tree map

3. Create a subplot with two rows to visualize two violin plots for the annual salary and weekly working hours, respectively. Compare in each case to what extent education has an impact. To exclude pensioners, only consider people younger than 65. Use a colormap that is suitable for colorblind people. **subplots()** can be used in combination with Seaborn's plot, by simply passing the **ax** argument with the respective axes. The following output will be generated after implementing this step:

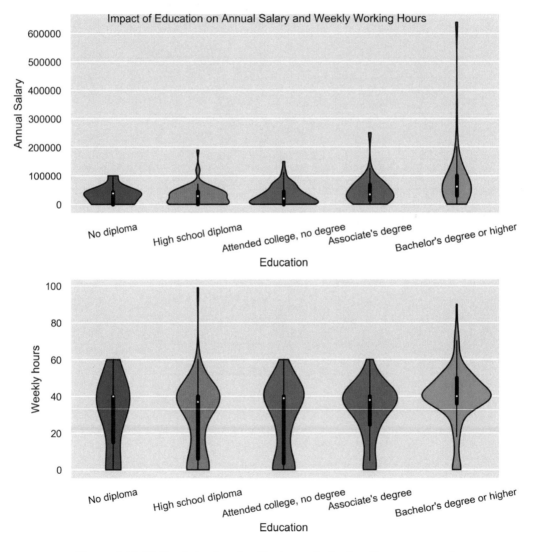

Figure 4.44: Violin plots showing the impact of education on annual salary and weekly working hours

> **NOTE**
>
> The solution to this activity can be found on page 432.

SUMMARY

In this chapter, we demonstrated how Seaborn helps to create visually appealing figures. We discussed various options for controlling Figure aesthetics, such as Figure style, controlling spines, and setting the context of visualizations. We talked about color palettes in detail. Further visualizations were introduced for univariate and bivariate distributions. Moreover, we discussed FacetGrids for creating multi-plots, and regression plots as a way to analyze the relationships between two variables. Finally, we discussed the Squarify library, which is used to create tree maps.

In the next chapter, we will work with a different category of data, called geospatial data. The prominent attribute of such a dataset is the presence of geo-coordinates that can be used to plot elements on a given position on a map. We will visualize poaching points, the density of cities around the world, and create a more interactive visualization that only displays data points of the currently selected country.

5

PLOTTING GEOSPATIAL DATA

OVERVIEW

By the end of this chapter, you will be able to utilize geoplotlib to create stunning geographical visualizations and identify the different types of geospatial charts. You will be able to demonstrate datasets containing geospatial data for plotting and create complex visualizations using tile providers and custom layers.

INTRODUCTION

geoplotlib is an open-source Python library for geospatial data visualizations. It has a wide range of geographical visualizations and supports hardware acceleration. It also provides performance rendering for large datasets with millions of data points. As discussed in earlier chapters, Matplotlib provides various ways to visualize geographical data.

However, Matplotlib is not designed for this task because its interfaces are complicated and inconvenient to use. Matplotlib also restricts how geographical data can be displayed. The **Basemap** and **Cartopy** libraries allow you to plot on a world map, but these packages do not support drawing on **map tiles**. Map tiles are underlying rectangular, square, or hexagonal tile slabs that are used to create a seamless map of the world, with lightweight, individually requested tiles that are currently in view.

geoplotlib, on the other hand, was designed precisely for this purpose; it not only provides **map tiles** but also allows for interactivity and simple animations. It provides a simple interface that allows access to compelling geospatial visualizations such as histograms, point-based plots, tessellations such as Voronoi or Delaunay, and choropleth plots.

In the exercises and activities in this chapter, we will use geoplotlib in combination with different real-world datasets to do the following:

- Highlight popular poaching spots in one area of Tanzania

- Discover dense areas within cities in Europe that have a high population

- Visualize values for the distinct states of the US

- Create a custom animated layer that displays the time series data of aircraft

To understand the concepts, design, and implementation of geoplotlib, take a brief look at its conceptual architecture. The two inputs that are fed to geoplotlib are your **data sources** and **map tiles**. The map tiles, as we'll see later, can be replaced by different providers. The outputs describe the possibility to not only render images inside Jupyter Notebooks but also to work in an interactive window that allows the **zooming** and **panning** of the maps. The schema of the components of geoplotlib looks as follows:

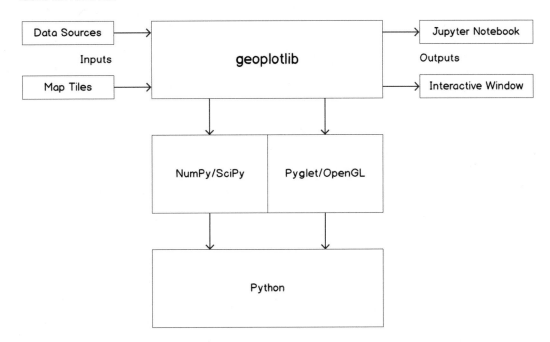

Figure 5.1: Conceptual architecture of geoplotlib

geoplotlib uses the concept of **layers** that can be placed on top of one another, providing a powerful interface for even complex visualizations. It comes with several common visualization layers that are easy to set up and use.

From the preceding diagram, we can see that **geoplotlib** is built on top of **NumPy/SciPy** and **Pyglet/OpenGL**. These libraries take care of numerical operations and rendering. Both components are based on Python, therefore enabling the use of the full Python ecosystem.

> **NOTE**
>
> All the datasets used in this chapter can be found at https://packt.live/3bzApYN. All the files of exercises and activities can be found here: https://packt.live/2UJRbyt.

All of the following examples are created with the **world_cities_pop.csv** dataset, which we will use for the exercises and activities later in this chapter. Before we can use it, we have to extract the **.zip** file that is included in the **Datasets** folder.

To use the **world_cities_pop** dataset, we need to add a **lat** and **lon** column. For the examples, we also want to filter our dataset down to contain only cities in Brazil. This will give us **dataset_filtered**. We will use this filtered-down dataset in the following examples:

```
# loading the Dataset with geoplotlib
dataset = pd.read_csv('../../Datasets/world_cities_pop.csv', \
                      dtype={'Region': np.str})


# Adding lat and lon column needed by geoplotlib
dataset['lat'] = dataset['Latitude']
dataset['lon'] = dataset['Longitude']


# filtering for cities in brasil
dataset_filtered = dataset[dataset['Country'] == 'br']
```

To run these examples yourself, please refer to **Examples.ipynb** in the **Examples** folder of the chapter.

THE DESIGN PRINCIPLES OF GEOPLOTLIB

Taking a closer look at the internal design of geoplotlib, we can see that it is built around three design principles:

- **Integration**: geoplotlib visualizations are purely Python-based. This means that generic Python code can be executed, and other libraries such as pandas can be used for **data wrangling** purposes. We can manipulate and enrich our datasets using pandas **DataFrames** and later convert them into a geoplotlib **DataAccessObject**, which we need for optimal compatibilities, as follows:

```
import pandas as pd
from geoplotlib.utils import DataAccessObject

# data wrangling with pandas DataFrames here
dataset_obj = DataAccessObject(dataset_filtered)
```

geoplotlib fully integrates into the Python ecosystem. This even enables us to plot geographical data inline inside our Jupyter Notebooks. This possibility allows us to design our visualizations quickly and iteratively.

- **Simplicity**: Looking at the example provided here, we can quickly see that geoplotlib abstracts away the complexity of plotting map tiles and already-provided layers such as **dot density** and **histogram**. It has a simple API that provides common visualizations. These visualizations can be created using custom data with only a few lines of code.

The core attributes of our datasets are **lat** and **lon** values. Latitude and longitude values enable us to index every single location on Earth. In geoplotlib, we need them to tell the library where on the map our elements need to be rendered. If our dataset comes with **lat** and **lon** columns, we can display each of those **data points**, for example, dots on a map with five lines of code.

In addition, we can use the **f_tooltip** argument to provide a popup for each point as an element of the column we provide as a source as follows:

```
# plotting our dataset as a dot density plot
import geoplotlib
from geoplotlib.utils import DataAccessObject

dataset_obj = DataAccessObject(dataset_filtered)
geoplotlib.dot(dataset_obj, \
               f_tooltip=lambda d:d['City'].title())

geoplotlib.show()
```

Executing this code will result in the following dot density plot:

Figure 5.2: Dot density layer of cities in Brazil and an overlay of the city on hovering

In addition to this, everyone who's used Matplotlib before will have no problems understanding geoplotlib. The syntax of geoplotlib is highly inspired by Matplotlib.

- **Performance**: As we mentioned before, geoplotlib can handle large amounts of data due to the use of NumPy for accelerated numerical operations and **OpenGL** for accelerated graphical rendering.

Next, we will create geographical visualizations without much effort and discover the advantages of using geoplotlib in combination with pandas. We will implement an exercise that plots the cities of the world and will be able to feel the performance of the library when plotting thousands of dots on our map.

GEOSPATIAL VISUALIZATIONS

Voronoi tessellation, **Delaunay triangulation**, and **choropleth plots** are a few of the geospatial visualizations that will be used in this chapter. An explanation for each of them is provided here.

VORONOI TESSELLATION

In a **Voronoi tessellation**, each pair of data points is separated by a line that is the same distance from both data points. The separation creates cells that, for every given point, marks which data point is closer. The closer the data points, the smaller the cells.

The following example shows how you can simply use the **voronoi** method to create this visualization:

```
# plotting our dataset as voronoi plot
geoplotlib.voronoi(dataset_filtered, line_color='b')
geoplotlib.set_smoothing(True)

geoplotlib.show()
```

As we can see, the code to create this visualization is relatively short.

After importing the dependencies we need, we read the dataset using the **read_csv** method of pandas (or geoplotlib). We then use it as data for our **voronoi** method, which handles all the complex logic of plotting the data on the map.

In addition to the data itself, we can set several parameters, such as general smoothing using the **set_smoothing** method. The smoothing of the lines uses anti-aliasing:

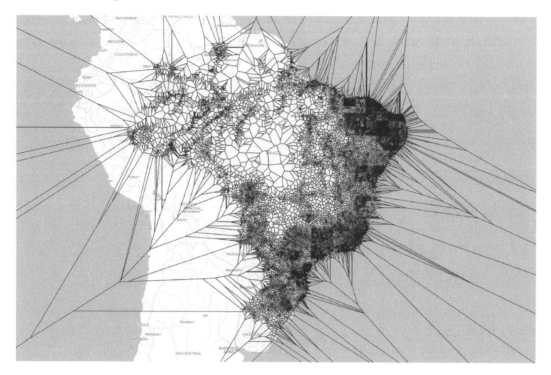

Figure 5.3: Voronoi plot of cities in Brazil to visualize population density

DELAUNAY TRIANGULATION

A **Delaunay triangulation** is related to Voronoi tessellation. When connecting each data point to every other data point that shares an edge, we end up with a plot that is triangulated. The closer the data points are to each other, the smaller the triangles will be. This gives us a visual clue about the density of points in specific areas. When combined with color gradients, we get insights about points of interest, which can be compared with a heatmap:

```
# plotting our dataset as a delaunay
geoplotlib.delaunay(dataset_filtered, cmap='hot_r')
geoplotlib.set_smoothing(True)

geoplotlib.show()
```

This example uses the same dataset as before, that is, population density in Brazil. The structure of the code is the same as in the **voronoi** example.

After importing the dependencies that we need, we read the dataset using the **read_csv** method and then use it as data for our **delaunay** method, which handles all of the complex logic of plotting data on the map.

In addition to the data itself, we can again use the **set_smoothing** method to smooth the lines using anti-aliasing.

The resulting visualization looks as follows:

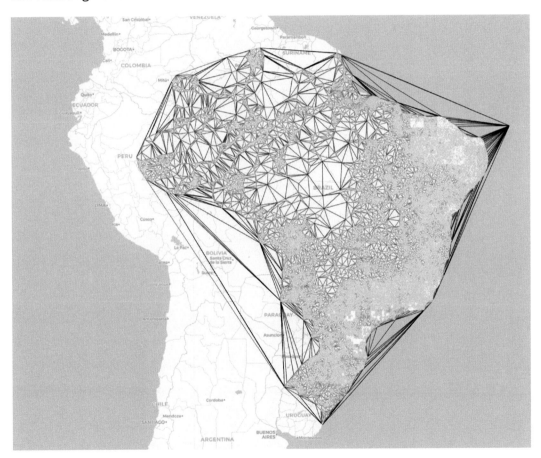

Figure 5.4: Delaunay triangulation of cities in Brazil to visualize population density

CHOROPLETH PLOT

This kind of geographical plot displays areas such as the states of a country in a shaded or colored manner. The shade or color of the plot is determined by a single data point or a set of data points. It gives an abstract view of a geographical area to visualize the relationships and differences between the different areas. In the following code and visual example, we can see that the unemployment rate determines the shade of each state of the US. The darker the shade, the higher the rate:

```python
from geoplotlib.colors import ColorMap
import json
"""

find the unemployment rate for the selected county, and convert it to
color
"""
def get_color(properties):
    key = str(int(properties['STATE'])) \
          + properties['COUNTY']
    if key in unemployment_rates:
        return cmap.to_color(unemployment_rates.get(key), \
                             .15, 'lin')
    else:
        return [0, 0, 0, 0]


# get unemployment data
with open('../../Datasets/unemployment.json') as fin:
    unemployment_rates = json.load(fin)
```

```
"""
plot the outlines of the states and color them using the unemployment
rate
"""
cmap = ColorMap('Reds', alpha=255, levels=10)
geoplotlib.geojson('../../Datasets/us_states_shapes.json', \
                   fill=True, color=get_color, \
                   f_tooltip=lambda properties: properties['NAME'])
geoplotlib.geojson('../../Datasets/us_states_shapes.json', \
                   fill=False, color=[255, 255, 255, 64])
geoplotlib.set_bbox(BoundingBox.USA)

geoplotlib.show()
```

We will cover what each line does in more detail later. However, to give you a better understanding of what is happening here, we will quickly cover the sections of the preceding code.

The first few lines import all the necessary dependencies, including geoplotlib and **json**, which will be used to load our dataset, which is provided in this format.

After the **import** statements, we see a **get_color** method. This method returns a color that has been determined by the unemployment rate of the given data point. This method defines how dark the red value will be. In the last section of the script, we read our dataset and use it with the **geojson** method.

The choropleth plot is one of the only visualizations that does not have a method assigned that is solely used for this kind of plot. We use the **geojson()** method to create more complex shapes than simple dots. By using the **f_tooltip** argument, we can also display the name of the city we are hovering over.

The **BoundingBox** object is an object to define the "corners" of the viewport. We can set an initial focus when running our visualization, which helps the user see what the visualization is about without panning around and zooming first.

Executing this code with the right example dataset provides the following visualization:

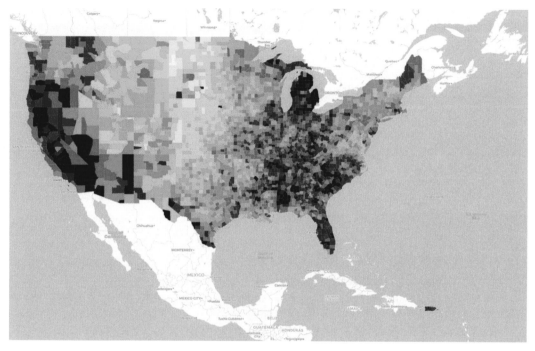

Figure 5.5: Choropleth plot of unemployment rates in the US; the darker the color, the higher the value

Next, we will implement an exercise to plot dot density and histograms.

EXERCISE 5.01: PLOTTING POACHING DENSITY USING DOT DENSITY AND HISTOGRAMS

In this exercise, we'll be looking at the primary use of geoplotlib's plot methods for **dot density**, **histograms**, and **Voronoi** diagrams. For this, we will make use of data on various poaching incidents that have taken place all over the world.

The dataset that we will be using here contains data from poaching incidents in Tanzania. The dataset consists of 268 rows and 6 columns (`id_report`, `date_report`, `description`, `created_date`, `lat`, and `lon`).

Each row is uniquely identified by **id_report**. The **date_report** column states what date the poaching incident took place on. On the other hand, the **created_date** column states the date on which the report was created. The **description** column provides basic information about the incident. The **lat** and **lon** columns state the geographical location of the place where the poaching took place.

Note that geoplotlib requires your dataset to have both **lat** and **lon** columns. These columns are the geographical data for latitude and longitude, which are used to determine how to plot the data. The following are the steps to perform:

1. Create an **Exercise5.01.ipynb** Jupyter Notebook within the **Chapter05/Exercise5.01** folder to implement this exercise.

2. First, import the dependencies that you will need. Use the **read_csv** method provided by geoplotlib to read the dataset as a CSV file into a **DataAccessObject**:

```
import geoplotlib
from geoplotlib.utils import read_csv
```

3. Load the **poaching_points_cleaned.csv** dataset from the **Datasets** folder using the pandas **read_csv** method as well:

```
dataset = read_csv('../../Datasets/poaching_points_cleaned.csv')
```

4. Print out the dataset and look at its type. What difference do you see compared to a pandas DataFrame? Let's take a look:

```
# looking at the dataset structure
dataset
```

The following figure shows the output of the preceding code:

```
DataAccessObject(['id_report', 'date_report', 'description', 'created_date', 'lat', 'lon'] x 268)
```

Figure 5.6: Dataset structure

The dataset is stored in a **DataAccessObject** class that's provided by geoplotlib. It does not have the same capabilities as a pandas **DataFrame**. Instead, it's meant for the simple and quick loading of data so that you can create a visualization. If we print out this object, we can see the differences better. It gives us a basic overview of what columns are present and how many rows the dataset has.

5. Convert the dataset into a pandas DataFrame to preprocess the data:

```
# csv import with pandas
import pandas as pd
pd_dataset = \
    pd.read_csv('../../Datasets/poaching_points_cleaned.csv')
pd_dataset.head()
```

The following figure shows the output:

	id_report	date_report	description	created_date	lat	lon
0	138	01/01/2005 12:00:00 AM	Poaching incident	2005/01/01 12:00:00 AM	-7.049359	34.841440
1	4	01/20/2005 12:00:00 AM	Poaching incident	2005/01/20 12:00:00 AM	-7.650840	34.480010
2	43	01/20/2005 12:00:00 AM	Poaching incident	2005/02/20 12:00:00 AM	-7.843202	34.005704
3	98	01/20/2005 12:00:00 AM	Poaching incident	2005/02/21 12:00:00 AM	-7.745846	33.948526
4	141	01/20/2005 12:00:00 AM	Poaching incident	2005/02/22 12:00:00 AM	-7.876673	33.690167

Figure 5.7: The first five entries of the dataset

6. Plot each row of our dataset as a single point on the map using a dot density layer by calling the **dot** method. Then, call the **show** method to render the map with a given layer:

```
# plotting our dataset with points
geoplotlib.dot(dataset)
geoplotlib.show()
```

The following figure shows the output:

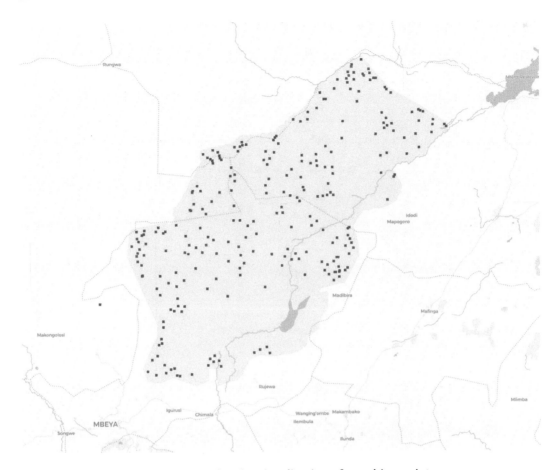

Figure 5.8: Dot density visualization of poaching points

Only looking at the **lat** and **lon** values in the dataset won't give us a very good idea of where on the map our elements are located or how far apart they are. We're not able to draw conclusions and get insights into our dataset without visualizing our data points on a map. When looking at the rendered map, we can instantly see that some areas have more incidents than others. This insight couldn't have been easily identified by simply looking at the numbers in the dataset itself.

7. Visualize the density using the **hist** method, which will create a **Histogram Layer** on top of our map tiles. Then, define a **binsize** of 20. This will allow us to set the size of the **hist** bins in our visualization:

```
# plotting our dataset as a histogram
geoplotlib.hist(dataset, binsize=20)
geoplotlib.show()
```

The following figure shows the output of the preceding code:

Figure 5.9: Histogram visualization of poaching points

Histogram plots give us a better understanding of the **density distribution** of our dataset. Looking at the final plot, we can see that there are some hotspots for poaching. It also highlights the areas without any poaching incidents.

8. Create a Voronoi plot using the same dataset. Use a color map **cmap** of **'Blues_r'** and define the **max_area** parameter as **1e5**:

```
# plotting a voronoi map
geoplotlib.voronoi(dataset, cmap='Blues_r', \
                   max_area=1e5, alpha=255)
geoplotlib.show()
```

The following figure shows the output of the preceding code:

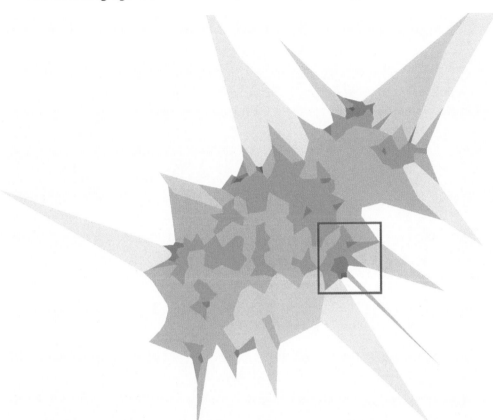

Figure 5.10: Voronoi visualization of poaching points

> **NOTE**
>
> To access the source code for this specific section, please refer to
> https://packt.live/2UlwGkT.
>
> This section does not currently have an online interactive example, and will
> need to be run locally.

Voronoi plots are good for visualizing the density of data points, too. Voronoi
introduces a little bit more complexity with several parameters, such as **cmap**, **max_
area**, and **alpha**. Here, **cmap** denotes the color of the map, **alpha** denotes the
color of the alpha, and **max_area** denotes a constant that determines the color of
the **Voronoi areas**.

If we compare this Voronoi visualization with the histogram plot, we can see that one area draws a lot of attention. The center-right edge of the plot shows quite a large dark blue area with an even darker center: something that could've easily been overlooked with the histogram plot.

We have now covered the basics of geoplotlib. It has many more methods, but they all have a similar API that makes using the other methods simple. Since we have looked at some very basic visualizations, it's now up to you to solve the first activity.

ACTIVITY 5.01: PLOTTING GEOSPATIAL DATA ON A MAP

In this activity, we will take our previously learned skills of plotting data with geoplotlib and apply them to our new **world_cities_pop.csv** dataset. We will find the dense areas of cities in Europe that have a population of more than 100,000 people:

1. Create an **Activity5.01.ipynb** Jupyter Notebook within the **Chapter05/Activity5.01** folder to implement this activity.

2. Import the dependencies and load the **world_cities_pop.csv** dataset from the **Datasets** folder using pandas.

3. List all the datatypes that are present in it and verify that they are correct. Then, map the **Latitude** and **Longitude** columns to **lat** and **lon**.

4. Now, plot the data points on a dot density plot.

5. Use the **agg** method of pandas to get the average number of cities per country.

6. Obtain the number of cities per country (the first 20 entries) and extract the countries that have a population of greater than zero.

7. Plot the remaining data on a dot plot.

8. Again, filter your remaining data for cities with a population of greater than 100,000.

9. To get a better understanding of the density of our data points on the map, use a **Voronoi tessellation layer**.

10. Filter down the data even further to only cities in countries such as Germany and Great Britain.

11. Finally, use a **Delaunay triangulation layer** to find the most densely populated areas.

Observe the expected output of the dot plot:

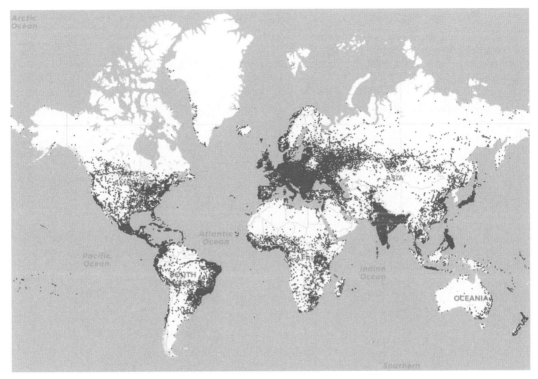

Figure 5.11: A dot density visualization of the reduced dataset

The following is the expected output of the Voronoi plot:

Figure 5.12: A Voronoi visualization of densely populated cities

The following is the expected output of the Delaunay triangulation:

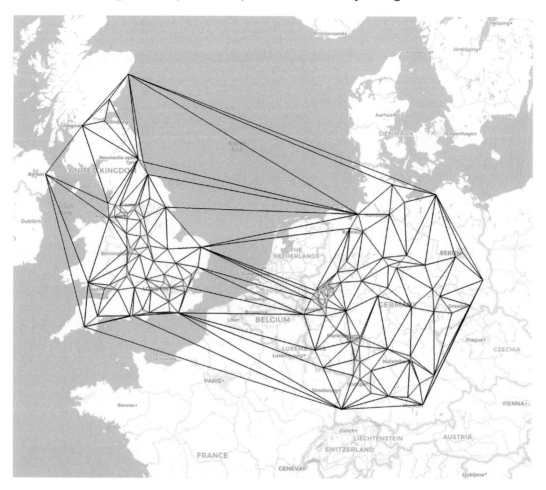

Figure 5.13: A Delaunay triangle visualization of cities in Germany and Great Britain

> **NOTE**
>
> The solution for this activity can be found on page 436.

You have now completed your first activity using geoplotlib. Note how we made use of different plots to get the information we required. Next, we will look at some more custom features of geoplotlib that will allow us to change the map tiles provider and create custom plotting layers.

THE GEOJSON FORMAT

The GeoJSON format is used to encode a variety of data structures, such as points, lines, and polygons with a focus on geographical visualization. The format has a defined structure that each valid file has to follow:

```
{
  "type": "Feature",
  "properties": {
    "name": "Dinagat Islands"
  },
  "geometry": {
    "type": "Point",
    "coordinates": [125.6, 10.1]
  }
}
```

Each object with additional properties, for example, an ID or name attribute, is a **Feature**. The **properties** attribute simply allows additional information to be added to the feature. The **geometry** attribute holds information about the type of feature we are working with, for example, a **Point**, and its specific coordinates. The coordinates define the positions for the "waypoints" of the given type. Those coordinates define the shape of the element to be displayed by the plotting library.

EXERCISE 5.02: CREATING A CHOROPLETH PLOT WITH GEOJSON DATA

In this exercise, we will work with **GeoJSON** data and also create a **choropleth visualization**. GeoJSON is especially useful for displaying statistical variables in shaded areas. In our case, the areas will be the outlines of the states of the USA.

Let's create a choropleth visualization with the given GeoJSON data:

1. Create an **Exercise5.02.ipynb** Jupyter Notebook within the **Chapter05/Activity5.02** folder to implement this exercise. Then, load the dependencies for this exercise:

```
# importing the necessary dependencies
import json
import geoplotlib
from geoplotlib.colors import ColorMap
from geoplotlib.utils import BoundingBox
```

2. Since the **geojson** method of geoplotlib only needs a path to the **us_states. json** dataset instead of a DataFrame or object, we don't need to load it. However, since we still want to see what kind of data we are handling, we must open the GeoJSON file and load it as a **json** object. We can then access its members using **simple indexing**:

```
# displaying the fourth entry of the states dataset
with open('../../Datasets/us_states.json') as data:
    dataset = json.load(data)

    fourth_state = dataset.get('features')[3]

    # only showing one coordinate instead of all points
    fourth_state['geometry']['coordinates'] = \
        fourth_state['geometry']['coordinates'][0][0]
    print(json.dumps(fourth_state, indent=4))
```

Our dataset contains a few properties. Only the state name, **NAME**, and the number of consensus areas, **CENSUSAREA**, are important for us in this exercise.

> **NOTE**
>
> Geospatial applications prefer GeoJSON files for persisting and exchanging geographical data.

3. Extract the names of all the states of the USA from the dataset. Next, print the number of states in the dataset and then print all the states as a list:

```
# listing the states in the dataset
with open('../../Datasets/us_states.json') as data:
    dataset = json.load(data)

    states = [feature['properties']['NAME'] for feature in \
            dataset.get('features')]
    print('Number of states:', len(states))
    print(states)
```

The following figure shows the output of the preceding code:

```
Number of states: 52
['Alabama', 'Alaska', 'Arizona', 'Arkansas', 'California', 'Colorado',
'Connecticut', 'Delaware', 'District of Columbia', 'Florida', 'Georgia'
, 'Hawaii', 'Idaho', 'Illinois', 'Indiana', 'Iowa', 'Kansas', 'Kentucky
', 'Louisiana', 'Maine', 'Maryland', 'Massachusetts', 'Michigan', 'Minn
esota', 'Mississippi', 'Missouri', 'Montana', 'Nebraska', 'Nevada', 'Ne
w Hampshire', 'New Jersey', 'New Mexico', 'New York', 'North Carolina',
'North Dakota', 'Ohio', 'Oklahoma', 'Oregon', 'Pennsylvania', 'Rhode Is
land', 'South Carolina', 'South Dakota', 'Tennessee', 'Texas', 'Utah',
'Vermont', 'Virginia', 'Washington', 'West Virginia', 'Wisconsin', 'Wyo
ming', 'Puerto Rico']
```

Figure 5.14: List of all cities in the US

4. If your GeoJSON file is valid, that is, if it has the expected structure, then use the **geojson** method of geoplotlib. Create a GeoJSON plot using the **geojson()** method of geoplotlib:

```
# plotting the information from the geojson file
geoplotlib.geojson('../../Datasets/us_states.json')
geoplotlib.show()
```

After calling the **show** method, the map will show up with a focus on North America. In the following diagram, we can already see the borders of each state:

Figure 5.15: Map with outlines of the states plotted

5. Rather than assigning a single value to each state, we want the darkness to represent the number of census areas. To do this, we have to provide a method for the **color** property. Map the **CENSUSAREA** attribute to a **ColorMap** class object with 10 levels to allow a good distribution of color. Provide a **maxvalue** of **300000** to the **to_color** method to define the upper limit of our dataset:

```
cmap = ColorMap('Reds', alpha=255, levels=10)
def get_color(properties):
    return cmap.to_color(properties[CENSUSAREA], \
                         maxvalue=300000,scale='lin')
```

As you can see in the code example, we can provide three arguments to our **ColorMap**. The first one, **'Reds'**, in our case, defines the basic coloring scheme. The **alpha** argument defines how opaque we want the color to be, **255** being 100% opaque, and **0** completely invisible. Those 8-bit values for the **Red**, **Green**, **Blue**, and **Alpha** (**RGBA**) values are commonly used in styling: they all range from 0 to 255. With the **levels** argument, we can define how many "steps," that is, levels of red values, we can map to.

6. Use the **us_states.json** file in the **Datasets** folder to visualize the different states. First, provide the color mapping to our **color** parameter and set the **fill** parameter to **True**. Then, draw a black outline for each state. Use the **color** argument and provide the RGBA value for black. Lastly, use the **USA** constant of the **BoundingBox** class to set the bounding box:

```
"""

plotting the shaded states and adding another layer which plots the
state outlines in white
our BoundingBox should focus the USA
"""

geoplotlib.geojson('../../Datasets/us_states.json', \
                   fill=True, color=get_color)
geoplotlib.geojson('../../Datasets/us_states.json', \
                   fill=False, color=[0, 0, 0, 255])

geoplotlib.set_bbox(BoundingBox.USA)
geoplotlib.show()
```

After executing the preceding steps, the expected output is as follows:

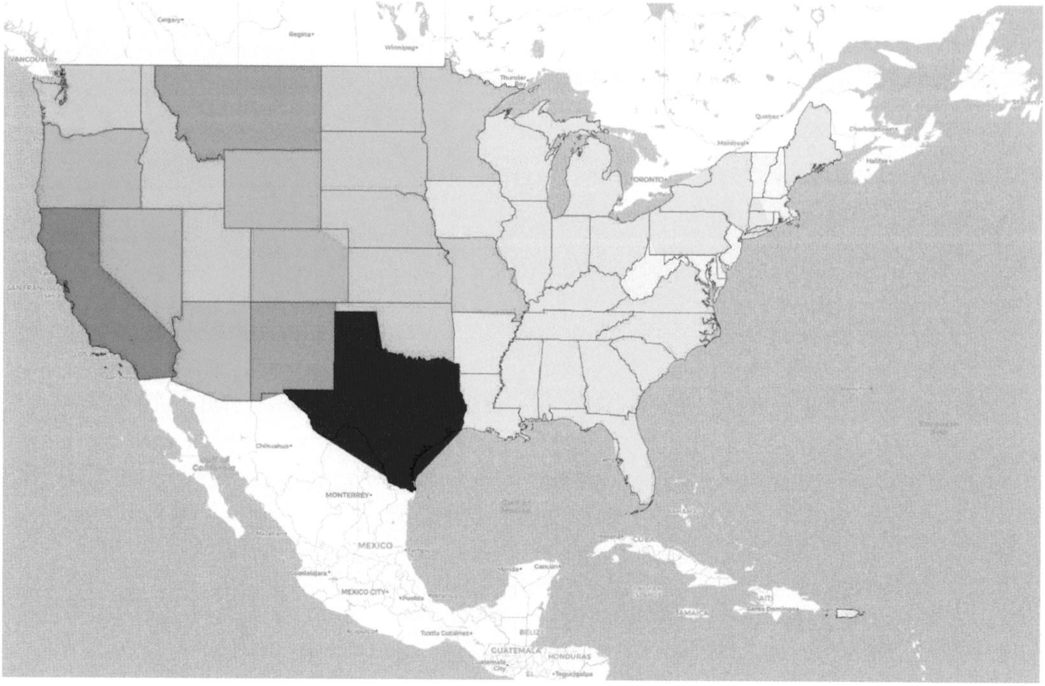

Figure 5.16: Choropleth visualization showing census areas in different states

A new window will open, displaying the country, USA, with the areas of its states filled with different shades of red. The darker areas represent higher census areas.

7. To give the user some more information about this plot, use the **f_tooltip** argument to provide a tooltip displaying the name and census area value of the state currently hovered over:

```
# adding the f_tooltip that
geoplotlib.geojson('../../Datasets/us_states.json', \
                fill=True, color=get_color, \
                f_tooltip=lambda properties: \
                        properties['NAME'] \
                        + ' - Census Areas: ' \
                        + str(properties['CENSUSAREA']))
```

```
geoplotlib.geojson('../../Datasets/us_states.json', \
                   fill=False, color=[0, 0, 0, 255])

geoplotlib.set_bbox(BoundingBox.USA)
geoplotlib.show()
```

The following is the output of the preceding code:

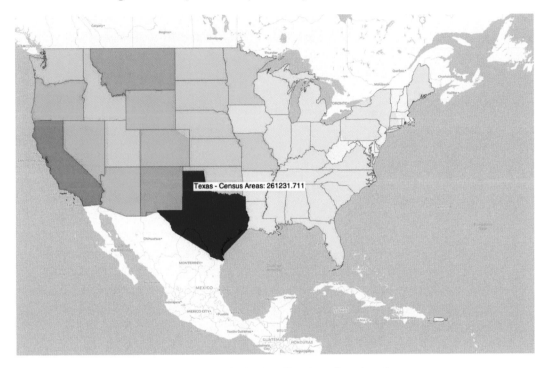

**Figure 5.17: A choropleth visualization showing the census
area value of the state hovered over**

Upon hovering, we will get a tooltip for each of the plotted areas displaying the name of the state and the census area value.

> **NOTE**
>
> To access the source code for this specific section, please refer to
> https://packt.live/30PX9Rh.
>
> This section does not currently have an online interactive example, and will
> need to be run locally.

You've already built different plots and visualizations using geoplotlib. In this exercise, we looked at displaying data from a GeoJSON file and creating a **choropleth plot**.

In the following topics, we will cover more advanced customizations that will give you the tools to create more powerful visualizations.

TILE PROVIDERS

geoplotlib supports the use of different **tile providers**. This means that any **OpenStreetMap** tile server can be used as a backdrop for our visualization. Some of the popular free tile providers include **Stamen Watercolor**, **Stamen Toner**, **Stamen Toner Lite**, and **DarkMatter**. Changing the tile provider can be done in two ways:

- **Make use of built-in tile providers**:

  geoplotlib contains a few built-in tile providers with shortcuts. The following code shows you how to use it:

  ```
  geoplotlib.tiles_provider('darkmatter')
  ```

- **Provide a custom object to the tiles_provider method**:

  By providing a custom object to geoplotlib's **tiles_provider()** method, you will not only get access to the **url** parameter from which the map tiles are being loaded but also see the **attribution** parameter displayed in the lower-right corner of the visualization. We are also able to set a distinct **caching directory** for the downloaded tiles. The following code demonstrates how to provide a custom object:

  ```
  geoplotlib.tiles_provider({\
                            'url': lambda zoom, \
                            xtile, ytile:
                            'http://a.tile.stamen.com/'\
                            'watercolor/%d/%d/%d.png' \
                            % (zoom, xtile, ytile),\
                            'tiles_dir': 'tiles_dir',
                            'attribution': \
                            'Python Data Visualization | Packt'\
  })
  ```

The caching in **tiles_dir** is mandatory since, each time the map is scrolled or zoomed into, we query new map tiles if they are not already downloaded. This can lead to the tile provider refusing your request due to too many requests occurring in a short period of time.

In the following exercise, we'll take a quick look at how to switch the map tile provider. It might not seem convincing at first, but it can take your visualizations to the next level if leveraged correctly.

EXERCISE 5.03: VISUALLY COMPARING DIFFERENT TILE PROVIDERS

In this exercise, we will switch the map tile provider for our visualizations. **geoplotlib** provides mappings for some of the most popular available map tiles. However, we can also provide a custom object that contains the **url** of some tile providers.

The following are the steps to perform the exercise:

1. Create an **Exercise5.03.ipynb** Jupyter Notebook within the **Chapter05/Exercise5.03** folder to implement this exercise. Import the necessary dependencies:

```
import geoplotlib
```

We won't use a dataset in this exercise since we want to focus on the map tiles and tile providers.

2. Display the map with the default tile provider:

```
geoplotlib.show()
```

The following figure shows the output of the preceding code:

Figure 5.18: World map with the default tile provider

This will display an empty world map since we haven't specified a tile provider. By default, it will use the **CartoDB Positron** map tiles.

3. Use the **tiles_provider** method and provide the **'darkmatter'** tiles:

```
# using map tiles from the dark matter tile provider
geoplotlib.tiles_provider('darkmatter')
geoplotlib.show()
```

geoplotlib provides several **shorthand accessors** to common map tile providers. The following figure shows the output:

Figure 5.19: World map with darkmatter map tiles

In this example, we used the **darkmatter** map tiles. As you can see, they are very dark and will make your visualizations pop out.

> **NOTE**
>
> We can also use different map tiles such as **watercolor**, **toner**, **toner-lite**, and **positron** in a similar way.

4. Use the **attribution** element of the **tiles_provider** argument object (the entity passed to the method) to provide a custom attribution:

```
geoplotlib.tiles_provider({
                          'url': lambda zoom, \
                          xtile, ytile: \
                          'http://a.tile.openstreetmap.fr/'\
                          'hot/%d/%d/%d.png' \
                          % (zoom, xtile, ytile),\
                          'tiles_dir': 'custom_tiles',
                          'attribution': 'Custom Tiles '\
                           'Provider - Humanitarian map style'\
})
geoplotlib.show()
```

The following figure shows the output of the preceding code:

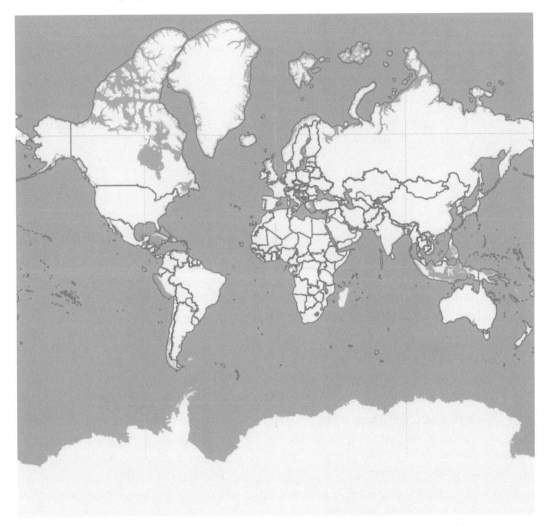

Figure 5.20: Humanitarian map tiles from the custom tile providers object

Some map tile providers have strict request limits, so you may see warning messages if you're zooming in too fast.

> **NOTE**
>
> To access the source code for this specific section, please refer to https://packt.live/3e6WjTT.
>
> This section does not currently have an online interactive example, and will need to be run locally.

You now know how to change the tile provider to give your visualization one more layer of customizability. This also introduces us to another layer of complexity. It all depends on the concept of our final product and whether we want to use the "default" map tiles or some artistic map tiles.

The next section will cover how to create custom layers that can go far beyond the ones we have described in this book. We'll look at the basic structure of the **BaseLayer** class and what it takes to create a custom layer.

CUSTOM LAYERS

Now that we have covered the basics of visualizing geospatial data with built-in layers and methods to change the tile provider, we will now focus on defining our custom layers. **Custom layers** allow you to create more complex data visualizations. They also help with adding more interactivity and animation to them. Creating a custom layer starts by defining a new class that extends the **BaseLayer** class that's provided by geoplotlib. Besides the **__init__** method, which initializes the class level variables, we also have to, at the very least, extend the **draw** method of the **BaseLayer** class already provided.

Depending on the nature of your visualization, you might also want to implement the **invalidate** method, which takes care of map projection changes such as zooming into your visualization. Both the **draw** and **invalidate** methods receive a **Projection** object that takes care of the latitude and longitude mapping on our two-dimensional viewport. These mapped points can be handed to an instance of a **BatchPainter** object that provides primitives such as points, lines, and shapes to draw those coordinates onto your map.

An example of a custom layer, comparable to what we will create, is this program, which plots the cities of a selected country as dots on the map. We have a given list of possible countries and can switch through them using the arrow keys:

```python
# importing the necessary dependencies
import pyglet
from geoplotlib.layers import BaseLayer
from geoplotlib.core import BatchPainter


countries = ['be', 'ch', 'de', 'es', 'fr', 'it', 'nl', 'pt']


class CountrySelectLayer(BaseLayer):

    def __init__(self, data, bbox=BoundingBox.WORLD):
        self.data = data
        self.view = bbox

        # start with germany
        self.country_num = 0

    def invalidate(self, proj):
        country_data = \
                    self.data[self.data['Country'] \
                    == countries[self.country_num]]
        self.painter = BatchPainter()

        x, y = proj.lonlat_to_screen(country_data['lon'], \
                country_data['lat'])
        self.painter.points(x, y, 2)

    def draw(self, proj, mouse_x, mouse_y, ui_manager):
        self.painter.batch_draw()

    def draw(self, proj, mouse_x, mouse_y, ui_manager):
        self.painter.batch_draw()
        ui_manager.info('Displaying cities in {}'.format\
                    (countries[self.country_num]))

    def on_key_release(self, key, modifiers):
        if key == pyglet.window.key.RIGHT:
```

```
            self.country_num = (self.country_num + 1) \
                            % len(countries)
            return True
        elif key == pyglet.window.key.LEFT:
            self.country_num = (self.country_num - 1) \
                            % len(countries)
            return True

        return False


    # bounding box that gets used when layer is created
    def bbox(self):
        return self.view



europe_bbox = BoundingBox(north=68.574309, \
                    west=-25.298424, \
                    south=34.266013, \
                    east=47.387123)
geoplotlib.add_layer(CountrySelectLayer(dataset, europe_bbox))
geoplotlib.show()
```

As we've seen several times before, we first import all the necessary dependencies for this plot, including geoplotlib. **BaseLayer** and **BatchPainter** are dependencies we haven't seen before, since they are only needed when writing custom layers.

BaseLayer is a class provided by geoplotlib that is extended by our custom **Layer** class. This concept is called inheritance. This means that our custom class has access to all the properties and methods defined in the **BaseLayer** class. This is necessary since geoplotlib requires a predefined structure for layers to make them plottable.

The **BatchPainter** class is another helper for our implementation that lets us trigger the drawing of elements onto the map.

When creating the custom layer, we simply provide the **BaseLayer** class in the parentheses to tell Python to extend the given class.

The class then needs to implement at least two of the provided methods, **__init__** and **draw**.

__init__ defines what happens when a new custom layer is instantiated. This is used to set the state of our layer; here, we define values such as our data to be used and create a **new BatchPainter** class.

The **draw** method is called every frame and draws the defined elements using the **BatchPainter** class.

In this method, we can do all sorts of calculations such as, in this case, filtering our dataset to only contain the values of the current active timestamp. In addition to that, we make the viewport follow our current **lat** and **lon** values by fitting the projection to a new **BoundingBox**.

Since we don't want to draw everything from scratch with every frame, we use the **invalidate** method, which only updates the points on the viewport. For example, changes such as zooming.

When using interaction elements, such as switching through our countries using the arrow keys, we can return either **True** or **False** from the **on_key_pressed** method to trigger the redrawing of all the points.

Once our class is defined, we can call the **add_layer** method of geoplotlib to add the newly defined layer to our visualization and finally call **show ()** to show the map.

When executing the preceding example code, we get a visualization that, upon switching the selected country with the arrow keys, draws the cities for the selected country using dots on the map:

Figure 5.21: The selection of cities in Germany

The following figure shows the cities in Spain after changing the selected country using the arrow keys:

Figure 5.22: The selection of cities in Spain after changing the country using the arrow keys

In the following exercise, we will create our animated visualization by using what we've learned about custom layers in the preceding example.

> **NOTE**
>
> Since geoplotlib operates on OpenGL, this process is highly performant and can even draw complex visualizations quickly.

EXERCISE 5.04: PLOTTING THE MOVEMENT OF AN AIRCRAFT WITH A CUSTOM LAYER

In this exercise, we will create a custom layer to display geospatial data and also animate your data points over time. We'll get a deeper understanding of how geoplotlib works and how layers are created and drawn. Our dataset contains both **spatial** and **temporal** information, which enables us to plot the flight's movement overtime on our map.

Let's create a custom layer **that** will allow us to display geospatial data and animate the data points over time:

1. Import **pandas** for the data import:

```
# importing the necessary dependencies
import pandas as pd
```

2. Use the **read_csv** method of **pandas** to load the **flight_tracking.csv** dataset from the **Datasets** folder:

```
dataset = pd.read_csv('../../Datasets/flight_tracking.csv')
```

3. Use the **head** method to list the first five rows of the dataset and to understand the columns:

```
# displaying the first 5 rows of the dataset
dataset.head()
```

	hex_ident	altitude(feet)	latitude	longitude	date	time	angle	distance(nauticalmile)	squawk	ground_speed(knotph)	track	callsign
0	40631C	14525	53.65947	-1.43819	2017/09/11	17:02:06.418	-120.77	11.27	6276.0	299.0	283.0	NaN
1	40631C	14525	53.65956	-1.43921	2017/09/11	17:02:06.875	-120.64	11.30	6276.0	299.0	283.0	NaN
2	40631C	14500	53.65979	-1.44066	2017/09/11	17:02:07.342	-120.43	11.32	6276.0	299.0	283.0	EZY63BT
3	40631C	14475	53.66025	-1.44447	2017/09/11	17:02:09.238	-119.94	11.40	6276.0	299.0	283.0	EZY63BT
4	40631C	14475	53.66044	-1.44591	2017/09/11	17:02:09.825	-119.75	11.43	6276.0	299.0	283.0	EZY63BT

Figure 5.23: The first five elements of the dataset

4. Rename the **latitude** and **longitude** columns to **lat** and **lon** by using the **rename** method provided by pandas:

```
# renaming columns latitude to lat and longitude to lon
dataset = dataset.rename(index=str, \
        columns={"latitude": "lat", "longitude": "lon"})
```

Take another look at the first five elements of the dataset, and observe that the names of the columns have changed to **lat** and **lon**:

```
# displaying the first 5 rows of the dataset
dataset.head()
```

	hex_ident	altitude(feet)	lat	lon	date	time	angle	distance(nauticalmile)	squawk	ground_speed(knotph)	track	callsign
0	40631C	14525	53.65947	-1.43819	2017/09/11	17:02:06.418	-120.77	11.27	6276.0	299.0	283.0	NaN
1	40631C	14525	53.65956	-1.43921	2017/09/11	17:02:06.875	-120.64	11.30	6276.0	299.0	283.0	NaN
2	40631C	14500	53.65979	-1.44066	2017/09/11	17:02:07.342	-120.43	11.32	6276.0	299.0	283.0	EZY63BT
3	40631C	14475	53.66025	-1.44447	2017/09/11	17:02:09.238	-119.94	11.40	6276.0	299.0	283.0	EZY63BT
4	40631C	14475	53.66044	-1.44591	2017/09/11	17:02:09.825	-119.75	11.43	6276.0	299.0	283.0	EZY63BT

Figure 5.24: The dataset with the lat and lon columns

5. Since we want to get a visualization over time in this activity, we need to work with **date** and **time**. If we take a closer look at our dataset, it shows us that **date** and **time** are separated into two columns. Combine **date** and **time** into a timestamp, using the **to_epoch** method already provided:

```
# method to convert date and time to an unix timestamp
from datetime import datetime
def to_epoch(date, time):
    try:
        timestamp = round(datetime.strptime('{} {}'.\
                      format(date, time), \
                      '%Y/%m/%d %H:%M:%S.%f').timestamp())
        return timestamp
    except ValueError:
        return round(datetime.strptime('2017/09/11 17:02:06.418', \
                      '%Y/%m/%d %H:%M:%S.%f').timestamp())
```

6. Use **to_epoch** and the **apply** method provided by the pandas DataFrame to create a new column called **timestamp** that holds the Unix timestamp:

```
"""

create a new column called timestamp with the to_epoch method applied
"""

dataset['timestamp'] = dataset.apply(lambda x: to_epoch\
                              (x['date'], x['time']), \
                              axis=1)
```

7. Take another look at our dataset. We now have a new column that holds the Unix timestamps:

```
# displaying the first 5 rows of the dataset
dataset.head()
```

	hex_ident	altitude(feet)	lat	lon	date	time	angle	distance(nauticalmile)	squawk	ground_speed(knotph)	track	callsign	timestamp
0	40631C	14525	53.65947	-1.43819	2017/09/11	17:02:06.418	-120.77	11.27	6276.0	299.0	283.0	NaN	1505142126
1	40631C	14525	53.65956	-1.43921	2017/09/11	17:02:06.875	-120.64	11.30	6276.0	299.0	283.0	NaN	1505142127
2	40631C	14500	53.65979	-1.44066	2017/09/11	17:02:07.342	-120.43	11.32	6276.0	299.0	283.0	EZY63BT	1505142127
3	40631C	14475	53.66025	-1.44447	2017/09/11	17:02:09.238	-119.94	11.40	6276.0	299.0	283.0	EZY63BT	1505142129
4	40631C	14475	53.66044	-1.44591	2017/09/11	17:02:09.825	-119.75	11.43	6276.0	299.0	283.0	EZY63BT	1505142130

Figure 5.25: The dataset with a timestamp column added

Since our dataset is now ready to be used with all the necessary columns in place, we can start writing our custom layer. This layer will display each point once it reaches the **timestamp** that's provided in the dataset. It will be displayed for a few seconds before it disappears. We'll need to keep track of the current timestamp in our custom layer. Consolidating what we learned in the theoretical section of this topic, we have an **__init__** method that constructs our custom **TrackLayer**.

8. In the **draw** method, filter the dataset for all the elements that are in the mentioned time range and use each element of the filtered list to display it on the map with color that's provided by the **colorbrewer** method.

Since our dataset only contains data from a specific time range and we're always incrementing the time, we want to check whether there are still any elements with **timestamps** after the current timestamp. If not, we want to set our current timestamp to the earliest timestamp that's available in the dataset. The following code shows how we can create a custom layer:

```
# custom layer creation
import geoplotlib
from geoplotlib.layers import BaseLayer
from geoplotlib.core import BatchPainter
from geoplotlib.colors import colorbrewer
from geoplotlib.utils import epoch_to_str, BoundingBox


class TrackLayer(BaseLayer):
    def __init__(self, dataset, bbox=BoundingBox.WORLD):
        self.data = dataset
        self.cmap = colorbrewer(self.data['hex_ident'], \
                                alpha=200)
        self.time = self.data['timestamp'].min()
        self.painter = BatchPainter()
        self.view = bbox
    def draw(self, proj, mouse_x, mouse_y, ui_manager):
        self.painter = BatchPainter()
        df = self.data.where((self.data['timestamp'] \
                              > self.time) \
                             & (self.data['timestamp'] \
                             <= self.time + 180))
```

```
        for element in set(df['hex_ident']):
            grp = df.where(df['hex_ident'] == element)
            self.painter.set_color(self.cmap[element])
            x, y = proj.lonlat_to_screen(grp['lon'], grp['lat'])
            self.painter.points(x, y, 15, rounded=True)
        self.time += 1
        if self.time > self.data['timestamp'].max():
            self.time = self.data['timestamp'].min()
        self.painter.batch_draw()
        ui_manager.info('Current timestamp: {}'.\
                        format(epoch_to_str(self.time)))

    # bounding box that gets used when the layer is created
    def bbox(self):
        return self.view
```

9. Define a custom **BoundingBox** that focuses our view on this area, since the dataset only contains data from the area around Leeds in the UK:

```
# bounding box for our view on Leeds
from geoplotlib.utils import BoundingBox
leeds_bbox = BoundingBox(north=53.8074, \
                         west=-3, \
                         south=53.7074 , \
                         east=0)
```

10. geoplotlib sometimes requires you to provide a **DataAccessObject** class instead of a pandas DataFrame. Use geoplotlib to convert any pandas DataFrame into a **DataAccessObject** class:

```
# displaying our custom layer using add_layer
from geoplotlib.utils import DataAccessObject
data = DataAccessObject(dataset)
geoplotlib.add_layer(TrackLayer(data, bbox=leeds_bbox))
geoplotlib.show()
```

The following is the output of the preceding code:

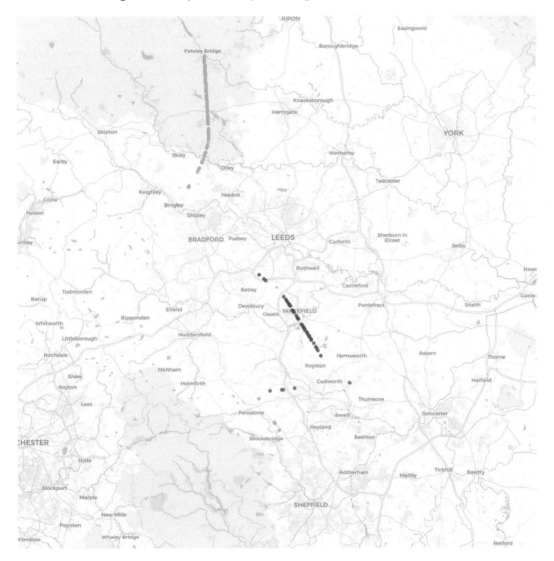

Figure 5.26: Final animated tracking map that displays the routes of the aircraft

> **NOTE**
>
> To access the source code for this specific section, please refer to
> https://packt.live/3htmztU.
>
> This section does not currently have an online interactive example, and will
> need to be run locally.

You have now completed the custom layer activity using geoplotlib. We've applied several preprocessing steps to shape the dataset as we want to have it. We've also written a custom layer to display spatial data in the temporal space. Our custom layer even has a level of animation. This is something we'll look into more in the following chapter about Bokeh. We will now implement an activity that will help us get more acquainted with custom layers in Bokeh.

ACTIVITY 5.02: VISUALIZING CITY DENSITY BY THE FIRST LETTER USING AN INTERACTIVE CUSTOM LAYER

In this last activity for geoplotlib, you'll combine all the methodologies learned in the previous exercises and the activity to create an interactive visualization that displays the cities that start with a given letter, by merely pressing the left and right arrow keys on your keyboard.

Since we use the same setup to create custom layers as the library does, you will be able to understand the library implementations of most of the layers provided by geoplotlib after this activity.

1. Create an **Activity5.02.ipynb** Jupyter Notebook within the **Chapter05/Activity5.02** folder to implement this activity.

2. Import the dependencies.

3. Load the **world_cities_pop.csv** dataset from the **Datasets** folder using pandas and look at the first five rows to understand its structure.

4. Map the **Latitude** and **Longitude** columns to **lat** and **lon**.

5. Filter the dataset to only contain European cities by using the given **europe_country_codes** list.

6. Compare the length of all data with the filtered data of Europe by printing the length of both.

7. Filter down the European dataset to get a dataset that only contains cities that start with the letter Z.

8. Print its length and the first five rows using the **head** method.

9. Create a dot density plot with a tooltip that shows the country code and the name of the city separated by a **-**. Use the **DataAccessObject** to create a copy of our dataset, which allows the use of **f_tooltip**. The following is the expected output of the dot density plot:

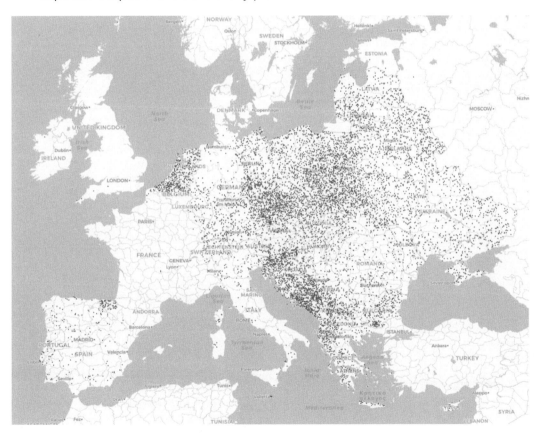

Figure 5.27: Cities starting with a Z in Europe as dots

10. Create a Voronoi plot with the same dataset that only contains cities that start with Z. Use the **'Reds_r'** color map and set the **alpha** value to **50** to make sure you still see the map tiles. The following is the expected output of the Voronoi plot:

Figure 5.28: Voronoi visualization of cities starting with a Z in Europe

11. Create a custom layer that plots all the cities in Europe dataset that starts with the provided letter. Make it interactive so that by using the left and right arrow keys, we can switch between the letters. To do that, first, filter the **self.data** dataset in the **invalidate** method using the current letter acquired from the **start_letters** array using **self.start_letter** indexing.

12. Create a new **BatchPainter()** function and project the **lon** and **lat** values to **x** and **y** values. Use the **BatchPainter** function to paint the points on the map with a size of **2**.

13. Call the **batch_draw()** method in the **draw** method and use the **ui_manager** to add an **info** dialog to the screen telling the user which starting letter is currently being used.

14. Check which key is pressed using **pyglet**: **pyglet.window.key.RIGHT**. If the right or left key is pressed, increment or decrement the **start_letter** value of the **FilterLayer** class accordingly. (Use **modulo** to allow rotation, which should happen when A->Z or Z->A). Make sure that you **return True** in the **on_key_release** method if you changed the **start_letter** to trigger a redrawing of the points.

15. Add the custom layer using the **add_layer** method and provide the given **europe_bbox** as a **BoundingBox** class.

The following is the expected output of the custom filter layer:

Figure 5.29: A custom filter layer displaying European cities starting with A

If we press the right arrow twice, we will see the cities starting with C instead:

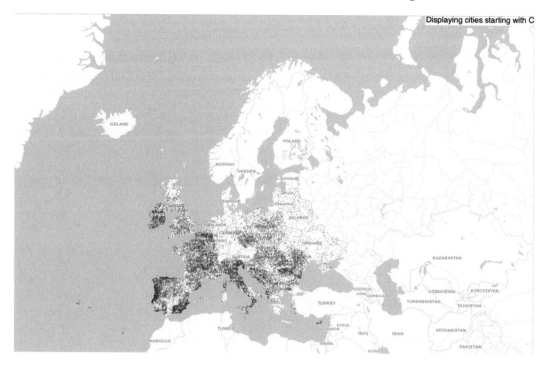

Figure 5.30: A custom filter layer displaying European cities starting with C

> **NOTE**
>
> The solution for this activity can be found on page 447.

This last activity has a custom layer that uses all the properties described by geoplotlib. All of the already provided layers by geoplotlib are created using the same structure. This means that you're now able to dig into the source code and create your own advanced layers.

SUMMARY

In this chapter, we covered basic and advanced concepts and methods of geoplotlib. It gave us a quick insight into internal processes, and we learned how to practically apply the library to our own problem statements. Most of the time, the built-in plots should suit your needs pretty well. If you're interested in building animated or even interactive visualizations, you will have to create custom layers that enable those features.

In the following chapter, we'll get some hands-on experience with the Bokeh library and build visualizations that can easily be integrated into web pages. Once we have finished using Bokeh, we'll conclude the chapter with an activity that allows you to work with a new dataset and a library of your choice so that you can come up with your very own visualization.

6

MAKING THINGS INTERACTIVE
WITH BOKEH

OVERVIEW

In this chapter, we will design interactive plots using the Bokeh library. By the end of this chapter, you will be able to use Bokeh to create insightful web-based visualizations and explain the difference between two interfaces for plotting. You will identify when to use the Bokeh server and create interactive visualizations.

INTRODUCTION

Bokeh is an interactive visualization library focused on modern browsers and the web. Other than Matplotlib or geoplotlib, the plots and visualizations we are going to create in this chapter will be based on JavaScript widgets. Bokeh allows us to create visually appealing plots and graphs nearly out of the box without much styling. In addition to that, it helps us construct performant interactive dashboards based on large static datasets or even streaming data.

Bokeh has been around since 2013, with *version 1.4.0* being released in November 2019. It targets modern web browsers to present interactive visualizations to users rather than static images. The following are some of the features of Bokeh:

- **Simple visualizations**: Through its different interfaces, it targets users of many skill levels, providing an API for quick and straightforward visualizations as well as more complex and extremely customizable ones.

- **Excellent animated visualizations**: It provides high performance and can, therefore, work on large or even streaming datasets, which makes it the go-to choice for animated visualizations and data analysis.

- **Inter-visualization interactivity**: This is a web-based approach; it's easy to combine several plots and create unique and impactful dashboards with visualizations that can be interconnected to create inter-visualization interactivity.

- **Supports multiple languages**: Other than Matplotlib and geoplotlib, Bokeh has libraries for both Python and JavaScript, in addition to several other popular languages.

- **Multiple ways to perform a task**: Adding interactivity to Bokeh visualizations can be done in several ways. The simplest built-in way is the ability to zoom and pan in and out of your visualization. This gives the users better control of what they want to see. It also allows users to filter and transform the data.

- **Beautiful chart styling**: The tech stack is based on Tornado in the backend and is powered by D3 in the frontend. D3 is a JavaScript library for creating outstanding visualizations. Using the underlying D3 visuals allows us to create beautiful plots without much custom styling.

Since we are using Jupyter Notebook throughout this book, it's worth mentioning that Bokeh, including its interactivity, is natively supported in Notebook.

CONCEPTS OF BOKEH

The basic concept of Bokeh is, in some ways, comparable to that of Matplotlib. In Bokeh, we have a figure as our root element, which has sub-elements such as a title, an axis, and **glyphs**. Glyphs have to be added to a figure, which can take on different shapes, such as circles, bars, and triangles. The following hierarchy shows the different concepts of Bokeh:

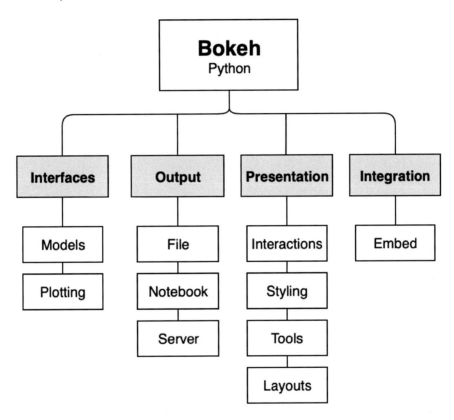

Figure 6.1: Concepts of Bokeh

INTERFACES IN BOKEH

The interface-based approach provides different levels of complexity for users that either want to create some basic plots with very few customizable parameters or want full control over their visualizations to customize every single element of their plots. This layered approach is divided into two levels:

- **Plotting**: This layer is customizable.

- **Models interface**: This layer is complex and provides an open approach to designing charts.

> **NOTE**
>
> The **models** interface is the basic building block for all plots.

The following are the two levels of the layered approach to interfaces:

- **bokeh.plotting**

  This mid-level interface has a somewhat comparable API to Matplotlib. The workflow is to create a figure and then enrich this figure with different glyphs that render data points in the figure. As in Matplotlib, the composition of sub-elements such as axes, grids, and the **inspector** (which provide basic ways of exploring your data through zooming, panning, and hovering) is done without additional configuration.

  The vital thing to note here is that even though its setup is done automatically, we can configure the sub-elements. When using this interface, the creation of the scene graph used by **BokehJS** is handled automatically too.

- **bokeh.models**

  This low-level interface is composed of two libraries: the JavaScript library called **BokehJS**, which gets used for displaying the charts in the browser, and the core plot creation Python code, which provides the developer interface. Internally, the definition created in Python creates JSON objects that hold the declaration for the JavaScript representation in the browser.

The **models** interface provides complete control over how Bokeh plots and **widgets** (elements that enable users to interact with the data displayed) are assembled and configured. This means that it is up to the developer to ensure the correctness of the **scene graph** (a collection of objects describing the visualization).

OUTPUT

Outputting Bokeh charts is straightforward. There are three ways this can be done:

- The **.show()** method: The primary option is to display the plot in an HTML page using this method.

- The inline **.show()** method: When using inline plotting with a Jupyter Notebook, the **.show()** method will allow you to display the chart inside your Notebook.

- The **.output_file()** method: You're also able to directly save the visualization to a file without any overhead using the **.output_file()** method. This will create a new file at the given path with a given name.

The most powerful way of providing your visualization is through the use of the Bokeh server.

BOKEH SERVER

Bokeh creates **scene graph** JSON objects that will be interpreted by the BokehJS library to create the visualization output. This process gives you a unified format for other languages to create the same Bokeh plots and visualizations, independently of the language used.

To create more complex visualizations and leverage the tooling provided by Python, we need a way to keep our visualizations in sync with one another. This way, we can not only filter data but also do calculations and operations on the server-side, which updates the visualizations in real-time.

In addition to that, since we will have an entry point for data, we can create visualizations that get fed by streams instead of static datasets. This design provides a way to develop more complex systems with even greater capabilities.

Looking at the scheme of this architecture, we can see that the documents are provided on the server-side, then moved over to the browser, which then inserts it into the BokehJS library. This insertion will trigger the interpretation by BokehJS, which will then create the visualization. The following diagram describes how the Bokeh server works:

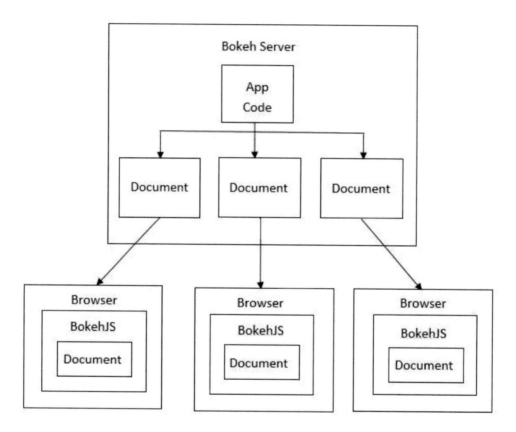

Figure 6.2: The Bokeh server

PRESENTATION

In Bokeh, presentations help make the visualization more interactive by using different features, such as interactions, styling, tools, and layouts.

Interactions

Probably the most exciting feature of Bokeh is its interactions. There are two types of interactions: **passive** and **active**.

Passive interactions are actions that the users can take that doesn't change the dataset. In Bokeh, this is called the **inspector**. As we mentioned before, the inspector contains attributes such as zooming, panning, and hovering over data. This tooling allows the user to inspect the data in more detail and might provide better insights by allowing the user to observe a zoomed-in subset of the visualized data points. The elements highlighted with a box in the following figure show the essential passive interaction elements provided by Bokeh. They include zooming, panning, and clipping data.

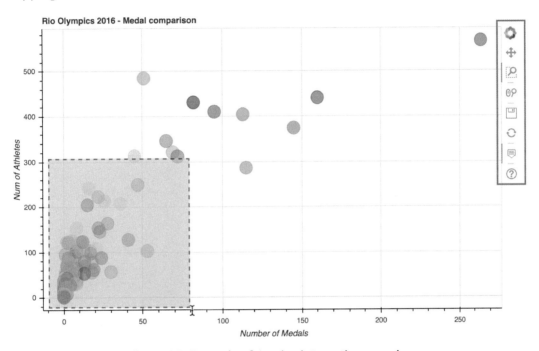

Figure 6.3: Example of passive interaction zooming

Active interactions are actions that directly change the displayed data. This includes actions such as selecting subsets of data or filtering the dataset based on parameters. **Widgets** are the most prominent of active interactions since they allow users to manipulate the displayed data with handlers. Examples of available widgets are buttons, sliders, and checkboxes.

Referring back to the subsection about the output styles, these widgets can be used in both the so-called standalone applications in the browser and the Bokeh server. This will help us consolidate the recently learned theoretical concepts and make things more transparent. Some of the interactions in Bokeh are tab panes, dropdowns, multi-selects, radio groups, text inputs, check button groups, data tables, and sliders. The elements highlighted with a red box in the following figure show a custom active interaction widget for the same plot we looked at in the example of passive interaction.

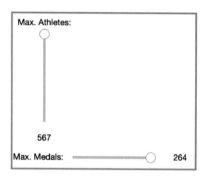

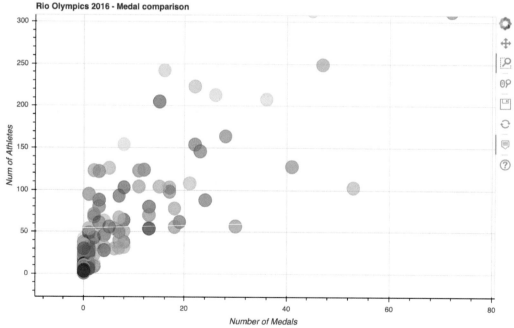

Figure 6.4: Example of custom active interaction widgets

INTEGRATING

Embedding Bokeh visualizations can take two forms:

- **HTML document**: These are the standalone HTML documents. These documents are self-contained, which means that all the necessary dependencies of Bokeh are part of the generated HTML document. This format is simple to generate and can be sent to clients or quickly displayed on a web page.

- **Bokeh applications**: Backed by a Bokeh server, these provide the possibility to connect to, for example, Python tooling for more advanced visualizations.

Bokeh is a little bit more complicated than Matplotlib with Seaborn and has its drawbacks like every other library. Once you have the basic workflow down, however, you're able to quickly extend basic visualizations with interactivity features to give power to the user.

> **NOTE**
>
> One interesting feature is the **to_bokeh** method, which allows you to plot Matplotlib figures with Bokeh without configuration overhead. Further information about this method is available at https://bokeh.pydata.org/en/0.12.3/docs/user_guide/compat.html.

In the following exercises and activities, we'll consolidate the theoretical knowledge and build several simple visualizations to explain Bokeh and its two interfaces. After we've covered the basic usage, we will compare the **plotting** and **models** interfaces and work with widgets that add interactivity to the visualizations.

BASIC PLOTTING

As mentioned before, the **plotting** interface of Bokeh gives us a higher-level abstraction, which allows us to quickly visualize data points on a grid.

To create a new plot, we have to define our imports to load the necessary dependencies:

```
# importing the necessary dependencies
import pandas as pd
from bokeh.plotting import figure, show
from bokeh.io import output_notebook

output_notebook()
```

Before we can create a plot, we need to import the dataset. In the examples in this chapter, we will work with a computer hardware dataset. It can be imported by using pandas' **read_csv** method.

```
# loading the Dataset with pandas
dataset = pd.read_csv('../../Datasets/computer_hardware.csv')
```

The basic flow when using the **plotting** interface is comparable to that of Matplotlib. We first create a figure. This figure is then used as a container to define elements and call methods on:

```
# adding an index column to use it for the x-axis
dataset['index'] = dataset.index

# plotting the cache memory levels as line
plot = figure(title='Cache per Hardware', \
              x_axis_label='Hardware index', \
              y_axis_label='Cache Memory')
plot.line(dataset['index'], dataset['cach'], line_width=5)

show(plot)
```

Once we have created a new figure instance using the imported **figure()** method, we can use it to draw lines, circles, or any glyph objects that Bokeh offers. Note that the first two arguments of the **plot.line** method is datasets that contain an equal number of elements to plot the element.

To display the plot, we then call the **show()** method we imported from the **bokeh.plotting** interface earlier on. The following figure shows the output of the preceding code:

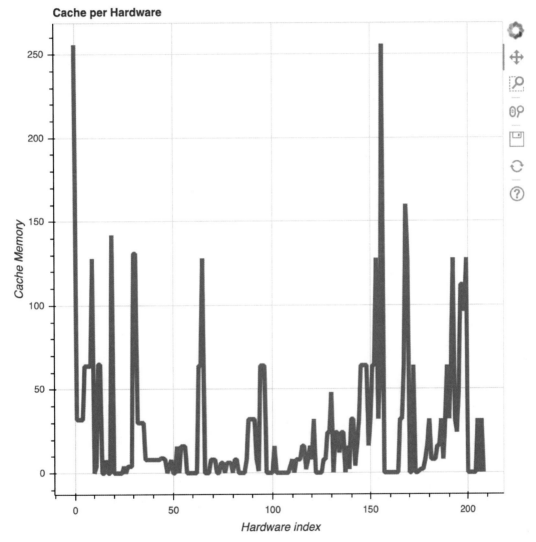

Figure 6.5: Line plot showing the cache memory of different hardware

Since the interface of different plotting types is unified, scatter plots can be created in the same way as line plots:

```
# plotting the hardware cache as dots
plot = figure(title='Cache per Hardware', \
              x_axis_label='Hardware', \
              y_axis_label='Cache Memory')
plot.scatter(dataset['index'], dataset['cach'], size=5, color='red')
show(plot)
```

The following figure shows the output of the preceding code:

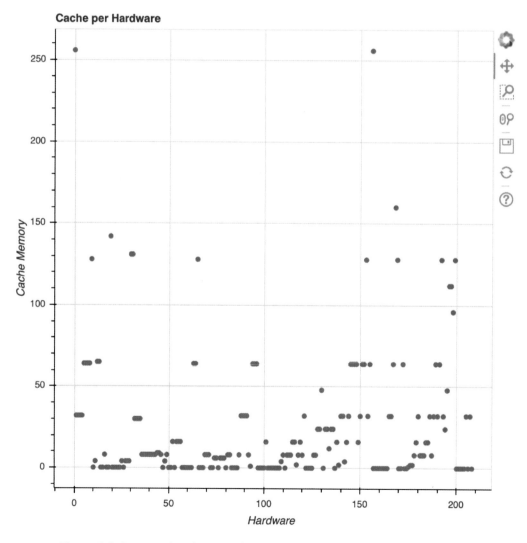

Figure 6.6: Scatter plot showing the cache memory of different hardware

In many cases, a visualization will have several attributes of a dataset plotted. A legend will help users understand which attributes they are looking at. Legends display a mapping between, for example, lines in the plot and according to information such as the hardware cache memory.

By adding a **legend_label** argument to the plot calls like **plot.line()**, we get a small box containing the information in the top-right corner (by default):

```
# plotting cache memory and cycle time with legend
plot = figure(title='Attributes per Hardware', \
              x_axis_label='Hardware index', \
              y_axis_label='Attribute Value')
plot.line(dataset['index'], dataset['cach'], \
          line_width=5, legend_label='Cache Memory')
plot.line(dataset['index'], dataset['myct'], line_width=5, \
          color='red', legend_label='Cycle time in ns')

show(plot)
```

The following figure shows the output of the preceding code:

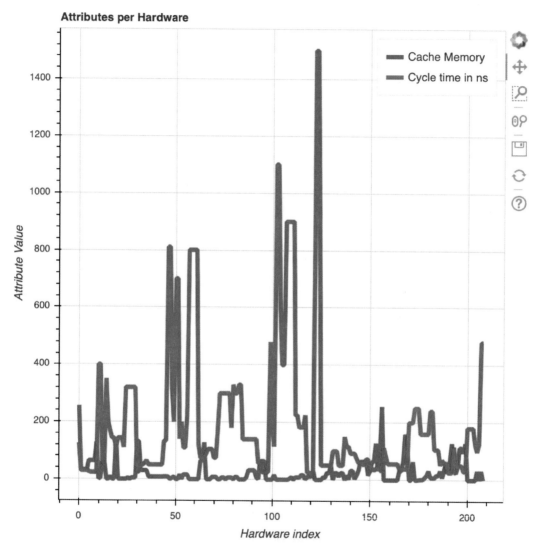

Figure 6.7: Line plots displaying the cache memory and cycle time per hardware with the legend

When looking at the preceding example, we can see that once we have several lines, the visualization can get cluttered.

We can give the user the ability to **mute**, meaning defocus, the clicked element in the legend.

Adding a **muted_alpha** argument to the line plotting and adding a **click_policy** of **mute** to our legend element are the only two steps needed:

```
# adding mutability to the legend
plot = figure(title='Attributes per Hardware', \
              x_axis_label='Hardware index', \
              y_axis_label='Attribute Value')
plot.line(dataset['index'], dataset['cach'], line_width=5, \
          legend_label='Cache Memory', muted_alpha=0.2)
plot.line(dataset['index'], dataset['myct'], line_width=5, \
          color='red', legend_label='Cycle time in ns', \
          muted_alpha=0.2)

plot.legend.click_policy="mute"

show(plot)
```

The following figure shows the output of the preceding code:

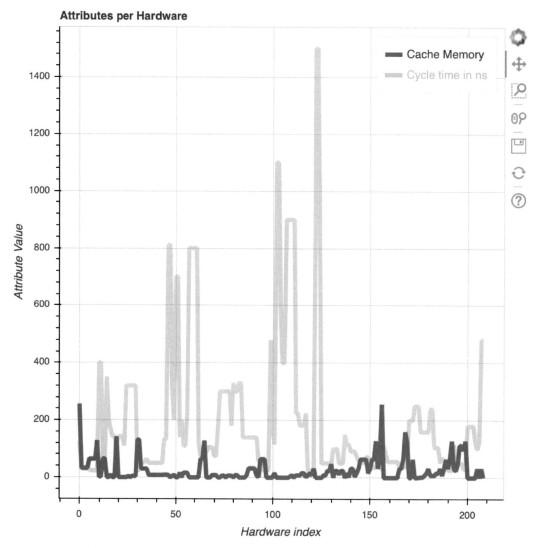

Figure 6.8: Line plots displaying the cache memory and cycle time per hardware with a mutable legend; cycle time is also muted

Next, we will do an exercise to plot the graph using Bokeh.

> **NOTE**
>
> All the exercises and activities in this chapter are developed using Jupyter Notebook. The files can be downloaded from the following link: https://packt.live/39txwH5. All the datasets used in this chapter can be found at https://packt.live/3bzApYN.

EXERCISE 6.01: PLOTTING WITH BOKEH

In this exercise, we want to use **bokeh.plotting** interface, which is focused on providing a simple interface for quick visualization creation. We will use **world_population** dataset. This dataset shows the population of different countries over the years. Follow these steps:

1. Create an **Exercise6.01.ipynb** Jupyter notebook within the **Chapter06/Exercise6.01** folder.

2. Import the figure (which will initialize a plot) and the **show** method (which displays the plot) from plotting our library:

```
import pandas as pd
from bokeh.plotting import figure, show
```

3. Import and call the **output_notebook** method from the **io** interface of Bokeh to display the plots inside a Jupyter Notebook:

```
from bokeh.io import output_notebook
output_notebook()
```

4. Use pandas to load the **world_population** dataset:

```
dataset = pd.read_csv('../../Datasets/world_population.csv', \
                      index_col=0)
```

5. Verify that our data has been successfully loaded by calling **head** on our DataFrame:

```
dataset.head()
```

The following figure shows the output:

Country Name	Country Code	Indicator Name	Indicator Code	1960	1961	1962	1963	1964	1965
Aruba	ABW	Population density (people per sq. km of land ...	EN.POP.DNST	NaN	307.972222	312.366667	314.983333	316.827778	318.666667
Andorra	AND	Population density (people per sq. km of land ...	EN.POP.DNST	NaN	30.587234	32.714894	34.914894	37.170213	39.470213
Afghanistan	AFG	Population density (people per sq. km of land ...	EN.POP.DNST	NaN	14.038148	14.312061	14.599692	14.901579	15.218206
Angola	AGO	Population density (people per sq. km of land ...	EN.POP.DNST	NaN	4.305195	4.384299	4.464433	4.544558	4.624228
Albania	ALB	Population density (people per sq. km of land ...	EN.POP.DNST	NaN	60.576642	62.456898	64.329234	66.209307	68.058066

Figure 6.9: Loading the top five rows of the world_population dataset using the head method

6. Populate our x-axis and y-axis with some data extraction. The x-axis will hold all the years that are present in our columns. The y-axis will hold the population density values of the countries. Start with Germany:

```
# preparing our data for Germany
years = [year for year in dataset.columns if not year[0].isalpha()]
de_vals = [dataset.loc[['Germany']][year] for year in years]
```

7. After extracting the necessary data, create a new plot by calling the Bokeh **figure** method. Provide parameters such as **title**, **x_axis_label**, and **y_axis_label** to define the descriptions displayed on our plot. Once our plot is created, we can add glyphs to it. Here, we will use a simple line. Set the **legend_label** parameter next to the x and y values to get an informative legend in our visualization:

```
"""
plotting the population density change in Germany in the given years
"""
plot = figure(title='Population Density of Germany', \
              x_axis_label='Year', \
              y_axis_label='Population Density')
plot.line(years, de_vals, line_width=2, legend_label='Germany')
show(plot)
```

The following figure shows the output of the preceding code:

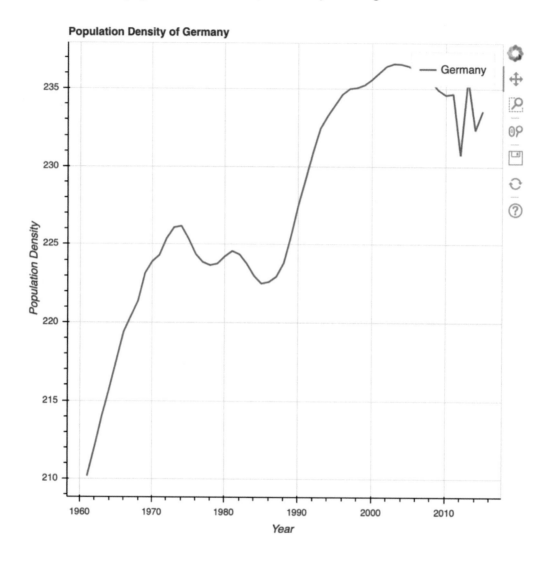

Figure 6.10: Creating a line plot from the population density data of Germany

8. Now add another country—in this case, **Switzerland**. Use the same technique that we used with **Germany** to extract the data for **Switzerland**:

```
# preparing the data for the second country
ch_vals = [dataset.loc[['Switzerland']][year] for year in years]
```

9. We can add several layers of glyphs on to our figure plot. We can also stack different glyphs on top of one another, thus giving specific and data-improved visuals. Add an orange line to the plot that displays the data from **Switzerland**. Also, plot orange circles for each data point of the **ch_vals** list and assign it the same **legend_label** to combine both representations, the line, and circles:

```
"""
plotting the data for Germany and Switzerland in one visualization,
adding circles for each data point for Switzerland
"""
plot = \
figure(title='Population Density of Germany and Switzerland', \
       x_axis_label='Year', y_axis_label='Population Density')
plot.line(years, de_vals, line_width=2, legend_label='Germany')
plot.line(years, ch_vals, line_width=2, color='orange', legend_
label='Switzerland')
plot.circle(years, ch_vals, size=4, line_color='orange', \
            fill_color='white', legend_label='Switzerland')
show(plot)
```

The following figure shows the output of the preceding code:

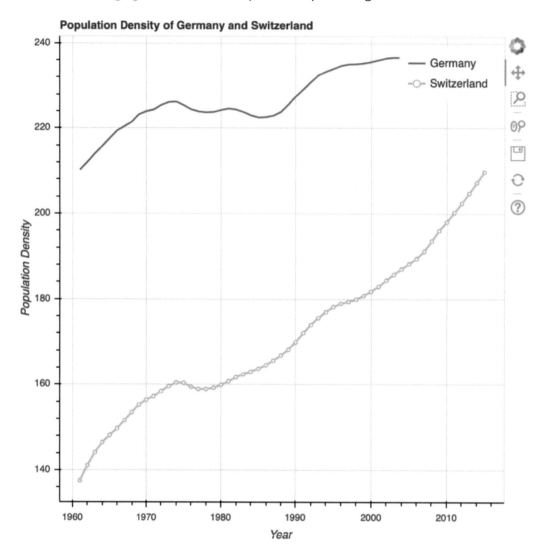

Figure 6.11: Adding Switzerland to the plot

10. When looking at a larger amount of data for different countries, it makes sense to have a plot for each of them separately. Use **gridplot layout**:

```
"""
plotting the Germany and Switzerland plot in two different
visualizations that are interconnected in terms of view port
"""
from bokeh.layouts import gridplot
plot_de = figure(title='Population Density of Germany', \
                 x_axis_label='Year', \
                 y_axis_label='Population Density', \
                 plot_height=300)

plot_ch = figure(title='Population Density of Switzerland', \
                 x_axis_label='Year', \
                 y_axis_label='Population Density', \
                 plot_height=300, x_range=plot_de.x_range, \
                 y_range=plot_de.y_range)

plot_de.line(years, de_vals, line_width=2)
plot_ch.line(years, ch_vals, line_width=2)
plot = gridplot([[plot_de, plot_ch]])
show(plot)
```

The following figure shows the output of the preceding code:

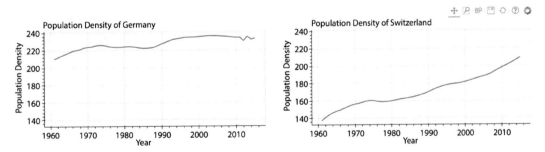

Figure 6.12: Using a gridplot to display the country plots next to each other

11. Realign the plots vertically by passing a two-dimensional array to the **gridplot** method:

```
# plotting the preceding declared figures in a vertical manner
plot_v = gridplot([[plot_de], [plot_ch]])
show(plot_v)
```

The following screenshot shows the output of the preceding code:

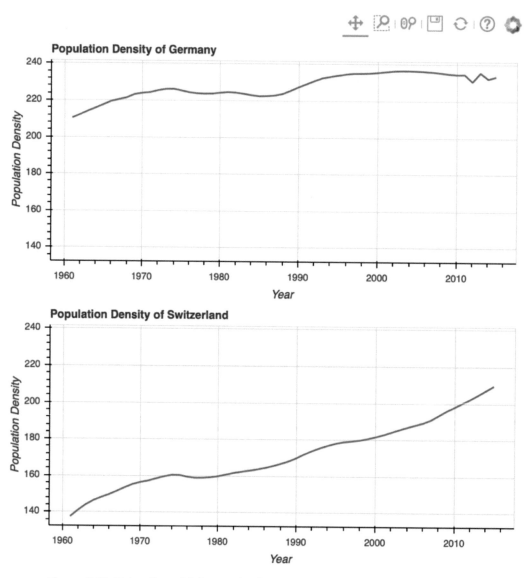

Figure 6.13: Using the gridplot method to arrange the visualizations vertically

We have now covered the very basics of Bokeh. Using the **plotting** interface makes it easy to get some quick visualizations in place. This helps you understand the data you're working with.

This simplicity is achieved by abstracting away complexity, and we lose much control by using the **plotting** interface. In the next exercise, we'll compare the **plotting** and **models** interfaces to show you how much abstraction is added to **plotting**.

Let's implement an exercise to compare the **plotting** and **models** interfaces.

EXERCISE 6.02: COMPARING THE PLOTTING AND MODELS INTERFACES

In this exercise, we want to compare the **plotting** and **models** interfaces. We will compare them by creating a basic plot with the high-level **plotting** interface and then recreate this plot by using the lower-level **models** interface. This will show us the differences between these two interfaces and set us up for the next exercises, in which we will need to understand how to use the **models** interface. Follow these steps:

1. Create an **Exercise6.02.ipynb** Jupyter Notebook within the **Chapter06/ Exercise6.02** folder to implement this exercise.

2. Import the **figure** (which will initialize a plot) and the **show** method (which displays the plot). Also, import and call the **output_notebook** method from the **io** interface of Bokeh to plot inline:

```
import numpy as np
import pandas as pd
from bokeh.io import output_notebook

output_notebook()
```

3. Use pandas to load our **world_population** dataset:

```
dataset = pd.read_csv('../../Datasets/world_population.csv', \
                      index_col=0)
```

4. Call **head** on our DataFrame to verify that our data has been successfully loaded:

```
dataset.head()
```

The following screenshot shows the output of the preceding code:

Country Name	Country Code	Indicator Name	Indicator Code	1960	1961	1962	1963	1964	1965
Aruba	ABW	Population density (people per sq. km of land ...	EN.POP.DNST	NaN	307.972222	312.366667	314.983333	316.827778	318.666667
Andorra	AND	Population density (people per sq. km of land ...	EN.POP.DNST	NaN	30.587234	32.714894	34.914894	37.170213	39.470213
Afghanistan	AFG	Population density (people per sq. km of land ...	EN.POP.DNST	NaN	14.038148	14.312061	14.599692	14.901579	15.218206
Angola	AGO	Population density (people per sq. km of land ...	EN.POP.DNST	NaN	4.305195	4.384299	4.464433	4.544558	4.624228
Albania	ALB	Population density (people per sq. km of land ...	EN.POP.DNST	NaN	60.576642	62.456898	64.329234	66.209307	68.058066

Figure 6.14: Loading the top five rows of the world_population dataset using the head method

5. Import **figure** and **show** to display our plot:

```
from bokeh.plotting import figure, show
```

6. Create three lists that have years present in the dataset, the mean population density for the whole dataset for each year, and the mean population density per year for **Japan**:

```
years = [year for year in dataset.columns if not year[0].isalpha()]
mean_pop_vals = [np.mean(dataset[year]) for year in years]
jp_vals = [dataset.loc[['Japan']][year] for year in years]
```

7. Use the plot element and apply our **glyphs** elements to it. Plot the global mean with a line and the mean of **Japan** with crosses. Set the legend location to the bottom-right corner:

```
plot = \
figure(title='Global Mean Population Density compared to Japan', \
       x_axis_label='Year', y_axis_label='Population Density')

plot.line(years, mean_pop_vals, line_width=2, \
          legend_label='Global Mean')
plot.cross(years, jp_vals, legend_label='Japan', line_color='red')

plot.legend.location = 'bottom_right'

show(plot)
```

The following screenshot shows the output of the preceding code:

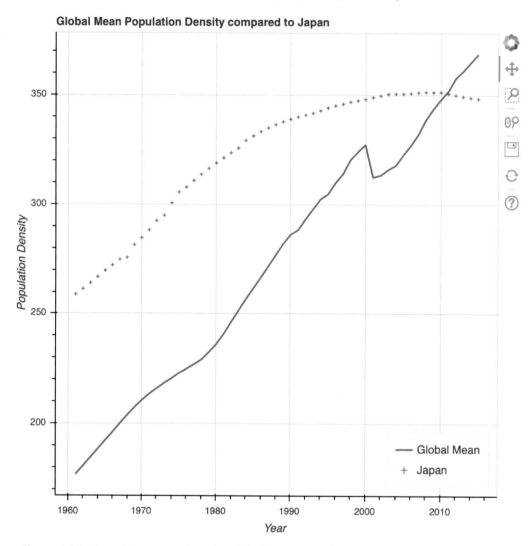

Figure 6.15: Line plots comparing the global mean population density with that of Japan

As we can see in the preceding diagram, we have many elements already in place. This means that we already have the right x-axis labels, the matching range for the y-axis, and our legend is nicely placed in the upper-right corner without much configuration.

Using the models Interface

The **models** interface is of a much lower level than other interfaces. We can already see this when looking at the list of imports we need for a comparable plot.

8. Import **Grid**, **Plot**, **LinearAxis**, **RangeId**, **Line**, **Cross**, **ColumnDataSource**, **SingleIntervalTicker**, **YearsTicker**, **the Glyphrenderer**, **Title**, **Legend**, and **LegendItem** from the submodules of the **models** interface:

```
# importing the models dependencies
from bokeh.io import show
from bokeh.models.grids import Grid
from bokeh.models.plots import Plot
from bokeh.models.axes import LinearAxis
from bokeh.models.ranges import Range1d
from bokeh.models.glyphs import Line, Cross
from bokeh.models.sources import ColumnDataSource
from bokeh.models.tickers import SingleIntervalTicker, YearsTicker
from bokeh.models.renderers import GlyphRenderer
from bokeh.models.annotations import Title, Legend, LegendItem
```

9. Before we build our plot, we have to find the **min** and **max** values for the y-axis since we don't want to have too large or too small a range of values. Get all the mean values for global and **Japan** without any invalid values. Get their smallest and largest values and pass them to the constructor of **Range1d**. For the x-axis, our list of years is pre-defined:

```
# defining the range for the x and y axis
extracted_mean_pop_vals = \
[val for i, val in enumerate(mean_pop_vals) \
 if i not in [0, len(mean_pop_vals) - 1]]

extracted_jp_vals = \
[jp_val['Japan'] for i, jp_val in enumerate(jp_vals) \
 if i not in [0, len(jp_vals) - 1]]

min_pop_density = min(extracted_mean_pop_vals)
min_jp_densitiy = min(extracted_jp_vals)
min_y = int(min(min_pop_density, min_jp_densitiy))
max_pop_density = max(extracted_mean_pop_vals)
```

```
max_jp_densitiy = max(extracted_jp_vals)
max_y = int(max(max_jp_densitiy, max_pop_density))
xdr = Range1d(int(years[0]), int(years[-1]))
ydr = Range1d(min_y, max_y)
```

10. Next, create two **Axis** objects, which will be used to display the axis lines and the label for the axis. Since we also want ticks between the different values, pass in a **Ticker** object that creates this setup:

```
axis_def = dict(axis_line_color='#222222', axis_line_width=1, \
                major_tick_line_color='#222222', \
                major_label_text_color='#222222', \
                major_tick_line_width=1)
x_axis = LinearAxis(ticker = SingleIntervalTicker(interval=10), \
                    axis_label = 'Year', **axis_def)
y_axis = LinearAxis(ticker = SingleIntervalTicker(interval=50), \
                    axis_label = 'Population Density', **axis_def)
```

11. Create the title by passing a **Title** object to the **title** attribute of the **Plot** object:

```
# creating the plot object
title = \
Title(align = 'left', \
      text = 'Global Mean Population Density compared to Japan')
plot = Plot(x_range=xdr, y_range=ydr, plot_width=650, \
            plot_height=600, title=title)
```

12. Try to display our plot now by using the **show** method. Since we have no renderers defined at the moment, we will get an error. We need to add elements to our plot:

```
"""
error will be thrown because we are missing renderers that are
created when adding elements
"""

show(plot)
```

The following screenshot shows the output of the preceding code:

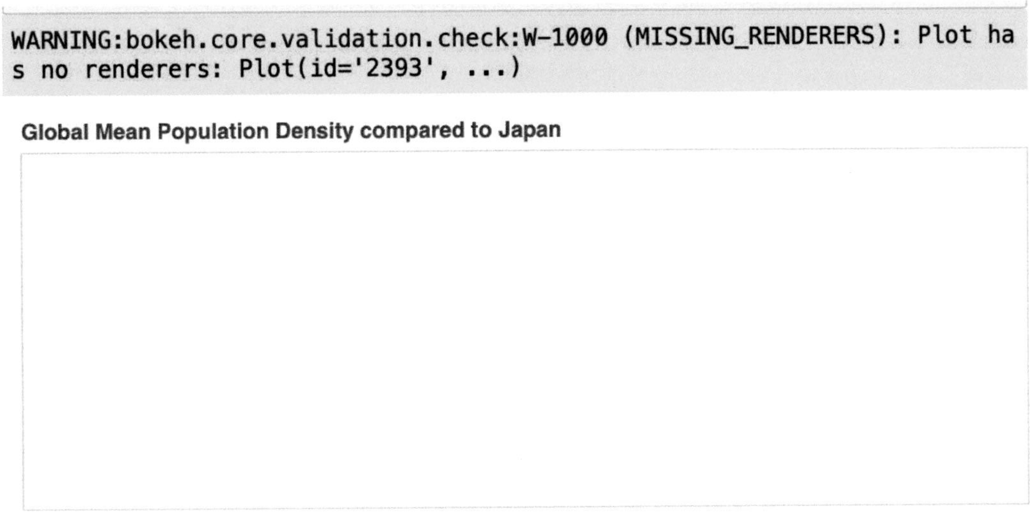

```
WARNING:bokeh.core.validation.check:W-1000 (MISSING_RENDERERS): Plot ha
s no renderers: Plot(id='2393', ...)
```

Global Mean Population Density compared to Japan

Figure 6.16: Empty plot with title

13. Insert the data into a **DataSource** object. This can then be used to map the data source to the **glyph** object that will be displayed in the plot:

```
# creating the data display
line_source = ColumnDataSource(dict(x=years, y=mean_pop_vals))
line_glyph = Line(x='x', y='y', line_color='#2678b2', \
                  line_width=2)
cross_source = ColumnDataSource(dict(x=years, y=jp_vals))
cross_glyph = Cross(x='x', y='y', line_color='#fc1d26')
```

14. Use the right **add** method to add objects to the plot. For layout elements such as the **Axis** objects, use the **add_layout** method. Glyphs, which display our data, have to be added with the **add_glyph** method:

```
plot.add_layout(x_axis, 'below')
plot.add_layout(y_axis, 'left')
line_renderer = plot.add_glyph(line_source, line_glyph)
cross_renderer = plot.add_glyph(cross_source, cross_glyph)
```

15. Show our plot again to see our lines are in place:

```
show(plot)
```

The following screenshot shows the output of the preceding code:

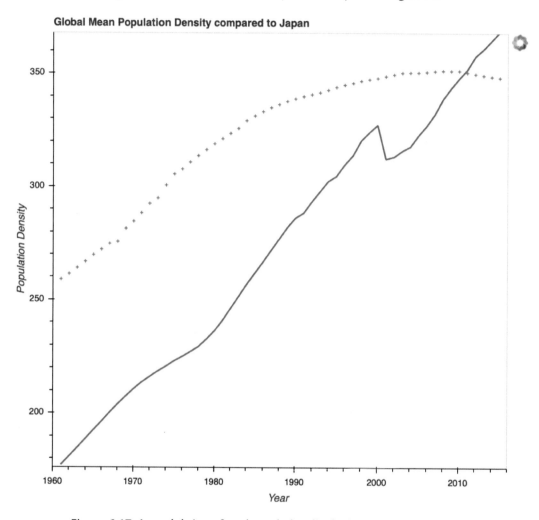

Figure 6.17: A models interface-based plot displaying the lines and axes

16. Use an object to add a legend to the plot. Each **LegendItem** object will be displayed in one line in the legend:

```
legend_items= [LegendItem(label='Global Mean', \
                          renderers=[line_renderer]), \
                LegendItem(label='Japan', \
                          renderers=[cross_renderer])]
legend = Legend(items=legend_items, location='bottom_right')
```

17. Create the grid by instantiating two **Grid** objects, one for each axis. Provide the tickers of the previously created **x** and **y** axes:

```
# creating the grid
x_grid = Grid(dimension=0, ticker=x_axis.ticker)
y_grid = Grid(dimension=1, ticker=y_axis.ticker)
```

18. Finally, use the **add_layout** method to add the grid and the legend to our plot. After this, display our complete plot, which will look like the one we created in the first task, with only four lines of code:

```
plot.add_layout(legend)
plot.add_layout(x_grid)
plot.add_layout(y_grid)
show(plot)
```

The following screenshot shows the output of the preceding code:

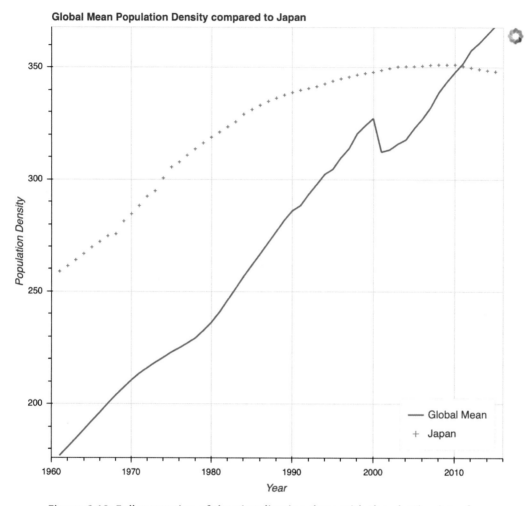

Figure 6.18: Full recreation of the visualization done with the plotting interface

As you can see, the **models** interface should not be used for simple plots. It's meant to provide the full power of Bokeh to experienced users that have specific requirements that need more than the **plotting** interface.

> **NOTE**
>
> To access the source code for this specific section, please refer to https://packt.live/3fq8plf.
>
> You can also run this example online at https://packt.live/2YHFOaD.

We have looked at the difference between the high-level **plotting** and low-level **models** interface now. This will help us understand the internal workings and potential future errors better. In this following activity, we'll use what we've already learned and created a basic visualization that plots the mean car price of each manufacturer from our dataset.

Next, we will color each data point with a color based on a given value. In Bokeh, like in geoplotlib, this can be done using **ColorMapper**.

ColorMapper can map specific values to a given color in the selected spectrum. By providing the minimum and maximum value for a variable, we define the range in which colors are returned:

```
# adding color based on the mean price to our elements
from bokeh.models import LinearColorMapper


color_mapper = LinearColorMapper(palette='Magma256', \
                                 low=min(dataset['cach']), \
                                 high=max(dataset['cach']))

plot = figure(title='Cache per Hardware', \
              x_axis_label='Hardware', \
              y_axis_label='Cache Memory')
plot.scatter(dataset['index'], dataset['cach'], \
             color={'field': 'y', 'transform': color_mapper}, \
             size=10)


show(plot)
```

The following screenshot shows the output of the preceding code:

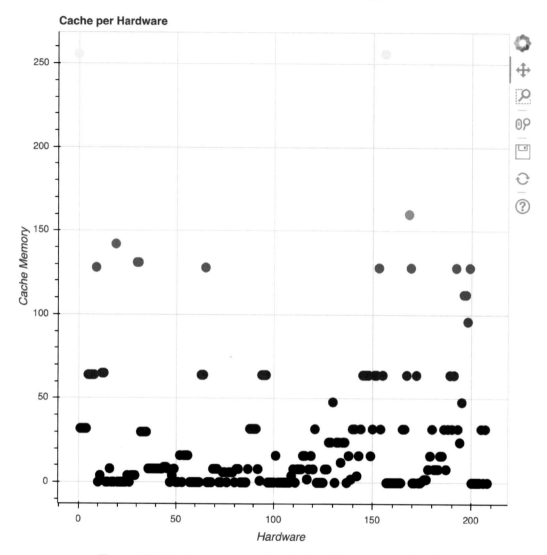

Figure 6.19: Cache memory colored using the amount of cache

Next, we will implement all the concepts related to Bokeh we have learned so far.

ACTIVITY 6.01: PLOTTING MEAN CAR PRICES OF MANUFACTURERS

This activity will combine everything that you have learned about Bokeh so far. We will use this knowledge to create a visualization that displays the mean price of each car manufacturer of our dataset.

Our automobile dataset contains the following columns:

- **make**: Manufacturer of the car

- **fuel-type**: Diesel or gas

- **num-of-doors**: Number of doors

- **body-style**: Body style of the car, for example, convertible

- **engine-location**: Front or rear

- **length**: Continuous from 141.1 to 208.1

- **width**: Continuous from 60.3 to 72.3

- **height**: Continuous from 47.8 to 59.8

- **num-of-cylinders**: Number of cylinders, for example, eight

- **horsepower**: Amount of horsepower

- **peak-rpm**: Maximum RPM

- **city-mpg**: Fuel consumption in the city

- **highway-mpg**: Fuel consumption on the highway

- **price**: Price of the car

Note that we will use only the **make** and **price** columns in our activity.

In the process, we will first plot all cars with their prices and then slowly develop a more sophisticated visualization that also uses color to visually focus the manufacturers with the highest mean prices.

1. Create an **Activity6.01.ipynb** Jupyter Notebook within the **Chapter06/Activity6.01** folder.

2. Import **pandas** with an alias and make sure to enable Notebook output using the **bokeh.io** interface.

3. Load the **automobiles.csv** dataset from the **Datasets** folder using pandas. Make sure that the dataset is loaded by displaying the first five elements of the dataset.

4. Import **figure** and **show** from Bokeh's **plotting** interface.

5. Add a new column **index** to our dataset by assigning it to the values from our **dataset.index**.

6. Create a new figure and plot each car using a scatter plot with the index and price column. Give the visualization a title of **Car prices** and name the x-axis **Car Index**. The y-axis should be named **Price**.

Grouping cars from manufacturers together

7. Group the dataset using **groupby** and the column **make**. Then use the **mean** method to get the mean value for each column. We don't want the make column to be used as an index, so provide the **as_index=False** argument to **groupby**.

8. Create a new figure with a title of **Car Manufacturer Mean Prices**, an x-axis of **Car Manufacturer**, and a y-label of **Mean Price**. In addition to that, handle the categorical data by providing the **x_range** argument to the figure with the **make** column.

9. Assign the value of **vertical** to the **xaxis.major_label_orientation** attribute of our **grouped_plot**. Call the show method again to display the visualization.

Adding color

10. Import and set up a new **LinearColorMapper** object with a palette of **Magma256**, and the min and max prices for the **low** and **high** arguments.

11. Create a new figure with the same **name**, **labels**, and **x_range** as before.

12. Plot each manufacturer and provide a **size** argument with a size of 15.

13. Provide the **color** argument to the **scatter** method and use the **field** and **transform** attributes to provide the column (y) and the **color_mapper**.

14. Set the label orientation to vertical.

The final output will look like this:

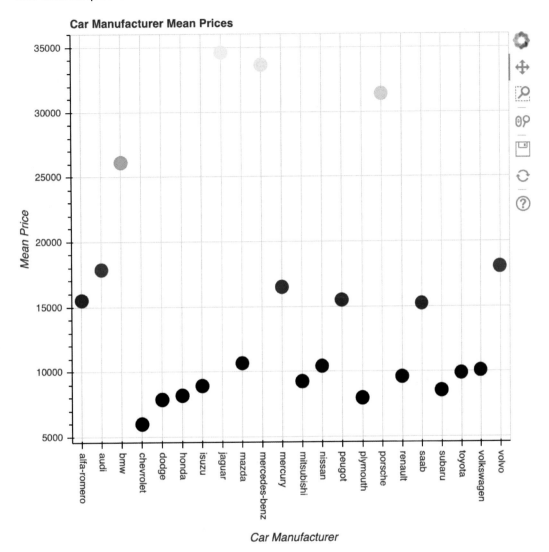

Figure 6.20: Final visualization displaying the mean car price for each manufacturer

NOTE

The solution for this activity can be found on page 456.

In the next section, we will create interactive visualizations that allow the user to modify the data that is displayed.

ADDING WIDGETS

One of the most powerful features of Bokeh is the ability to use **widgets** to interactively change the data that's displayed in a visualization. To understand the importance of interactivity in your visualizations, imagine seeing a static visualization about stock prices that only shows data for the last year.

If you're interested in seeing the current year or even visually comparing it to the recent and coming years, static plots won't be suitable. You would need to create one plot for every year or even overlay different years on one visualization, which would make it much harder to read.

Comparing this to a simple plot that lets the user select the date range they want, we can already see the advantages. You can guide the user by restricting values and only displaying what you want them to see. Developing a story behind your visualization is very important, and doing this is much easier if the user has ways of interacting with the data.

Bokeh widgets work best when used in combination with the Bokeh server. However, using the Bokeh server approach is beyond the content of this book, since we would need to work with simple Python files. Instead, we will use a hybrid approach that only works with the Jupyter Notebook.

We will look at the different widgets and how to use them before going in and building a basic plot with one of them. There are a few different options regarding how to trigger updates, which are also explained in this section. The widgets that will be covered in the following exercise are explained in the following table:

Value	Widget	Example
Boolean	Checkbox	False
String	Text	'Input Text'
Int value, Int range	IntSlider	5, (0, 100), (0, 10, 1)
Float value, Float range	FloatSlider	1.0, (0.0, 100.0), (0.0, 10.0, 0.5)
List or Dict	Dropdown	['Option1', 'Option2'], {'one':1,'two':2}

Figure 6.21: Some of the basic widgets with examples

The general way to create a new widget visible in a Jupyter Notebook is to define a new method and wrap it into an **interact** widget. We'll be using the "syntactic sugar" way of adding a decorator to a method—that is, by using annotations. This will give us an interactive element that will be displayed after the executable cell, like in the following example:

```
# importing the widgets
from ipywidgets import interact, interact_manual

# creating an input text
@interact(Value='Input Text')
def text_input(Value):
    print(Value)
```

The following screenshot shows the output of the preceding code:

| Value | Input Text |

Input Text

Figure 6.22: Interactive text input

In the preceding example, we first import the interact element from the **ipywidgets** library. This then allows us to define a new method and annotate it with the **@interact** decorator.

The **Value** attribute tells the interact element which widget to use based on the data type of the argument. In our example, we provide a string, which will give us a **TextBox** widget. We can refer to the preceding table to determine which **Value** data type will return which widget.

The print statement in the preceding code prints whatever has been entered in the textbox below the widget.

> **NOTE**
>
> The methods that we can use interact with always have the same structure. We will look at several examples in the following exercise.

EXERCISE 6.03: BUILDING A SIMPLE PLOT USING BASIC INTERACTIVITY WIDGETS

This first exercise of the *Adding Widgets* topic will give you a gentle introduction to the different widgets and the general concept of how to use them. We will quickly go over the most common widgets, sliders, checkboxes, and dropdowns to understand their structure.

1. Create an **Exercise6.03.ipynb** Jupyter Notebook within the **Chapter06/Exercise6.03** folder to implement this exercise.

2. Import and call the **output_notebook** method from Bokeh's **io** interface to display the plots inside Jupyter Notebook:

```
# make bokeh display figures inside the notebook
from bokeh.io import output_notebook
output_notebook()
```

Looking at Basic Widgets

3. In this first task, we will add interactive widgets to the interactive element of IPython. Import the necessary **interact** and **interact_manual** elements from **ipywidgets**:

```
# importing the widgets
from ipywidgets import interact, interact_manual
```

4. Create a checkbox widget and print out the result of the interactive element:

```
@interact(Value=False)
def checkbox(Value=False):
    print(Value)
```

The following screenshot shows the output of the preceding code:

Value

False

Figure 6.23: Interactive checkbox that will switch from False to True if checked

> **NOTE**
>
> **@interact()** is called a **decorator**. It wraps the annotated method into the interact component. This allows us to display and react to the change of the drop-down menu. The method will be executed every time the value of the dropdown changes.

5. Create a dropdown using a list of options, **['Option1', 'Option2', 'Option3', 'Option4'] as the @interact decorator value**:

```
# creating a dropdown
options=['Option1', 'Option2', 'Option3', 'Option4']

@interact(Value=options)
def dropdown(Value=options[0]):
    print(Value)
```

The following screenshot shows the output of the preceding code:

Option1

Figure 6.24: Interactive dropdown

6. Create a text input using a value of **'Input Text'** as the **@interact** decorator value:

```
# creating an input text
@interact(Value='Input Text')
def text_input(Value):
    print(Value)
```

The following screenshot shows the output of the preceding code:

Value | Input Text

Input Text

Figure 6.25: Interactive text input

7. Create two widgets, a dropdown and a checkbox with the same value, as in the last two tasks:

```
# multiple widgets with default layout
options=['Option1', 'Option2', 'Option3', 'Option4']


@interact(Select=options, Display=False)
def uif(Select, Display):
    print(Select, Display)
```

The following screenshot shows the output of the preceding code:

Select   Option1   ⌄

☐ Display

```
Option1 False
```

Figure 6.26: Two widgets are displayed vertically by default

8. Create an **int** slider using a range value of **(0,100)** as the **@interact** decorator value:

```
# creating an int slider with dynamic updates
@interact(Value=(0, 100))
def slider(Value=0):
    print(Value)
```

The following screenshot shows the output of the preceding code:

Value ⚪━━━━━━━━━   0

0

Figure 6.27: Interactive int slider

9. Create an int slider using values of 0 and 100 as the @**interact** decorator min and max values. Set **continuous_update** to false to only trigger an update on mouse release:

```
# creating an int slider that only triggers on mouse release
from ipywidgets import IntSlider
slider=IntSlider(min=0, max=100, continuous_update=False)

@interact(Value=slider)
def slider(Value=0.0):
    print(Value)
```

The following screenshot shows the output of the preceding code:

0

Figure 6.28: Interactive int slider that only triggers upon mouse release

> **NOTE**
>
> Although the outputs of *Figure 6.27* and *Figure 6.28* look the same, in *Figure 6.28*, the slider triggers only upon mouse release.

10. Use the @**interact_manual** decorator, which adds an execution button to the output that triggers a manual update of the plot. Create an int slider using a range value of **(0.0,100.0,0.5)** as the decorator value to set a step size of **0.5**:

```
# creating a float slider 0.5 steps with manual update trigger
@interact_manual(Value=(0.0, 100.0, 0.5))
def slider(Value=0.0):
    print(Value)
```

The following screenshot shows the output of the preceding code:

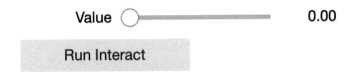

Figure 6.29: Interactive int slider with a manual update trigger

---

NOTE

Compared to the previous cells, this one contains the `interact_manual` decorator instead of interact. This will add an execution button that will trigger the update of the value instead of triggering with every change. This can be really useful when working with larger datasets, where the recalculation time would be large. Because of this, you don't want to trigger the execution for every small step, but only once you have selected the correct value.

NOTE

To access the source code for this specific section, please refer to https://packt.live/3e8G60B.

You can also run this example online at https://packt.live/37ANwXT.

After looking at several example widgets and how to create and use them in the previous exercise, we will now use a real-world **stock_price** dataset to create a basic plot and add simple interactive widgets.

EXERCISE 6.04: PLOTTING STOCK PRICE DATA IN TABS

In this exercise, we will revisit the essential widgets and build a simple plot that will display the first 25 data points for the selected stock. We will display the stocks that can be changed with a drop-down menu.

The dataset of this exercise is a **stock_prices** dataset. This means that we will be looking at data over a range of time. As this is a large and variable dataset, it will be easier to show and explain widgets such as slider and dropdown on it. The dataset is available in the **Datasets** folder of the GitHub repository; here is the link to it: https://packt.live/3bzApYN. Follow these steps:

1. Create an **Exercise6.04.ipynb** Jupyter Notebook in the **Chapter06/Exercise6.04** folder to implement this exercise.

2. Import the **pandas** library:

```
import pandas as pd
```

3. Import and call the **output_notebook** method from Bokeh's **io** interface to display the plots inside Jupyter Notebook:

```
from bokeh.io import output_notebook
output_notebook()
```

4. After downloading the dataset and moving it into the **Datasets** folder of this chapter, import our **stock_prices.csv** data:

```
dataset = pd.read_csv('../../Datasets/stock_prices.csv')
```

5. Test whether the data has been loaded successfully by executing the **head** method on the dataset:

```
dataset.head()
```

The following screenshot shows the output of the preceding code:

	date	symbol	open	close	low	high	volume
0	2016-01-05 00:00:00	WLTW	123.430000	125.839996	122.309998	126.250000	2163600.0
1	2016-01-06 00:00:00	WLTW	125.239998	119.980003	119.940002	125.540001	2386400.0
2	2016-01-07 00:00:00	WLTW	116.379997	114.949997	114.930000	119.739998	2489500.0
3	2016-01-08 00:00:00	WLTW	115.480003	116.620003	113.500000	117.440002	2006300.0
4	2016-01-11 00:00:00	WLTW	117.010002	114.970001	114.089996	117.330002	1408600.0

Figure 6.30: Loading the top five rows of the stock_prices dataset using the head method

Since the date column has no information about the hour, minute, and second, we want to avoid displaying them in the visualization later on and display the year, month, and day.

6. Create a new column that holds the formatted short version of the date value. Print out the first five rows of the dataset to see the new column, **short_date**:

```
# mapping the date of each row to only the year-month-day format
from datetime import datetime
def shorten_time_stamp(timestamp):
    shortened = timestamp[0]
    if len(shortened) > 10:
        parsed_date=datetime.strptime(shortened, \
                             '%Y-%m-%d %H:%M:%S')
        shortened=datetime.strftime(parsed_date, '%Y-%m-%d')
    return shortened
dataset['short_date'] = \
dataset.apply(lambda x: shorten_time_stamp(x), axis=1)

dataset.head()
```

The following screenshot shows the output of the preceding code:

	date	symbol	open	close	low	high	volume	short_date
0	2016-01-05 00:00:00	WLTW	123.430000	125.839996	122.309998	126.250000	2163600.0	2016-01-05
1	2016-01-06 00:00:00	WLTW	125.239998	119.980003	119.940002	125.540001	2386400.0	2016-01-06
2	2016-01-07 00:00:00	WLTW	116.379997	114.949997	114.930000	119.739998	2489500.0	2016-01-07
3	2016-01-08 00:00:00	WLTW	115.480003	116.620003	113.500000	117.440002	2006300.0	2016-01-08
4	2016-01-11 00:00:00	WLTW	117.010002	114.970001	114.089996	117.330002	1408600.0	2016-01-11

Figure 6.31: Dataset with the added short_date column

> **NOTE**
>
> The execution of the cell will take a moment since it's a fairly large dataset. Please be patient.

Creating a Basic Plot and Adding a Widget

In this task, we will create a basic visualization with the stock price dataset. This will be your first interactive visualization in which you can dynamically change the stock that is displayed in the graph. We will get used to one of the aforementioned interactive widgets: the drop-down menu. It will be the main point of interaction for our visualization.

7. Import the already-familiar figure and show methods from the **plotting** interface. Since we also want to have a panel with two tabs displaying different plot styles, also import the **Panel** and **Tabs** classes from the **models** interface:

```
from ipywidgets import interact
from bokeh.models.widgets import Panel, Tabs
from bokeh.plotting import figure, show
```

To better structure, our notebook, write an adaptable method that gets a subsection of stock data as an argument and builds a two-tab **Pane** object that lets us switch between the two views in our visualization.

8. Create two tabs. The first tab will contain a line plot of the given data, while the second will contain a circle-based representation of the same data. Create a legend that will display the name of the currently viewed stock:

```
# method to build the tab-based plot
def get_plot(stock):
    stock_name=stock['symbol'].unique()[0]

    line_plot=figure(title='Stock prices', \
                    x_axis_label='Date', \
                    x_range=stock['short_date'], \
                    y_axis_label='Price in $USD')
    line_plot.line(stock['short_date'], stock['high'], \
                legend_label=stock_name)
    line_plot.xaxis.major_label_orientation = 1

    circle_plot=figure(title='Stock prices', \
                    x_axis_label='Date', \
                    x_range=stock['short_date'], \
                    y_axis_label='Price in $USD')
    circle_plot.circle(stock['short_date'], stock['high'], \
                legend_label=stock_name)
    circle_plot.xaxis.major_label_orientation = 1

    line_tab=Panel(child=line_plot, title='Line')
    circle_tab=Panel(child=circle_plot, title='Circles')
    tabs = Tabs(tabs=[ line_tab, circle_tab ])

    return tabs
```

9. Get a list of all the stock names in our dataset by using the **unique** method for our symbol column:

```
# extracting all the stock names
stock_names=dataset['symbol'].unique()
```

Once we have done this, use this list as an input for the interact element.

10. Add the drop-down widget in the decorator and call the method that returns our visualization in the show method with the selected stock. Only provide the first 25 entries of each stock. By default, the stock of Apple should be displayed; its symbol in the dataset is **AAPL**. This will give us a visualization that is displayed in a pane with two tabs. The first tab will display an interpolated line, and the second tab will display the values as circles:

```
# creating the dropdown interaction and building the plot
@interact(Stock=stock_names)
def get_stock_for(Stock='AAPL'):
    stock = dataset[dataset['symbol'] == Stock][:25]
    show(get_plot(stock))
```

The following screenshot shows the output of the preceding code:

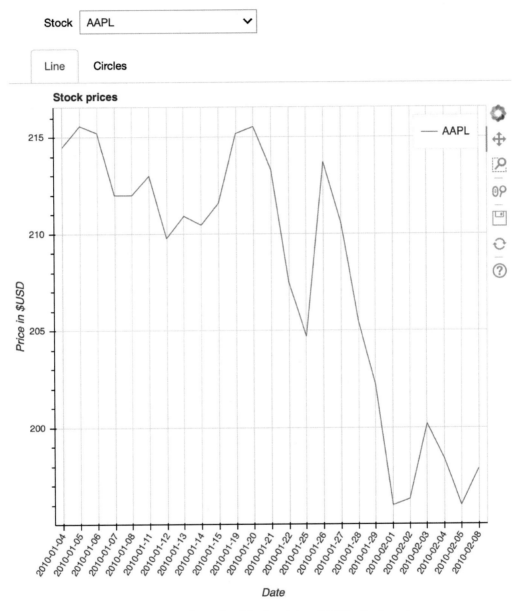

Figure 6.32: Line tab with the data of AAPL displayed

The following screenshot shows the output of the code in step 11:

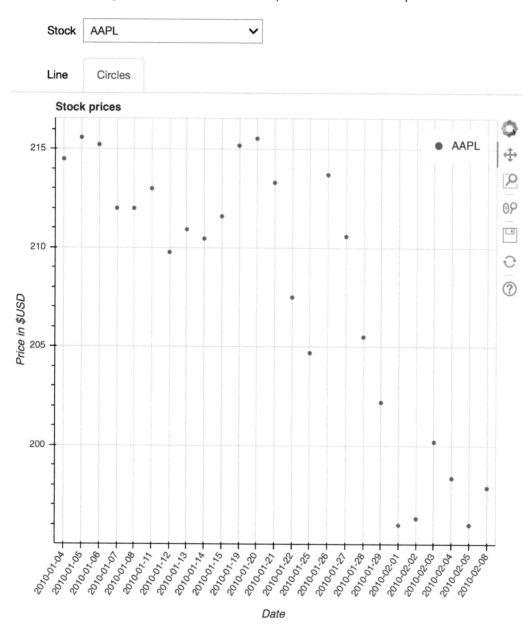

Figure 6.33: Circle tab with the data of AAPL displayed

> **NOTE**
>
> We can already see that each date is displayed on the x-axis. If we want to display a bigger time range, we have to customize the ticks on our x-axis. This can be done using ticker objects.

> **NOTE**
>
> To access the source code for this specific section, please refer to https://packt.live/3fnfPvl.
>
> You can also run this example online at https://packt.live/3d7RqsH.

We have now covered the very basics of widgets and how to use them in a Jupyter Notebook.

> **NOTE**
>
> If you want to learn more about using widgets and which widgets can be used in Jupyter, visit https://ipywidgets.readthedocs.io/en/latest/examples/Using%20Interact.html and https://ipywidgets.readthedocs.io/en/stable/examples/Widget%20List.html.

In the following activity, we will make use of the Bokeh **DataSource** to add a tooltip overlay to our plot that is displayed upon hovering over the data points. **DataSource** can be helpful in several cases, for example, displaying a tooltip on hovering the data points. In most cases, we can use pandas DataFrames to feed data into our plot, but for certain features, such as tooltips, we have to use **DataSource**:

```python
# using a ColumnDataSource to display a tooltip on hovering
from bokeh.models.sources import ColumnDataSource

data_source = \
ColumnDataSource(data=dict(vendor_name=dataset['vendor_name'], \
                           model=dataset['model'], \
                           cach=dataset['cach'], \
                           x=dataset['index'], \
                           y=dataset['cach']))

TOOLTIPS=[('Vendor', '@vendor_name'), ('Model', '@model'), \
          ('Cache', '@cach')]

plot = figure(title='Cache per Hardware', \
              x_axis_label='Hardware', \
              y_axis_label='Cache Memory', tooltips=TOOLTIPS)
plot.scatter('x', 'y', size=10, color='teal', source=data_source)

show(plot)
```

The following screenshot shows the output of the preceding code:

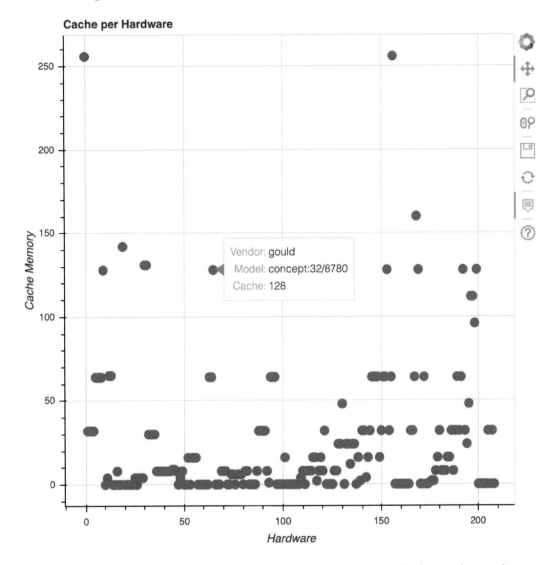

Figure 6.34: Cache memory plotted as dots with tooltip overlay displaying the vendor, model, and amount of memory

In the next activity, we will learn to extend plots using widgets.

ACTIVITY 6.02: EXTENDING PLOTS WITH WIDGETS

In this activity, you will combine what you have already learned about Bokeh. You will also need the skills you have acquired while working with pandas for additional DataFrame handling. We will create an interactive visualization that lets us explore the results of the 2016 Rio Olympics.

Our dataset contains the following columns:

- **id**: Unique ID of the athlete
- **name**: Name of the athlete
- **nationality**: Nationality of the athlete
- **sex**: Male or female
- **dob**: Date of birth of the athlete
- **height**: Height of the athlete
- **weight**: Weight of the athlete
- **sport**: Category the athlete is competing in
- **gold**: Number of gold medals the athlete won
- **silver**: Number of silver medals the athlete won
- **bronze**: Number of bronze medals the athlete won

We want to use the **nationality**, **gold**, **silver**, and **bronze** columns to create a custom visualization that lets us dig through the Olympians.

Our visualization will display each country that participated in a coordinate system where the x-axis represents the number of medals won and the y-axis represents the number of athletes. Using interactive widgets, we will be able to filter the displayed countries by both the maximum number of medals won and the maximum amount of athletes axes.

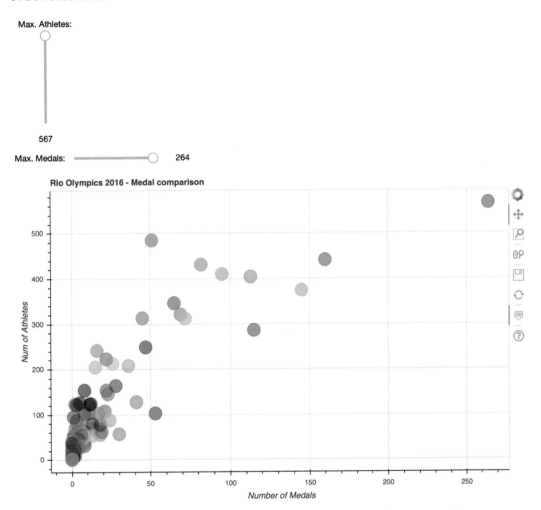

Figure 6.35: Final interactive visualization that displays the scatter plot

There are many options when it comes to choosing which interactivity to use. We will focus on only two widgets to make it easier for you to understand the concepts. In the end, we will have a visualization that allows us to filter countries for the number of medals and athletes they placed in the Olympics and upon hovering over the single data points, receive more information about each country:

1. Create an **Activity6.02.ipynb** Jupyter Notebook within the **Chapter06/ Activity6.02** folder.

2. Enable notebook output using the **bokeh.io** interface. Import pandas and load the dataset and make sure that the dataset is loaded by displaying the first five elements of the dataset.

3. Import **figure** and **show** from Bokeh and **interact** and **widgets** from **ipywidgets** to get started.

4. Load our **olympia2016_athletes.csv** dataset from the **Datasets** folder and set up the interaction elements. Scroll down until you reach the cell that says **getting the max number of medals and athletes of all countries**. Extract the two numbers from the dataset.

5. Create widgets for **IntSlider** for the maximum number of athletes (orientation vertical) and **IntSlider** for the maximum number of medals (orientation horizontal).

6. Set up the **@interact** method, which will display the complete visualization. The only code we will write here is to **show** the return value of the **get_plot** method that gets all the interaction element values as parameters.

7. Implement the decorator method, move up in the Notebook, and work on the **get_plot** method.

8. First, filter our countries dataset that contains all the countries that placed athletes in the Olympic games. Check whether they have a lower or equal number of medals and athletes than our max values passed as arguments.

9. Create our **DataSource** and use it for the tooltips and the printing of the circle glyphs.

10. After that, create a new plot using the figure method that has the following attributes: title set to **Rio Olympics 2016 - Medal comparison**, **x_ axis_label** set to **Number of Medals**, and **y_axis_label** set to **Num of Athletes**.

11. Execute every cell starting from the **get_plot** cell to the bottom—again, making sure that all implementations are captured.

12. When executing the cell that contains the **@interact** decorator, you will see a scatter plot that displays a circle for every country displaying additional information, such as the **shortcode** of the country, the number of athletes, and the number of gold, silver, and bronze medals.

> **NOTE**
>
> The solution for this activity can be found on page 465.

As we mentioned before, when working with interactive features and Bokeh, you might want to read up about the Bokeh server a little bit more. It will give you more options to express your creativity by creating animated plots and visualizations that can be explored by several people at the same time.

SUMMARY

In this chapter, we have looked at another option for creating visualizations with a whole new focus: web-based Bokeh plots. We also discovered ways in which we can make our visualizations more interactive and give the user the chance to explore data in a different way.

As we mentioned in the first part of this chapter, Bokeh is a comparably new tool that empowers developers to use their favorite language to create easily portable visualizations for the web. After working with Matplotlib, Seaborn, geoplotlib, and Bokeh, we can see some standard interfaces and similar ways to work with those libraries. After studying the tools that are covered in this book, it will be simple to understand new plotting tools.

In the next and final chapter, we will introduce a new real-life dataset to create visualizations. This last chapter will allow you to consolidate the concepts and tools that you have learned about in this book and further enhance your skills.

7

COMBINING WHAT WE HAVE LEARNED

OVERVIEW

In this chapter, we will apply all the concepts that we have learned in all the previous chapters. We will use three new datasets in combination with practical activities for Matplotlib, Seaborn, geoplotlib, and Bokeh. By the end of this chapter, you will be able to apply your skills in Matplotlib and Seaborn. We will create a time series with Bokeh, and finally, we will analyze geospatial data with geoplotlib. We will conclude this chapter with a summary that recaps what we've learned throughout the book.

INTRODUCTION

In recent chapters, we've learned about some of the most widely used and state-of-the-art visualization libraries for Python. In the previous chapter, we advanced from simple static plots to building interactive visualizations using Bokeh, which allowed us to gain control over what is displayed to the users.

To consolidate what we have learned, we will provide you with three sophisticated activities. Each activity uses one of the libraries that we have covered in this book. Each activity has a more extensive dataset than we have used before, which will prepare you to work with real-world examples.

In the first activity, we will consolidate the acquired knowledge in Matplotlib and Seaborn. For a quick recap, Matplotlib allows the generation of various plot types with just a few lines of code. Seaborn is based on Matplotlib and provides a high-level interface for creating visually appealing charts. It dramatically extends Matplotlib with predefined visualization styles and color palettes.

> **NOTE**
>
> All activities will be developed in the Jupyter Notebook or Jupyter Lab. Please download the GitHub repository with all the prepared templates and datasets from https://packt.live/2tSthph.

ACTIVITY 7.01: IMPLEMENTING MATPLOTLIB AND SEABORN ON THE NEW YORK CITY DATABASE

In this activity, we will visualize data pertaining to New York City (NYC) and compare it to the state of New York and the United States (US), including visualizing the median household income, plotting the average wage by gender and for different job categories, visualizing the wage distribution, and much more. The goal of this activity is to combine everything you've learned about Matplotlib and Seaborn to create self-explanatory, nice-looking plots.

The American Community Survey (ACS) Public-Use Microdata Samples (PUMS) dataset (one-year estimate from 2017) from https://www.census.gov/programs-surveys/acs/technical-documentation/pums/documentation.2017.html is used.

Download the following datasets and place the extracted CSV file in the **Datasets** subdirectory: https://www2.census.gov/programs-surveys/acs/data/pums/2017/1-Year/csv_pny.zip and https://www2.census.gov/programs-surveys/acs/data/pums/2017/1-Year/csv_hny.zip.

In this activity, the New York Population Records (**../../Datasets/acs2017/pny.csv**) and New York Housing Unit Records (**../../Datasets/acs2017/hny.csv**) datasets are used. The first dataset contains information about the New York population, and the second dataset contains information about housing units. The dataset contains data for about 1% of the population and housing units. Due to the extensive amount of data, we do not provide the datasets for the whole of the US; instead, we will provide the required information related to the US, if necessary. The **PUMS_Data_Dictionary_2017.pdf** PDF gives an overview and description of all variables. A further description of the codes can be found in **ACSPUMS2017CodeLists.xls**:

1. Create an **Activity7.01.ipynb** Jupyter Notebook in the **Chapter07/Activity7.01** folder to implement this activity. Import all the necessary libraries.

2. Use pandas to read both CSV files located in the **Datasets** folder.

3. Use the given PUMA (public use microdata area code based on the 2010 census definition, which are areas with populations of 100k or more) ranges to further divide the dataset into NYC districts (Bronx, Manhattan, Staten Island, Brooklyn, and Queens):

```
# PUMA ranges
bronx = [3701, 3710]
manhatten = [3801, 3810]
staten_island = [3901, 3903]
brooklyn = [4001, 4018]
queens = [4101, 4114]
nyc = [bronx[0], queens[1]]
```

4. In the dataset, each sample has a certain **weight** that reflects the **weight** for the total dataset. Therefore, we cannot simply calculate the median. Use the given **weighted_median** function in the following code to compute the median:

```python
# Function for a 'weighted' median
def weighted_frequency(values, weights):
    weighted_values = []
    for value, weight in zip(values, weights):
        weighted_values.extend(np.repeat(value, weight))
    return weighted_values
def weighted_median(values, weights):
    return np.median(weighted_frequency(values, weights))
```

5. In this subtask, we will create a plot containing multiple subplots that visualize information with regard to NYC wages. Before we create the plots, some data wrangling is necessary.

6. Compute the average wage by gender for the given occupation categories for the population of NYC:

```python
occ_categories = ['Management,\nBusiness,\nScience,\nand Arts'\
                  '\nOccupations', 'Service\nOccupations', \
                  'Sales and\nOffice\nOccupations', \
                  'Natural Resources,\nConstruction,\nand '\
                  'Maintenance\nOccupations', \
                  'Production,\nTransportation,\nand Material '\
                  'Moving\nOccupations']

occ_ranges = {'Management, Business, Science, and Arts Occupations': \
              [10, 3540], 'Service Occupations': [3600, 4650], \
              'Sales and Office Occupations': [4700, 5940], \
              'Natural Resources, Construction, and Maintenance '\
              'Occupations': [6000, 7630], \
              'Production, Transportation, and Material Moving '\
              'Occupations': [7700, 9750]}
```

7. Compute the wage frequencies for New York and NYC. Use the following yearly wage intervals: 10k steps between 0 and 100k, 50k steps between 100k and 200k, and >200k:

```
wage_bins = {'<$10k': [0, 10000], '$10-20k': [10000, 20000], \
             '$20-30k': [20000, 30000], \
             '$30-40k': [30000, 40000], \
             '$10-20k': [40000, 50000], \
             '$50-60k': [50000, 60000], \
             '$60-70k': [60000, 70000], \
             '$70-80k': [70000, 80000], \
             '$80-90k': [80000, 90000], \
             '$90-100k': [90000, 100000], \
             '$100-150k': [100000, 150000], \
             '$150-200k': [150000, 200000], \
             '>$200k': [200000, np.infty]}
```

8. Create a plot containing multiple subplots that visualize information with regard to NYC wages. Now, visualize the median household income for the US, New York, NYC, and its districts. Next, visualize the average wage by gender for the given occupation categories for the population of NYC. Then, visualize the wage distribution for New York and NYC. Lastly, use the following yearly wage intervals: 10k steps between 0 and 100k, 50k steps between 100k and 200k, and >200k.

Following is the expected output:

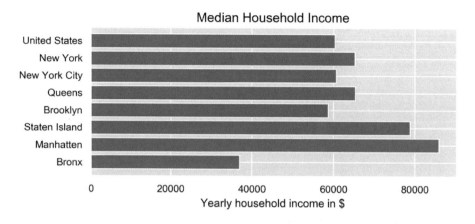

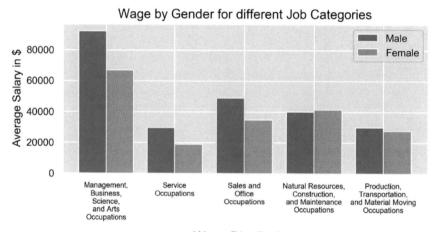

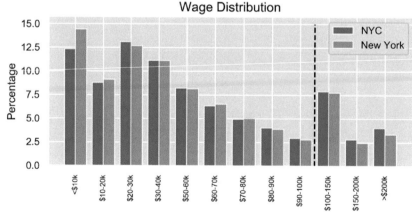

Figure 7.1: Wage statistics for New York City in comparison with New York and the United States

9. Use a tree map to visualize the percentage for the given occupation subcategories for the population of NYC:

```
occ_subcategories = \
{'Management,\nBusiness,\nand Financial': [10, 950], \
 'Computer, Engineering,\nand Science': [1000, 1965], \
 'Education,\nLegal,\nCommunity Service,'\
 '\nArts,\nand Media': [2000, 2960], \
 'Healthcare\nPractitioners\nand\nTechnical': [3000, 3540], \
 'Service': [3600, 4650], \
 'Sales\nand Related': [4700, 4965], \
 'Office\nand Administrative\nSupport': [5000, 5940], \
 '': [6000, 6130], \
 'Construction\nand Extraction': [6200, 6940], \
 'Installation,\nMaintenance,\nand Repair': [7000, 7630], \
 'Production': [7700, 8965], \
 'Transportation\nand Material\nMoving': [9000, 9750]}
```

Following is the expected output:

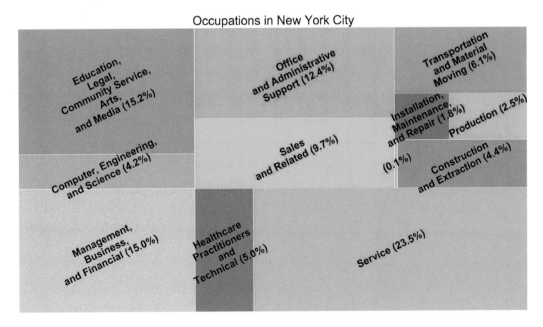

Figure 7.2: Occupations in NYC

10. Use a heatmap to show the correlation between difficulties (self-care difficulty, hearing difficulty, vision difficulty, independent living difficulty, ambulatory difficulty, veteran service-connected disability, and cognitive difficulty) and age groups (<5, 5-11, 12-14, 15-17, 18-24, 25-34, 35-44, 45-54, 55-64, 65-74, and 75+) in NYC. Following is the expected output:

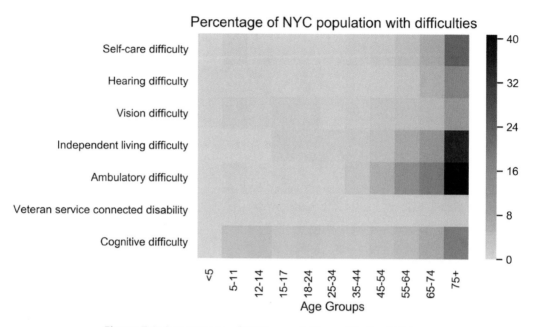

Figure 7.3: Percentage of NYC population with disabilities

> **NOTE**
>
> The solution to this activity can be found on page 472.

In the next section, we will perform an activity on Bokeh using a real-life scenario.

BOKEH

Stock price data is one of the most exciting types of data for many people. When thinking about its nature, we can see that it is highly dynamic and continually changing. To understand it, we need high levels of interactivity to not only look at the stocks of interest, but also to compare different stocks, see their traded volume, and the highs/lows of the given dates and whether it rose or sunk the day before that.

Considering all of the features mentioned previously, we need to use a highly customizable visualization tool. We also need the possibility to add different widgets to enable interactivity. In this activity, we will, therefore, use Bokeh to create a candlestick visualization with several interactivity widgets to enable a better exploration of our data. Please make sure the Bokeh version you are using is *1.4.0*.

ACTIVITY 7.02: VISUALIZING STOCK PRICES WITH BOKEH

In this activity, we will implement all the skills of Bokeh that we have learned. You will also need the skills you have acquired while working with pandas. We will create an interactive visualization that displays a candlestick plot, which is often used when handling stock price data. We will be able to compare two stocks with one another by selecting them from dropdowns. A **RangeSlider** will allow us to restrict the displayed date range in the requested year, 2016. Depending on what graph we choose, we will either see the candlestick visualization or a simple line plot displaying the volume of the selected stock:

1. Create an **Activity7.02.ipynb** Jupyter Notebook in the **Chapter07/ Activity7.02** folder to implement this activity.

2. Import pandas and enable notebook output by using the **bokeh.io** interface.

3. Load the downloaded **stock_prices** dataset.

4. Make sure that the dataset is loaded by displaying the first five elements of the dataset.

5. Use the **datetime** library to create a column, **short_date**, in our DataFrame that holds the information from the date column without the hour, minute, and second information.

6. Validate by displaying the first five elements of the updated DataFrame.

7. Import **figure** and **show** from Bokeh and **interact** and **widgets** from **ipywidgets** to get started.

8. Execute the cells from top to bottom until you reach the cell that has the comment **#extracting the necessary data**. Start your implementation there.

9. Get the unique stock names from the dataset. Filter out the dates from 2016. Only get unique dates from 2016. Create a list that contains the strings **open- close** and **volume**, which will be used for the radio buttons to switch between the two plots.

10. After extracting the necessary data, set up the interaction elements. Create widgets for the following: a dropdown for the first stock name (the default value will be **AAPL**) and a dropdown for the second stock name that will be compared to the first (the default value will be **AON**).

11. Also, set up a **SelectionRangeSlider** to select the range of dates we want to display in our plot (the default values displayed will be 0 to 25).

12. Define a **RadioButtons** attribute to choose between the candlestick plot and the plot that displays the traded volume (the default value will be **open-close**, which will display the candlestick plot.)

13. Set up the **@interact** method that finally displays the complete visualization. Provide the interaction elements that have just been set up with the **@ interact** decorator and call the **show** method with the **get_plot** method we executed before.

14. After implementing the decorated method, move up in our notebook and work on the **add_candle_plot** method. Start with the so-called candlestick visualization, which is often used with stock price data. Calculate the mean for every (**high/low**) pair and then plot those data points with a line with the given color. Next, set up an **add_candle_plot** that gets a **plot** object, a **stock_ name**, a **stock_range** columns containing the data of only the selected date range that was defined with the widgets, and a color for the line. Create a segment that creates the vertical line, and either a green or red **vbar** to color code whether the close price is lower than the open price. Once the candles are created, draw a continuous line running through the mean **high, low** point of each candle.

15. Move on and implement the line plot in the cell that contains the **get_plot** method. Plot a line for the data from **stock_1** with a blue color. Plot a line for the data from **stock_2** with an orange color.

16. Before finalizing this activity, add mutability to our legend, which changes the way elements are displayed upon clicking on one of the displayed elements in the legend of the visualization. The resulting visualization should look somewhat like the following image:

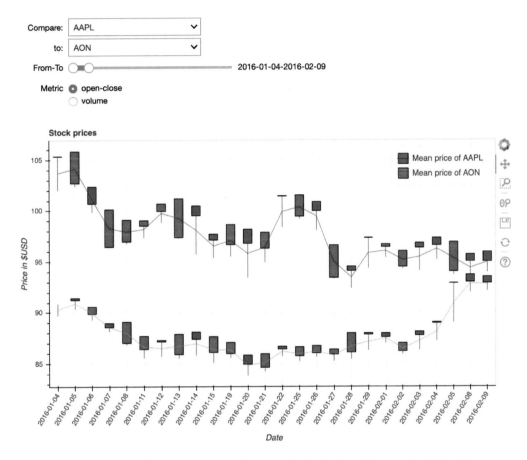

Figure 7.4: Final interactive visualization that displays the candlestick plot

The following figure shows the final interactive visualization of volume plot:

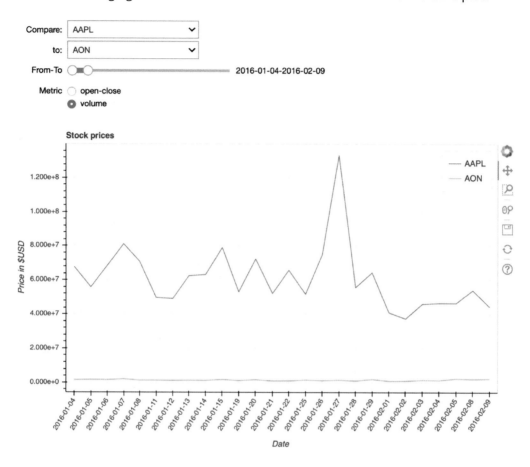

Figure 7.5: Final interactive visualization that displays the volume plot

NOTE

The solution to this activity can be found on page 484.

As we mentioned before, when working with interactive features and Bokeh, you might want to read up about the Bokeh server a little bit more. It will give you more options to create animated plots and visualizations that can be explored by several people at the same time.

GEOPLOTLIB

The dataset that is used in this activity is from Airbnb, which is publicly available online. Accommodation listings have two predominant features: latitude and longitude. Those two features allow us to create geospatial visualizations that give us a better understanding of attributes such as the distribution of accommodation across each city.

In this activity, we will use geoplotlib to create a visualization that maps each accommodation to a dot on a map. Each dot is colored based on either the price or rating of that listing. The two attributes can be switched by pressing the left and right keys on the keyboard.

ACTIVITY 7.03: ANALYZING AIRBNB DATA WITH GEOPLOTLIB

In this activity, we will implement all the geoplotlib skills that we have learned. We will use Airbnb listing data to determine the most expensive and best-rated regions of accommodation in the New York area. We will write a custom layer with which we can switch between the price and the review score of each accommodation. In the end, we will be able to see the hotspots for the most expensive and best-rated accommodation across New York.

In theory, we should see a price increase the closer we get to the center of Manhattan. It will be very fascinating to see whether the ratings for the given accommodations also increase as we get closer to the center of Manhattan:

1. Create an **Activity7.03.ipynb** Jupyter Notebook in the **Chapter07/ Activity7.03** folder to implement this activity. First, make sure you import the necessary dependencies.

2. Load the **airbnb_new_york.csv** dataset using pandas. If your system is a little bit slower, just use the **airbnb_new_york_smaller.csv** dataset with fewer data points.

3. Understand the dataset by observing the variables and the first few entries.

4. Since our dataset once again has columns that are named **Latitude** and **Longitude** instead of **lat** and **lon**, rename those columns to their short versions.

5. To use a color map that changes color based on the price of accommodation, we need a value that can easily be compared and checked whether it's smaller or bigger than any other listing.

Therefore, create a new column called **dollar_price** that will hold the value of the price column as float. Make sure to fill all the **NaN** values of the **price** column with **$0.0**, and **review_scores_rating** column with **0.0** by using the **fillna()** method of the dataset.

6. This dataset has 96 columns. When working with such a huge dataset, it makes sense to think about what data we really need and create a subsection of our dataset that only holds the data we need. Print all the columns that are available and an example for that column to decide what information is suitable.

7. Trim down the number of columns our working dataset has by creating a subsection of the columns with **id**, **latitude** (as **lat**), **longitude** (as **lon**), **price** (in $), and **review_scores_rating**.

8. Print the first five rows of the trimmed down the dataset.

9. Create a new **DataAccessObject** object with the newly created subsection of the dataset. Use it to plot out a dot map. The expected output is as follows:

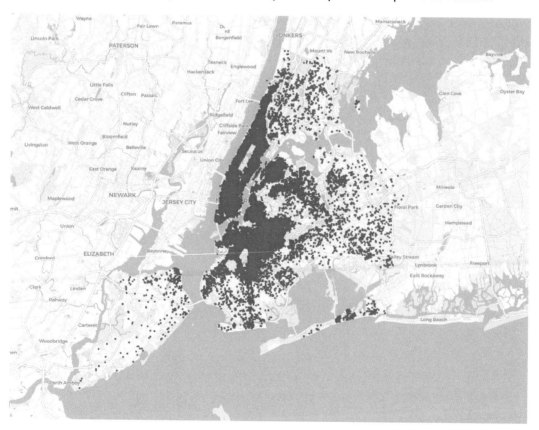

Figure 7.6: Simple dot map created from the points

10. Create a new **ValueLayer** class that extends the geoplotlib **BaseLayer** class.

11. Initiate the following instance variables in the **__init__** method of the **ValueLayer** class: first, **self.data**, which holds the dataset; second, **self.display**, which holds the currently selected attribute name; third, **self.painter**, which holds an instance of the **BatchPainter** class; fourth, **self.view**, which holds the **BoundingBox** function; and lastly, **self.cmap**, which holds a color map with the **jet color** schema, and an alpha of 255 and 100 levels:

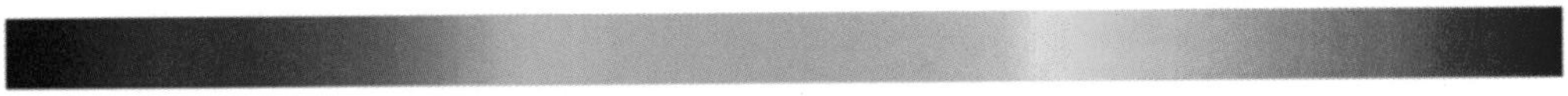

Figure 7.7: Jet color map scale

12. Implement the **bbox**, **draw**, and **on_key_release** methods from the **ValueLayer** class. First, return the **self.view** variable in the **bbox** method. Then, set the **ui_manager.info** text to **Use left and right to switch between the displaying of price and ratings. Currently displaying: dollar_price** or **review_scores_rating**, depending on what the **self.display** variable holds. Next, in the **on_key_release** method, check whether the left or right key is pressed and switch the **self.display** variable between **dollar_price** or **review_scores_rating**. Lastly, return **True** if the left or the right key has been pressed to trigger redrawing the dots, otherwise return **False**.

13. Given the data, plot each point on the map with a color that is defined by the currently selected attribute, either **price** or **rating**. First, in the **invalidate** method, assign a new **BatchPainter()** function to the **self.painter** variable. Second, get the max value of the dataset given the current **self.display** variable. Third, use a log scale if **dollar_price** is used, otherwise use a lin scale. Fourth, map the value to color using the **cmap** object we defined in the **__init__** method and plot each point with the given color onto the map with a size of **5**.

This is not the most efficient solution, but it will do for now.

14. Create a new **BoundingBox** function focused on New York by using `north=40.897994, west=-73.999040, south=40.595581, east=-73.95040`. In addition to a custom **BoundingBox**, we will use the **darkmatter** tile provider that we looked at in *Chapter 5, Plotting Geospatial Data*. Provide the **BoundingBox** function to the **ValueLayer** class when adding a new layer to geoplotlib.

The following is an expected output that shows a dot map with color based on rating:

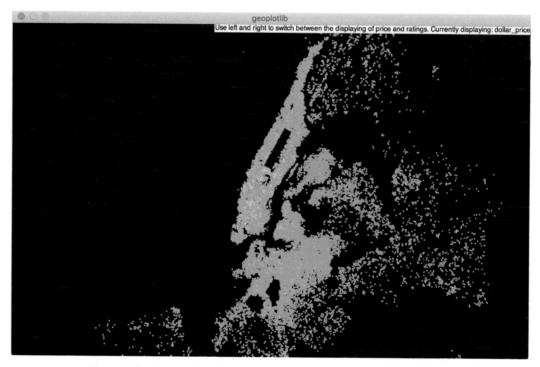

Figure 7.8: New York Airbnb dot map, colored based on the price

The following is an expected output that shows a dot map with color based on rating:

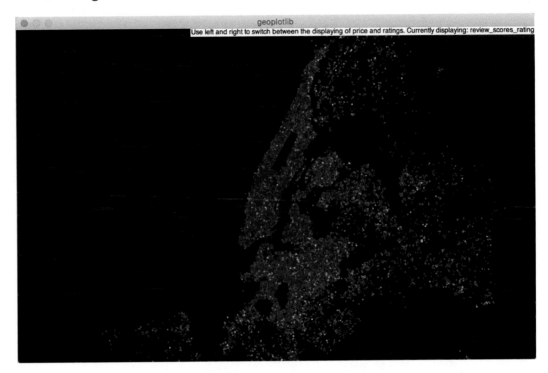

Figure 7.9: New York Airbnb dot map, colored based on the ratings

NOTE

The solution to this activity can be found on page 493.

As we can now see, writing custom layers for geoplotlib is a good approach for focusing on the attributes that you are interested in.

SUMMARY

This chapter gave us a short overview and recap of everything that was covered in this book based on three extensive practical activities. In *Chapter 1, The Importance of Data Visualization and Data Exploration*, we started with a Python library journey that we used as a guide throughout the whole book. We first talked about the importance of data and visualizing this data to get meaningful insights from it and gave a quick recap of different statistical concepts.

Through several activities, we learned how to import and handle datasets with NumPy and pandas. In *Chapter 2, All You Need to Know about Plots*, we discussed various plot/chart visualizations and which visualizations are best for displaying certain information. We mentioned the use case, design practices, and practical examples for each plot type.

In *Chapter 3, A Deep Dive into Matplotlib*, we thoroughly covered Matplotlib and started with the basic concepts. Next, we dived deeper into the numerous possibilities for enriching visualizations with text. Emphasis was put on explaining almost all plotting functions Matplotlib offers using practical examples. Furthermore, we talked about different ways to create layouts. The chapter was rounded off by demonstrating how you can visualize images and write mathematical expressions.

Chapter 4, Simplifying Visualizations Using Seaborn, covered Seaborn, which is built on top of Matplotlib and provides a higher-level abstraction to make insightful visualizations. With several examples, we showed you how Seaborn can simplify the creation of visualizations. We also introduced further plots, such as heatmaps, violin plots, and correlograms. Finally, we used Squarify to create tree maps.

Visualizing geospatial data was covered in *Chapter 5, Plotting Geospatial Data,* using geoplotlib. Understanding how geoplotlib is structured internally explained why we had to work with the pyglet library when adding interactivity to our visualizations. We worked with different datasets and built both static and interactive visualizations for geospatial data.

In *Chapter 6, Making Things Interactive with Bokeh*, we focused on working with Bokeh, which targets modern web browsers to present interactive visualizations. Starting with simple examples, we explored the most significant advantage of Bokeh, namely, interactive widgets.

We ended the book with this chapter, applying all the skills that we've learned through three real-life datasets.

With the conclusion of this book, you should now have the practical knowledge and skills to design your own data visualizations using various Python libraries such as NumPy, pandas, Matplotlib, Seaborn, geoplotlib, and Bokeh.

APPENDIX

CHAPTER 1: THE IMPORTANCE OF DATA VISUALIZATION AND DATA EXPLORATION

ACTIVITY 1.01: USING NUMPY TO COMPUTE THE MEAN, MEDIAN, VARIANCE, AND STANDARD DEVIATION OF A DATASET

Solution:

1. Import NumPy:

```
import numpy as np
```

2. Load the **normal_distribution.csv** dataset by using the **genfromtxt** method from NumPy:

```
dataset = np.genfromtxt('../../Datasets/normal_distribution.csv', \
                        delimiter=',')
```

3. First, print a subset of the first two rows of the dataset:

```
dataset[0:2]
```

The output of the preceding code is as follows:

```
array([[ 99.14931546, 104.03852715, 107.43534677,  97.85230675,
         98.74986914,  98.80833412,  96.81964892,  98.56783189],
       [ 92.02628776,  97.10439252,  99.32066924,  97.24584816,
         92.9267508 ,  92.65657752, 105.7197853 , 101.23162942]])
```

Figure 1.57: First two rows of the dataset

4. Load the dataset and calculate the mean of the third row. Access the third row by using index 2, **dataset[2]**:

```
np.mean(dataset[2])
```

The output of the preceding code is as follows:

```
100.20466135250001
```

5. Index the last element of an ndarray in the same way a regular Python list can be accessed. **dataset[:, -1]** will give us the last column of every row:

```
np.mean(dataset[:,-1])
```

The output of the preceding code is as follows:

```
100.4404927375
```

6. Get a submatrix of the first three elements of every row of the first three columns by using the double-indexing mechanism of NumPy, which gives us an interface to extract sub-selection:

```
"""
calculate the mean of the intersection of the first 3 rows \
and first 3 columns
"""
np.mean(dataset[0:3, 0:3])
```

The output of the preceding code is as follows:

```
97.87197312333333
```

7. Calculate the median of the last row of the dataset. Don't use the length of the dataset as the index:

```
np.median(dataset[-1])
```

The output of the preceding code is as follows:

```
99.18748092
```

8. Use reverse indexing define a range to get the last three columns using **dataset[:, -3:]**:

```
np.median(dataset[:, -3:])
```

The output of the preceding code is as follows:

```
99.47332349999999
```

9. To aggregate the values along an axis to calculate the rows, use **axis=1**:

```
np.median(dataset, axis=1)
```

The output of the preceding code is as follows:

```
array([ 98.77910163,  97.17512034,  98.58782879, 100.68449836,
       101.00170737,  97.76908825, 101.85002253, 100.04756697,
       102.24292555,  99.59514997, 100.4955753 ,  99.8860714 ,
        99.00647994,  98.67276177, 102.44376222,  96.61933565,
       104.0968893 , 100.72023043,  98.70877396,  99.75008654,
       104.89344428, 101.00634942,  98.30543801,  99.18748092])
```

Figure 1.58: Using axis to calculate the median of each row

10. Calculate the variance for each column using **axis=0**:

```
np.var(dataset, axis=0)
```

The output of the preceding code is as follows:

```
array([23.64757465, 29.78886109, 20.50542011, 26.03204443, 28.38853175,
       19.09960817, 17.67291174, 16.17923204])
```

Figure 1.59: Variance across each column

11. Calculate the variance of the intersection of the last two rows and the first two columns. When only looking at a very small subset of the matrix (2x2) elements, we can apply what we learned in the statistical overview to observe that the value is way smaller than the whole dataset:

```
np.var(dataset[-2:, :2])
```

The output of the preceding code is as follows:

```
4.674691991769191
```

The values of the variance might seem a little bit strange at first. You can always go back to the *Measures of Dispersion* section to recap what you've learned so far.

> **NOTE**
>
> A small subset of a dataset does not display the attributes of the whole.

12. Calculate the standard deviation of the dataset. Just remember that the variance is not the standard deviation:

```
np.std(dataset)
```

The output of the preceding code is as follows:

```
4.838197554269257
```

> **NOTE**
>
> To access the source code for this specific section, please refer to https://packt.live/3hroPlv.
>
> You can also run this example online at https://packt.live/30MIyG8.

ACTIVITY 1.02: FOREST FIRE SIZE AND TEMPERATURE ANALYSIS

Solution:

1. Import the necessary libraries:

```
import pandas as pd
```

2. Use the **read_csv** method to load the **forestfires.csv** dataset:

```
dataset = pd.read_csv('../../Datasets/forestfires.csv')
```

3. Print the first two rows of the dataset to get a feeling for its structure:

```
dataset[0:2]
```

The output of the preceding code is as follows:

	X	Y	month	day	FFMC	DMC	DC	ISI	temp	RH	wind	rain	area
0	7	5	mar	fri	86.2	26.2	94.3	5.1	8.2	51	6.7	0.0	0.0
1	7	4	oct	tue	90.6	35.4	669.1	6.7	18.0	33	0.9	0.0	0.0

Figure 1.60: Printing the first two rows of the dataset

Derive insights from the sizes of forest fires

4. Filter the dataset so that it only contains rows that have an area value of **>0** since our dataset contains several rows with an area of 0 and we only want to look at rows that have an area larger than 0 for now:

```
area_dataset= dataset[dataset["area"] > 0]
area_dataset
```

The output of the preceding code is as follows:

	X	Y	month	day	FFMC	DMC	DC	ISI	temp	RH	wind	rain	area
138	9	9	jul	tue	85.8	48.3	313.4	3.9	18.0	42	2.7	0.0	0.36
139	1	4	sep	tue	91.0	129.5	692.6	7.0	21.7	38	2.2	0.0	0.43
140	2	5	sep	mon	90.9	126.5	686.5	7.0	21.9	39	1.8	0.0	0.47
141	1	2	aug	wed	95.5	99.9	513.3	13.2	23.3	31	4.5	0.0	0.55
142	8	6	aug	fri	90.1	108.0	529.8	12.5	21.2	51	8.9	0.0	0.61
...	...	...	...	...	...	...	...	...	...	...	...	...	...
509	5	4	aug	fri	91.0	166.9	752.6	7.1	21.1	71	7.6	1.4	2.17
510	6	5	aug	fri	91.0	166.9	752.6	7.1	18.2	62	5.4	0.0	0.43
512	4	3	aug	sun	81.6	56.7	665.6	1.9	27.8	32	2.7	0.0	6.44
513	2	4	aug	sun	81.6	56.7	665.6	1.9	21.9	71	5.8	0.0	54.29
514	7	4	aug	sun	81.6	56.7	665.6	1.9	21.2	70	6.7	0.0	11.16

270 rows × 13 columns

Figure 1.61: Filtered dataset with only rows that have an area of larger than 0

5. Get the mean, min, max, and std of the area column and see what information this gives you. First, let's find the mean value:

```
area_dataset["area"].mean()
```

Following is the output of the code:

```
24.600185185185182
```

Get the smallest area value from our dataset:

```
area_dataset["area"].min()
```

The output of the preceding code is as follows:

```
0.09
```

Get the largest area value from our dataset:

```
area_dataset["area"].max()
```

The output of the preceding code is as follows:

```
1090.84
```

Get the standard deviation of values in our dataset:

```
area_dataset["area"].std()
```

The output of the preceding code is as follows:

```
86.50163460412126
```

6. Sort the filtered dataset using the area column and print the last 20 entries using the **tail** method to see how many very large values it holds:

```
area_dataset.sort_values(by=["area"]).tail(20)
```

The output of the preceding code is as follows:

	X	Y	month	day	FFMC	DMC	DC	ISI	temp	RH	wind	rain	area
469	6	3	apr	sun	91.0	14.6	25.6	12.3	13.7	33	9.4	0.0	61.13
228	4	6	sep	sun	93.5	149.3	728.6	8.1	28.3	26	3.1	0.0	64.10
473	9	4	jun	sat	90.5	61.1	252.6	9.4	24.5	50	3.1	0.0	70.32
392	1	3	sep	sun	91.0	276.3	825.1	7.1	21.9	43	4.0	0.0	70.76
229	8	6	aug	sat	92.2	81.8	480.8	11.9	16.4	43	4.0	0.0	71.30
457	1	4	aug	wed	91.7	191.4	635.9	7.8	19.9	50	4.0	0.0	82.75
293	7	6	jul	tue	93.1	180.4	430.8	11.0	26.9	28	5.4	0.0	86.45
230	4	4	sep	wed	92.9	133.3	699.6	9.2	26.4	21	4.5	0.0	88.49
231	1	5	sep	sun	93.5	149.3	728.6	8.1	27.8	27	3.1	0.0	95.18
232	6	4	sep	tue	91.0	129.5	692.6	7.0	18.7	43	2.7	0.0	103.39
233	9	4	sep	tue	84.4	73.4	671.9	3.2	24.3	36	3.1	0.0	105.66
234	4	5	sep	sat	92.5	121.1	674.4	8.6	17.7	25	3.1	0.0	154.88
377	2	2	aug	sat	93.7	231.1	715.1	8.4	21.9	42	2.2	0.0	174.63
420	8	8	aug	wed	91.7	191.4	635.9	7.8	26.2	36	4.5	0.0	185.76
235	8	6	aug	sun	91.4	142.4	601.4	10.6	19.6	41	5.8	0.0	196.48
236	2	2	sep	sat	92.5	121.1	674.4	8.6	18.2	46	1.8	0.0	200.94
237	1	2	sep	tue	91.0	129.5	692.6	7.0	18.8	40	2.2	0.0	212.88
479	7	4	jul	mon	89.2	103.9	431.6	6.4	22.6	57	4.9	0.0	278.53
415	8	6	aug	thu	94.8	222.4	698.6	13.9	27.5	27	4.9	0.0	746.28
238	6	5	sep	sat	92.5	121.1	674.4	8.6	25.1	27	4.0	0.0	1090.84

Figure 1.62: 20 largest entries sorted by area

7. Get the median of the **area** column and visually compare it to the mean value:

```
area_dataset["area"].median()
```

The output of the preceding code is as follows:

```
6.37
```

Finding the month with the most forest fires

8. List all the **month** values present in the dataset to compare the number of fires and the **temperature** and get a list of unique values from the **month** column of the dataset:

```
months = dataset["month"].unique()


months
```

The output of the preceding code is as follows:

```
array(['mar', 'oct', 'aug', 'sep', 'apr', 'jun', 'jul', 'feb', 'jan',
       'dec', 'may', 'nov'], dtype=object)
```

Figure 1.63: List of month values present in the dataset

9. Get the amount of entries for the **month** of March using the shape member of our DataFrame:

```
dataset[dataset["month"] == "mar"].shape[0]
```

The output of the preceding code is as follows:

```
54
```

10. Now, iterate over all months, filter our dataset for rows containing the given month, and calculate the mean temperature. Print a statement containing the number of fires, the mean temperature, and the month:

```
for month in months:
    month_dataset = dataset[dataset["month"] == month]
    fires_in_month = month_dataset.shape[0]
    avg_tmp_in_month = int(month_dataset["temp"].mean())

    print(str(fires_in_month) + " fires in " + month \
          + " with a mean temperature of ~" \
          + str(avg_tmp_in_month) + "°C")
```

The output of the preceding code is as follows:

```
54 fires in mar with a mean temperature of ~13°C
15 fires in oct with a mean temperature of ~17°C
184 fires in aug with a mean temperature of ~21°C
172 fires in sep with a mean temperature of ~19°C
9 fires in apr with a mean temperature of ~12°C
17 fires in jun with a mean temperature of ~20°C
32 fires in jul with a mean temperature of ~22°C
20 fires in feb with a mean temperature of ~9°C
2 fires in jan with a mean temperature of ~5°C
9 fires in dec with a mean temperature of ~4°C
2 fires in may with a mean temperature of ~14°C
1 fires in nov with a mean temperature of ~11°C
```

Figure 1.64: Amount of forest fires and mean temperature for each month

NOTE

To access the source code for this specific section, please refer to https://packt.live/2NeLJ1H.

You can also run this example online at https://packt.live/3d7RUiv.

CHAPTER 2: ALL YOU NEED TO KNOW ABOUT PLOTS

ACTIVITY 2.01: EMPLOYEE SKILL COMPARISON

Solution:

1. Bar charts and radar charts are great for comparing multiple variables for multiple groups.

2. **Suggested response:** The bar chart is great for comparing the skill attributes of the different employees, but it is not the best choice when it comes to getting an overall impression of an employee, due to the fact that the skills are not displayed directly next to one another.

   The radar chart is great for this scenario because you can both compare performance across employees and directly observe the individual performance for each skill attribute.

3. **Suggested response:**

   For both the bar and radar charts, adding a title and labels would help to understand the plots better. Additionally, using different colors for the different employees in the radar chart would help to keep the different employees apart.

ACTIVITY 2.02: ROAD ACCIDENTS OCCURRING OVER TWO DECADES

Solution:

1. **Suggested response:** If we look at *Figure 2.20*, we can see that the years 2000 and 2015 have the lightest colored squares overall. These are the two years that have the lowest accident rates.

2. **Suggested response:** If we look at the trend for each month, that is, January, April, July, and October for the past two decades, we can see a decreasing trend in the number of accidents taking place in January.

The activity about road accidents gave you a simple example of how to use heatmaps to illustrate the relationship between multiple variables. In the next section, we will cover composition plots.

ACTIVITY 2.03: SMARTPHONE SALES UNITS

Solution:

1. **Suggested response:** If we compare the performance of each manufacturer in the third and fourth quarters, we come to the conclusion that Apple has performed exceptionally well. Their sales units have risen at a higher rate from the third quarter to the fourth quarter for both 2016 and 2017 when compared with that of other manufacturers.

2. **Suggested response:** If we look at the trends in the sales units of each manufacturer, we can see that after the third quarter of 2017, the sales units of all the companies except Xiaomi have shown an inconsistency. If we look at the performance of Xiaomi, there has been an upward trend after the first quarter of the year 2017. The sales of Apple and Samsung are exhibiting a downward trend while the sales of Huawei and Xiaomi are showing an upward trend. It is predicted that these trends will continue.

3. **Suggested response:** Using a stacked area chart would additionally directly visualize the overall trend of smartphone sales. A small drawback is that it would be more difficult to read absolute smartphone sales numbers for an individual company.

ACTIVITY 2.04: FREQUENCY OF TRAINS DURING DIFFERENT TIME INTERVALS

Solution:

1. **Suggested response:** Most trains arrive at 4 p.m. and 6 p.m.

2. **Suggested response:** The histogram appears as follows:

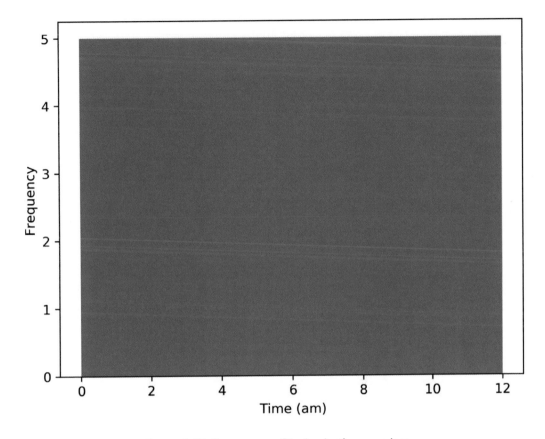

Figure 2.47: Frequency of trains in the morning

ACTIVITY 2.05: ANALYZING VISUALIZATIONS

Solution:

FIRST VISUALIZATION

Suggested response:

1. The proposed visualization has multiple faults. First, a pie chart is supposed to show part-of-a-whole relations, which is not the case for this task since we only consider the top 30 YouTube music channels and not all channels. Second, 30 values are too many to visualize within a pie chart. Third, the labels overlap. Also, it is difficult to quantify the slices as there is no unit of measurement specified.

2. An improvement would be to use a bar chart. For example, in the following horizontal bar chart, it is easier to tell the number of subscribers in millions for each YouTube channel:

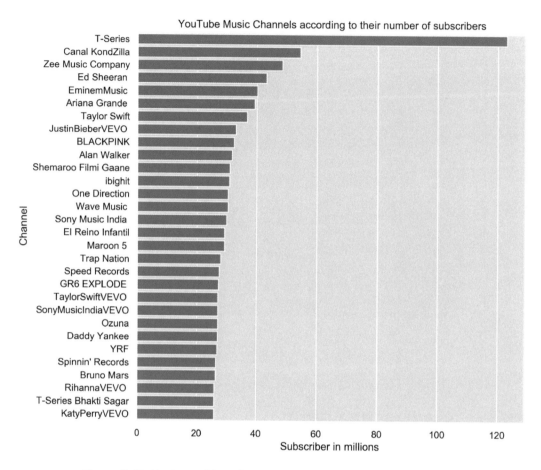

Figure 2.48: Horizontal bar chart showing YouTube music channels

SECOND VISUALIZATION

Suggested response:

1. This is also an example of using the wrong chart type. A line chart was used to compare different categories that do not have any temporal relation. Furthermore, informative guides such as legends and labels are missing.

2. The following diagram shows how the data should have been represented using a comparative bar chart:

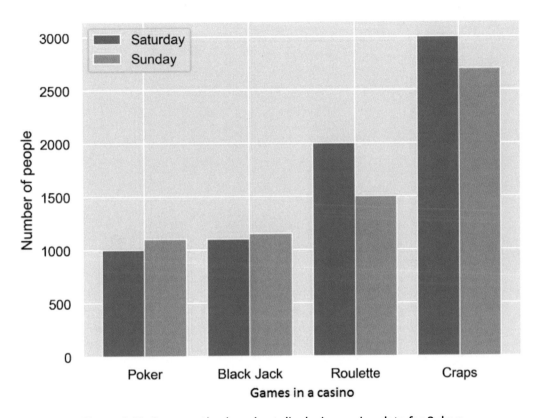

Figure 2.49: Comparative bar chart displaying casino data for 2 days

ACTIVITY 2.06: CHOOSING A SUITABLE VISUALIZATION

Solution:

Since it was asked of us to visualize the median, the interquartile ranges, and the underlying density of populations from different income groups, violin plots are the best choice as they visualize both summary statistics and a kernel density estimate. The density plot only shows the density, whereas box plots only illustrate summary statistics.

CHAPTER 3: A DEEP DIVE INTO MATPLOTLIB

ACTIVITY 3.01: VISUALIZING STOCK TRENDS BY USING A LINE PLOT

Solution:

Visualize a stock trend by using a line plot:

1. Create an **Activity3.01.ipynb** Jupyter notebook in the **Chapter03/Activity3.01** folder to implement this activity.

2. Import the necessary modules and enable plotting within the Jupyter notebook:

```
# Import statements
import matplotlib.pyplot as plt
import numpy as np
import pandas as pd


%matplotlib inline
```

3. Use pandas to read the datasets (**GOOGL_data.csv**, **FB_data.csv**, **AAPL_data.csv**, **AMZN_data.csv**, and **MSFT_data.csv**) located in the **Datasets** folder. The **read_csv()** function reads a .csv file into a DataFrame:

```
# load datasets
google = pd.read_csv('../../Datasets/GOOGL_data.csv')
facebook = pd.read_csv('../../Datasets/FB_data.csv')
apple = pd.read_csv('../../Datasets/AAPL_data.csv')
amazon = pd.read_csv('../../Datasets/AMZN_data.csv')
microsoft = pd.read_csv('../../Datasets/MSFT_data.csv')
```

4. Use **Matplotlib** to create a line chart that visualizes the closing prices for the past 5 years (whole data sequence) for all five companies. Add labels, titles, and a legend to make the visualization self-explanatory. Use the **plt.grid()** function to add a grid to your plot:

```
# Create figure
plt.figure(figsize=(16, 8), dpi=300)
# Plot data
plt.plot('date', 'close', data=google, label='Google')
plt.plot('date', 'close', data=facebook, label='Facebook')
plt.plot('date', 'close', data=apple, label='Apple')
plt.plot('date', 'close', data=amazon, label='Amazon')
plt.plot('date', 'close', data=microsoft, label='Microsoft')
```

```
# Specify ticks for x and y axis
plt.xticks(np.arange(0, 1260, 40), rotation=70)
plt.yticks(np.arange(0, 1450, 100))
# Add title and label for y-axis
plt.title('Stock trend', fontsize=16)
plt.ylabel('Closing price in $', fontsize=14)
# Add grid
plt.grid()
# Add legend
plt.legend()
# Show plot
plt.show()
```

Following is the output of the code:

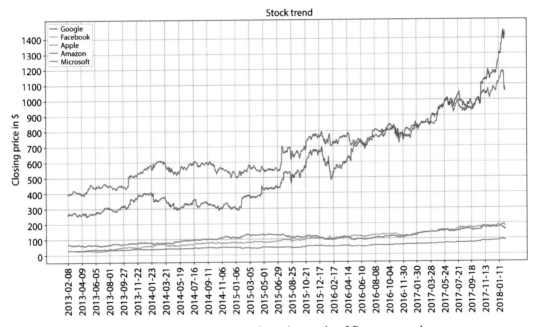

Figure 3.50: Visualization of stock trends of five companies

From the preceding diagram, we can see that the stock prices of Google and Amazon are high compared to Facebook, Microsoft, and Apple.

> **NOTE**
>
> To access the source code for this specific section, please refer to
> https://packt.live/2Y35oHT.
>
> You can also run this example online at https://packt.live/3hxuyGj.

ACTIVITY 3.02: CREATING A BAR PLOT FOR MOVIE COMPARISON

Solution:

Create a bar plot for comparing the ratings of different movies:

1. Create an **Activity3.02.ipynb** Jupyter notebook in the **Chapter03/ Activity3.02** folder to implement this activity.

2. Import the necessary modules and enable plotting within the Jupyter notebook:

```
# Import statements
import numpy as np
import pandas as pd
import matplotlib.pyplot as plt
%matplotlib inline
```

3. Use pandas to read the data located in the **Datasets** folder:

```
# Load dataset
movie_scores = pd.read_csv('../../Datasets/movie_scores.csv')
```

4. Use Matplotlib to create a visually appealing bar plot comparing the two scores for all five movies. Use the movie titles as labels for the x-axis. Use percentages at intervals of 20 for the y-axis, and minor ticks at intervals of 5. Add a legend and a suitable title to the plot:

```
# Create figure
plt.figure(figsize=(10, 5), dpi=300)
# Create bar plot
pos = np.arange(len(movie_scores['MovieTitle']))
width = 0.3
plt.bar(pos - width / 2, movie_scores['Tomatometer'], \
        width, label='Tomatometer')
plt.bar(pos + width / 2, movie_scores['AudienceScore'], \
        width, label='Audience Score')
# Specify ticks
```

```
plt.xticks(pos, rotation=10)
plt.yticks(np.arange(0, 101, 20))
# Get current Axes for setting tick labels and horizontal grid
ax = plt.gca()
# Set tick labels
ax.set_xticklabels(movie_scores['MovieTitle'])
ax.set_yticklabels(['0%', '20%', '40%', '60%', '80%', '100%'])
# Add minor ticks for y-axis in the interval of 5
ax.set_yticks(np.arange(0, 100, 5), minor=True)
# Add major horizontal grid with solid lines
ax.yaxis.grid(which='major')
# Add minor horizontal grid with dashed lines
ax.yaxis.grid(which='minor', linestyle='--')
# Add title
plt.title('Movie comparison')
# Add legend
plt.legend()
# Show plot
plt.show()
```

The output is as follows:

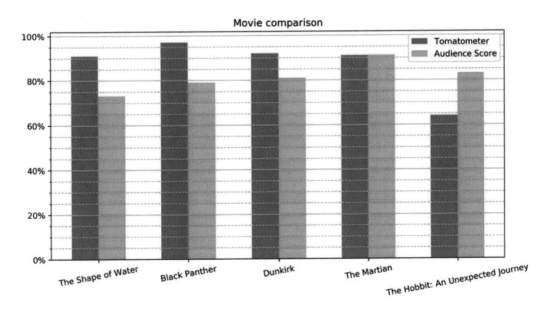

Figure 3.51: Bar plot comparing scores of five movies

In the preceding output, we can see that the audience liked the movie "The Hobbit: An Unexpected Journey" when compared to other movies that were rated high by Tomatometer.

> **NOTE**
>
> To access the source code for this specific section, please refer to https://packt.live/30NVXhs.
>
> You can also run this example online at https://packt.live/3fu2e5X.

ACTIVITY 3.03: CREATING A STACKED BAR PLOT TO VISUALIZE RESTAURANT PERFORMANCE

Solution:

Let's create a stacked bar chart to visualize the performance of a restaurant:

1. Create an **Activity3.03.ipynb** Jupyter notebook in the **Chapter03/ Activity3.03** folder to implement this activity.

   Navigate to the path of this file and type in the following at the command-line terminal: **jupyter-lab**.

2. Import the necessary modules and enable plotting within the Jupyter notebook:

```
# Import statements
import pandas as sb
import numpy as np
import matplotlib.pyplot as plt
import seaborn as sns
%matplotlib inline
```

   Note that we have imported the Seaborn library to load the built-in dataset that the library provides.

3. Load the dataset:

```
# Load dataset
bills = sns.load_dataset('tips')
```

4. Use the given dataset and create a matrix where the elements contain the sum of the total bills for each day and are split by smokers/non-smokers:

```
days = ['Thur', 'Fri', 'Sat', 'Sun']
days_range = np.arange(len(days))
smoker = ['Yes', 'No']

bills_by_days = [bills[bills['day'] == day] for day in days]

bills_by_days_smoker = \
[[bills_by_days[day][bills_by_days[day]['smoker'] == s] \
  for s in smoker] for day in days_range]

total_by_days_smoker = \
[[bills_by_days_smoker[day][s]['total_bill'].sum() \
  for s in range(len(smoker))] for day in days_range]

totals = np.asarray(total_by_days_smoker)
```

Here, the **asarray()** function is used to convert any list into an array.

5. Create a stacked bar plot, stacking the summed total bills separated by smoker and non-smoker for each day. Add a legend, labels, and a title:

```
# Create figure
plt.figure(figsize=(10, 5), dpi=300)
# Create stacked bar plot
plt.bar(days_range, totals[:, 0], label='Smoker')
plt.bar(days_range, totals[:, 1], bottom=totals[:, 0], \
        label='Non-smoker')
# Add legend
plt.legend()
# Add labels and title
plt.xticks(days_range)
ax = plt.gca()
ax.set_xticklabels(days)
ax.yaxis.grid()
plt.ylabel('Daily total sales in $')
plt.title('Restaurant performance')
# Show plot
plt.show()
```

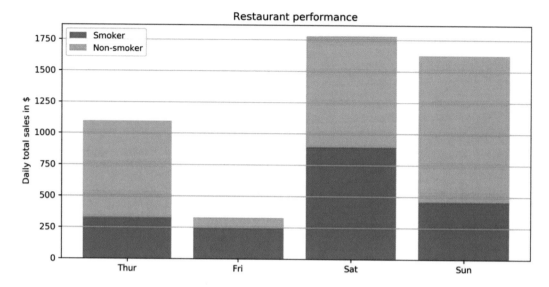

Figure 3.52: Stacked bar chart showing restaurant performance on different days

In the preceding output, we can see that the highest sales were made on Saturday by both smokers and non-smokers.

> **NOTE**
>
> To access the source code for this specific section, please refer to https://packt.live/3ea2IxY.
>
> You can also run this example online at https://packt.live/3htcMEI.

ACTIVITY 3.04: COMPARING SMARTPHONE SALES UNITS USING A STACKED AREA CHART

Solution:

Let's compare the sales units of smartphone manufacturers using a stacked area chart:

1. Create an **Activity3.04.ipynb** Jupyter notebook in the **Chapter03/Activity3.04** folder to implement this activity.

2. Import the necessary modules and enable plotting within the Jupyter notebook:

```
# Import statements
import pandas as pd
import numpy as np
import matplotlib.pyplot as plt
%matplotlib inline
```

3. Use pandas to read the data located in the **Datasets** folder:

```
# Load dataset
sales = pd.read_csv('../../Datasets/smartphone_sales.csv')
```

4. Create a visually appealing stacked area chart. Add a legend, labels, and a title:

```
# Create figure
plt.figure(figsize=(10, 6), dpi=300)
# Create stacked area chart
labels = sales.columns[2:]
plt.stackplot('Quarter', 'Apple', 'Samsung', 'Huawei', \
              'Xiaomi', 'OPPO', data=sales, labels=labels)
# Add legend
plt.legend()
# Add labels and title
plt.xlabel('Quarters')
plt.ylabel('Sales units in thousands')
plt.title('Smartphone sales units')
# Show plot
plt.show()
```

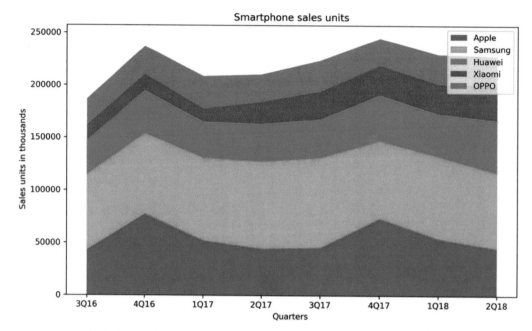

Figure 3.53: Stacked area chart comparing sales units of different smartphone
manufacturers

In the preceding output, we can see a comparison of five smartphone units. We
can see that Samsung has the highest sales and it would be safe to invest in it.

> **NOTE**
>
> To access the source code for this specific section, please refer to
> https://packt.live/2CckMJC.
>
> You can also run this example online at https://packt.live/3hvKQQ7.

ACTIVITY 3.05: USING A HISTOGRAM AND A BOX PLOT TO VISUALIZE INTELLIGENCE QUOTIENT

Solution:

Let's visualize the IQ of different groups using a histogram and a box plot:

1. Import the necessary modules and enable plotting within a Jupyter notebook:

```
# Import statements
import numpy as np
import matplotlib.pyplot as plt
%matplotlib inline
```

2. Use the following IQ scores for the following plots:

```
# IQ samples
iq_scores = [126,  89,  90, 101, 102,  74,  93, 101,  66, \
             120, 108,  97,  98, 105, 119,  92, 113,  81, \
             104, 108,  83, 102, 105, 111, 102, 107, 103,  \
              89,  89, 110,  71, 110, 120,  85, 111,  83, \
             122, 120, 102,  84, 118, 100, 100, 114,  81, \
             109,  69,  97,  95, 106, 116, 109, 114,  98,  \
              90,  92,  98,  91,  81,  85,  86, 102,  93, \
             112,  76,  89, 110,  75, 100,  90,  96,  94, \
             107, 108,  95,  96,  96, 114,  93,  95, 117, \
             141, 115,  95,  86, 100, 121, 103,  66,  99,  \
              96, 111, 110, 105, 110,  91, 112, 102, 112,  75]
```

3. Plot a histogram with 10 bins for the given IQ scores. IQ scores are normally distributed with a mean of 100 and a standard deviation of 15. Visualize the mean as a vertical solid red line, and the standard deviation using dashed vertical lines. Add labels and a title:

```
# Create figure
plt.figure(figsize=(6, 4), dpi=150)
# Create histogram
plt.hist(iq_scores, bins=10)
plt.axvline(x=100, color='r')
plt.axvline(x=115, color='r', linestyle= '--')
plt.axvline(x=85, color='r', linestyle= '--')
# Add labels and title
plt.xlabel('IQ score')
```

```
plt.ylabel('Frequency')
plt.title('IQ scores for a test group of a hundred adults')
# Show plot
plt.show()
```

Following is the output of the code:

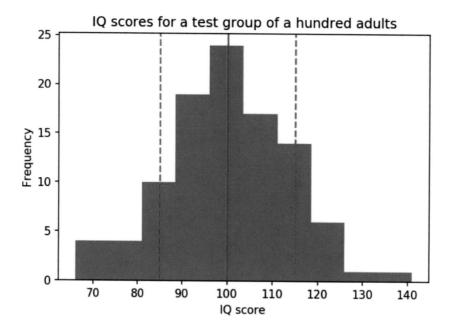

Figure 3.54: Histogram for an IQ test

4. Create a box plot to visualize the IQ scores. Add labels and a title:

```
# Create figure
plt.figure(figsize=(6, 4), dpi=150)
# Create histogram
plt.boxplot(iq_scores)
# Add labels and title
ax = plt.gca()
ax.set_xticklabels(['Test group'])
plt.ylabel('IQ score')
plt.title('IQ scores for a test group of a hundred adults')
# Show plot
plt.show()
```

Following is the output of the code:

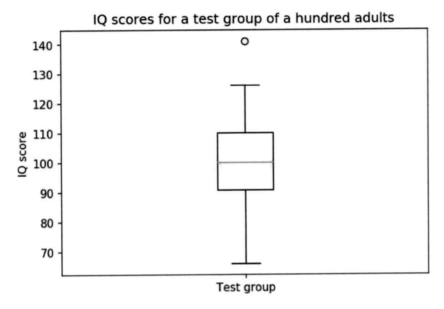

Figure 3.55: Box plot for IQ scores

5. The following are IQ scores for different test groups that we can use as data:

```
group_a = [118, 103, 125, 107, 111,  96, 104,  97,  96, \
           114,  96,  75, 114, 107,  87, 117, 117, 114, \
           117, 112, 107, 133,  94,  91, 118, 110, 117, \
            86, 143,  83, 106,  86,  98, 126, 109,  91, \
           112, 120, 108, 111, 107,  98,  89, 113, 117, \
            81, 113, 112,  84, 115,  96,  93, 128, 115, \
           138, 121,  87, 112, 110,  79, 100,  84, 115, \
            93, 108, 130, 107, 106, 106, 101, 117,  93, \
            94, 103, 112,  98, 103,  70, 139,  94, 110, \
           105, 122,  94,  94, 105, 129, 110, 112,  97, \
           109, 121, 106, 118, 131,  88, 122, 125,  93,  78]

group_b = [126,  89,  90, 101, 102,  74,  93, 101,  66, 120, \
           108,  97,  98, 105, 119,  92, 113,  81, 104, 108, \
            83, 102, 105, 111, 102, 107, 103,  89,  89, 110, \
            71, 110, 120,  85, 111,  83, 122, 120, 102, 84, \
           118, 100, 100, 114,  81, 109,  69,  97,  95, 106, \
           116, 109, 114,  98,  90,  92,  98,  91,  81,  85, \
            86, 102,  93, 112,  76,  89, 110,  75, 100,  90, \
```

```
                96,  94, 107, 108,  95,  96,  96, 114, 93,  95, \
               117, 141, 115,  95,  86, 100, 121, 103,  66, 99, \
                96, 111, 110, 105, 110,  91, 112, 102, 112,  75]

group_c = [108,  89, 114, 116, 126, 104, 113,  96,  69, 121, \
           109, 102, 107, 122, 104, 107, 108, 137, 107, 116, \
            98, 132, 108, 114,  82,  93,  89,  90,  86,  91, \
            99,  98,  83,  93, 114,  96,  95, 113, 103,  81, \
           107,  85, 116,  85, 107, 125, 126, 123, 122, 124, \
           115, 114,  93,  93, 114, 107, 107,  84, 131,  91, \
           108, 127, 112, 106, 115,  82,  90, 117, 108, 115, \
           113, 108, 104, 103,  90, 110, 114,  92, 101,  72, \
           109,  94, 122,  90, 102,  86, 119, 103, 110,  96, \
            90, 110,  96,  69,  85, 102,  69,  96, 101,  90]

group_d = [93,  99,  91, 110,  80, 113, 111, 115,  98,  74, \
           96,  80,  83, 102,  60,  91,  82,  90,  97, 101, \
           89,  89, 117,  91, 104, 104, 102, 128, 106, 111, \
           79,  92,  97, `101, 106, 110,  93,  93, 106, 108, \
           85,  83, 108,  94,  79,  87, 113, 112, 111, 111, \
           79, 116, 104,  84, 116, 111, 103, 103, 112,  68, \
           54,  80,  86, 119,  81,  84,  91,  96, 116, 125, \
           99,  58, 102,  77,  98, 100,  90, 106, 109, 114, \
          102, 102, 112, 103,  98,  96,  85,  97, 110, 131, \
           92,  79, 115, 122,  95, 105,  74,  85,  85,  95]
```

6. Create a box plot for each of the IQ scores of different test groups. Add labels and a title:

```
# Create figure
plt.figure(figsize=(6, 4), dpi=150)
# Create histogram
plt.boxplot([group_a, group_b, group_c, group_d])
# Add labels and title
ax = plt.gca()
ax.set_xticklabels(['Group A', 'Group B', 'Group C', 'Group D'])
plt.ylabel('IQ score')
plt.title('IQ scores for different test groups')
# Show plot
plt.show()
```

Following is the output of the code:

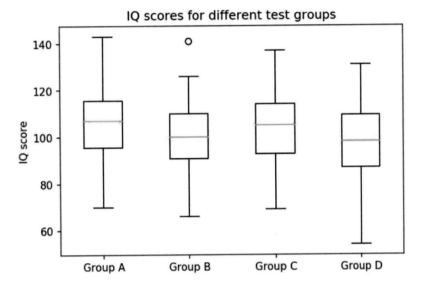

Figure 3.56: Box plot for IQ scores of different test groups

> **NOTE**
>
> To access the source code for this specific section, please refer to
> https://packt.live/3e80Wx4.
>
> You can also run this example online at https://packt.live/2UOfoCM.

ACTIVITY 3.06: CREATING A SCATTER PLOT WITH MARGINAL HISTOGRAMS

Solution:

1. Import the necessary modules and enable plotting within a Jupyter notebook:

```
# Import statements
import pandas as pd
import numpy as np
import matplotlib.pyplot as plt
%matplotlib inline
```

2. Use pandas to read the data located in the **Datasets** folder:

```
# Load dataset
data = pd.read_csv('../../Datasets/anage_data.csv')
```

3. Filter the data so that you end up with samples containing a body mass and a maximum longevity as the given dataset is not complete. Select all the samples of the **aves** class and with a body mass smaller than 20,000:

```
# Preprocessing
longevity = 'Maximum longevity (yrs)'
mass = 'Body mass (g)'
data = data[np.isfinite(data[longevity]) \
        & np.isfinite(data[mass])]
# Sort according to class
aves = data[data['Class'] == 'Aves']
aves = data[data[mass] < 20000]
```

4. Create a Figure with a constrained layout. Create a **gridspec** of size 4x4. Create a scatter plot of size 3x3 and marginal histograms of size 1x3 and 3x1. Add labels and a Figure title:

```
# Create figure
fig = plt.figure(figsize=(8, 8), dpi=150, \
                    constrained_layout=True)
# Create gridspec
gs = fig.add_gridspec(4, 4)
# Specify subplots
histx_ax = fig.add_subplot(gs[0, :-1])
histy_ax = fig.add_subplot(gs[1:, -1])
scatter_ax = fig.add_subplot(gs[1:, :-1])
# Create plots
scatter_ax.scatter(aves[mass], aves[longevity])
histx_ax.hist(aves[mass], bins=20, density=True)
histx_ax.set_xticks([])
histy_ax.hist(aves[longevity], bins=20, density=True, \
                orientation='horizontal')
histy_ax.set_yticks([])
# Add labels and title
plt.xlabel('Body mass in grams')
plt.ylabel('Maximum longevity in years')
fig.suptitle('Scatter plot with marginal histograms')
# Show plot
plt.show()
```

The following is the output of the code:

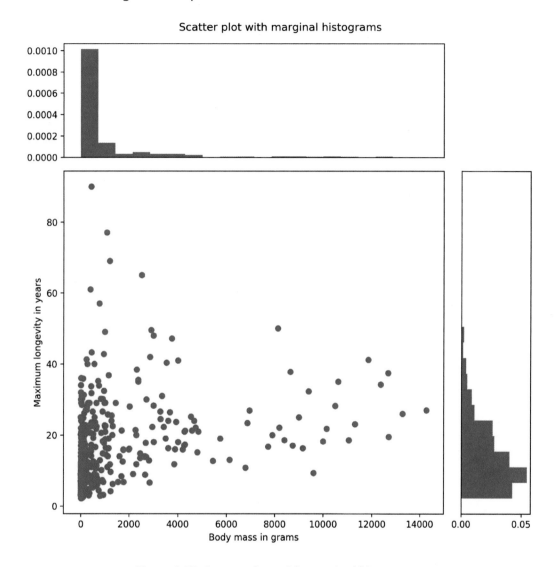

Figure 3.57: Scatter plots with marginal histograms

ACTIVITY 3.07: PLOTTING MULTIPLE IMAGES IN A GRID

Solution:

1. Import the necessary modules and enable plotting within a Jupyter notebook:

```
# Import statements
import os
import numpy as np
import matplotlib.pyplot as plt
import matplotlib.image as mpimg
%matplotlib inline
```

2. Load all four images from the **Datasets** folder:

```
# Load images
img_filenames = sorted(os.listdir('../../Datasets/images'))
imgs = [mpimg.imread(os.path.join('../../Datasets/images', \
                     img_filename)) \
                 for img_filename in img_filenames]
```

3. Visualize the images in a 2x2 grid. Remove the axes and give each image a label:

```
# Create subplot
fig, axes = plt.subplots(2, 2)
fig.figsize = (6, 6)
fig.dpi = 150
axes = axes.ravel()
# Specify labels
labels = ['coast', 'beach', 'building', 'city at night']
# Plot images
for i in range(len(imgs)):
    axes[i].imshow(imgs[i])
    axes[i].set_xticks([])
    axes[i].set_yticks([])
    axes[i].set_xlabel(labels[i])
```

The following is the output of the code:

Figure 3.58: Visualizing images in a 2x2 grid

> **NOTE**
>
> To access the source code for this specific section, please refer to https://packt.live/3hxvFWv.
>
> You can also run this example online at https://packt.live/2zABMrY.

CHAPTER 4: SIMPLIFYING VISUALIZATIONS USING SEABORN

ACTIVITY 4.01: USING HEATMAPS TO FIND PATTERNS IN FLIGHT PASSENGERS' DATA

Solution:

Find the patterns in the flight passengers' data with the help of a heatmap:

1. Create an **Activity4.01.ipynb** Jupyter notebook in the **Chapter04/ Activity4.01** folder to implement this activity.

2. Import the necessary modules and enable plotting within a Jupyter notebook:

```
%matplotlib inline
import numpy as np
import pandas as pd
import matplotlib.pyplot as plt
import seaborn as sns
sns.set()
```

3. Use pandas to read the **flight_details.csv** dataset located in the **Datasets** folder. The given dataset contains the monthly figures for flight passengers for the years 1949 to 1960:

```
data = pd.read_csv("../../Datasets/flight_details.csv")
```

4. Now, we can use the **pivot()** function to transform the data into a format that is suitable for heatmaps:

```
data = data.pivot("Months", "Years", "Passengers")
data = data.reindex(['January', 'February', 'March', \
                     'April', 'May', 'June', 'July', \
                     'August', 'September', 'October', \
                     'November', 'December'])
```

5. Use the **heatmap()** function of the Seaborn library to visualize this data. Within this function, we pass parameters such as DataFrame and colormap. Since we got data from the preceding code, we will pass it as a **DataFrame** in the **heatmap()** function. Also, we will create our own colormap and pass it as a second parameter to this function:

```
plt.figure(dpi=200)
# you can use any sequential color palette
sns.heatmap(data, cmap=sns.cubehelix_palette(rot=-.3, \
                                             as_cmap=True))
```

```
plt.title("Flight Passengers from 1949 to 1960")
plt.show()
```

The following is the output of the code:

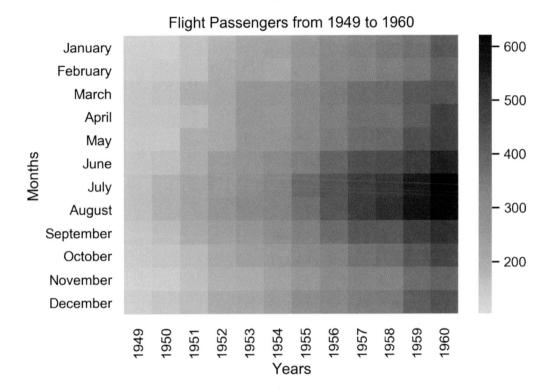

Figure 4.45: Heatmap of flight passengers' data

The heatmap reveals an increasing number of flight passengers from year to year as well as increased demand for flights during the summer months.

> **NOTE**
>
> To access the source code for this specific section, please refer to https://packt.live/2UOMTov.
>
> You can also run this example online at https://packt.live/3ftSPLy.

ACTIVITY 4.02: MOVIE COMPARISON REVISITED

Solution:

Compare the movie scores for five different movies by using a bar plot that's been provided by the Seaborn library:

1. Create an **Activity4.02.ipynb** Jupyter notebook in the **Chapter04/ Activity4.01** folder to implement this activity.

2. Import the necessary modules and enable plotting within a Jupyter notebook:

```
%matplotlib inline
import numpy as np
import pandas as pd
import matplotlib.pyplot as plt
import seaborn as sns
```

3. Use the **read_csv()** function of pandas to read the **movie_scores.csv** dataset located in the **Datasets** folder:

```
mydata = pd.read_csv("../../Datasets/movie_scores.csv", \
                     index_col=0)
```

4. Construct a DataFrame from this given data. This can be done with the help of the **pd.DataFrame()** function provided by pandas. The following code gives us a better idea of this:

```
movie_scores = \
pd.DataFrame({"Movie Title": list(mydata["MovieTitle"]) * 2, \
             "Score": list(mydata["AudienceScore"]) \
             + list(mydata["Tomatometer"]), \
             "Type": ["Audience Score"] \
             * len(mydata["AudienceScore"]) + ["Tomatometer"] \
             * len(mydata["Tomatometer"])})
```

5. Make use of the **barplot()** function provided by Seaborn. Provide **Movies** and **Scores** as parameters so that their data is displayed on both axes. Provide **Type** as **hue** to use subgroups. The final parameter requires a DataFrame as input. Thus, we provide the **movie_scores** DataFrame that we obtained from the previous step.

   The following code provides a better understanding of this:

```
sns.set()
plt.figure(figsize=(10, 5), dpi=300)
```

```
# Create bar plot
ax = sns.barplot("Movie Title", "Score", hue="Type", \
                 data=movie_scores)
plt.xticks(rotation=10)
# Add title
plt.title("Movies Scores comparison")
plt.xlabel("Movies")
plt.ylabel("Scores")
# Show plot
plt.show()
```

The following is the output of the code:

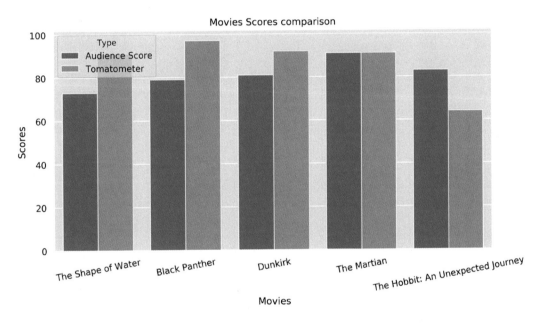

Figure 4.46: Movie scores comparison

We compared the ratings of Audience Score and Tomatometer for five different movies and concluded that the ratings matched for the movie **The Martian**.

ACTIVITY 4.03: COMPARING IQ SCORES FOR DIFFERENT TEST GROUPS BY USING A VIOLIN PLOT

Solution:

Compare IQ scores among different test groups using the Seaborn library:

1. Create an **Activity4.03.ipynb** Jupyter notebook from the **Chapter04/ Activity4.03** folder to implement this activity.

2. Import the necessary modules and enable plotting within a Jupyter notebook:

```
%matplotlib inline
import numpy as np
import pandas as pd
import matplotlib.pyplot as plt
import seaborn as sns
```

3. Use the **read_csv()** function of pandas to read the data located in the **Datasets** folder:

```
mydata = pd.read_csv("../../Datasets/iq_scores.csv")
```

4. Access the data of each test group in the column. Convert this into a list using the **tolist()** method. Once the data of each test group has been converted into a list, assign this list to the variables of each respective test group:

```
group_a = mydata[mydata.columns[0]].tolist()
group_b = mydata[mydata.columns[1]].tolist()
group_c = mydata[mydata.columns[2]].tolist()
group_d = mydata[mydata.columns[3]].tolist()
```

5. Print the variables of each group to check whether the data inside it has been converted into a list. This can be done with the help of the **print()** function:

```
print(group_a)
```

Following is the output of the code:

```
[118, 103, 125, 107, 111, 96, 104, 97, 96, 114, 96, 75, 114, 107, 87, 117, 117, 114, 117, 112, 107, 133, 9
4, 91, 118, 110, 117, 86, 143, 83, 106, 86, 98, 126, 109, 91, 112, 120, 108, 111, 107, 98, 89, 113, 117, 8
1, 113, 112, 84, 115, 96, 93, 128, 115, 138, 121, 87, 112, 110, 79, 100, 84, 115, 93, 108, 130, 107, 106,
106, 101, 117, 93, 94, 103, 112, 98, 103, 70, 139, 94, 110, 105, 122, 94, 94, 105, 129, 110, 112, 97, 109,
121, 106, 118, 131, 88, 122, 125, 93, 78]
```

Figure 4.47: Values of Group A

Print data of group b:

```
print(group_b)
```

Following is the output of the code:

```
[126, 89, 90, 101, 102, 74, 93, 101, 66, 120, 108, 97, 98, 105, 119, 92, 113, 81, 104, 108, 83, 102, 105,
111, 102, 107, 103, 89, 89, 110, 71, 110, 120, 85, 111, 83, 122, 120, 102, 84, 118, 100, 100, 114, 81, 10
9, 69, 97, 95, 106, 116, 109, 114, 98, 90, 92, 98, 91, 81, 85, 86, 102, 93, 112, 76, 89, 110, 75, 110, 90,
96, 94, 107, 108, 95, 96, 96, 114, 93, 95, 117, 141, 115, 95, 86, 100, 121, 103, 66, 99, 96, 111, 110, 10
5, 110, 91, 112, 102, 112, 75]
```

Figure 4.48: Values of Group B

Print data of group c:

```
print(group_c)
```

Following is the output of the code:

```
[108, 89, 114, 116, 126, 104, 113, 96, 69, 121, 109, 102, 107, 122, 104, 107, 108, 137, 107, 116, 98, 132,
108, 114, 82, 93, 89, 90, 86, 91, 99, 98, 83, 93, 114, 96, 95, 113, 103, 81, 107, 85, 116, 85, 107, 125, 1
26, 123, 122, 124, 115, 114, 93, 93, 114, 107, 107, 84, 131, 91, 108, 127, 112, 106, 115, 82, 90, 117, 10
8, 115, 113, 108, 104, 103, 90, 110, 114, 92, 101, 72, 109, 94, 122, 90, 102, 86, 119, 103, 110, 96, 90, 1
10, 96, 69, 85, 102, 69, 96, 101, 90]
```

Figure 4.49: Values of Group C

Print data of group d:

```
print(group_d)
```

Following is the output of the code:

```
[93, 99, 91, 110, 80, 113, 111, 115, 98, 74, 96, 80, 83, 102, 60, 91, 82, 90, 97, 101, 89, 89, 117, 91, 10
4, 104, 102, 128, 106, 111, 79, 92, 97, 101, 106, 110, 93, 93, 106, 108, 85, 83, 108, 94, 79, 87, 113, 11
2, 111, 111, 79, 116, 104, 84, 116, 111, 103, 103, 112, 68, 54, 80, 86, 119, 81, 84, 91, 96, 116, 125, 99,
58, 102, 77, 98, 100, 90, 106, 109, 114, 102, 102, 112, 103, 98, 96, 85, 97, 110, 131, 92, 79, 115, 122, 9
5, 105, 74, 85, 85, 95]
```

Figure 4.50: Values of Group D

6. Once we get the data for each test group, we need to construct a DataFrame from this given data. This can be done with the help of the **pd.DataFrame()** function that's provided by pandas:

```
data = pd.DataFrame({'Groups': ['Group A'] * len(group_a) \
                    + ['Group B'] * len(group_b) + ['Group C'] \
                    * len(group_c) + ['Group D'] \
                    * len(group_d), \
                    'IQ score': group_a + group_b + group_c \
                    + group_d})
```

7. Now, since we have the DataFrame, we need to create a violin plot using the **violinplot()** function that's provided by Seaborn. Within this function, we need to specify the titles for both the axes along with the DataFrame we are using. The title for the x-axis will be **Groups**, and the title for the y-axis will be **IQ score**. As far as the DataFrame is concerned, we will pass **data** as a parameter. Here, **data** is the DataFrame that we obtained from the previous step:

```
plt.figure(dpi=150)
# Set style
sns.set_style('whitegrid')
# Create boxplot
sns.violinplot('Groups', 'IQ score', data=data)
# Despine
sns.despine(left=True, right=True, top=True)
# Add title
plt.title('IQ scores for different test groups')
# Show plot
plt.show()
```

The following is the output of the code:

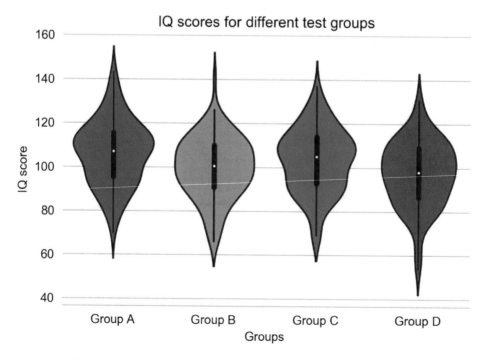

Figure 4.51: Violin plot showing IQ scores of different groups

The **despine()** function helps to remove the top and right spines from the plot. Here, we have also removed the left spine. Using the **title()** function, we have set the title for our plot. The **show()** function helps to visualize the plot.

> **NOTE**
>
> To access the source code for this specific section, please refer to https://packt.live/30OU8ka.
>
> You can also run this example online at https://packt.live/2Y6G04g.

ACTIVITY 4.04: VISUALIZING THE TOP 30 MUSIC YOUTUBE CHANNELS USING SEABORN'S FACETGRID

Solution:

Visualize the total number of subscribers and the total number of views for the top 30 YouTube channels by using the **FacetGrid()** function that's provided by the Seaborn library:

1. Create an **Activity4.04.ipynb** Jupyter notebook in the **Chapter04/ Activity4.04** folder to implement this activity.

2. Import the necessary modules and enable plotting within a Jupyter notebook:

```
%matplotlib inline
import numpy as np
import pandas as pd
import matplotlib.pyplot as plt
import seaborn as sns
```

3. Use the **read_csv()** function of pandas to read the data located in the **Datasets** folder:

```
mydata = pd.read_csv("../../Datasets/YouTube.csv")
```

4. Access the data of each test group in the column. Convert this into a list by using the **tolist()** method. Once the data of each test group has been converted into a list, assign this list to variables of each respective test group:

```
channels = mydata[mydata.columns[0]].tolist()
subs = mydata[mydata.columns[1]].tolist()
views = mydata[mydata.columns[2]].tolist()
```

5. Print the variables of each group to check whether the data inside it has been converted into a list. This can be done with the help of the **print()** function:

```
print(channels)
```

Following is the output of the code:

```
['T-Series', 'Canal KondZilla', 'Zee Music Company', 'Ed Sheeran ', 'EminemMusic ', 'Ariana Grande ', 'Taylor Swift', 'JustinBieberVEVO ', ' BLACKPINK', 'Alan Walker', 'Shemaroo Filmi Gaane', 'ibighit', 'One Direction', 'Wave Music ', 'Sony Music India ', 'El Reino Infantil', 'Maroon 5 ', 'Trap Nation', 'Speed Records', 'GR6 EXPLODE ', 'TaylorSwiftVEVO ', 'SonyMusicIndiaVEVO', 'Ozuna', 'Daddy Yankee', 'YRF', "Spinnin' Records", 'Bruno Mars', 'RihannaVEVO ', 'T-Series Bhakti Sagar', 'KatyPerryVEVO']
```

Figure 4.52: List of YouTube channels

Printing the number of subscribers for each channel:

```
print(subs)
```

Following is the output of the code:

```
[123.0, 54.5, 48.5, 43.2, 40.2, 39.3, 36.8, 33.1, 32.4, 31.7, 31.0, 30.9, 30.4, 30.4, 29.9, 29.2, 29.2, 27.9, 27.4, 27.2, 27.0, 27.0, 27.0, 26.9, 26.8, 26.4, 26.3, 25.9, 25.8, 25.8]
```

Figure 4.53: List of subscribers for each YouTube channel

Printing the number of views for each channel:

```
print(views)
```

```
[94410, 27860, 22689, 18905, 773, 953, 310, 19326, 8112, 7470, 14708, 7659, 356, 20569, 12077, 26159, 294, 10195, 13769, 13341, 18096, 12577, 13059, 9796, 14253, 15738, 11411, 14768, 10552, 18603]
```

Figure 4.54: List of views for each YouTube channel

6. Once we get the data for **channels**, **subs**, and **views**, we need to construct a DataFrame from the given data. This can be done with the help of the **pd.DataFrame()** function that's provided by pandas:

```
data = pd.DataFrame({'YouTube Channels': channels + channels, \
                     'Subscribers in millions': subs + views, \
                     'Type': ['Subscribers'] * len(subs) \
                     + ['Views'] * len(views)})
```

7. Now, since we have the DataFrame, we need to create a FacetGrid using the **FacetGrid()** function that's provided by Seaborn. Here, **data** is the DataFrame, which we obtained from the previous step:

```
sns.set()
g = sns.FacetGrid(data, col='Type', hue='Type', \
                  sharex=False, height=8)
g.map(sns.barplot, 'Subscribers in millions', 'YouTube Channels')
plt.show()
```

The following is the output of the code:

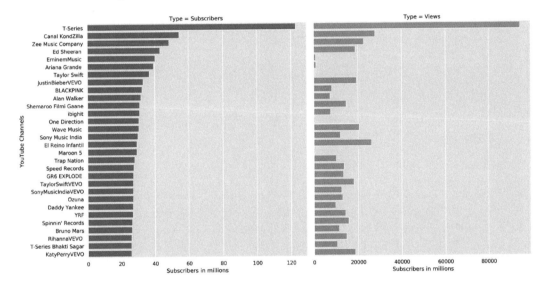

Figure 4.55: Subscribers and views of the top 30 YouTube channels

We can conclude that the YouTube channel T-Series has both the highest number of subscribers and views in the music category.

> **NOTE**
>
> To access the source code for this specific section, please refer to https://packt.live/3d9qLLU.
>
> You can also run this example online at https://packt.live/37A5xFY.

ACTIVITY 4.05: LINEAR REGRESSION FOR ANIMAL ATTRIBUTE RELATIONS

Solution:

Visualize the linear relationship between maximum longevity and body mass in the regression plot by using the **regplot()** function that's provided by the Seaborn library:

1. Create an **Activity4.05.ipynb** Jupyter notebook in the **Chapter04/ Activity4.05** folder to implement this activity.

2. Import the necessary modules and enable plotting within a Jupyter notebook:

```
%matplotlib inline
import numpy as np
import pandas as pd
import matplotlib.pyplot as plt
import seaborn as sns
```

3. Use the **read_csv()** function of pandas to read the data located in the **Datasets** folder:

```
mydata = pd.read_csv("../../Datasets/anage_data.csv")
```

4. Filter the data so that you end up with samples containing a body mass and maximum longevity. Only consider samples for the **Mammalia** class and a body mass of less than 200,000. This preprocessing can be seen in the following code:

```
longevity = 'Maximum longevity (yrs)'
mass = 'Body mass (g)'
data = mydata[mydata['Class'] == 'Mammalia']
data = data[np.isfinite(data[longevity]) \
        & np.isfinite(data[mass]) & (data[mass] < 200000)]
```

5. Once the preprocessing is done, plot the data using the **regplot()** function that's provided by the Seaborn library. There are three parameters inside the **regplot()** function that have to be specified. The first two parameters are **mass** and **longevity**, wherein the body mass data will be shown on the x-axis, and the maximum longevity data will be shown on the y-axis. For the third parameter, provide the DataFrame obtained from the previous step:

```
# Create figure
sns.set()
plt.figure(figsize=(10, 6), dpi=300)
# Create a scatter plot
```

```
sns.regplot(mass, longevity, data=data)
# Show plot
plt.show()
```

The following is the output of the code:

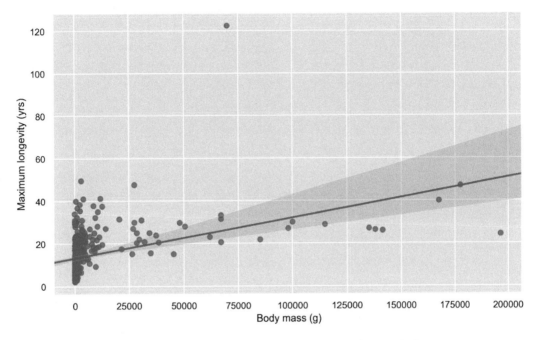

Figure 4.56: Linear regression for animal attribute relations

We can conclude that there is a linear relationship between body mass and maximum longevity for the **Mammalia** class.

> **NOTE**
>
> To access the source code for this specific section, please refer to https://packt.live/2UNM5Ax.
>
> You can also run this example online at https://packt.live/30Nf9Mk.

ACTIVITY 4.06: VISUALIZING THE IMPACT OF EDUCATION ON ANNUAL SALARY AND WEEKLY WORKING HOURS

Solution:

You're asked to determine whether education has an influence on annual salary and weekly working hours. You ask 500 people in the state of New York about their age, annual salary, weekly working hours, and their education. You first want to know the percentage for each education type, so therefore you use a tree map. Two violin plots will be used to visualize the annual salary and weekly working hours. Compare in each case to what extent education has an impact.

It should also be taken into account that all visualizations in this activity are designed to be suitable for colorblind people. In principle, this is always a good idea to bear in mind:

1. Create an **Activity4.06.ipynb** Jupyter notebook from the **Chapter04/ Activity4.06** folder to implement this activity. Navigate to the path of this file and type in the following at the command-line terminal: **jupyter-lab**.

2. Import the necessary modules and enable plotting within a Jupyter notebook:

```
%matplotlib inline
import numpy as np
import pandas as pd
import matplotlib.pyplot as plt
import seaborn as sns
import squarify
sns.set()
```

3. Use the **read_csv()** function of pandas to read the **age_salary_hours. csv** dataset located in the **Datasets** folder:

```
data = pd.read_csv("../../Datasets/age_salary_hours.csv")
```

4. Use a tree map to visualize the percentages for each education type:

```
# Compute percentages from dataset
degrees = set(data['Education'])
percentages = []
for degree in degrees:
    percentages.append(data[data['Education'] == degree].shape[0])
percentages = np.array(percentages)
```

```
percentages = ((percentages / percentages.sum()) * 100)

# Create labels for tree map
labels = [degree + '\n({0:.1f}%)'.format(percentage) \
          for degree, percentage in zip(degrees, percentages)]

# Create figure
plt.figure(figsize=(9, 6), dpi=200)
squarify.plot(percentages, label=labels, \
              color=sns.color_palette('colorblind', \
                                      len(degrees)))
plt.axis('off')
# Add title
plt.title('Degrees')
# Show plot
plt.show()
```

The following is the output of the code:

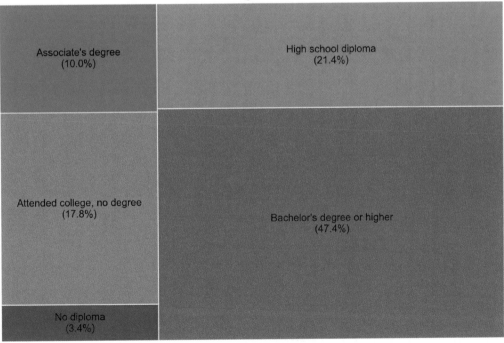

Figure 4.57: Tree map

5. Create a subplot with two rows to visualize two violin plots for the annual salary and weekly working hours, respectively. Compare in each case to what extent education has an impact. To exclude pensioners, only consider people younger than 65. Use a colormap that is suitable for colorblind people. **subplots()** can be used in combination with Seaborn's plot, by simply passing the **ax** argument with the respective axes:

```
ordered_degrees = sorted(list(degrees))
ordered_degrees = [ordered_degrees[4], ordered_degrees[3], \
                    ordered_degrees[1], ordered_degrees[0], \
                    ordered_degrees[2]]
data = data.loc[data['Age'] < 65]
# Set color palette to colorblind
sns.set_palette('colorblind')
# Create subplot with two rows
fig, ax = plt.subplots(2, 1, dpi=200, figsize=(8, 8))
sns.violinplot('Education', 'Annual Salary', data=data, \
               cut=0, order=ordered_degrees, ax=ax[0])
ax[0].set_xticklabels(ax[0].get_xticklabels(), rotation=10)
sns.violinplot('Education', 'Weekly hours', data=data, \
               cut=0, order=ordered_degrees, ax=ax[1])
ax[1].set_xticklabels(ax[1].get_xticklabels(), rotation=10)
plt.tight_layout()
# Add title
fig.suptitle('Impact of Education on Annual Salary and '\
             'Weekly Working Hours')
# Show figure
plt.show()
```

The following is the output of the code:

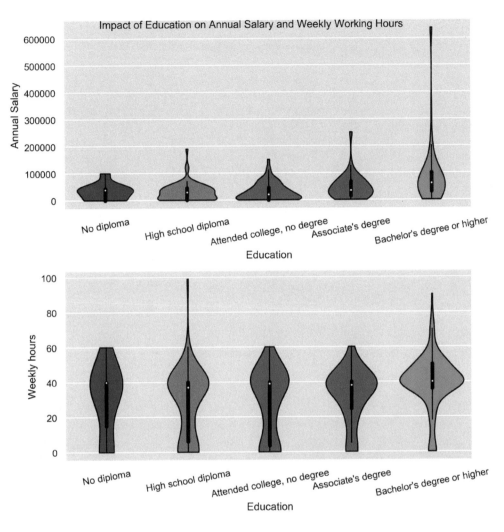

Figure 4.58: Violin plots showing the impact of education on annual salary and weekly working hours

The preceding output helps us to analyze the impact of education on annual salary and weekly working hours.

> **NOTE**
>
> To access the source code for this specific section, please refer to
> https://packt.live/2AIDJ66.
>
> You can also run this example online at https://packt.live/3fw499U.

CHAPTER 5: PLOTTING GEOSPATIAL DATA

ACTIVITY 5.01: PLOTTING GEOSPATIAL DATA ON A MAP

Solution:

Let's plot the geospatial data on a map and find the densely populated areas of cities in Europe that have population of more than 100,000:

1. Create an **Activity5.01.ipynb** Jupyter notebook in the **Chapter05/Activity5.01** folder to implement this activity and then import the necessary dependencies:

    ```
    import numpy as np
    import pandas as pd
    import geoplotlib
    ```

2. Load the **world_cities_pop.csv** dataset from the **Datasets** folder using pandas:

    ```
    #loading the Dataset (make sure to have the dataset downloaded)
    dataset = pd.read_csv('../../Datasets/world_cities_pop.csv', \
                          dtype = {'Region': np.str})
    ```

    > **NOTE**
    >
    > If we import our dataset without defining the **dtype** attribute of the **Region** column as a **String** type, we will get a warning telling us that it has a mixed datatype. We can get rid of this warning by explicitly defining the type of the values in this column, which we can do by using the **dtype** parameter.

3. Check the **dtype** attribute of each column using the **dtypes** attribute of a DataFrame:

    ```
    # looking at the data types of each column
    dataset.dtypes
    ```

The following figure shows the output of the preceding code:

```
Country          object
City             object
AccentCity       object
Region           object
Population      float64
Latitude        float64
Longitude       float64
dtype: object
```

Figure 5.31: The datatypes of each column of the dataset

> **NOTE**
>
> Here, we can see the datatypes of each column. Since the **String** type is not a primitive datatype, it's displayed as an object.

4. Use the **head()** method of a pandas DataFrame to display the first five entries:

```
# showing the first 5 entries of the dataset
dataset.head()
```

The following figure shows the output of the preceding code:

	Country	City	AccentCity	Region	Population	Latitude	Longitude
0	ad	aixas	Aixàs	06	NaN	42.483333	1.466667
1	ad	aixirivali	Aixirivali	06	NaN	42.466667	1.500000
2	ad	aixirivall	Aixirivall	06	NaN	42.466667	1.500000
3	ad	aixirvall	Aixirvall	06	NaN	42.466667	1.500000
4	ad	aixovall	Aixovall	06	NaN	42.466667	1.483333

Figure 5.32: The first five entries of the dataset

5. Map the **Latitude** and **Longitude** columns into the **lat** and **lon** columns by using simple code:

```
# mapping Latitude to lat and Longitude to lon
dataset['lat'] = dataset['Latitude']
dataset['lon'] = dataset['Longitude']
```

Most datasets won't be in the format that you desire. Some of them might have their **Latitude** and **Longitude** values hidden in a different column. This is where the data wrangling skills of *Chapter 1, The Importance of Data Visualization and Data Exploration*, are required.

6. Our dataset is now ready for the first plotting. Use a **DotDensityLayer** to see all of our data points:

```
# plotting the whole dataset with dots
geoplotlib.dot(dataset)
geoplotlib.show()
```

The following figure shows the output of the preceding code:

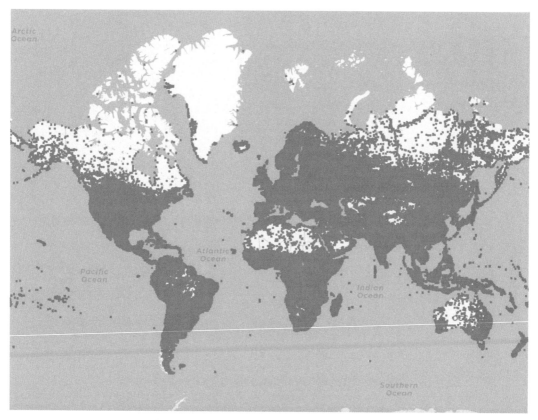

Figure 5.33: Dot density visualization of all the cities

7. Before we start breaking down our data to get a better and more workable dataset, we want to understand the outlines of all of our data. Display the number of countries and the number of cities that our dataset holds:

```
# amount of countries and cities
print(len(dataset.groupby(['Country'])), 'Countries')
print(len(dataset), 'Cities')
```

The following figure shows the output of the preceding code:

```
234 Countries
3173958 Cities
```

8. Use the **size()** method, which returns a **Series** object, to see each grouped element on its own:

```
# amount of cities per country (first 20 entries)
dataset.groupby(['Country']).size().head(20)
```

The following figure shows the output of the preceding code:

```
Country
ad          92
ae         446
af       88749
ag         183
ai          42
al       15123
am        2890
an         269
ao       19560
ar        8738
at       14788
au       10941
aw         115
az       11223
ba       15999
bb         536
bd       26414
be       16218
bf       10468
bg       20106
dtype: int64
```

Figure 5.34: The number of cities per country

9. Display the average number of cities per country using the **agg** method of pandas:

```
# average num of cities per country
dataset.groupby(['Country']).size().agg('mean')
```

The following figure shows the output of the preceding code:

```
13563.923076923076
```

Reduce the amount of data we are working with by removing all the cities that don't have a population value, meaning a population of 0, in this case:

```
# filter for countries with a population entry (Population > 0)
dataset_with_pop = dataset[(dataset['Population'] > 0)]
print('Full dataset:', len(dataset))
print('Cities with population information:', \
      len(dataset_with_pop))
```

The following figure shows the output of the preceding code:

```
Full dataset: 3173958
Cities with population information: 47980
```

> **NOTE**
>
> Breaking down and filtering your data is one of the most important aspects of getting good insights. Cluttered visualizations can hide information.

10. Display the first five items of the new dataset to get a basic indication of what the values in the **Population** column will look like:

```
# displaying the first 5 items from dataset_with_pop
dataset_with_pop.head()
```

The following figure shows the output of the preceding code:

	Country	City	AccentCity	Region	Population	Latitude	Longitude	lat	lon
6	ad	andorra la vella	Andorra la Vella	07	20430.0	42.500000	1.516667	42.500000	1.516667
20	ad	canillo	Canillo	02	3292.0	42.566667	1.600000	42.566667	1.600000
32	ad	encamp	Encamp	03	11224.0	42.533333	1.583333	42.533333	1.583333
49	ad	la massana	La Massana	04	7211.0	42.550000	1.516667	42.550000	1.516667
53	ad	les escaldes	Les Escaldes	08	15854.0	42.500000	1.533333	42.500000	1.533333

Figure 5.35: The first five items of the reduced dataset

11. Now, take a look at our reduced dataset with the help of a dot density plot:

```
"""
showing all cities with a defined population \
with a dot density plot
"""
geoplotlib.dot(dataset_with_pop)
geoplotlib.show()
```

The following is the output of the code:

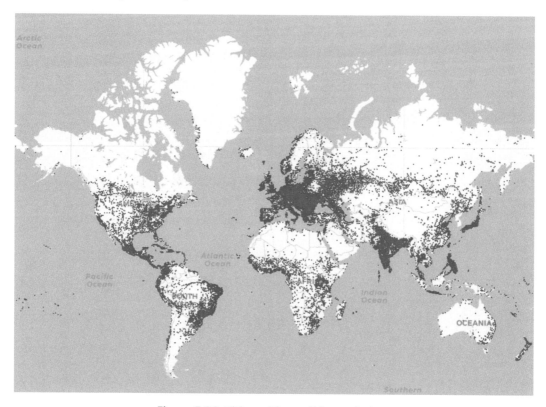

Figure 5.36: Cities with a valid population

On the new dot plot, we can already see some improvements in terms of clarity. However, we still have too many dots on our map. Given the activity definition, we can filter our dataset further by only looking at cities with a population of more than **100k**.

12. Filter the dataset to contain only cities with a population of more than **100k**:

```
# dataset with cities with a population of >= 100k
dataset_100k = \
dataset_with_pop[(dataset_with_pop['Population'] >= 100000)]
print('Cities with a population of 100k or more:', \
      len(dataset_100k))
```

The following figure shows the output of the preceding code:

```
Cities with a population of 100k or more: 3527
```

13. In addition to just plotting our **100k** dataset, fix our viewport to a specific bounding box. Since our data is spread across the world, use the built-in **WORLD** constant of the **BoundingBox** class:

```
"""
displaying all cities >= 100k population with a fixed bounding box
(WORLD) in a dot density plot
"""

from geoplotlib.utils import BoundingBox

geoplotlib.dot(dataset_100k)
geoplotlib.set_bbox(BoundingBox.WORLD)
geoplotlib.show()
```

The following figure shows the output of the preceding code:

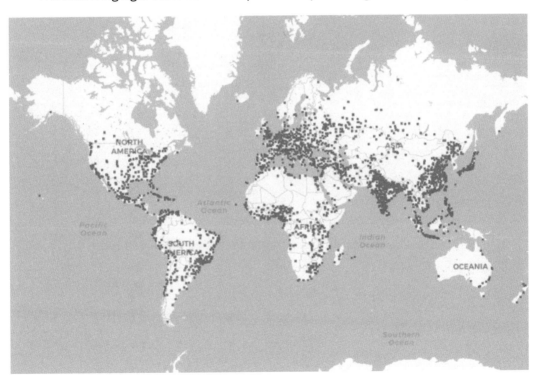

Figure 5.37: Dot density visualization of cities with a population of 100,000 or more

14. Compare the output with the previous plots; it gives us a better view of where the highest number of cities with a population of more than 100,000 is. Find the areas of these cities that are the most densely packed using a **Voronoi** plot:

```
# using filled voronoi to find dense areas
geoplotlib.voronoi(dataset_100k, cmap='hot_r', \
                   max_area=1e3, alpha=255)
geoplotlib.show()
```

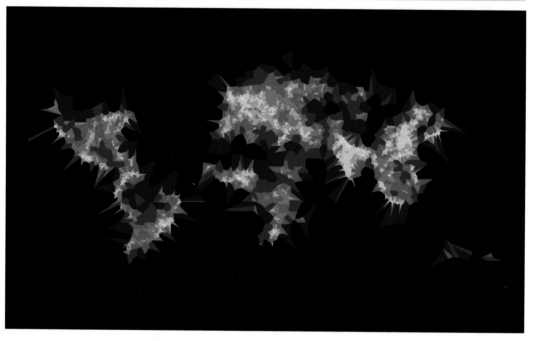

Figure 5.38: A Voronoi visualization of densely populated cities

The resulting visualization is exactly what we were searching for. On the Voronoi plot, we can see clear tendencies. Germany, Great Britain, Nigeria, India, Japan, Java, the East Coast of the USA, and Brazil stick out. We can now filter our data and only look at those countries to find the ones that are best suited to this scenario.

> **NOTE**
>
> You can also create a custom colormap gradient with the **ColorMap** class.

15. Filter the dataset to only countries in Europe, such as Germany and Great Britain. Use the **or** operator when adding a filter to our data. This will allow us to filter for Germany and Great Britain at the same time:

```
# filter 100k dataset for cities in Germany and GB
dataset_europe = dataset_100k[(dataset_100k['Country'] == 'de') \
              | (dataset_100k['Country'] == 'gb')]
print('Cities in Germany or GB with population >= 100k:', \
      len(dataset_europe))
```

The following is the output of the preceding code:

```
Cities in Germany or GB with population >= 100k: 150
```

16. Use Delaunay triangulation to find the areas that have the most densely packed cities:

```
"""
using Delaunay triangulation to find the most densely populated area
"""
geoplotlib.delaunay(dataset_europe, cmap='hot_r')
geoplotlib.show()
```

By using a **hot_r** color map, we can quickly get a good visual representation and make the areas of interest pop out. Here, the areas around Cologne, Birmingham, and Manchester really stick out:

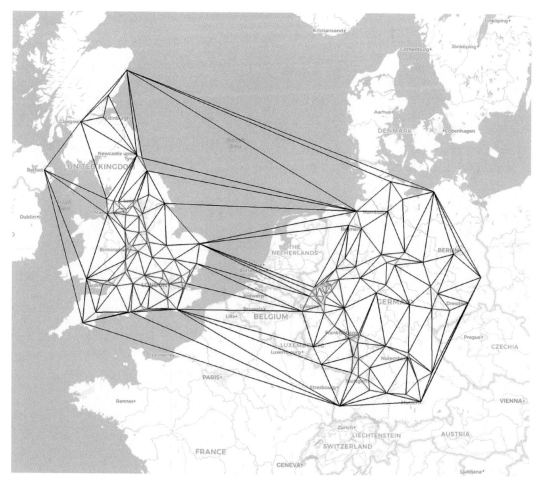

Figure 5.39: A Delaunay triangle visualization of cities in Germany and Great Britain

ACTIVITY 5.02: VISUALIZING CITY DENSITY BY THE FIRST LETTER USING AN INTERACTIVE CUSTOM LAYER

Solution:

1. Create an **Activity5.02.ipynb** Jupyter notebook in the **Chapter05/Activity5.02** folder to implement this activity, and then import the necessary dependencies:

```
# importing the necessary dependencies
import numpy as np
import pandas as pd
import geoplotlib
```

2. Load the **world_cities_pop.csv** dataset from the **Datasets** folder using pandas:

```
dataset = pd.read_csv('../../Datasets/world_cities_pop.csv', \
                      dtype = {'Region': np.str})
```

> **NOTE**
>
> If we import our dataset without defining the **dtype** parameter of the **Region** column as a **String** type, we will get a warning telling us that it has a mixed datatype. We can get rid of this warning by explicitly defining the type of the values in this column, which we can do by using the **dtype** parameter.

3. Check the **dtype** parameter of each column using the **dtypes** attribute of a DataFrame:

```
# looking at the first 5 rows of the dataset
dataset.head()
```

The following figure shows the output of the preceding code:

	Country	City	AccentCity	Region	Population	Latitude	Longitude
0	ad	aixas	Aixàs	06	NaN	42.483333	1.466667
1	ad	aixirivali	Aixirivali	06	NaN	42.466667	1.500000
2	ad	aixirivall	Aixirivall	06	NaN	42.466667	1.500000
3	ad	aixirvall	Aixirvall	06	NaN	42.466667	1.500000
4	ad	aixovall	Aixovall	06	NaN	42.466667	1.483333

Figure 5.40: The first five rows of the dataset

4. Prepare our dataset to be usable by geoplotlib by assigning two new columns, **lat** and **lon**. Map the **Latitude** and **Longitude** columns into **lat** and **lon** columns, which are used by geoplotlib:

```
# mapping Latitude to lat and Longitude to lon
dataset['lat'] = dataset['Latitude']
dataset['lon'] = dataset['Longitude']
```

5. Focus your attention on European countries and their cities. A list of all European countries is as follows:

```
# 2 letter country codes of europe without russia
europe_country_codes = ['al', 'ad', 'at', 'by', 'be', 'ba', \
                        'bg', 'hr', 'cy', 'cz', 'dk', 'ee', \
                        'fo', 'fi', 'fr', 'de', 'gi', 'gr', \
                        'hu', 'is', 'ie', 'im', 'it', 'xk', \
                        'lv', 'li', 'lt', 'lu', 'mk', 'mt', \
                        'md', 'mc', 'me', 'nl', 'no', 'pl', \
                        'pt', 'ro', 'sm', 'rs', 'sk', 'si', \
                        'es', 'se', 'ch', 'ua', 'gb', 'va']
```

6. Given this list, we want to use filtering to get a dataset that only contains European cities. The filtering works exactly as we learned in *Chapter 01, The Importance of Data Visualization and Data Exploration*. Use the **europe_country_codes** column to filter down our dataset by using the **isin()** method as a condition for our DataFrame:

```
# filtering the dataset for countries in europe
europe_dataset = \
dataset[dataset['Country'].isin(europe_country_codes)]
```

7. Print both the length of our whole dataset and the filtered down dataset:

```
# printing the length of both datasets
print('Whole World data', len(dataset))
print('Europe data', len(europe_dataset))
```

The following figure shows the output of the preceding code:

```
Whole World data 3173958
Europe data 682348
```

8. As preparation for our interactive visualization, we want to do a test run with cities that start with the letter Z. Filter down our Europe dataset by using **europe_dataset['AccentCity'].str.startswith('Z')** as a filter condition. Print out the number of cities starting with Z and the first five rows of our filtered dataset:

```
# plotting the whole dataset with dots
cities_starting_z = \
europe_dataset[europe_dataset['AccentCity'].str.startswith('Z')]

print('Cities starting with Z:', len(cities_starting_z))
cities_starting_z.head()
```

The following figure shows the output of the preceding code:

```
Cities starting with Z: 13218
```

	Country	City	AccentCity	Region	Population	Latitude	Longitude	lat	lon
104206	al	zaane	ZÄane	44	NaN	40.932778	19.783056	40.932778	19.783056
104207	al	zabarzani	Zabarzani	40	NaN	40.427778	20.269167	40.427778	20.269167
104208	al	zabarzan	Zabarzan	40	NaN	40.427778	20.269167	40.427778	20.269167
104209	al	zaberzane	Zabërzanë	40	NaN	40.427778	20.269167	40.427778	20.269167
104210	al	zaberzan i siperm	Zaberzan i Sipërm	40	NaN	40.427778	20.269167	40.427778	20.269167

Figure 5.41: The dataset only containing cities starting with Z

We want to take a quick look at the cities starting with **Z** in the dataset using a **DotDensity** plot and also get some information about the cities using the previously seen **f_tooltip** argument. To use the **f_tooltip** argument, we need to wrap our dataset in **DataAccessObject**.

9. Create a new **DataAccessObject** from our cities with the **Z** dataset, visualize it with a dot plot, and use a tooltip that outputs the **Country** and **City** name separated by a – (for example, **Ch - Zürich**):

```
# using dot density to plot a point for each city
from geoplotlib.utils import DataAccessObject

geoplotlib_data = DataAccessObject(cities_starting_z)
geoplotlib.dot(geoplotlib_data, f_tooltip=lambda d: '{} \
            - {}'.format(d['Country'].upper(), \
            d['City']).title())
geoplotlib.show()
```

The following figure shows the output of the preceding code:

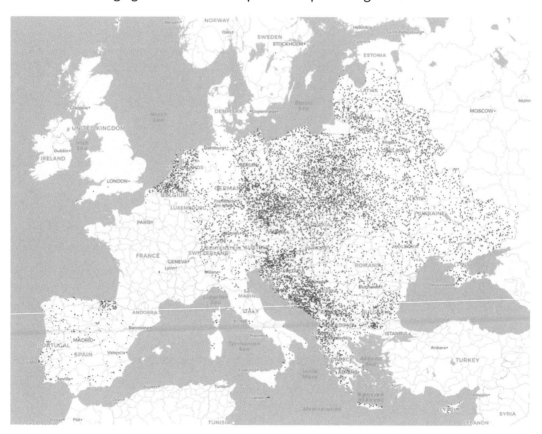

Figure 5.42: A dot density plot of cities starting with Z in Europe

10. As a second step, we want to use a **voronoi** plot to display the density of cities starting with the letter Z. Create a new **voronoi** plot using a color map of **Reds_r**, max area of **1e5**, and an **alpha** value of **50** so that we can still see the mapping peeking through:

```
"""
displaying the density of cities stating with \
z using a voronoi plot
"""
geoplotlib.voronoi(cities_starting_z, cmap='Reds_r', \
                   max_area=1e5, alpha=50)
geoplotlib.show()
```

The following figure shows the output of the preceding code:

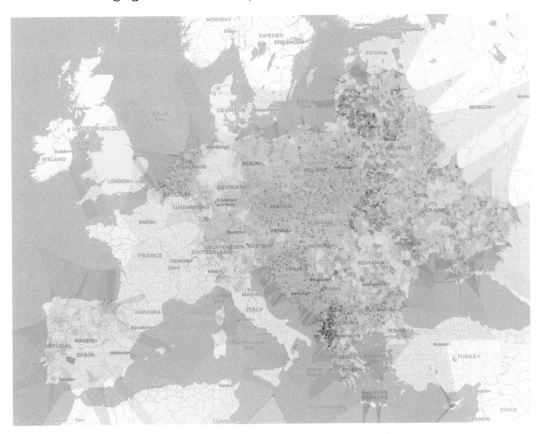

Figure 5.43: A Voronoi plot showing the density of cities starting with Z in Europe

Now we will create an interactive visualization that displays each city, as a dot, that starts with the currently selected first letter. The letter selected by default will be **A**. We need a way to iterate through the letters using the left and right arrows. As described in the introductory *Custom Layers* section, we can make use of the **on_key_release** method, which is specifically designed for this.

11. Filter the **self.data** dataset in the **invalidate** method using the current letter acquired from the **start_letters** array using the **self.start_letter** index:

```python
# custom layer creation
import pyglet
import geoplotlib
from geoplotlib.layers import BaseLayer
from geoplotlib.core import BatchPainter
from geoplotlib.utils import BoundingBox


start_letters = ['A', 'B', 'C', 'D', 'E', 'F', 'G', 'H', 'I', \
                 'H', 'K', 'L', 'M', 'N', 'O', 'P', 'Q', 'R', \
                 'S', 'T', 'U', 'V', 'W' , 'X', 'Y', 'Z']


class FilterLayer (BaseLayer):
    def __init__(self, dataset, bbox=BoundingBox.WORLD):
        self.data = dataset
        self.start_letter = 0
        self.view = bbox


    def invalidate(self, proj):
        start_letter_data = self.data[self.data['AccentCity']\
                            .str.startswith\
                            (start_letters[self.start_letter])]
```

12. Create a new **BatchPainter()** function and project the **lon** and **lat** values to the **x** and **y** values. Use the **BatchPainter** function to paint the points on the map with a size of **2**:

```python
        self.painter = BatchPainter()
        x, y = proj.lonlat_to_screen(start_letter_data['lon'], \
                                     start_letter_data['lat'])
        self.painter.points(x, y, 2)
```

13. Call the **batch_draw()** method in the **draw** method and use the **ui_manager** to add an **info** dialog to the screen telling the user which starting letter is currently being used:

```
def draw(self, proj, mouse_x, mouse_y, ui_manager):
    self.painter.batch_draw()
    ui_manager.info('Displaying cities starting with {}'\
                    .format(start_letters[self.start_letter]))
```

14. Check which key is pressed using **pyglet**, **pyglet.window.key.RIGHT**. If the right or left key is pressed, increment or decrement the **start_letter** value of the **FilterLayer** class accordingly. (Use **modulo** to allow rotation, which should happen when A->Z or Z->A). Make sure that you **return True** in the **on_key_release** method if you changed the **start_letter** value to trigger a redrawing of the points:

```
def on_key_release(self, key, modifiers):
    if key == pyglet.window.key.RIGHT:
        self.start_letter = (self.start_letter + 1) \
                            % len(start_letters)
        return True
    elif key == pyglet.window.key.LEFT:
        self.start_letter = (self.start_letter - 1) \
                            % len(start_letters)
        return True

    return False


# bounding box that gets used when the layer is created
def bbox(self):
    return self.view
```

15. Now call the **add_layer()** method of geoplotlib, providing our custom layer with the given **BoundingBox** class of Europe:

```
# using Delaunay triangulation to find the densest area
europe_bbox = BoundingBox(north=68.574309, west=-25.298424, \
                          south=34.266013, east=47.387123)


geoplotlib.add_layer(FilterLayer(europe_dataset, europe_bbox))
geoplotlib.show()
```

The following figure shows the output of the preceding code:

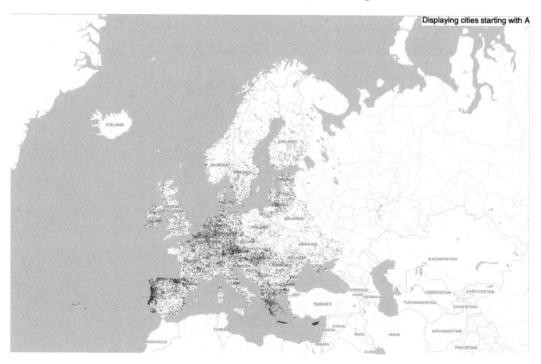

Figure 5.44: A dot density plot of cities starting with A in Europe in the custom layer

Pressing the right arrow key twice will lead to the custom layer plotting the cities starting with a C:

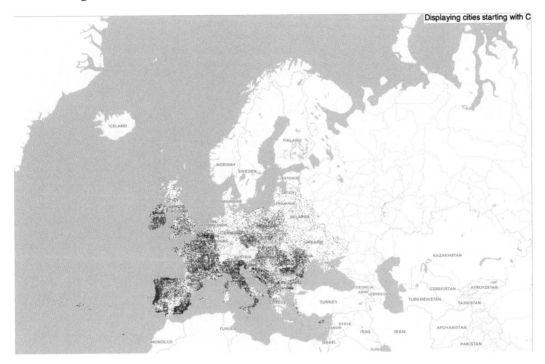

Figure 5.45: A dot density plot of cities starting with C in Europe in the custom layer

> **NOTE**
>
> To access the source code for this specific section, please refer to https://packt.live/2Y63NBi.
>
> This section does not currently have an online interactive example, and will need to be run locally.

CHAPTER 6: MAKING THINGS INTERACTIVE WITH BOKEH

ACTIVITY 6.01: PLOTTING MEAN CAR PRICES OF MANUFACTURERS

Solution:

1. Create an **Activity6.01.ipynb** Jupyter notebook in the **Chapter06/ Activity6.01** folder.

2. Import the necessary libraries:

```
import pandas as pd
from bokeh.io import output_notebook


output_notebook()
```

3. Load the **automobiles.csv** dataset from the **Datasets** folder:

```
dataset = pd.read_csv('../../Datasets/automobiles.csv')
```

4. Use the **head** method to print the first five rows of the dataset:

```
dataset.head()
```

The following figure shows the output of the preceding code:

	make	fuel-type	num-of-doors	body-style	engine-location	length	width	height	num-of-cylinders	horsepower	peak-rpm	city-mpg	highway-mpg	price
0	alfa-romero	gas	two	convertible	front	168.8	64.1	48.8	four	111	5000	21	27	13495
1	alfa-romero	gas	two	convertible	front	168.8	64.1	48.8	four	111	5000	21	27	16500
2	alfa-romero	gas	two	hatchback	front	171.2	65.5	52.4	six	154	5000	19	26	16500
3	audi	gas	four	sedan	front	176.6	66.2	54.3	four	102	5500	24	30	13950
4	audi	gas	four	sedan	front	176.6	66.4	54.3	five	115	5500	18	22	17450

Figure 6.36: Loading the top five rows of the automobile dataset

Plotting each car with its price

1. Use the **plotting** interface of Bokeh to do some basic visualization first. Let's plot each car with its price. Import **figure** and **show** from the **bokeh.plotting** interface:

```
from bokeh.plotting import figure, show
```

2. First, use the index as our x-axis since we just want to plot each car with its price. Create a new column in our dataset that uses **dataset.index** as values:

```
dataset['index'] = dataset.index
```

Once we have our usable index column, we can plot our cars.

3. Create a new figure and plot each car using a scatter plot with the index and price column. Give the visualization a title of **Car prices** and name the x-axis **Car Index**. Name the y-axis **Price**:

```
plot = figure(title='Car prices', x_axis_label='Car Index', \
              y_axis_label='Price')
plot.scatter(dataset['index'], dataset['price'])
show(plot)
```

The following screenshot shows the output of the preceding code:

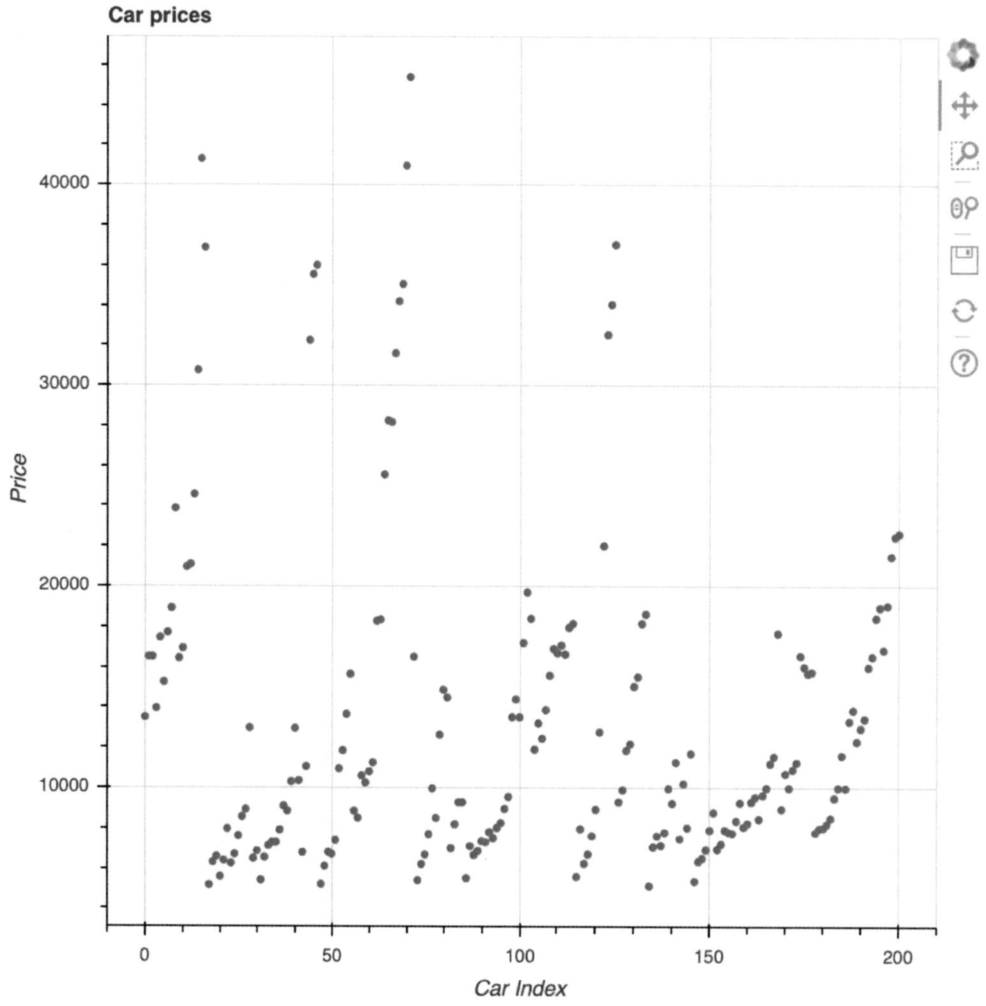

Figure 6.37: One point for each car

Grouping cars from manufacturers together

1. Group the dataset using **groupby** and the **make** column. Then use the **mean**
    method to get the mean value for each column. We don't want the **make**
    column to be used as an index, so provide the **as_index=False** argument to
    groupby. Print out the grouped average dataset to see how it differs from the
    initial dataset:

```
grouped_average = dataset.groupby(['make'], as_index=False).mean()
grouped_average
```

The following screenshot shows the output of the preceding code:

	make	length	width	height	city-mpg	highway-mpg	price	index
0	alfa-romero	169.600000	64.566667	50.000000	20.333333	26.666667	15498.333333	1.0
1	audi	184.766667	68.850000	54.833333	19.333333	24.500000	17859.166667	5.5
2	bmw	184.500000	66.475000	54.825000	19.375000	25.375000	26118.750000	12.5
3	chevrolet	151.933333	62.500000	52.400000	41.000000	46.333333	6007.000000	18.0
4	dodge	160.988889	64.166667	51.644444	28.000000	34.111111	7875.444444	24.0
5	honda	160.769231	64.384615	53.238462	30.384615	35.461538	8184.692308	35.0
6	isuzu	171.650000	63.500000	52.450000	24.000000	29.000000	8916.500000	42.5
7	jaguar	196.966667	69.933333	51.133333	14.333333	18.333333	34600.000000	45.0
8	mazda	170.805882	65.588235	53.358824	25.705882	31.941176	10652.882353	55.0
9	mercedes-benz	195.262500	71.062500	55.725000	18.500000	21.000000	33647.000000	67.5
10	mercury	178.400000	68.000000	54.800000	19.000000	24.000000	16503.000000	72.0
11	mitsubishi	168.030769	65.253846	50.692308	24.923077	31.153846	9239.769231	79.0
12	nissan	170.988889	65.088889	53.633333	27.000000	32.944444	10415.666667	94.5
13	peugot	191.136364	68.390909	57.181818	22.454545	26.636364	15489.090909	109.0
14	plymouth	164.900000	64.271429	51.971429	28.142857	34.142857	7963.428571	118.0
15	porsche	168.900000	65.825000	51.250000	17.500000	25.500000	31400.500000	123.5
16	renault	179.150000	66.550000	52.850000	23.000000	31.000000	9595.000000	126.5
17	saab	186.600000	66.500000	56.100000	20.333333	27.333333	15223.333333	130.5
18	subaru	168.858333	64.950000	53.750000	26.333333	30.750000	8541.250000	139.5
19	toyota	171.934375	65.090625	53.721875	27.500000	32.906250	9885.812500	161.5
20	volkswagen	172.533333	65.616667	55.183333	28.583333	34.916667	10077.500000	183.5
21	volvo	188.800000	67.963636	56.236364	21.181818	25.818182	18063.181818	195.0

Figure 6.38: New grouped dataset with mean values for columns

Note that we are dealing with categorical data, the manufacturer name, this time.

2. Create a new figure with a title of **Car Manufacturer Mean Prices**, an x-axis of **Car Manufacturer**, and a y-axis of **Mean Price**. In addition to that, handle the categorical data by providing the **x_range** argument to the figure with the **make** column:

```
# plotting the manufacturers and their mean car prices
grouped_plot = figure(title='Car Manufacturer Mean Prices', \
                      x_axis_label='Car Manufacturer', \
                      y_axis_label='Mean Price', \
                      x_range=grouped_average['make'])
grouped_plot.scatter(grouped_average['make'], \
                     grouped_average['price'])

show(grouped_plot)
```

The following screenshot shows the output of the preceding code:

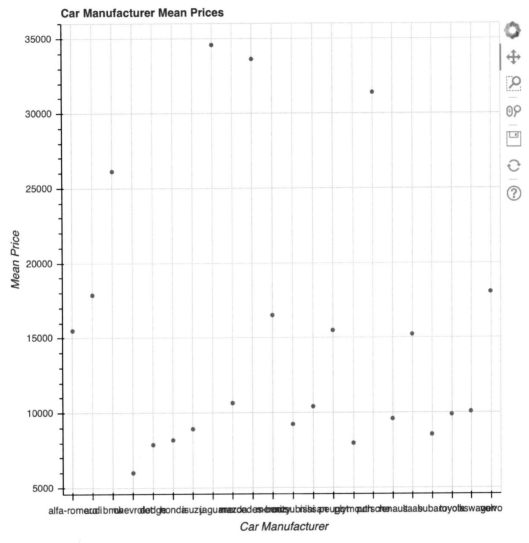

Figure 6.39: Car manufacturers with their mean car prices

By default, the axis labels are aligned horizontally.

3. Assign the value of **vertical** to the **xaxis.major_label_orientation** attribute of our **grouped_plot**. Call the show method again to display the visualization:

```
grouped_plot.xaxis.major_label_orientation = "vertical"
show(grouped_plot)
```

The following screenshot shows the output of the preceding code:

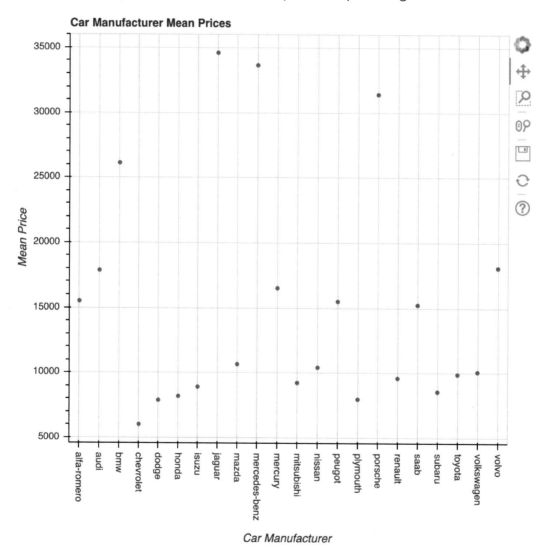

Figure 6.40: Car manufacturers with their mean car prices and vertical make labels

Adding color

To give the user a little bit more information about the data, we want to add some color based on the mean price of each manufacturer. In addition to that, we also want to increase the size of the points to make them pop more.

4. Import and set up a new **LinearColorMapper** with a palette of **Magma256**, and the min and max prices for the **low** and **high** arguments.

5. Create a new figure with the same name, labels, and **x_range** as before. Plot each manufacturer and provide a **size** argument with a size of 15. Provide the **color** argument to the **scatter** method and use the **field** and **transform** attributes to provide the column (y) and **color_mapper**. As we've done before, set the label orientation to vertical:

```
# adding color based on the mean price to our elements
from bokeh.models import LinearColorMapper


color_mapper = \
LinearColorMapper(palette='Magma256', \
                  low=min(grouped_average['price']), \
                  high=max(grouped_average['price']))


grouped_colored_plot = \
figure(title='Car Manufacturer Mean Prices', x_axis_label='Car \
        Manufacturer', y_axis_label='Mean Price', \
        x_range=grouped_average['make'])
grouped_colored_plot.scatter(grouped_average['make'], \
                             grouped_average['price'], \
                             color={'field': 'y', \
                                    'transform': color_mapper}, \
                             size=15)


grouped_colored_plot.xaxis.major_label_orientation = "vertical"


show(grouped_colored_plot)
```

The following screenshot shows the output of the preceding code:

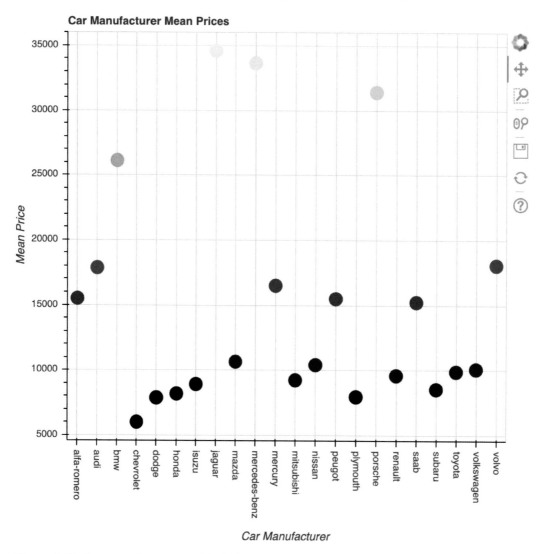

Figure 6.41: Car manufacturers with their mean car prices colored based on the mean price

You've built a full visualization to display data of different car manufacturers. We worked with basic plotting elements such as the **scatter** method and categorical data. In addition to that, we also discovered how to use ColorMappers, similar to what we did with geoplotlib, to give our data points colors based on specific values, such as the mean price.

> **NOTE**
>
> To access the source code for this specific section, please refer to https://packt.live/3hxyHdr.
>
> You can also run this example online at https://packt.live/30L3Fsw.

ACTIVITY 6.02: EXTENDING PLOTS WITH WIDGETS

Solution:

1. Create an **Activity6.02.ipynb** Jupyter notebook in the **Chapter06/ Activity6.02** folder.

2. Import the necessary libraries:

```
import pandas as pd
```

3. Import and call the **output_notebook** method from the **io** interface of Bokeh:

```
from bokeh.io import output_notebook
output_notebook()
```

4. Load our **olympia2016_athletes.csv** dataset from the **Datasets** folder:

```
dataset = pd.read_csv('../../Datasets/olympia2016_athletes.csv')
```

5. Call **head** on the DataFrame to test that our data has been successfully loaded:

```
dataset.head()
```

The following figure shows the output of the preceding code:

	id	name	nationality	sex	dob	height	weight	sport	gold	silver	bronze
0	736041664	A Jesus Garcia	ESP	male	10/17/69	1.72	64.0	athletics	0	0	0
1	532037425	A Lam Shin	KOR	female	9/23/86	1.68	56.0	fencing	0	0	0
2	435962603	Aaron Brown	CAN	male	5/27/92	1.98	79.0	athletics	0	0	1
3	521041435	Aaron Cook	MDA	male	1/2/91	1.83	80.0	taekwondo	0	0	0
4	33922579	Aaron Gate	NZL	male	11/26/90	1.81	71.0	cycling	0	0	0

Figure 6.42: Loading the top five rows of the olympia2016_athletes dataset using the head method

Building an Interactive Visualization

6. Import **figure** and show from the **plotting** interface and **interact**, as a **decorator**, from the **widgets** interface:

```
from bokeh.plotting import figure, show, ColumnDataSource
from ipywidgets import interact, widgets
```

7. Get a list of unique countries and one for the number of athletes and the number of medals per country. Use the **groupby** method of your dataset to achieve this:

```
countries = dataset['nationality'].unique()
athletes_per_country = dataset.groupby('nationality').size()
medals_per_country = dataset.groupby('nationality')\
                     ['gold', 'silver','bronze'].sum()
```

Before we go in and implement the plotting for this visualization, we want to set up our widgets and the @**interact** method that will display the plot upon execution. Execute this empty **get_plot()** method cell and then move on to the widget creation. We will implement this later.

8. Use two **IntSlider** widgets that will control the max numbers for the number of athletes and/or medals a country is allowed to have in order to be displayed in the visualization. Get the maximum number of medals of all the countries and the maximum number of athletes of all the countries:

```
max_medals = medals_per_country.sum(axis=1).max()
max_athletes = athletes_per_country.max()
```

9. Use those maximum numbers as the maximum for two **IntSlider** widgets. Display the **max_athletes_slider** in a vertical orientation and the **max_medals_slider** in a horizontal orientation. In the visualization, they should be described as **Max. Athletes** and **Max. Medals**:

```
# setting up the interaction elements
max_athletes_slider=\
widgets.IntSlider(value=max_athletes, min=0, max=max_athletes, \
                  step=1, description='Max. Athletes:', \
                  continuous_update=False, \
                  orientation='vertical', \
                  layout={'width': '100px'})


max_medals_slider=\
widgets.IntSlider(value=max_medals, min=0, max=max_medals, \
                  step=1, description='Max. Medals:', \
                  continuous_update=False, \
                  orientation='horizontal')
```

10. After setting up the widgets, implement the method that will be called with each update of the interaction widgets. Use the **@interact** decorator for this. Instead of value ranges or lists, provide the variable names of our already created widgets in the decorator:

```
@interact(max_athletes=max_athletes_slider, \
          max_medals=max_medals_slider)
def get_olympia_stats(max_athletes, max_medals):
    show(get_plot(max_athletes, max_medals))
```

Since we have already set up the empty method that will return a plot, we can call **show()** with the method call inside it to show the result once it is returned from the **get_plot** method.

11. Scroll up and implement the plotting we skipped in a previous step. The two arguments passed are **max_athletes** and **max_medals**. First, filter our countries dataset, which contains all the countries that placed athletes in the Olympic games. Check whether they have less than or equal medals and athletes than our max values, which were passed as arguments. Once we have a filtered dataset, create our **DataSource**. This **DataSource** will be used both for the tooltips and the printing of the circle glyphs.

> **NOTE**
>
> There is extensive documentation on how to use and set up tooltips that you can and use, which can be accessed with the following link:
> https://bokeh.pydata.org/en/latest/docs/user_guide/tools.html.

12. Create a new plot using the **figure** method that has the following attributes: title set to **'Rio Olympics 2016 - Medal comparison'**, **x_axis_label** set to **'Number of Medals'**, and **y_axis_label** set to **'Num of Athletes'**:

```
# creating the scatter plot
def get_plot(max_athletes, max_medals):
    filtered_countries=[]
    for country in countries:
        if (athletes_per_country[country] <= max_athletes and \
            medals_per_country.loc[country].sum() <= max_medals):
            filtered_countries.append(country)

    data_source=get_datasource(filtered_countries)
    TOOLTIPS=[('Country', '@countries'), ('Num of Athletes', '@y'), \
              ('Gold', '@gold'), ('Silver', '@silver'), \
              ('Bronze', '@bronze')]

    plot=figure(title='Rio Olympics 2016 - Medal comparison', \
                x_axis_label='Number of Medals', \
                y_axis_label='Num of Athletes', \
                plot_width=800, plot_height=500, tooltips=TOOLTIPS)

    plot.circle('x', 'y', source=data_source, size=20, \
                color='color', alpha=0.5)
    return plot
```

13. Display every country with a different color by randomly creating the colors with a six-digit hex code. The following method does this:

```
"""
get a 6 digit random hex color to differentiate the countries better
"""

import random
def get_random_color():
    return '#%06x' % random.randint(0, 0xFFFFFF)
```

14. Use a Bokeh **ColumnDataSource** object to handle our data and make it easily accessible for our tooltip and glyphs. We want to display additional information in a tooltip, so add the **color** field, which holds the required amount of random colors; the **countries** field, which holds the filtered list of countries; the **gold**, **silver**, and **bronze** fields, which hold the number of **gold**, **silver**, and **bronze** medals for each country, respectively; the **x** field, which holds the summed number of medals for each **country**; and the **y** field, which holds the number of athletes for each **country**, to our **DataSource** object:

```
# build the datasource
def get_datasource(filtered_countries):
    return ColumnDataSource(data=dict(
        color=[get_random_color() for _ in filtered_countries], \
            countries=filtered_countries, \
            gold=[medals_per_country.loc[country]['gold'] \
                for country in filtered_countries],
            silver=[medals_per_country.loc[country]['silver'] \
                for country in filtered_countries],
            bronze=[medals_per_country.loc[country]['bronze'] \
                for country in filtered_countries],
            x=[medals_per_country.loc[country].sum() \
                for country in filtered_countries],
            y=[athletes_per_country.loc[country].sum() \
                for country in filtered_countries]))
```

15. Execute the last cell with our @**interact** decorator once more. This time, it will display our scatter plot with our interactive widgets. We will see each country in a different color. Upon hovering over them, we will get more information about each country, such as its short name, number of athletes, and the number of gold, silver, and bronze medals they earned. The resulting visualization should look as follows:

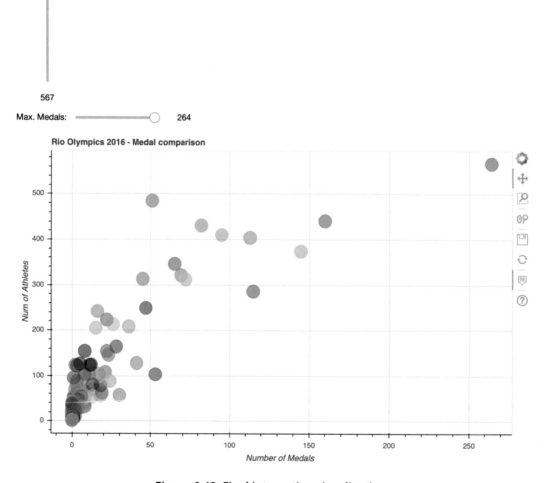

Figure 6.43: Final interactive visualization

You've built a full visualization to display and explore data from the 2016 Olympics. We added two widgets to our visualization, which allowed us to filter the displayed countries.

> **NOTE**
>
> To access the source code for this specific section, please refer to https://packt.live/2CdiAl5.
>
> You can also run this example online at https://packt.live/3fuWEQQ.

CHAPTER 7: COMBINING WHAT WE HAVE LEARNED

ACTIVITY 7.01: IMPLEMENTING MATPLOTLIB AND SEABORN ON THE NEW YORK CITY DATABASE

Solution:

1. Create an **Activity7.01.ipynb** Jupyter Notebook in the **Chapter07/ Activity7.01** folder to implement this activity. Import all the necessary libraries:

```
# Import statements
import pandas as pd
import numpy as np
import seaborn as sns
import matplotlib
import matplotlib.pyplot as plt
import squarify
sns.set()
```

2. Use pandas to read both CSV files located in the **Datasets** folder:

```
p_ny = pd.read_csv('../../Datasets/acs2017/pny.csv')
h_ny = pd.read_csv('../../Datasets/acs2017/hny.csv')
```

3. Use the given PUMA (public use microdata area code based on the 2010 census definition, which are areas with populations of 100,000 or more) ranges to further divide the dataset into NYC districts (Bronx, Manhattan, Staten Island, Brooklyn, and Queens):

```
# PUMA ranges
bronx = [3701, 3710]
manhatten = [3801, 3810]
staten_island = [3901, 3903]
brooklyn = [4001, 4017]
queens = [4101, 4114]
nyc = [bronx[0], queens[1]]
def puma_filter(data, puma_ranges):
    return data.loc[(data['PUMA'] >= puma_ranges[0]) \
                    & (data['PUMA'] <= puma_ranges[1])]
h_bronx = puma_filter(h_ny, bronx)
h_manhatten = puma_filter(h_ny, manhatten)
h_staten_island = puma_filter(h_ny, staten_island)
```

```
h_brooklyn = puma_filter(h_ny, brooklyn)
h_queens = puma_filter(h_ny, queens)
p_nyc = puma_filter(p_ny, nyc)
h_nyc = puma_filter(h_ny, nyc)
```

4. Use the given **weighted_median** function in the following code to compute the median:

```
# Function for a 'weighted' median
def weighted_frequency(values, weights):
    weighted_values = []
    for value, weight in zip(values, weights):
        weighted_values.extend(np.repeat(value, weight))
    return weighted_values
def weighted_median(values, weights):
    return np.median(weighted_frequency(values, weights))
```

5. In this subtask, we will create a plot containing multiple subplots that visualize information with regard to NYC wages. Before we create the plots, some data wrangling is necessary:

```
# Median household income in the US
us_income_median = 60336


# Data wrangling for median household income
income_adjustement = h_ny.loc[0, ['ADJINC']].values[0] / 1e6

def median_household_income(data):
    query = data.loc[np.isfinite(data['HINCP']), \
                     ['HINCP', 'WGTP']].values
    return np.round(weighted_median(query[:, 0], query[:, 1]) \
                    * income_adjustement)

h_ny_income_median = median_household_income(h_ny)
h_nyc_income_median = median_household_income(h_nyc)
h_bronx_income_median = median_household_income(h_bronx)
h_manhatten_income_median = median_household_income(h_manhatten)
h_staten_island_income_median = \
median_household_income(h_staten_island)
h_brooklyn_income_median = median_household_income(h_brooklyn)
h_queens_income_median = median_household_income(h_queens)
```

6. Compute the average wage by gender for the given occupation categories for the population of NYC:

```python
occ_categories = ['Management,\nBusiness,\nScience,\nand '\
                  'Arts\nOccupations', 'Service\nOccupations', \
                  'Sales and\nOffice\nOccupations', \
                  'Natural Resources,\nConstruction,\nand '\
                  'Maintenance\nOccupations', \
                  'Production,\nTransportation,\nand Material '\
                  'Moving\nOccupations']

occ_ranges = \
{'Management, Business, Science, and Arts '\
 'Occupations': [10, 3540], \
 'Service Occupations': [3600, 4650], \
 'Sales and Office Occupations': [4700, 5940], \
 'Natural Resources, Construction, and '\
 'Maintenance Occupations': [6000, 7630], \
 'Production, Transportation, and Material '\
 'Moving Occupations': [7700, 9750]}

def wage_by_gender_and_occupation(data, gender):
    weighted_wages = []
    for occ in occ_ranges.values():
        query = data.loc[(data['OCCP'] >= occ[0]) \
                        & (data['OCCP'] <= occ[1]) \
                        & (data['SEX'] == gender), \
                        ['WAGP', 'PWGTP']]
        weight_sum = np.sum(query['PWGTP'])
        weighted_wages.append(np.round(np.sum(query['WAGP'] \
                              * (query['PWGTP'] / weight_sum))))
    return weighted_wages

wages_male = wage_by_gender_and_occupation(p_nyc, 1)
wages_female = wage_by_gender_and_occupation(p_nyc, 2)
```

7. Compute the wage frequencies for New York and NYC. Use the following yearly wage intervals: 10k steps between 0 and 100k, 50k steps between 100k and 200k, and >200k:

```
wage_bins = {'<$10k': [0, 10000], '$10-20k': [10000, 20000], \
             '$20-30k': [20000, 30000], \
             '$30-40k': [30000, 40000], \
             '$10-20k': [40000, 50000], \
             '$50-60k': [50000, 60000], \
             '$60-70k': [60000, 70000], \
             '$70-80k': [70000, 80000], \
             '$80-90k': [80000, 90000], \
             '$90-100k': [90000, 100000], \
             '$100-150k': [100000, 150000], \
             '$150-200k': [150000, 200000], \
             '>$200k': [200000, np.infty]}


def wage_frequency(data):
    # Only consider people who have a job: salary > 0
    valid = data.loc[np.isfinite(data['WAGP']) \
                    & (data['WAGP'] > 0), ['WAGP', 'PWGTP']]
    overall_sum = np.sum(valid['PWGTP'].values)
    frequency = []
    for wage_bin in wage_bins.values():
        query = data.loc[(data['WAGP'] \
                * income_adjustement > wage_bin[0]) \
                & (data['WAGP'] \
                * income_adjustement <= wage_bin[1]), \
                ['PWGTP']].values
        frequency.append(np.sum(query) / overall_sum)
    return frequency


wages_nyc = wage_frequency(p_nyc)
wages_ny = wage_frequency(p_ny)
```

8. Create a plot containing multiple subplots that visualize information with regard to NYC wages. Now, visualize the median household income for the US, New York, NYC, and its districts. Next, visualize the average wage by gender for the given occupation categories for the population of NYC. Then, visualize the wage distribution for New York and NYC. Lastly, use the following yearly wage intervals: 10k steps between 0 and 100k, 50k steps between 100k and 200k, and >200k:

```
# Create figure with three subplots
fig, (ax1, ax2, ax3) = plt.subplots(3, 1, figsize=(7, 10), \
                                     dpi=300)


# Median household income
ax1.set_title('Median Household Income', fontsize=14)
x = np.arange(8)
ax1.barh(x, [h_bronx_income_median, h_manhatten_income_median, \
            h_staten_island_income_median, \
            h_brooklyn_income_median, \
            h_queens_income_median, h_nyc_income_median, \
            h_ny_income_median, us_income_median])
ax1.set_yticks(x)
ax1.set_yticklabels(['Bronx', 'Manhatten', 'Staten Island', \
                    'Brooklyn', 'Queens', 'New York City', \
                    'New York', 'United States'])
ax1.set_xlabel('Yearly household income in $')


# Wage by gender in common jobs
ax2.set_title('Wage by Gender for different Job Categories', \
              fontsize=14)
x = np.arange(5) + 1
width = 0.4
ax2.bar(x - width / 2, wages_male, width=width, label='Male')
ax2.bar(x + width / 2, wages_female, width=width, label='Female')
ax2.legend()
```

```
ax2.set_xticks(x)
ax2.set_xticklabels(occ_categories, rotation=0, fontsize=8)
ax2.set_ylabel('Average Salary in $')


# Wage distribution
ax3.set_title('Wage Distribution', fontsize=14)
x = np.arange(len(wages_nyc)) + 1
width = 0.4
ax3.bar(x - width / 2, np.asarray(wages_nyc) \
        * 100, width=width, label='NYC')
ax3.bar(x + width / 2, np.asarray(wages_ny) \
        * 100, width=width, label='New York')
ax3.legend()
ax3.set_xticks(x)
ax3.set_xticklabels(wage_bins.keys(), rotation=90, fontsize=8)
ax3.set_ylabel('Percentage')
ax3.vlines(x=9.5, ymin=0, ymax=15, linestyle='--')


# Overall figure
fig.tight_layout()
plt.show()
```

The following diagram shows the output of the preceding code:

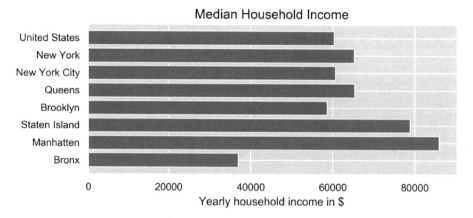

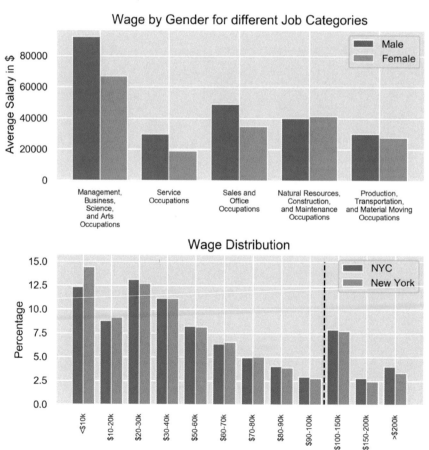

Figure 7.10: Wage statistics for NYC in comparison with New York and the United States

9. Use a tree map to visualize the percentage for the given occupation subcategories for the population of NYC:

```
# Data wrangling for occupations
occ_subcategories = \
{'Management,\nBusiness,\nand Financial': [10, 950], \
 'Computer, Engineering,\nand Science': [1000, 1965], \
 'Education,\nLegal,\nCommunity Service,\nArts,\nand '\
 'Media': [2000, 2960], \
 'Healthcare\nPractitioners\nand\nTechnical': [3000, 3540],
 'Service': [3600, 4650],
 'Sales\nand Related': [4700, 4965],
 'Office\nand Administrative\nSupport': [5000, 5940],
 '': [6000, 6130],
 'Construction\nand Extraction': [6200, 6940],
 'Installation,\nMaintenance,\nand Repair': [7000, 7630],
 'Production': [7700, 8965],
 'Transportation\nand Material\nMoving': [9000, 9750]}


def occupation_percentage(data):
    percentages = []
    overall_sum = np.sum(data.loc[(data['OCCP'] >= 10) \
                         & (data['OCCP'] <= 9750), \
                         ['PWGTP']].values)
    for occ in occ_subcategories.values():
        query = data.loc[(data['OCCP'] >= occ[0]) \
                        & (data['OCCP'] <= occ[1]), \
                        ['PWGTP']].values
        percentages.append(np.sum(query) / overall_sum)
    return percentages
occ_percentages = occupation_percentage(p_nyc)


# Visualization of tree map
plt.figure(figsize=(18, 10), dpi=300)
df = pd.DataFrame({'percentage': occ_percentages, \
                   'group': list(occ_subcategories.keys())})
df['group'] = df['group'] + ' (' \
            + (np.round(df['percentage'] * 1000) \
            / 10).astype('str') + '%)'
```

```
blues = [matplotlib.cm.Blues((i + 2) * 30) for i in range(4)]
greens = [matplotlib.cm.Greens((i + 2) * 40) for i in range(1)]
oranges = [matplotlib.cm.Oranges((i + 2) * 40) for i in range(2)]
purples = [matplotlib.cm.Purples((i + 2) * 40) for i in range(3)]
reds = [matplotlib.cm.Reds((i + 2) * 40) for i in range(2)]
colors = blues + greens + oranges + purples + reds
squarify.plot(sizes=df['percentage'], label=df['group'], \
              color=colors, text_kwargs={'fontsize': 20, \
                                'rotation': 25, \
                                'fontweight': 'bold'})
plt.axis('off')
plt.title('Occupations in New York City', fontsize=24)
plt.savefig('tree_map.png', dpi=300, bbox_inches='tight')
```

The following diagram shows the output of the preceding code:

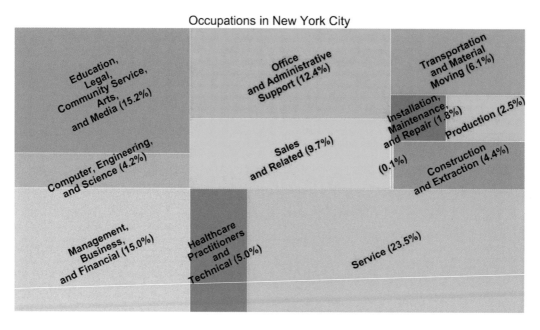

Figure 7.11: Occupations in NYC

> **NOTE**
>
> Please note that the terms here addressed refer solely to the classifications of disabilities as defined by the US Census Bureau (accessible through the following link: https://www.census.gov/topics/health/disability/guidance/data-collection-acs.html). This language does not reflect the views or intentions of Packt or its affiliates.
>
> **Independent living difficulty**: Because of a physical, mental, or emotional problem, having difficulties performing errands alone, such as visiting a doctor's office or shopping (DOUT).
>
> **Ambulatory difficulty**: Having serious difficulty walking or climbing stairs (DPHY).
>
> **Self-care difficulty**: Having difficulty bathing or dressing (DDRS).

10. Use a heatmap to show the correlation between the different disability types (self-care difficulty, hearing difficulty, vision difficulty, independent living difficulty, ambulatory difficulty, veteran service-connected disability, and cognitive difficulty) and age groups (<5, 5-11, 12-14, 15-17, 18-24, 25-34, 35-44, 45-54, 55-64, 65-74, 75+) in New York City:

```
# Data wrangling for New York City population difficulties
difficulties = {'Self-care difficulty': 'DDRS', \
                'Hearing difficulty': 'DEAR', \
                'Vision difficulty': 'DEYE', \
                'Independent living difficulty': 'DOUT', \
                'Ambulatory difficulty': 'DPHY', \
                'Veteran service connected disability': 'DRATX', \
                'Cognitive difficulty': 'DREM'}


age_groups = {'<5': [0, 4], '5-11': [5, 11], '12-14': [12, 14], \
              '15-17': [15, 17], '18-24': [18, 24], \
              '25-34': [25, 34], '35-44': [35, 44], \
              '45-54': [45, 54], '55-64': [55, 64], \
              '65-74': [65, 74], '75+': [75, np.infty]}
```

```python
def difficulty_age_array(data):
    array = np.zeros((len(difficulties.values()), \
                      len(age_groups.values())))
    for d, diff in enumerate(difficulties.values()):
        for a, age in enumerate(age_groups.values()):
            age_sum = np.sum(data.loc[(data['AGEP'] >= age[0]) \
                      & (data['AGEP'] <= age[1]), \
                      ['PWGTP']].values)
            query = data.loc[(data['AGEP'] >= age[0]) \
                    & (data['AGEP'] <= age[1]) \
                    & (data[diff] == 1), ['PWGTP']].values
            array[d, a] = np.sum(query) / age_sum
    return array


array = difficulty_age_array(p_nyc)


# Heatmap
plt.figure(dpi=300 , \
           cmap=sns.cubehelix_palette(rot=-.3, as_cmap=True))
ax = sns.heatmap(array * 100)
ax.set_yticklabels(difficulties.keys(), rotation=0)
ax.set_xticklabels(age_groups.keys(), rotation=90)
ax.set_xlabel('Age Groups')
ax.set_title('Percentage of NYC population with difficulties', \
             fontsize=14)
plt.show()
```

The following diagram shows the output of the preceding code:

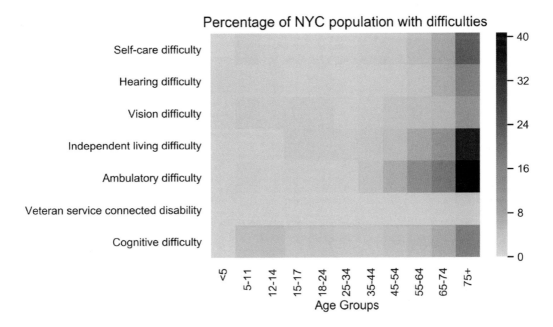

Figure 7.12: Percentage of NYC population with disabilities

NOTE

To access the source code for this specific section, please refer to https://packt.live/3e7xU0z.

This section does not currently have an online interactive example, and will need to be run locally.

ACTIVITY 7.02: VISUALIZING STOCK PRICES WITH BOKEH

Solution:

1. Create an **Activity7.02.ipynb** Jupyter Notebook from the **Chapter07/Activity7.02** folder to implement this activity.

2. Import pandas and enable the notebook output for Bokeh:

```
# importing the necessary dependencies
import pandas as pd
from bokeh.io import output_notebook

output_notebook()
```

3. After downloading the dataset and moving it into the **Datasets** folder, import our **stock_prices.csv** data:

```
# loading the Dataset with geoplotlib
dataset = pd.read_csv('../../Datasets/stock_prices.csv')
```

4. Check the first five rows on our DataFrame to make sure that our data has been loaded successfully:

```
# looking at the dataset
dataset.head()
```

The following diagram shows the output of the preceding code:

	date	symbol	open	close	low	high	volume
0	2016-01-05 00:00:00	WLTW	123.430000	125.839996	122.309998	126.250000	2163600.0
1	2016-01-06 00:00:00	WLTW	125.239998	119.980003	119.940002	125.540001	2386400.0
2	2016-01-07 00:00:00	WLTW	116.379997	114.949997	114.930000	119.739998	2489500.0
3	2016-01-08 00:00:00	WLTW	115.480003	116.620003	113.500000	117.440002	2006300.0
4	2016-01-11 00:00:00	WLTW	117.010002	114.970001	114.089996	117.330002	1408600.0

Figure 7.13: Head of our imported data

5. Since the **date** column has no information regarding the hour, minute, and second (all 00:00:00), avoid displaying them in the visualization later on by simply displaying the year, month, and day. Create a new column that holds the formatted short version of the date value. Display the first five elements of the dataset again to validate your new column:

```
# mapping the date of each row to only the year-month-day format
from datetime import datetime
def shorten_time_stamp(timestamp):
    shortened = timestamp[0]
    if len(shortened) > 10:
        parsed_date=datetime.strptime(shortened, \
                                      '%Y-%m-%d %H:%M:%S')
        shortened=datetime.strftime(parsed_date, '%Y-%m-%d')
    return shortened

dataset['short_date'] = \
dataset.apply(lambda x: shorten_time_stamp(x), axis=1)
# looking at the dataset with shortened date
dataset.head()
```

The following diagram shows the output of the preceding code:

	date	symbol	open	close	low	high	volume	short_date
0	2016-01-05 00:00:00	WLTW	123.430000	125.839996	122.309998	126.250000	2163600.0	2016-01-05
1	2016-01-06 00:00:00	WLTW	125.239998	119.980003	119.940002	125.540001	2386400.0	2016-01-06
2	2016-01-07 00:00:00	WLTW	116.379997	114.949997	114.930000	119.739998	2489500.0	2016-01-07
3	2016-01-08 00:00:00	WLTW	115.480003	116.620003	113.500000	117.440002	2006300.0	2016-01-08
4	2016-01-11 00:00:00	WLTW	117.010002	114.970001	114.089996	117.330002	1408600.0	2016-01-11

Figure 7.14: Dataset with an added short_date column

> **NOTE**
>
> The execution of the cell will take a moment since it's a fairly large dataset. Please, be patient.

6. To create our visualization, we need some additional imports. Import **figure** and show this from the plotting interface. The widgets, as we saw in *Chapter 6, Making Things Interactive with Bokeh*, come from the **ipywidgets** library. Import the **@interact** decorator and the **widgets** interface, which gives us access to the different widgets:

```
# importing the necessary dependencies
from bokeh.plotting import figure, show
from ipywidgets import interact, widgets
```

7. Scroll down to the cell that says **#extracting the necessary data** before implementing the plotting. Make sure that you execute the cells below that, even though this will simply pass and do nothing for now. Extract the following information: a list of unique stock names that are present in the dataset, a list of all **short_dates** that are in 2016, a sorted list of unique dates generated from the previous list of dates from 2016, and a list with the values **open-close** and **volume**:

```
# extracting the necessary data
stock_names=dataset['symbol'].unique()
dates_2016=dataset[dataset['short_date'] >= '2016-01-01']\
            ['short_date']
unique_dates_2016=sorted(dates_2016.unique())
value_options=['open-close', 'volume']
```

8. Given the extracted information from the preceding cell, define **widgets** and provide the available options for it. Create a dropdown with the **stock_names**, which, by default, should have the AAPL stock selected, named **Compare:**. The second dropdown also uses **stock_names**, but, by default, should have the AON stock selected, named **to**:

```
# setting up the interaction elements
drp_1=widgets.Dropdown(options=stock_names, \
                       value='AAPL', \
                       description='Compare:')
drp_2=widgets.Dropdown(options=stock_names, \
                       value='AON', description='to:')
```

9. Create a **SelectionRange** slider, which will allow us to select a range of dates from the extracted list of unique 2016 dates. By default, set the first 25 dates as selected and name it **From-To**. Disable the **continuous_update** parameter. Adjust the layout width to **500px** to make sure that the dates are displayed correctly:

```
range_slider=\
widgets.SelectionRangeSlider(options=unique_dates_2016, \
                            index=(0,25), \
                            continuous_update=False, \
                            description='From-To', \
                            layout={'width': '500px'})
```

10. Add a **RadioButtons** group that provides the **open-close** and **volume** options. By default, **open-close** should be selected, named **Metric**:

```
range_slider=\
widgets.SelectionRangeSlider(options=unique_dates_2016, \
                            index=(0,25), \
                            continuous_update=False, \
                            description='From-To', \
                            layout={'width': '500px'})
value_radio=widgets.RadioButtons(options=value_options, \
                            value='open-close', \
                            description='Metric')
```

> **NOTE**
>
> As we mentioned in *Chapter 6, Making Things Interactive with Bokeh*, we can also make use of the widgets that are described here: https://ipywidgets.readthedocs.io/en/stable/examples/Widget%20List.html.

11. After setting up the widgets, implement the method that will be called with each update of the interactive widgets. Use the @**interact** decorator for this.

    Instead of value ranges or lists, provide the variable names of our already created widgets in the decorator. The method will get four arguments: **stock_1**, **stock_2**, **date**, and **value**.

    Since we have already set up the empty method that will return the preceding plot, call **show()** with the method call inside to show the result once it is returned from the **get_stock_for_2016** method. Now, create the **interact** method:

    ```
    @interact(stock_1=drp_1, stock_2=drp_2, date=range_slider, \
            value=value_radio)
    def get_stock_for_2016(stock_1, stock_2, date, value):
        show(get_plot(stock_1, stock_2, date, value))
    ```

12. Start with the so-called candlestick visualization, which is often used with stock price data. Calculate the mean for every (**high/low**) pair and then plot those data points with a line with the given color. Next, set up an **add_candle_plot** function that gets a **plot** object, a **stock_name** parameter, a **stock_range** parameter containing the data of only the selected date range that was defined with the widgets, and a color for the line. Create a segment that creates the vertical line, and either a green or red **vbar** to color code whether the close price is lower than the open price. Once the candles are created, draw a continuous line running through the mean (**high, low**) point of each candle:

    ```
    def add_candle_plot(plot, stock_name, stock_range, color):
        inc_1 = stock_range.close > stock_range.open
        dec_1 = stock_range.open > stock_range.close
        w = 0.5
        plot.segment(stock_range['short_date'], stock_range['high'], \
                    stock_range['short_date'], stock_range['low'], \
                    color="grey")
        plot.vbar(stock_range['short_date'][inc_1], w, \
                stock_range['high'][inc_1], \
                stock_range['close'][inc_1], \
                fill_color="green", line_color="black", \
                legend_label=('Mean price of ' + stock_name))
    ```

```
    plot.vbar(stock_range['short_date'][dec_1], w, \
        stock_range['high'][dec_1], \
        stock_range['close'][dec_1], \
        fill_color="red", line_color="black", \
        legend_label=('Mean price of ' + stock_name))
stock_mean_val=stock_range[['high', 'low']].mean(axis=1)

    plot.line(stock_range['short_date'], stock_mean_val, \
        legend_label=('Mean price of ' + stock_name), \
        line_color=color, alpha=0.5)
```

> **NOTE**
>
> Make sure to reference the example provided in the Bokeh library here. You can adapt the code in there to our arguments: https://bokeh.pydata.org/en/latest/docs/gallery/candlestick.html.

13. After you have implemented the **add_candle_plot** method, scroll down and rerun the **@interact** cell. You will now see the candles being displayed for the two selected stocks. The final missing step is implementing the plotting of the lines if the **volume** value is selected.

14. Add an interactive legend that allows us to **mute**, meaning gray out, each stock in the visualization:

```
# method to build the plot
def get_plot(stock_1, stock_2, date, value):
    #[..]
    plot.xaxis.major_label_orientation = 1
    plot.grid.grid_line_alpha=0.3
    if value == 'open-close':
        add_candle_plot(plot, stock_1_name, \
                    stock_1_range, 'blue')
        add_candle_plot(plot, stock_2_name, \
                    stock_2_range, 'orange')
```

```
    if value == 'volume':
    plot.line(stock_1_range['short_date'], \
            stock_1_range['volume'], \
            legend_label=stock_1_name, muted_alpha=0.2)
    plot.line(stock_2_range['short_date'], \
            stock_2_range['volume'], \
            legend_label=stock_2_name, muted_alpha=0.2, \
            line_color='orange')
    plot.legend.click_policy="mute"

    return plot
```

> **NOTE**
>
> To make our legend interactive, please take a look at the documentation for the legend feature: https://bokeh.pydata.org/en/latest/docs/user_guide/interaction/legends.html.
>
> The complete code for this step can be found on GitHub: https://github.com/PacktWorkshops/The-Data-Visualization-Workshop/blob/master/Chapter07/Activity7.02/Activity7.02.ipynb.

15. After our implementation has finished, execute the last cell with our **@interact** decorator once more. This time, it will display our candlestick plot and, once we switch to the volume RadioButton, we will see the volumes displayed that have been traded at the given dates. The resulting visualization should look something like this:

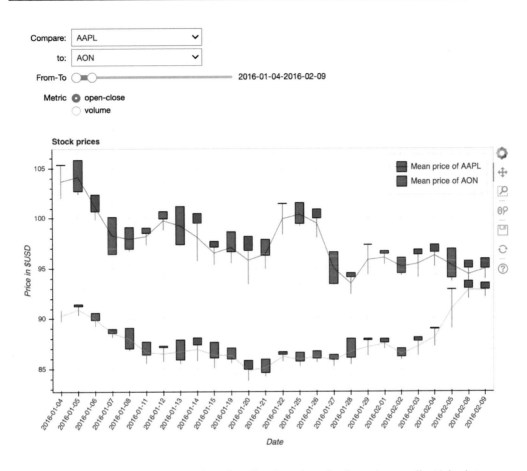

Figure 7.15: Final interactive visualization that displays the candlestick plot

The following diagram shows the final interactive visualization of the volume plot:

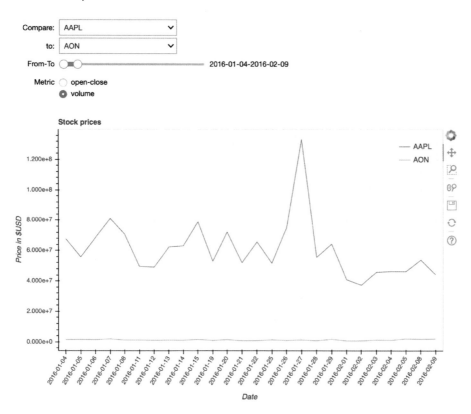

Figure 7.16: Final interactive visualization that displays the volume plot

You have now built a full visualization to display and explore stock price data. We added several widgets to our visualization that allows us to select "to be compared" stocks, restrict the displayed data to a specific date range, and even display two different kinds of plots.

> **NOTE**
>
> To access the source code for this specific section, please refer to https://packt.live/37ADxSM.
>
> You can also run this example online at https://packt.live/3e83pHQ.

ACTIVITY 7.03: ANALYZING AIRBNB DATA WITH GEOPLOTLIB

Solution:

1. Create an **Activity7.03.ipynb** Jupyter Notebook in the **Chapter07/ Activity7.03** folder to implement this activity. Import **NumPy**, **pandas**, and **geoplotlib** first:

```
# importing the necessary dependencies
import numpy as np
import pandas as pd
import geoplotlib
```

2. Use the **read_csv** method of pandas to load the **.csv** file. If your computer is a little slow, use the smaller dataset:

```
# loading the Dataset
dataset = pd.read_csv('../../Datasets/airbnb_new_york.csv')
# dataset = pd.read_csv('../../Datasets/airbnb_new_york_smaller.csv')
```

3. Observe the structure of our dataset by looking at the features provided:

```
# print the first 5 rows of the dataset
dataset.head()
```

The following diagram shows the output of the preceding code:

	id	listing_url	scrape_id	last_scraped	name	summary	space	description	experiences_offered	neighborhood_overview	...
0	21456	https://www.airbnb.com/rooms/21456	20181206022948	2018-12-06	Light-filled classic Central Park	An adorable, classic, clean, light-filled one-...	An adorable, classic, clean, light-filled one-...	An adorable, classic, clean, light-filled one-...	none	Diverse. Great coffee shops and restaurants, n...	...
1	2539	https://www.airbnb.com/rooms/2539	20181206022948	2018-12-06	Clean & quiet apt home by the park	Renovated apt home in elevator building.	Spacious, renovated, and clean apt home, one b...	Renovated apt home in elevator building. Spaci...	none	Close to Prospect Park and Historic Ditmas Park	...
2	21644	https://www.airbnb.com/rooms/21644	20181206022948	2018-12-06	Upper Manhattan, New York	A great space in a beautiful neighborhood- min...	Nice room in a spacious pre-war apartment in u...	A great space in a beautiful neighborhood- min...	none	I love that the neighborhood is safe to walk a...	...
3	3330	https://www.airbnb.com/rooms/3330	20181206022948	2018-12-06	++ Brooklyn Penthouse Guestroom ++	This is a spacious, clean, furnished master be...	Room Features: - clean, hardwood floors - 2 la...	This is a spacious, clean, furnished master be...	none	Location is GREAT!! Right off the L train in t...	...
4	21794	https://www.airbnb.com/rooms/21794	20181206022948	2018-12-06	COZY QUIET room 4 DOOGLERS!	It's comfy & has a loft bed & a chaise lounge,...	This is the smaller room of the two I have ava...	It's comfy & has a loft bed & a chaise lounge,...	none	GREAT Central Location. On 15th street between...	...

5 rows × 96 columns

Figure 7.17: Displaying the first five elements of the dataset

4. Remember that geoplotlib needs **latitude** and **longitude** columns with the names **lat** and **lon**. We will, therefore, add new columns for **lat** and **lon** and assign the corresponding value columns to them:

```
# mapping Latitude to lat and Longitude to lon
dataset['lat'] = dataset['latitude']
dataset['lon'] = dataset['longitude']
```

5. In order to use a color map that changes color based on the price of accommodation, we need a value that can easily be compared and checked whether it's smaller or bigger than any other listing. Therefore, create a new column called **dollar_price** that will hold the value of the price column as a float. Make sure to fill all the **NaN** values of the **price** column and the **review_scores_rating** column with **0.0** by using the **fillna()** method of the dataset:

```
# convert string of type $<numbers> to <nubmers> of type float
def convert_to_float(x):
    try:
        value=str.replace(x[1:], ',', '')
        return float(value)
    except:
        return 0.0


"""
create new dollar_price column with the price as a number \
and replace the NaN values by 0 in the rating column
"""

dataset['price'] = dataset['price'].fillna('$0.0')
dataset['review_scores_rating'] = \
dataset['review_scores_rating'].fillna(0.0)
dataset['dollar_price'] = \
dataset['price'].apply(lambda x: convert_to_float(x))
```

6. This dataset has 96 columns. When working with such a huge dataset, it makes sense to think about what data we need and creates a subsection of our dataset that only holds the data we need. Before we can do that, we'll take a look at all available columns and an example for that column. This will help us decide what information is suitable:

```
# print the col name and the first entry per column
for col in dataset.columns:
    print('{}\t{}'.format(col, dataset[col][0]))
```

The following diagram shows the output of the preceding code:

```
id       2515
listing_url      https://www.airbnb.com/rooms/2515
scrape_id        20181206022948
last_scraped     2018-12-06
name     Stay at Chez Chic budget room #1
summary  Step into our artistic spacious apartment and enjoy your artistic Guest room with original artwork from NY artists. Shared with my little family hov
entral Park — the busy city minutes away but sleeping in quiet at night!
space    -PLEASE BOOK DIRECTLY. NO NEED TO SEND A REQUEST FOR DATES> CALENDAR IS UP TO DATE> ALL AIRBNB RESERVATIONS WILL BE HONORED> Nice, comfortable, and
ize bed. In very nice apartment on central Park North 4th floor walk-up. same place as Chez chic #2, max capacity of the rooms 2 people). You will share the
cated one block from Subway 2/3,B/C on 110th street, Bus M1,2,3,4 at the corner, central park across the street.  Your room: full size bed (sleeps two), des
provided. Iron/air dryer provided. Separate Full bathroom shared with guestroom room #2. Access to the Kitchen from 8AM weekdays or anytime during the weeke
n the evening.   The apartment: spacious newly renovated, hardwood floors,3BD, 2Bath apartment with Living r
description      Step into our artistic spacious apartment and enjoy your artistic Guest room with original artwork from NY artists. Shared with my little fa
t from Central Park — the busy city minutes away but sleeping in quiet at night! -PLEASE BOOK DIRECTLY. NO NEED TO SEND A REQUEST FOR DATES> CALENDAR IS UP
and clean private guest room with shared bathroom (2 people max) — full size bed. In very nice apartment on central Park North 4th floor walk-up. same place
the apt with me and my little family. Daily cleaning in common areas. Located one block from Subway 2/3,B/C on 110th street, Bus M1,2,3,4 at the corner, cer
desk, Digital Tv/DVD, wifi internet, A/C, closet and desk. Sheets/Towels provided. Iron/air dryer provided. Separat
experiences_offered      none
neighborhood_overview    nan
notes    Please no cooking at night but you can warm up food in the microwave and use the kitchen
transit  Subway 2.3.B.C. at 110th street around the corner and bus M.2.3.4 at the corner
access   Guests will have their PRIVATE BATHROOM (NOTE: Shared between June 22-Aug 22) (shared with 2nd guestroom if there are guests), and the kitchen
interaction      We will have a list of Harlem restaurants and points of interest ready for you, as well as a subway map of NYC and pratical infos.
house_rules      no-smoking/please take off your shoes: cleaning fees $40
thumbnail_url    nan
medium_url        nan
picture_url      https://a0.muscache.com/im/pictures/d0489e42-4333-4360-911f-413d503fe146.jpg?aki_policy=large
xl_picture_url   nan
host_id 2758
```

Figure 7.18: Each column header with an example entry from the dataset

7. Trim down the number of columns our working dataset has by creating a subsection of the columns with **id**, **latitude** as **lat**, **longitude** as **lon**, **price** in $, and **review_scores_rating**:

```
"""
create a subsection of the dataset with the above-mentioned columns
"""
columns=['id', 'lat', 'lon', 'dollar_price', \
        'review_scores_rating']
sub_data=dataset[columns]
```

8. Print the first five rows of the trimmed down dataset:

```
# print the first 5 rows of the dataset
sub_data.head()
```

The following diagram shows the output of the preceding code:

	id	lat	lon	dollar_price	review_scores_rating
0	2515	40.799205	-73.953676	59.0	93.0
1	21456	40.797642	-73.961775	140.0	94.0
2	2539	40.647486	-73.972370	149.0	98.0
3	2595	40.753621	-73.983774	225.0	95.0
4	21644	40.828028	-73.947308	89.0	100.0

Figure 7.19: Displaying the first five rows after keeping only five columns

9. Create a new **DataAccessObject** object with the newly created subsection of the dataset. Use it to plot out a dot map:

```
"""

import DataAccessObject and create a data object \
as an instance of that class
"""

from geoplotlib.utils import DataAccessObject
data = DataAccessObject(sub_data)
# plotting the whole dataset with dots
geoplotlib.dot(data)
geoplotlib.show()
```

The following diagram shows the output of the preceding code:

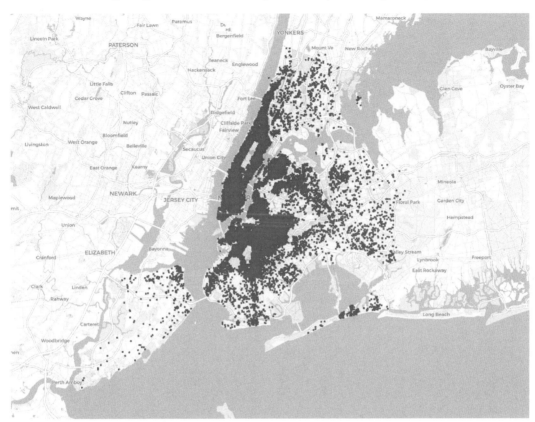

Figure 7.20: Simple dot map created from the points

10. The final step is to write the custom layer. Define a **ValueLayer** class that extends the **BaseLayer** object of geoplotlib. For the interactive feature mentioned, we require an additional import. **pyglet** provides us with the option to act on key presses:

```
# custom layer creation
import pyglet
import geoplotlib
from geoplotlib.layers import BaseLayer
from geoplotlib.core import BatchPainter
from geoplotlib.colors import ColorMap
from geoplotlib.utils import BoundingBox

class ValueLayer(BaseLayer):
```

```python
    def __init__(self, dataset, bbox=BoundingBox.WORLD):
        # initialize instance variables
        pass


    def invalidate(self, proj):
        """
        draw the points with the color based on the \
        selected attribute
        """
        pass


    def draw(self, proj, mouse_x, mouse_y, ui_manager):
        # display the ui manager info
        pass


    def on_key_release(self, key, modifiers):
        """
        check if left or right keys are pressed \
        to switch to other attribute
        """
        pass


    def bbox(self):
        # bounding box that gets used when the layer is created
        pass
```

11. Initiate the following instance variables in the **__init__** method of the
    ValueLayer class: first, **self.data**, which holds the dataset; second, **self.
    display**, which holds the currently selected attribute name; third, **self.
    painter**, which holds an instance of the **BatchPainter** class; fourth, **self.
    view**, which holds the **BoundingBox** function; and lastly, **self.cmap**, which
    holds a color map with the **jet color** schema and an alpha of 255 and
    100 levels:

```python
# custom layer creation
import pyglet
import geoplotlib
from geoplotlib.layers import BaseLayer
from geoplotlib.core import BatchPainter
from geoplotlib.colors import ColorMap
from geoplotlib.utils import BoundingBox
```

```
class ValueLayer(BaseLayer):

    def __init__(self, dataset, bbox=BoundingBox.WORLD):
        # initialize instance variables
        self.data = dataset
        self.display = 'dollar_price'
        self.painter = BatchPainter()
        self.view = bbox
        self.cmap = ColorMap('jet', alpha=255, levels=100)
```

12. Implement the **bbox**, **draw**, and **on_key_release** method for the
   ValueLayer class. First, return the **self.view** variable in the **bbox**
   method. Then, set the **ui_manager.info** text to **Use left and right
   to switch between the displaying of price and ratings.
   Currently displaying: dollar_price** or **review_scores_rating**,
   depending on what the **self.display** variable holds, and lastly, in the
   on_key_release method, check whether the left or right key is pressed and
   switch the **self.display** variable between **dollar_price** or **review_
   scores_rating**. Next, return **True** if the left or the right key has been
   pressed to trigger redrawing of the dots, otherwise return **False**. The full
   custom layer notebook cell will look like this:

```
# custom layer creation
import pyglet
import geoplotlib
from geoplotlib.layers import BaseLayer
from geoplotlib.core import BatchPainter
from geoplotlib.colors import ColorMap
from geoplotlib.utils import BoundingBox


class ValueLayer(BaseLayer):

    def __init__(self, dataset, bbox=BoundingBox.WORLD):
        # initialize instance variables
        self.data = dataset
        self.display = 'dollar_price'
        self.painter = BatchPainter()
        self.view = bbox
        self.cmap = ColorMap('jet', alpha=255, levels=100)
```

```
    def invalidate(self, proj):
        """
        draw the points with the color based \
        on the selected attribute
        """
        pass

    def draw(self, proj, mouse_x, mouse_y, ui_manager):
        # display the ui manager info
        ui_manager.info('Use left and right to switch between '\
                        'the displaying of price and ratings. '\
                        'Currently displaying: {}'\
                        .format(self.display))
        self.painter.batch_draw()

    def on_key_release(self, key, modifiers):
        """
        check if left or right keys are pressed \
        to switch to other attribute
        """
        if key == pyglet.window.key.LEFT \
        or key == pyglet.window.key.RIGHT:
            self.display = 'dollar_price' if self.display \
            != 'dollar_price' else 'review_scores_rating'
            return True
        return False

    def bbox(self):
        # bounding box that gets used when a layer is created
        return self.view
```

13. Given the data, plot each point on the map with a color that is defined by the currently selected attribute, either **price** or **rating**. First, in the **invalidate** method, assign a new **BatchPainter()** function to the **self.painter** variable. Second, get the max value of the dataset given the current **self. display** variable. Third, use a **log** scale if **dollar_price** is used, otherwise use a **lin** scale. Lastly, map the value to color using the **cmap** object we defined in the **__init__** method and plot each point with the given color onto the map with a size of **5**:

```python
# custom layer creation
import pyglet
import geoplotlib
from geoplotlib.layers import BaseLayer
from geoplotlib.core import BatchPainter
from geoplotlib.colors import ColorMap
from geoplotlib.utils import BoundingBox


class ValueLayer(BaseLayer):

    def __init__(self, dataset, bbox=BoundingBox.WORLD):
        # initialize instance variables
        self.data = dataset
        self.display = 'dollar_price'
        self.painter = BatchPainter()
        self.view = bbox
        self.cmap = ColorMap('jet', alpha=255, levels=100)


    def invalidate(self, proj):
        """
        paint every point with a color that represents \
        the currently selected attributes value
        """
        self.painter = BatchPainter()
        max_val = max(self.data[self.display])
        scale = 'log' if self.display == 'dollar_price' else 'lin'

        for index, id in enumerate(self.data['id']):
            # log scale can't start at 0, must be 1
            min_val = max(self.data[self.display][index], 1)

            color = self.cmap.to_color(min_val, max_val, scale)
            self.painter.set_color(color)
            lat, lon = self.data['lon'][index], \
                        self.data['lat'][index]
            x, y = proj.lonlat_to_screen(lat, lon)
            self.painter.points(x, y, 5)
```

```
    def draw(self, proj, mouse_x, mouse_y, ui_manager):
        # display the ui manager info
        ui_manager.info('Use left and right to switch between \
                        'the displaying of price and ratings. '\
                        'Currently displaying: {}'\
                        .format(self.display))
        self.painter.batch_draw()

    def on_key_release(self, key, modifiers):
        """
        check if left or right keys are pressed to \
        switch to other attribute
        """
        if key == pyglet.window.key.LEFT \
        or key == pyglet.window.key.RIGHT:
            self.display = 'dollar_price' if self.display \
                           != 'dollar_price' \
                           else 'review_scores_rating'
            return True
        return False

    # bounding box that gets used when layer is created
    def bbox(self):
        return self.view
```

14. Create a new **BoundingBox** function focused on New York by using
    **north=40.897994, west=-73.999040, south=40.595581,
    east=-73.95040**. Use the **darkmatter** tile provider that we looked at in
    Chapter 5, Plotting Geospatial Data. Provide the **BoundingBox** function to the
    ValueLayer class when adding a new layer to geoplotlib:

```
# bounding box for our view on New York
from geoplotlib.utils import BoundingBox
ny_bbox = BoundingBox(north=40.897994, west=-73.999040, \
                      south=40.595581, east=-73.95040)


# displaying our custom layer using add_layer
geoplotlib.tiles_provider('darkmatter')
geoplotlib.add_layer(ValueLayer(data, bbox=ny_bbox))
geoplotlib.show()
```

After launching our visualization, we can see that our viewport is focused on New York. Every accommodation is displayed with one dot. Each dot is colored, based on either its price or (upon clicking the right or left arrow) the rating. We can see that the general color gets closer to yellow/orange the closer we get to central Manhattan. On the other hand, in the rating visualization, we can see that the accommodation in central Manhattan appears to be rated lower than the accommodation outside:

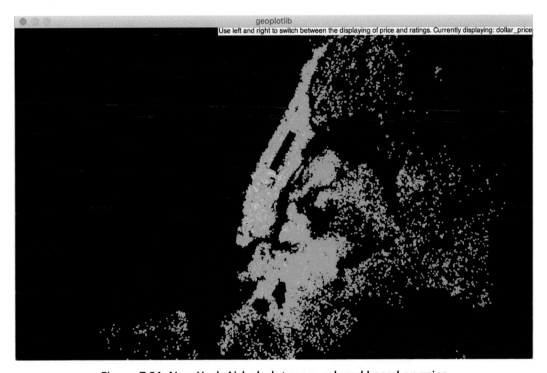

Figure 7.21: New York Airbnb dot map, colored based on price

The following diagram shows a dot map with color based on rating:

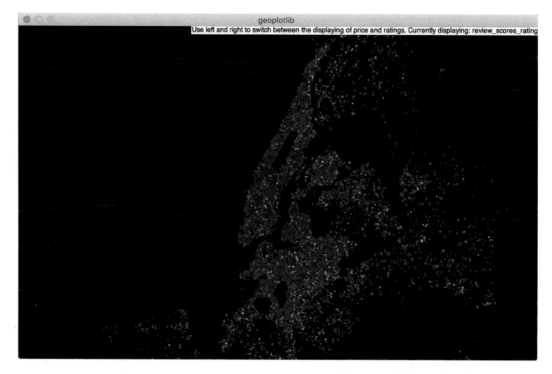

Figure 7.22: New York Airbnb dot map, colored based on ratings

You have just created an interactive visualization by writing your custom layer to display and visualize price and rating information for Airbnb accommodations spread across New York.

NOTE

To access the source code for this specific section, please refer to https://packt.live/3eioPSA.

This section does not currently have an online interactive example, and will need to be run locally.

INDEX